October 1996

Ask Me If I Care

*Voices from an
American High School*

*For Anne & Andrew :
I can tell
you care !*

NANCY J. RUBIN

and a cast of hundreds

Nancy Rubin

1⊜

TEN SPEED PRESS
Berkeley, California

Askmecaree@aol.com

PERMISSIONS:

"Are You Happy to Be Gay?" Copyright © 1992 by Creators Syndicate Inc. Reprinted by permission of Ann Landers and Creators Syndicate.

Excerpts from "Facts about Television," 1993. Reprinted by permission of Ben Fishbaine and Sonoma County TV Turn-Off.

Excerpts from *The State of America's Children Yearbook 1994*. Copyright © 1994 by Children's Defense Fund. Reprinted by permission of Children's Defense Fund, Washington, D.C.

Excerpts from the *Adolescent and Young Adult Fact Book*. Copyright © 1991 By Children's Defense Fund. Reprinted by permission of the Children's Defense Fund, Washington, D.C.

Excerpts from *Demystifying Homosexuality: A Teaching Guide about Lesbians and Gay Men*. Copyright © 1984 by Irvington Publishers, Inc. Reprinted by permission of Irvington Publishers, Inc.

"Ethnic identity as defined by survey participants" excerpted from "Love, Lineage, and the Conflicts of Adoption," 1993. Reprinted by permission of Johanna Metzgar.

Excerpts from *Uppers, Downers, All Arounders: Physical and Mental Effects of Psychoactive Drugs*. Copyright © 1993 by William E. Cohen and Darryl S. Inaba. Reprinted by permission of CNS Productions/Paul J. Steinbroner–Publisher, Ashland, Oregon.

Excerpt from *In Love and In Danger: A Teen's Guide to Breaking Free of Abusive Relationships* by Barrie Levy. Copyright © 1993 by Barrie Levy. Reprinted by permission of Seal Press.

"A Mother's Day Message" by Marian Wright Edelman. Copyright © 1994 by Children's Defense Fund. Reprinted with permission of *Parade*.

🔟

TEN SPEED PRESS
P.O. Box 7123
Berkeley, California 94707

Book design by Nancy Austin
All photographs including cover by Jonathan Chester/ Extreme Images, with the exception of page 396.

Photographs on page 396 by Jesse Grant, Oakland, CA.

Library of Congress Cataloging-in-Publication Data

Rubin, Nancy J., 1946–
    Ask me if I care : voices from an American high school / Nancy J. Rubin, and a cast of hundreds.
        p. cm.
    Includes index.
    ISBN 0-89815-597-5
    1. High school students—United States—Attitudes. 2. Rubin, Nancy J., 1946– . I. Title.
LA229.R82 1994
373.18'1'0973—dc20   93–47610
                                                      CIP

First Ten Speed Press printing, 1994

Manufactured in the United States of America

1 2 3 4 5 6 — 98 97 96 95 94

This book is dedicated to:

My mother and father,
with all my love;

All my students,
with deep appreciation for letting me
into your lives;

Those whose work appears in this book,
with thanks for letting others share in
your private thoughts.

CONTENTS

ACKNOWLEDGMENTS

I am so grateful for the lifelong love and support of my family, which has been such a positive influence in my life and so very special to me: my sister and brother and their spouses, my nieces, nephews, cousins, second cousins, aunts, uncles, great aunts, etc.

To my uncle, Ben Benjamin, who encouraged me, back in 1977, to write this book.

To my grandfather (who lived to be 102) and my Uncle Bill; I feel so blessed to have had them in my life. Their wisdom, values, and love I will always cherish. The way they lived their lives was a great lesson to me.

This year my parents will celebrate their fifty-seventh wedding anniversary and their love and devotion to one another, to their children and all family members, to their friends, and to those less fortunate, have been the greatest influence on my life; by example, they have been role models and perfect teachers. I thank them with all my heart.

Everyone at Ten Speed with whom I have worked has made this project a real joy for me—never have I felt such teamwork and support. I am deeply grateful to George Young and Phil Wood for taking on this project.

I wish to thank Nicole Geiger for her incredible enthusiasm, loving support, and wonderful guidance. Without her perseverance and encouragement this book would not exist.

I wish to thank Jackie Wan for her insight and expertise. Her humor and wisdom made working together a delightful experience.

To Nancy Austin, Anna Erickson, and Jeanne Pimentel for their creativity and great ideas, and for being such an integral part of the team. Also to Cybele Knowles, Catherine Jacobes, and Cynthia Harris for their hard work and expertise.

To Pat Cody and Pamela Drake for taking an interest in my work and taking the initiative to get the book published. I greatly appreciate their time and effort on my behalf.

To Devin Kalile Grayson, Class of 1988, who provided the title for this book, and whose writing and friendship I have long enjoyed.

To the hundreds of speakers who have volunteered to speak in my classes and share some part of their lives, thank you for all that you have contributed. The Pacific Center for Human Growth and the New Bridge Foundation have provided panels of speakers for over a decade.

Special thanks to Chuck Small, the longest running speaker (and the funniest) and a great friend and confidant for over twenty years.

To Paul Steinbroner, whose sound data and good-natured assistance helped immensely.

To my dear friends who have each given so much to me throughout the years. Special thanks to Harvey Caplan and Gail Reinhart for giving me valuable feedback on the manuscript.

To the Berkeley Unified School District for having the foresight to create a class like Social Living and so many other innovative programs. I have always been so grateful to work in a district which supports the freedom of expression and the discussion of controversial issues.

To the Berkeley High School staff—especially those of you who, like me, have worked under eight different principals—I applaud your fortitude in our mutual efforts to survive on the front lines.

FOREWORD

Nancy Rubin is a legend in her own time. Her Social Living class at Berkeley High School is famous among local teenagers for being a place where no question is too embarrassing to be asked, and where every individual is respected and heard. Nancy taught several young people in my own extended family who deeply appreciated her candor, her humor, her acceptance of them, and her willingness to extend a hand and offer advice.

As Mayor of Berkeley, I spent a great deal of time talking and working with Nancy's students and other young people like them. I came to this, as she did, via a circuitous route—in my case, the growing problem of youth violence. We are increasingly terrified of the society we have created and the children we have neglected. As I became determined to find solutions to this problem in Berkeley, I found out that almost no one had asked the young people themselves what was wrong and what *they* thought could be done to change it. Nancy's students and others entered my world through task forces and meetings with teenagers as I sought solutions to my city's problems. I have heard them speak out loud many of the hopes and concerns they share through their writing in this book.

During my own rebellious teenage years in the 1950s you might say many of us felt *over*-attended to. We were eager to test tightly drawn limits and wanted *less* structure and *less* attention. Listening to kids today, I hear that structure and attention are what they crave more than anything else. Too many of them come from homes where anything goes and no one cares. Their ideas for solutions are realistic and modest: they want a safe place to be after school, some help with their homework, someone to talk with about their problems. Not much to ask from the richest nation in the world.

What is to be done? Nancy Rubin shares her experience with her kids and allows them to share theirs—openly and honestly. That's a good start. She makes a positive difference in each individual's life, and in so doing, moves community life forward in a positive way that benefits us all.

Gifted teachers like Nancy Rubin can contribute enormously to making effective public policy. Too often serious issues are studied, but rarely does anyone bother to ask the input of the people who are in the center of the storm—the educators. In my new job as Regional Representative of the United States Department of Education, one of the heartening signs of new direction is Secretary Richard Riley's "teacher in residence" who serves on his policy staff and is working to ensure that teachers' voices are heard in every major policy debate. This is another step forward.

Ask Me If I Care is a book that works on all levels. It is good sociology, good "best practice" for teachers and parents, and a fascinating look at the private stories that put today's policy issues in perspective in the most eloquent way possible.

I put down *Ask Me If I Care* and pick up the *New York Times*. The lead story is about a nationwide poll of teenagers in which young people's major concerns include the topics in this book: violence, substance abuse, weapons in school, and little attention at home. This book puts a human face on those statistics. It underscores the fact that our children are angry, hopeful, and very frightened. They are asking us for attention, structure, guidance, love—and we ignore them at our peril.

—LONI HANCOCK
Secretary's Representative,
United States Department of Education, Region IX
Mayor of Berkeley, 1986–1994

INTRODUCTION

Every Friday, as my students noisily depart for the weekend, I shout over their conversations to remind them "Don't drink and drive"… "Just say no"…"If you can't say no, use condoms"…"Buckle up"…"Always wear a helmet!" I've said this so many times, it's gotten to be a joke with them. Some of them playfully throw it back at me: "Nancy, don't get pregnant this weekend!"…"Don't get too drunk, Nancy!" I love this lighthearted banter, but at the same time, I hope that they are taking me seriously, because it's no joke: these are difficult, dangerous times to be a teen. And there's a lot more to it than just buckling up a seat belt.

I teach a course called Social Living at an urban public high school. It's a nine-week crash course intended to help students deal with some of the major problems they will almost inevitably have to deal with as teenagers and young adults: sexuality, alcohol and drug use, sexually transmitted diseases, family relationships, violence, stress, self-esteem, racial prejudice. In addition, we cover other issues as they arise in classroom discussions, or in response to something in the news, a holiday, or an upcoming school event.

When I first started teaching this course some eighteen years ago, I was given the assignment just one week before school was to start. To say I was shocked would be an understatement. I was credentialed to teach the visually impaired and for the past five years had been working with blind students at Berkeley High School (BHS), with a class load of ten students. Now, without warning, I was to instruct *150* students a day on a broad range of controversial subjects for which I had absolutely no training. It was a challenging transition, to say the least. Fortunately, the other Social Living teachers generously shared their worksheets and speakers lists with me and gave me suggestions on classroom activities, but I have to admit that I relied a great deal on films that first semester!

Sometime during that first year, as I experimented with different approaches and tried to discover my own style of teaching, I stumbled upon the idea of having the students keep journals. I would assign a topic and have them write their responses in class. It was a revelation in more ways than one. I was amazed by the honesty and intensity of my students' writings, and the humor, pain, anguish, love, and confusion expressed in the journals deeply affected me. I was also shocked and dismayed by what some of the writings revealed—the tremendous burdens many of these young people were carrying, and the horrendous life problems they were trying to solve.

I began to collect entries that seemed particularly expressive to me, and then decided to share some of them with my classes, without identifying the writers of course. I found that the students were as touched by what they were hearing as I had been: they understood that their own peers were revealing their deepest secrets and doubts. Whenever I read from the journals, I could always sense a different atmosphere in the room and an involvement that was rarely there at other times.

© 1978 United Feature Syndicate, Inc.

Reprinted with permission

I'm writing a journal of my life. My mom has promised to burn it if anything should ever happen to me.

Some students found relief in discovering that they were not alone with their problems, or that, by comparison, their problems were not as bad as they originally thought. Others became more sensitive to the burdens that their classmates carry. I found this method of sharing ideas to be a powerful approach to teaching, and the students' writings very quickly became an integral part of my course.

From the very beginning, my school allowed me complete freedom in handling controversial material and made no attempt to censor my choice of topics or speakers. Eighteen years ago, this was a rarity: very few other schools permitted open discussion about homosexuality or birth control methods, for instance, or if such taboo topics were to be broached, there were so many safeguards as to make the exchange of information largely ineffective. Originally my intent was to publish a collection of journal entries in order to make the information from my class available to adolescents who did not have access to a comprehensive health and family life class like mine. It still is, but now my focus has widened. Now I want to reach the adult population as well, and share with them what has come out of my classroom experiences.

Our young people are exposed to so much at an early age and are being forced to grow up very fast. Every day, the newspapers report staggering statistics on the number of AIDS cases, teen pregnancies, gang pressures, accidental shootings, the latest drug craze, child abuse. As adults, I think we must offer our support for the teens in our lives, but I don't think we can do this effectively without first understanding how they perceive their world.

It is often difficult to establish open communication across the generation gap, and that is probably why most adults are only dimly aware of the real problems that our young people face today. The tendency is to stereotype all teenagers as being concerned only about their clothes and cars, or their boyfriends and girlfriends, or what music will be played at the next dance. But anyone who reads some of the journal entries in this book, and listens in vicariously on some of our classroom discussions, will soon find that there is much more going on inside the average teenager's head than is outwardly apparent. Behind the masks that so many of them wear, and behind their familiar response of "Whatever," they do care—a great deal—about finding meaning in their existence, about understanding their world.

A Few Words about the Journals

All the journal entries included in this book are used with the written permission of their authors. Minor corrections in spelling, grammar, and punctuation have been made in order to make the material more readable, and some of the longer entries have been trimmed, but other than that, the entries have been as faithfully reproduced as was possible. I have kept the original language and included any embellishments that could be reproduced in type. In addition to the journal entries, there are some writings that came out of anonymous surveys where students can write about their problems or experiences, ask questions, or comment on the class. These, too, are used with the writers' permission.

Some of the entries were written many years ago, so there may be a few references to events long past, or some language that seems dated. If the message was relevant and the point of view well stated, I did not consider this a problem.

Selecting the material to be included was a difficult process. I have thousands of journal entries in my collection, and if space permitted, I would have included them all, as each has its own charm and unique viewpoint, and each has its own special meaning for me. This, of course, was not possible. Instead, I tried to select a balanced representation that would show all sides of the various issues.

To protect my students and their friends and relatives, names have been removed or masked. In a few cases, the writer requested that their real name be used, but otherwise, the only information provided is the sex and age of each writer.

WHAT IS BERKELEY HIGH SCHOOL?

BERKELEY HIGH SCHOOL has an enrollment of approximately 2,400 students in grades nine through twelve, and a staff that includes 140 classroom teachers and 12 special education teachers, 70 percent of whom hold advanced degrees. The school is situated on a seventeen-acre campus near downtown Berkeley. The facilities include a football field, two gymnasiums,

and a theater, in addition to regular classrooms and offices, and a number of portable buildings. Many of the buildings are old and in need of repair. A gymnasium that was built in 1927 is still in use, as is a complex of classrooms that was built in 1933. Ironically, a 1965 structure was damaged in the 1989 earthquake and is the only one that will have to be torn down and replaced.

The city of Berkeley has one of the most diverse populations of any city its size in the United States. BHS is the only public high school in this city of 120,000 people, and as such, it reflects the diversity of the city. Its students come from widely varied cultural and ethnic backgrounds (eighty-three different languages are spoken in the homes from which its students come), and from families that fall in the highest income brackets to those that are indigent (16 percent of its

students come from households on AFDC, a state welfare program for families with dependent children). Their parents represent every level of education from Nobel laureates from the nearby University of California campus to the illiterate.

Serving this heterogeneous population has always been a challenge. In part, this has been met by adding courses, departments, and programs as the needs have become manifest, evaluating their effectiveness, and making adjustments based on these evaluations. For instance, in an effort to identify students who need extra help, all ninth-grade students are required to take a core course in English and history. Those who have difficulty are routed into "back-up" tutorial classes instead of being automatically passed on. This has reduced the number of D's and F's by 14 percent. A similar program operates in the Mathematics Department.

The list of classes that are offered at BHS would run on for pages (in addition to the "basics," there is everything from wood shop to Pascal, from accounting to photography). And space permits naming only a few of its many programs:

- an on-site health center

- an on-site child-care facility which has been in operation for over 20 years and was the first of its kind in the country

- the Computer Academy, designed specifically for at-risk students (a Biotech Academy and a Finance Academy will be functioning soon, too)

- a small cafeteria that is part of the restaurant services training program of the Career Education Department

- an African-American Studies Department that was created over 20 years ago which is the only one of its kind at the high school level.

- a Chicano/Latino Studies Department

- a Women's Studies Department

- the Arts Department, encompassing music, drama, dance, and fine arts

- 27 varsity sports, including crew and rugby

- 75 extracurricular clubs

- 2 newspapers and 1 literary magazine, all student run

- an award-winning jazz ensemble

- a concert chorale

BHS has traditionally placed a strong emphasis on academics. It offers a broad range of basic and advanced courses in laboratory sciences, social sciences, mathematics, history, English, and foreign languages. (To give an example of the depth of its programs, it offers French and Spanish through the fifth year, Latin and German through the fourth year, and Kiswahili through the third year.) Its students have always scored well on the SAT, and 85 percent of its graduates go on to college. (For the past twelve years, BHS has been the second largest feeder school to U.C. Berkeley).

Still, the school recognizes that it has not been able to reach all students. Eighty-five percent of them miss at least one class a day; about one hundred drop out each year (a 4 percent dropout rate). Within the constraints of available resources, BHS staff and administration continue to evaluate the curriculum and the services the school provides and to adjust to the changing needs. Its goal has been and always will be to help each student succeed to his or her highest potential.

(Profile based on 1993–94 statistics.)

WHAT IS A TEENAGER?

I can't explain myself I'm afraid, sir, because
I'm not myself you see.
—ALICE IN WONDERLAND (TO THE CATERPILLAR)

To FIND OUT HOW they view themselves, I recently asked my students to complete the sentence: "A teenager is...." These were their responses:

...misunderstood and unjustly stereotyped.

...both an adult and a child.

...a person who has an open mind.

...a person inbetween a child and a adult, always trying to find a nice medium. But most of the time it's not there.

...a fluxuating mass of hormones.

...a part of life that I wish I could pass up.

...many things, everyone is different. How can you ask this question? You're just continuing to try and stereotype teenagers. This question means nothing. Have you ever thought that maybe one of the largest problems "teenagers" have is that people are always trying to put them in categories. What is it that so magically happens at 20? How, aside from age, am I different exactly from an adult? Think more about these questions, they're not always as "hip" as you think!

This last boy was absolutely right, of course—everyone is different. And I agree with him that one of the reasons teenagers often feel misunderstood is that the adult world tends to operate on the basis of stereotypes and generalizations.

For instance, demographers and marketers look at teens in terms of numbers:

- Teen population, 1992: 24.08 million (about 10% of total population)
- Projected population, 1994: 25 million
- Projected spending by teens in 1994: $89 billion ($57 billion from wages earned, $32 billion from allowances)
- In 1992, teens spent $3 billion on athletic shoes alone
- Number of high school students, 1994: 12 million

The "average" teenager could be positively described as someone who...

- makes an effort to get schoolwork done
- has a part-time job or does volunteer work
- is responsible for getting own meals (including shopping and preparation)
- takes part in extracurricular activity (sports, music, church)
- is concerned about family, friends, school, and the future
- helps out around the house

However, the "typical" teenager is often portrayed by the media in more negative terms, as someone who...

- will only eat pizza, burritos, and french fries
- dresses in the sloppiest, most outrageous clothes possible
- watches TV or talks on the phone all day
- never puts anything away
- either argues over everything or refuses to talk
- never thinks beyond the weekend
- is only concerned about self

Yes, some teens are sloppy and lazy, and some think mainly about their appearance, or their boyfriends or girlfriends, but there is much more going on in their heads. Here are some of my students' responses when asked "What I think about the most is...."

> ...being on stage with Prince because that's a dream of mine.

> ...my girlfriend, my religion Islam, Kung Fu, school work.

> ...basketball and sometimes music and girls.

> ...right now, school, grades, living up to my own and my parents' expectations.

> ...money, boys, my overweightness, my parents, school, my sister, my appearance.

> ...right now, about the guy I like. I don't know how to get his attention.

> ...all the stress I'm under.

> ...sex, my appearance, my future, the weekend.

> ...what people think of me.

> ...the future, girls, who might be thinking of me.

> ...my heritage, that's what gives me power. Life, where I'm going, what I'm doing, and just everyday shit.

> ...my abortion tomorrow.

Perhaps we'd be better off if we avoided labeling people, as the boy above intimated, and concentrated instead on listening to each other with respect and exchanging ideas freely.

1 | Welcome to Social Living

PINECREST, CALIFORNIA, is situated in the Sierra, about a three-hour drive from the San Francisco Bay Area. Here, the University of California Alumni Association operates the Lair of the Golden Bear, a summer camp for its members and their families. From the time I was six years old I have been fortunate to have started almost every summer at this camp with my family—my parents and my older sister and brother.

The Lair seems the embodiment of traditional family values—a week's vacation in God's country, with all family members sleeping in a wood-frame cabin with just a canvas top and a flap for a door. Rarely do you hear a parent yelling at a child or a couple arguing. There are all the typical camp activities, an idyllic setting, and a wonderful spirit of camaraderie and tradition.

For the last ten years, I've been spending the last week of summer at the Lair, too. I make this second trip specifically to energize myself and to prepare mentally and emotionally to return to the joys, challenges, and frustrations of teaching at an inner-city high school. I find a balance at camp that helps me make the transition back to the stresses of teaching.

All too soon, though, I'm back in Berkeley, and another perfect summer fades into memory. The pine forest is replaced by the harsh reality of broken glass and boarded-up windows, "tags" sprayed over murals, and trash on the floors. Campfires are replaced by garbage can fires. The laughter of kids playing in the creek is replaced by "bitch," "nigga," and the newest slang echoing through the hallways and stairwells. I cannot imagine very many of my students being able to last a couple of days, let alone a week, in a one-room cabin with their family.

Although I've been teaching for many years, I still get a rush of excitement on the first day of school. And the doubts that plagued me as a novice plague me to this day: Will I be able to reach my new students—all two hundred of them? They will have such diverse backgrounds and experiences and expectations. Will I be able to handle the myriad problems that I will face? Though I keep trying, there is no way to prepare myself for the first day of school. Fortunately, a former student comes running up, throws her arms around me, and says, "Nancy, how was your summer? It's great to see you!" and once again I feel connected and inspired.

I get to my classroom very early to make sure that everything is set up the way I like it. As I open the door, I am relieved to find that only a few of the hundreds of posters, photos, album covers, cartoons, and pictures have fallen off the walls, ceiling, and cabinets. I have collected items from magazines and from my travels all over the world, and my students have brought in their own favorites to decorate the room. For me, my room is a haven from the noise and institutional drabness that permeates most of the school. Since I spend more of my waking hours at work than at home, and "entertain" more at school than at home, I have put considerable time, effort, and money into making my classroom a warm, comfortable, and interesting environment.

Then I notice that the combination deskchairs are arranged in straight rows with a large oak teacher's desk in the front—the classic classroom seating. Did someone use my room over the summer? I was promised that it would not be used. I prefer a less formal configuration, and I move the thirty-four chairs into two rows in the shape of a wide horseshoe with my chair at the opening. There are at least six different styles of desks which coordinate nicely with the crooked, broken blinds. I walk around to make sure that the desktops are clean. The older wood desks are riddled with hand-carved names, profanities, and drawings. It takes a very sharp instrument to penetrate the tops of the newer desks—most of them have remained fairly free of damage.

From the corner of my eye I notice something moving on the floor. A dead mouse is being devoured by thousands of ants! It is not a pretty sight and the first bell will be ringing in twenty minutes. I call for the janitor, and he actually shows up in time to remove the mouse—he scrounges some cardboard from the trash (left there since June?), scoops up the rodent, and throws it out the back door which opens onto some dead space between two buildings. I wait for him to return to clean up the ants and perhaps take some measures to prevent any further invasions of non-two-legged creatures. He never returns!

The bell rings; I open my door and stand at the entrance of my "home away from home" and greet each student as he or she enters. I have my class list with me and ask for their names. Since few students pronounce their names clearly, and many of the names are one-of-a-kind, finding them on the list is not an easy task. Everyone seems to arrive at once and some try to take seats before I have gotten their names. Most of the students are seated and are talking or looking at the books, magazines, and pictures in the room. Most are a bit shy, cooperative, and respectful. If only the latter two qualities would last! I take my seat with the blackboard behind me where I have written:

WELCOME TO SOCIAL LIVING
1ST 9 WEEKS
NANCY RUBIN

I introduce myself to my new class and request that everyone call me Nancy. Most students go along with Nancy, but if they prefer to call me Ms. Rubin, that is also fine. A couple of students in the past have made up their own names for me: among those that are printable are Grandma and Sweetheart.

I ask the students to be patient, as it may take me awhile to learn their names and how to pronounce each one properly. On any given class list I will encounter a wonderful variety of foreign or ethnic names, as well as original, creative names, such as Akua, Cliethel, Eyana, Giaour, Jinho, Juni, Kanitha, Klondike, Lysistrat, Marisol, Monsoon, Navoto, Neffitriia, Paz, Prince Charles, Quo Vadis, Rainbow, Sabra, Seul, Sumaka, Tamarind, Taufiq, Uyunda, Xa, Yaxchilan, Yen-Binyh, or Zara. Jennifers, Joshuas, and Jasons are still in abundance, but rarely do I have a Mary, Sally, or Sandy!

On the first day, I like to get right into the guts of the content of the class rather than talk about the rules and requirements. I ask the girls to take their chairs and sit together in a circle as far away from the boys as possible. I tell the boys to form their own circle. I go over to the girls and ask them to come up with a list of questions that they would like to ask the boys. I tell them that so often I hear girls say things like "All boys ever want is sex," or "My parents are far more protective of me than of my younger brother." Here is their chance to ask boys what they think and how they feel about certain issues—why they act the way they do! I give one of the girls a piece of paper and ask her to take notes for the group.

Then I go over to the boys and tell them they are to do just the opposite. They laugh when I suggest they ask the girls, "Why can't you go alone to the restroom? Why do you always go in groups?" (This question *always* comes up from the males. Girls respond by saying, "To borrow makeup...to help each other with our hair...for safety reasons...and to talk about you—our dates!")

Generally, the girls' list is two or three times as long as the boys' list. Sometimes the guys just stare at each other or pass the paper around and write down a question whereas the girls usually begin talking and laughing immediately. When they seem ready, I ask everyone to turn their chairs around so that the two groups are facing each other. I suggest that the girls begin by asking the boys any question from their list. I encourage everyone to respond so that many different opinions are expressed. When the girls seem satisfied with the responses to their first question, the boys then ask a question from their list and the girls reply.

Sometimes I head off questions that are inappropriate or too personal: "How many of you girls have had sex? Raise your hands." "Do you enjoy oral sex?" To these I may say that most people do not want to talk publicly about their sexual lives—and often will lie about it!—but later on I will give them statistics about the number of teenagers who are sexually active, and we will discuss oral sex. For now though, I want the group leader to find a question that does not invade anyone's private life. Still, the tone is set that this will be a very open class, with as many people participating as possible, and each of us learning from one another rather than by my lecturing.

On the second day of class, I give each student a list of rules and regulations that I have entitled "Don't Say I Never Told You This!!!" Social Living is a required course—all students must pass it in order to graduate—and I am aware that many students are here just to get the grade and move on. Because of this I decided long ago to concentrate on content, and keep the logistics as simple as possible, so I have few rules and assign very little homework. Still, to be sure there are no misunderstandings, I go over the entire sheet with each class.

I apologize to the class that some of the items on the list seem so obvious ("Bring a pen and notebook paper to class every day." "You should appear awake!"). I don't want to be treating them like second-graders, but from past experience I have found it necessary to explain in detail exactly what I expect and what the consequences will be for failure to follow through. As we go through the list I tell them that if they feel any of the rules are unfair we should discuss them. When I get to "No eating, drinking, or gum chewing," someone says, "Why can't we chew gum?" I find gum popping and bubble blowing very distracting. No matter how many times I defend my point of view, gum chewing is my biggest battle on a daily basis. As one colleague remarked, better gum than guns.

I tell them that the only way to flunk the class is to be absent too many times. Last semester one out of three students flunked. Some students sit up a bit straighter and begin to really focus in on what I am saying. A student asks, "How could anyone flunk Social Living? That would be pretty embarrassing!" I repeat, "Just by accumulating too many cuts or absences."

After we've reviewed all the rules, I ask them to read the following paragraph and sign it:

I understand the above rules, regulations, and requirements. I further understand that there will be CONSEQUENCES to inappropriate behavior. I understand that the easiest way to irritate Nancy is to chew gum, come in late, disrespect anyone in the classroom, and to do anything that detracts from a supportive, safe, and fun environment for learning and sharing. Notes and phone calls home will take place as needed.

The last paragraph on the sheet is a statement of my commitment to the class:

I promise to make class as interesting as possible. I will provide speakers, up-to-date videos, factual handouts, and give you the opportunity to ask any questions about any topic. I will not give any tests or quizzes. I expect your cooperation in the above rules. Please make your requests/complaints known to me as they occur.

For the final bit of business, I pass out a letter that students are to give to their parents. It explains the goals and content of this class and states that their child may be excused from taking Social Living "due to conflict of religious training and beliefs or personal moral convictions." I want them to feel comfortable in my class and if they or their parents or guardians have any concerns, they should let me know. I can only recall three or four students ever asking to be excused from the class. I would like each student to be here for his or her own personal growth—not just for the grade or the credits, but I do have to be realistic. One student wrote me this note:

> Don't take this offensively but the only reason I'm taking this class is to graduate from Berkeley High. Some of the things we'll be talking about in this class are against my religious beliefs (and I have some strong religious beliefs) however they are a part of society. Most of the topics really don't affect me, but there are some that do. I was surprised my mom actually signed the paper.

Business done with, I hand out the Autobiographical Information worksheet *(see Appendix),* which is their first journal assignment, and let them use the rest of the period to fill it out. The bell rings and thirty-four students abruptly leave. I will repeat this exact same scenario four more times today—and an additional fifteen times before the end of the school year!

It's only the second day of school, and one student is already on my case, challenging me in a very hostile way. I talk to his counselor later and she discovers that he was greatly offended by a poster in my room. (The poster is of two men—they are models posing for a safer sex ad for the San Francisco AIDS Foundation. It was given to me by a former student who had had it signed by the photographer.) We discuss at great length the pros and cons of the student remaining in Social Living. We decide that for now he should drop the class because his behavior has been known to be extremely volatile.

Day 3: We continue working on the lists of questions from the first day. In fourth period, we are talking about the importance of virginity to many females and somehow get onto the subject of female circumcision. A male student sitting to my right gets up and asks permission to go to the restroom. I say sure and while the words are coming out of my mouth his knees buckle under him, he falls backwards, hits his head, and is out cold! Did he faint? Epileptic seizure? Drug overdose? I have taken CPR but it was a long time ago. I have thirty-five pairs of eyes watching my response. Several male students try to be very helpful by wanting to get Zack up and walking—I firmly say, "Don't move him. Go for help—the Health Center is directly across the hall." I can see he is breathing. I dismiss the class early as it is only a few minutes before the bell. Zack later tells me that his only pain is from embarrassment. The nurse never did arrive but a student supervisor finally did. (We have a number of student supervisors on the staff; their function is to patrol the school and act as troubleshooters.) Zack hasn't missed a day of class since and I am determined to update my CPR skills! The Health Center is hoping to equip the nurse with a walkie-talkie.

Day 4: Today I explain the "journal cover" project—one of only two homework assignments they are required to do in the course of the nine weeks. They are to cover a standard folder with a collage of pictures and/or words. They may use anything to decorate it—concert tickets, photos of friends, campaign buttons—anything except nudes. I show them a variety of excellent covers done by former students: some are covered completely with fashion photos, others with sports photos, and a few contain nothing but images of booze, cigarettes, and fancy cars.

Many students will have quotes from Malcolm X, Magic Johnson, rap artists, or their own poetry or lyrics. Anonymous quotes, cut out from magazines, grace most covers:

- I'm just not ready to get involved

- Condoms? No problem!

- My mom's going through menopause right now so it's sort of like having two teenagers in the house

- AIDS is spread through blood, semen and ignorance

- Rather than starve your body, expand your mind!

And my favorite:

- The quality of education depends more on what's going on at home than in the school. And more on what is going on in the student than what is going on in the teacher.

I explain that the cover should reflect this period of their life, and tell them that they will get the folder back with all their journal entries at the end of the nine weeks. Someone usually asks why I still have all these folders if everything gets returned. I explain that over the eighteen years that I've been teaching this course, some students have transferred out without taking their journals, some have given me their work because they do not want their "nosy" parents getting into their personal business, and others have gifted me with their covers because I found them so original and creative. I encourage everyone to have fun with this assignment because I hope they will enjoy looking back on it years later—especially if they become parents of teens!

In addition to the outside cover, a current photo is required. I find these pictures very helpful when I read through all the journals at the end of the course: with two hundred students, it's easy to get names confused. It is fascinating to see what kind of photo each student chooses—many are school IDs, but some will show the student with family or friends, partying, modeling, kissing, and even getting high. Each journal cover and photograph tells me something special about the student, but what is most revealing will be what is written on the pages inside. But that comes later. Both the journal cover and photo are due in one week.

Switching gears now, I have the students complete the second journal assignment, which is to answer this question:

When I graduate from BHS...(explain your plans for life after high school—job? college? military? children? marriage? travel? etc.). How realistic are these plans?

I assure the students that they need not agonize over this assignment: it's not meant to be a heavy question. It's okay not to know what you're going to be and it's okay to change your plans anytime in the course of your life. Most people do. When I was their age, I would have said, "When I graduate from high school, I plan to go to U.C., get married, have a couple of kids, and become a child physical therapist." I ended up doing only one of those things—graduating from the University of California at Berkeley. If they keep their journals, this particular entry may be fun to look back at years from now.

Day 5: Today I have the students introduce themselves to their classmates and tell a little about themselves. Sometimes I have each student interview another student, then introduce that student to the class. These introductions, along with the open discussions we have held in the past few days, leave us feeling quite comfortable with one another.

A student lingers after one class to say that she already knows that she can trust me. She needs to talk. She has missed her period and thinks that she might be pregnant. But there is more to the story. The possible pregnancy was due to a rape during the summer. Together we call Planned Parenthood and Bay Area Women Against Rape—the local rape crisis counseling center. She seems relieved to have shared this secret, and I feel good that she trusted me and was willing to seek more help. Already the serenity of summer has become a very distant memory.

I keep one boy after another class because he was being somewhat disruptive and when we have dealt with this issue he says that he has a question for me. His girlfriend had been raped and he wasn't quite sure how to act with her. He tells me he is a Christian and plans to keep his virginity until he is married. Everything he says indicates that he treated her in a very sensitive and caring manner. I tell him that she was lucky to have such an understanding boyfriend. As soon as he leaves, another young man wants to talk. His friend is suicidal and she lives in another city. We talk about how he could possibly handle the situation.

After school, two former students—both gay—come by to visit. They ask how the Gay and Lesbian Support Group is doing—something I was asked to sponsor many years ago. I tell them that we have some new members and a cosponsor—a teacher who came out to his students last spring. They ask me how it came about that he chose to come out of the closet. I tell them that during class one of his students yelled out, "Are you a fuckin' faggot?" and he responded, "No, I am a proud black gay man." We talk about this and the fact that recently the issue of homosexuality has hit some new raw nerves. Social Living teachers have invited gay and lesbian speakers into their classes since the course was first developed in 1967, but only recently did the issue become so volatile with some students. We talk a little longer, then I excuse myself as I need to be at a meeting.

Each day students are adding and dropping classes and I am still searching for chairs to accommodate the forty-one students now attending my seventh period. The vice-principal finally locates some but says I had better act quickly because other teachers need them. There is no one in the school to help me move them. On any given day, in addition to being a teacher, I must also fill the role of nurse (do you have a Band-Aid? condom? maxi-pad?), crisis counselor (rape, suicide, pregnancy), mediator ("These girls are going to beat me up"), policewoman ("Please put the dice away," "No smoking on campus," "You can't park here"), or, as in this case, janitor. I seek out another vice-principal and with her help get the last few chairs I need for the next day. A seventh style of combination deskchair has been added to my collection!

Right now I am feeling positive about all of my classes and feeling great joy and satisfaction in teaching. I can easily cope with listening to the stories that are shared privately with me between classes, at lunch, and after school—like the two girls who told me they were pregnant, one of whom already has a baby, or the teenage father who was using a condom but the girl still got pregnant. What should he do? We talked about what she was planning on doing and he was sure that she would make him a father for the second time—at the age of fifteen. Two babies by two different females.

Most of the time I can hear about these painful predicaments and move on. It comes with the job of teaching this class. I open up personal, controversial, or seldom-talked-about issues and kids want to talk, and the topics can push a lot of buttons. It always feels good to connect on such a deep level and know that I might be helping and hopefully leading my students or their friends to further healing.

In nine weeks, which usually come down to some thirty-eight to forty actual teaching days, we will attempt to cover everything from birth to death—sexuality, relationships, abuse (sexual, emotional, and physical), STDs/AIDS, drugs and alcohol, stress reduction, suicide prevention, self-image, grief, and loss. Obviously we could spend a whole semester on any one of these topics, but, since that's not possible, I try to cut to the core of each topic. I hope that the information provided, together with the variety of opinions expressed, will lead the students to open up their minds to new perspectives and personal insight.

Each class will move at a different pace, even though for my own sanity I would rather have all five classes doing approximately the same material. I have taught this class to some 10,000 students, and what makes it exciting and always new for me is that each class period has a different chemistry, each student has a wealth of experience to contribute, and each represents a new challenge. In one class, there could be a few students who feel the need to be very intimidating, hostile, and negative. The very next group could be just the opposite—the students incredibly open and supportive of one another and the class so positive, powerful, and really magical that I wish I could keep them all day.

2 | **Sexuality**

NOW THAT THE GROUND RULES of the course have been established, and we've had time to get acquainted with each other, it's time to get into the body of the course. I almost always address the topic of human sexuality first because sex is a fun and engaging way to start. My students are curious, mystified, fearful, pressured, sometimes preoccupied. Even on the list of questions they draw up on the first day of school, typically 95 percent of the questions will have something to do with sex. They are often misinformed (or uninformed) and confused—the constant bombardment of suggestive lyrics and of sexual images and messages in movies, TV, and advertising being responsible for much of this confusion. Most of them will form at least one romantic relationship during their teen years, so they need to have all the facts in order to make wise choices and to protect themselves.

On my part, if I ever need a rationale for spending the amount of time on sex education that I do (about two out of the nine weeks), there are plenty of statistics to prove the need:

- Approximately 25% of 15-year-old girls and 33% of 15-year-old boys have had sexual intercourse. Among all adolescents, 77% of females and 86% of males are sexually active by age 20.

- 1.1 million teenage girls get pregnant each year: 1 out of 10 girls under the age of 20.

- 3 million teens—1 out of 6—are infected with a sexually transmitted disease every year.

- At least 40,000 teenage girls drop out of school each year because of pregnancy.

Or to put it in slightly different terms:

- Every day 8,400 teenagers become sexually active.
- Every day teenagers give birth to 1,340 babies, and teens younger than 15 give birth to 29 babies.
- Every day an estimated 1,115 teenagers have abortions.
- Every day 480 teenagers contract syphilis or gonorrhea.

So today I plan to get started on the topic of sex and have the students write a journal entry on that topic. But first, I need to explain the process of journal writing to them. I hand out the Journal Assignments sheet *(see Appendix),* which consists of four pages, and I tell them not to panic—we won't use all of the questions. During the nine weeks we usually only have time for twenty journal assignments, and they've already completed two of them. I keep a running list of the assignments on the board for the benefit of those who are absent. There are certain questions I always assign—others I select based on where each group seems to be heading, or particular holidays, unusual incidents at school, or current events (e.g., earthquakes, fires, wars). The journal entries are to be kept in the journal folder, which is due later this week.

I tell my students that the main purpose of writing in a journal is to get in touch with their feelings. I explain that the process of getting thoughts onto paper can help clarify feelings, release different emotions, and put things in perspective. As someone once told me, paper is the perfect listener. Many students are very open in class but others have difficulty giving voice to their feelings. Often students will brag or cover up in class but will usually write very truthfully in their journals. Countless entries have ended with "I never told this to anyone before" or "I am so glad you asked us to write about this today."

When they are writing in their journals, they don't need to worry about spelling or grammar. It is also okay if they want to include drawings, slang, poetry, etc.; the important thing is to describe their thoughts, feelings, opinions, and values. I assure the students that the journal is strictly private. If they do not want me to read what they have written, they can simply fold the entry up and I will not read it. If they do not trust me, they can staple it shut or even use some superglue!

I use the journals as a way of communicating with my students. Whenever anyone wants me to read what they have written, I will take their journal home, read it, respond, and return it the next day. Otherwise, they are to collect all the writings until the end of the seventh week, at which time they are to turn in the completed journals, and I will read them *all* and return them by the end of the nine-week course.

In the first class, a girl asks if we can finish the questions we started on the first day, instead of beginning to write in the journals, and there is a chorus of approval. I generally like to keep all the classes in the same place, but at the same time I am not rigid about sticking to strict schedules if I feel that the discussion is important. So in this class I set aside the journal assignment and we pick up where we left off that day. The girls ask the guys:

> Why do you act so macho in front of your friends? Why do you have sex, get the female pregnant, and leave? Why do you lie so much? Why do you think that our bad emotions always have something to do with PMS? How do you feel about girls asking you out?

The guys ask the girls:

> How does being a woman affect your life? What do you look for in a man? Why do you go for those dirty-ass drug dealers with no education?

The bell rings and someone asks if we can finish answering the questions tomorrow. I tell them that I don't plan to come to school on Saturday!

In the next class, we get ready to work on this journal question:

> **Sex...when and how did you learn about it? What was your reaction? How do you feel about sexuality now—in the media, teenage sexuality, homosexuality/bisexuality, romance, virginity, etc.?**

To head off complaints, I acknowledge that this is rather a broad question—actually a series of questions—and they don't need to address all parts of it. Before they start writing, I'll read them quite a few journal entries from former students, which will give them some ideas for writing their own responses. For now, I just want them to have the journal question in the back of their minds.

For each journal assignment, I always read a variety of entries that I have collected from previous students' journals. I try to balance out these selections to encourage my students to interpret the topic as freely as possible. The selections I read could be from someone who was in my class as recently as last quarter, or as long ago as ten years: the important thing is that they be relevant to today's teenagers, and that they be expressed clearly or in a way that will evoke some kind of response. Since I read over six hundred journals every school year, I have a feel for what is meaningful to my students.

Students are almost always willing to share, through their writing, things that they are too shy or embarrassed to talk about openly in class. I estimate that 98 percent of the students who have been approached have allowed me to use what they have written. (I always get written permission to use the material before I present it in class. Often students will write at the beginning of their journals, "You may use anything from my journal.")

Reading journal entries always sparks a certain amount of discussion, and occasionally we will get sidetracked. Each time I have to determine whether or not the discussion will be worthwhile. I like the spontaneity that arises from students, but I must be careful that it is not a ploy to avoid a topic that some may think is too painful or boring, or not pertinent to their lives. I always feel rushed and would love the luxury of a semester class to be able to cover everything the students want to talk about, and in further depth than is possible in the short time we have together.

The sample entries that I've chosen to read today cover a broad range of subjects all having to do with the general topic of sexuality. Most were written in answer to the journal question on sex, but some were written in the form of letters to fulfill a different journal assignment. Glancing at the first entry, I see that it has a four-letter word in it, which reminds me that I need to explain my viewpoint on profanity and censorship. I apologize in advance in case this kind of language offends anyone, but I feel strongly that it is important for me to read these selections as they were written. If I read "bleep" every time I come across a "bad" word, the writings will lose their impact.

I begin with two letters that two different girls wrote to their boyfriends:

Dear Boyfriend:

What's up with our relationship? I mean when we first started out it was fine. I mean up until about a month and a half ago. When I found you were dating other girls. And you say you love me. You stupid ass. Sometimes I wonder if all you want me for is a place to stay. Why do you treat me like fucking shit? Call me names (bitch, ho', fat) I mean why? Am I that damn bad? I realize I'm not the best woman in the world. You want to know something? Deep down I think you are still cheating on me. Every time you come over you turn off your pager or hide it. Why? Is it something you don't want me to see? And don't blame it on the battery. Why don't we ever go anywhere grown-up together? A night on the town in San Francisco sounds fine. You don't even call me back when I page you. Why? G., you hurt me so much but I always try to outweigh the bad with the good even though it doesn't always seem like it. What must I do to get more attention from you? Please tell me. Well, I'm about to go but I love you so very, very much. Oh, I think because you know I love you so much you treat me like shit, pure shit. I love you G.

Love,
Female, 17

There are audible groans in the room, especially from the females. "How can she stay with him?" "Fool!" I ask if anyone in the class is in a relationship like this—or knows someone who is. Half a dozen hands go up. Before I start reading the next entry I ask them to consider which male might make the better boyfriend!

Dear Boyfriend:

I'm so glad I met you this year. Why did it take so long for you to come along? You make me feel real good about myself. No boy has ever talked to me about safe sex the way you did (and still do). When you said we should both go to the doctor and get checked so we can have sex without a condom I felt really comfortable. Even though we haven't had sex yet I feel like that's something we don't even need. Even though that's what we both want. We get along real good and I bet every time we pass by some of your or my friends they probably all think that we have sex all the time. I guess because of the way we're always hugging on each other in the halls or in the courtyard. Damn I feel really lucky to have found you. Just because I say we don't need to have sex, doesn't change our needs, because I know I can't wait 'til we do it. I promise it will be worth the wait for both of us.

Sincerely,
Your appreciative girlfriend
Female, 18

There is a collective sigh—a feeling of "isn't that sweet." It's not sarcastic, but rather, "wow, she's lucky." Last I heard, this couple was still together after eighteen months and she said, "the relationship is even better"—and she is no longer a virgin.

The next selection, I tell the class, represents what many guys feel. In class, most guys who talk will tend to brag or at least make it known that they are having sex. But many of the guys are virgins and most feel fine about it.

I'm still a virgin but it does not bother me. For a while, I really wanted to "have sex" soon because I thought it would be with someone special, that loved me, and that I felt safe with. I'm very conscious of what other people think of me—a very negative characteristic—and so I'd want it to be with someone who thinks I'm special too—but right now I don't think I'd have time for a major relationship, because of the time committed to each other. In other ways I think a good relationship would be great for me, psychologically, to have someone who wants to be a part of my life, and I a part of theirs.

I'm not worried any more about "having sex" soon. I would like to develop a close relationship with someone before I graduate and when the two of us really felt we loved each other that much. Because I really do believe making love is a very close, personal thing and really want the first time to be special for me and my girlfriend. Oh, and I would hope that she would be a virgin too so we could share it together.

Male, 15

My problem is that I got a girl pregnant. Well, that wasn't so bad because I could support it, but I got another pregnant. If only I could have known the first one was pregnant, if me and the first girl didn't

get into an argument I would have never went and had sexual intercourse with another.

Signed BAD LUCK. What should I do? (I'm confused.)
Male, 17

The class takes on a new level of quietness as they realize that what
they are hearing is very personal and private. I continue.

I've been pregnant before. Twice. I feel so ashamed saying that! Both
were with the same guy. The first time was our fault because we didn't
use birth control, but the second time we did, only it didn't work. The
first time was hard because I didn't tell my parents and having their
support would have helped a whole lot! I didn't tell simply because I
was ashamed. It was also hard enough already just dealing with being
sexual. I had abortions both times. My boyfriend was very supportive,
but at the time it didn't feel like enough because he has a hard time
expressing his feelings and he was scared, and it was hard for both of
us to be supportive of the other one while both of us were feeling so
rotten.

The second time, I told my parents, and that made so much of a
difference!!! My boyfriend came with me both times to have my abortions, and the second time both him and my mom held my hands. It
hurt like hell. Especially emotionally. I love J. and I hated to kill a part
of us. I'm glad though that it was him who was there for me. In some
ways it has really brought us closer together, but if I could do it over,
Shit! I would be more careful.

Female, 15

Being a young teenage mother is very hard. I never thought that being
a mother is so hard but now I see that it's not easy. I love my son
dearly. I do what is necessary for my son's needs. I do know that he
needs to be taught also, just like me. If I had to start all over again I
would have never had a baby. I don't plan on having another child in
the future. So as of now today I'll always be his mother, and love him
dearly.

I advise that no teenager should have a baby at a young age like me.
Female, 16

In each class I am aware that what I read may hit home—how many girls are currently thinking they are pregnant? How many boys are wondering what they will do if their girlfriend is pregnant? I think about the teen father I spoke to last week. His girlfriend has decided to keep the baby and he fears that he will be forced back to the streets to deal drugs. For him, that is the only way he sees to support the child he already has and the future baby. He doesn't want to go back to dealing and wants to stay in school, but the pressures are just too great. I suggested alternatives but he's too overwhelmed to see any way out but his own. He has stopped coming to class. I wonder what has happened to him.

I go on to the next entry:

I'm 15 years old and a virgin. My virginity to me is as precious as gold. And I am very surprised that I have kept it this long. I'm not going to be ridiculous and save it for my husband on our wedding night because I'm scared that I wouldn't be able to wait that long, in fact by the time Christmas comes I doubt if I'll be a virgin. But what makes it so funny to me is that as soon as I turned 14 my mother put me on the pill because she was a pregnant teen (16). I have a steady boyfriend (my first love) and I told him that I was a virgin (because he didn't ask). He means a lot to me and I love him. And he loves me and he doesn't pressure me into trying to have sex with him. He has already told me that whenever I'm ready he's ready and he'll wait until the end of time if he has to. Even though I'm on the pill I am going to make him wear a rubber (condom) because I don't know who he has had sex with before me. And when we make love I want it to be special not just gang bang then it's over. I already know that it's going to hurt like hell but I think that I could deal with it. I just want it to be right and make sure that he is the right one.

Female, 15

A girl raises her hand and asks, "How many teens have sex?" I tell her that it really varies in terms of age—there is a big difference between fourteen-year-olds and nineteen-year-olds. There are differences between males and females and between races. I tell her that I will put some statistics on the board tomorrow.

I also tell her that the statistics only show how many have had sexual intercourse. I think a more interesting study would be a follow-up, perhaps a year later, to see how many felt it was worthwhile: "If you could go back in time, would you choose to do it again?" I rarely hear anyone say, "I wish I had had sex with so and so." I frequently hear, "I wish I had waited," or "What a bitch/asshole she/he turned out to be."

> I guess there are two definitions for that word sex. One through love and [the] other for variable reasons (to hold on, peer pressure, experience, etc.). It's annoying because at our age we don't know the difference and a lot of the time relationships become dependent on sex, not compatibility, enjoyment of company, or love but mainly sex. Sometimes I wonder if relationships could last without it. It's a beautiful thing to share but not if you have to lose your respect. Sometimes I really do wonder. We use it to reassure ourselves that we are appealing and loved at this age but a lot of the time it doesn't even matter if you are or aren't. Sex is emphasized too much in this society and I think a lot of people feel as I do about it. The meaning of LOVE is LOST to sex. There is such less pressure in a friendship than in a relationship—lovers come and go—but friends are eternal.
>
> Female, 15

I always remind students—especially the girls—about the statement "lovers come and go—but friends are eternal." Put another way, often a girl will ignore her friends when she has a boyfriend, but when the romance breaks up she most often looks to those same friends for comfort. "But how are the friends feeling at this point?" I ask. "This happened to me and I really resented how she ignored me and this wasn't the first time she acted this way," says a girl who still seems pissed off about it. I sum up by suggesting that it is important to keep a balance in your relationships and to remember that your friends will generally be around long after a romantic relationship is over—if you treat them right!

Switching to another aspect of relationships and sexuality, I read the following entry:

> I have been a lesbian ever since I was born. I realized that I was gay when I was about eight years old. I can remember liking my fifth grade teacher. My feeling for girls did not bother me. I felt special, different

from all the other girls. They were into boys and I was into girls. I thought that that was so neat. As I have become older I have come out to my mother. It flipped her out. It made me feel hurt—to her I had become a whole new person. She started calling me names and things like that were the hardest things I will ever face in my life. Being gay is great and I love it. I'm glad to be a lesbian. I hope someday people will be able to set their fears aside and accept us as they would accept a heterosexual couple—because we are human beings and not freaks.

Female, 15

Several hands go up and I call on the boy with the baseball cap on backwards, Walkman around his neck, and dark glasses shielding his eyes. "How would she know she was a lesbian ever since she was born?" I respond, "Let me assume you are straight—" He jumps in with "I'm 100 percent heterosexual, I'm straight." "Have you always known you were straight?" "YES!" he quickly answers. I continue, "Many gay people also feel that they have always been homosexual, and most go through much self-doubt, sometimes self-loathing because society gives out the message that it is not okay to be homosexual. I acknowledge that people have more to say on the subject of homosexuality (we could get hopelessly sidetracked here) and explain that we will spend more time on this later. Right now I wish to finish reading the cross section of journal writings.

I have slept twice with a guy (different ones) overnight. It is the nicest, nicest thing in the world to fall asleep in someone's arms and wake up in the morning to find he wasn't a dream at all and that you're still lying beside him. Also, being half woken up in the early morning by a shower of kisses. What bliss!

Female, 15

Many students remember the exact moment they first heard about sex. For many, learning about the body and sexuality has been a very natural part of lives, while others had a dramatic or at least memorable introduction! I think it is interesting that many parents teach their kids about their body by saying, "This is my nose," pointing to their nose, "and these are my eyes," pointing to their eyes, and then they proceed to name all the basic body parts until they get to the genitals, which they usually call "down there." Very few students learn terms such as vulva, clitoris, or penis from their parents. The next entry, which was written by a girl who had a "down there" mother, is one of my all-time favorites. I ask the students to picture themselves back in elementary school:

> I remember when I was in the second grade, I went to school, as I always went to school and learned one word that was to change my life forever. I was on the playground and this boy who I was friends with said, "Wanna fuck?" I said, "Not right now, I'm playing Battlestar Galactica." Well, that night, needless to say, my curiosity got the best of me, and boy—did it kill the cat. I went up to my mom, thinking it was either some sort of ball game, food, or commonly used expression and said, "Hey, Mom, wanna fuck?" Well she slapped my hand and said, "Don't use such foul language that you don't know." Well, being more inquisitive I said, "What does 'fuck' mean?" Well she started talking about boys and their instruments and how I'm not supposed to play them until I get married. Well, you know where this led. I thought that it was really neat that boys could play music with their private parts when girls couldn't.
>
> Female, 16

In some classes the kids are falling out of their seats laughing while others don't seem to think my favorite is very funny. It always amazes me how each class has a totally different chemistry and personality. With that final selection then, I give the class the rest of the period to write their journal entry on sex, reminding them that they do *not* have to write about their personal experiences or lack of experiences. I tell them, "You might want to write about sex and the media or how you feel about sex education in the schools. Remember, if you don't want me to read what you wrote, simply fold your paper."

The Sexuality Worksheet

On the next class day, I pass out the Sexuality Worksheet *(see Appendix)*, a list of over thirty questions that will be the focus of our attention for the next week or so. I put this worksheet together to make sure I cover all the basics with each class. It is so easy to get off the subject and forget what was covered the previous day or last week, and there are certain critical issues I want to be sure to cover.

The questions on the worksheet run the gamut from douching and bleeding during pregnancy and first intercourse to the cost of raising a child from birth to age eighteen. The specific facts that each question elicits are not nearly as important as the discussions that follow as I read each one out loud. Each class responds differently: one might spend fifteen or twenty minutes on a single item, and just a few minutes on another, while the reverse might be true in the next class. And I, too, will have more to say on certain key questions than on others.

The first question reads:

The word "pregnant" was censored from TV in the fifties.
True or false?

We talk about the difference between the TV shows and lyrics of today and those of the past as the answer to this question is True. For instance, when the Rolling Stones appeared on "The Ed Sullivan Show" back in the '60s, they were asked to change the lyrics from "Let's spend *the night* together" to "Let's spend *some time* together." Then I ask for some of the bolder lyrics of current songs and raps, and the classroom comes alive with students outdoing one another with the most graphic lines, often accompanied by spontaneous imitations of favorite MTV idols. We talk about the media and sexual messages and how their parents and grandparents may be shocked at the difference between the American Bandstand of the past and current music videos. It *is* a vastly different world.

Question number two brings us face to face with what is undoubtedly one of the major social concerns in the U.S. today:

More than _____ teenagers become pregnant each year in the U.S.

Someone says 3,000 to 4,000; someone else offers 100,000. Higher, I hint. Half a million someone shouts. I tell them the answer is 1.1 million. Even though everyone seems to know someone who has gotten pregnant, the class seems stunned that the figure is so high. And stunned by another fact: that the U.S. has the highest teenage pregnancy rate of any industrialized nation.

This next question is one I always allow plenty of time for:

At what age should a person stop having sex?

Many students guess around fifty years old although the youngest age I ever heard was thirty-seven! Those who set it at fifty usually say it's because that is when a woman goes through menopause. When they pick any age above fifty-five, their reasoning is that people that age are just too OLD! Most students correctly say people can be sexually active throughout their lives—with exceptions due to some health or drug problems. The point I'm trying to make—and one that I will repeat a number of times—is that they have the rest of their lives to be sexually active and, considering the rampant growth of sexually transmitted diseases (including AIDS) among teens, and the fact that over one million teenage girls get pregnant each year, their wisest course might be to postpone sex. I state it again differently. "You have decades left to be sexually active—wait for the right person, the right time, and what is right for your personal, moral, and religious values."

Teen Pregnancies

I use the next question to bolster my argument for postponing sex:

For teens: 6 in 10 pregnancies result in live births; 3 in 10 are terminated by abortion; 1 in 10 ends in miscarriage; 1 in 6 of the live births is given up for adoption. True or False?

The answer is True, and I explain why I think this information is important. I ask the class if anyone knows someone who got pregnant while using contraception, and there are several replies. "My mom was using a diaphragm and here I am!" "My auntie was on the pill and got pregnant." "My friend was using foam and her boyfriend a condom and she now has a little girl." My point is that if a guy has sex with a girl she can get pregnant, even if they are using some kind of protection. Furthermore, even if they have discussed the possibility of abortion if she got pregnant, five times out of ten—half the time—the girl will keep the baby. So the girl will become a teenage mother with a minimum commitment of eighteen years to her child. And the boy?

Often he will not be involved in the parenting at all. Paraphrasing one of Jesse Jackson's adages, someone says, "Any guy can make a baby, but it takes a man to raise a baby." I suggest that a few minutes of pleasure isn't worth the risk of having a baby at this age.

As we go through the worksheet, I stop to give statistics or to read old journal entries that will help illustrate certain points I'm trying to make. There are many letters on the topic of teen pregnancies. In the next one, a pregnant teen imagines what her unborn baby would write to her:

Dear Mom,

I wish you could've thought about creating me before I even came to be. I'm not mad but slightly pissed that you could have sex without a condom and <u>not</u> think of me. Well I guess I can't complain, you are the one who is going to bring me into the world. But I can already sense that my father is hardly going to be placed in my life. I guess I'll try my best to make you happy even though the time might be rough. I'm glad that there are no regrets. No matter what we go through.

I'll always love my mommy.
Love You Always,
Your Child
P.S. It's just me and you against the world.
Female, 17

....

No, I was not using birth control. Yes, I wanted to become pregnant at one point. But when I got pregnant it was a shock. Then I thought about it and said I'm not ready for this. Everyone seems to think when they have this adorable baby that the baby is not going to cry and it's going to be OK. Well it's bullshit. After I had my daughter I got on birth control. It was not my cup of tea. All I did was get fat and feel like I'm pregnant. I feel some teenagers get pregnant because they want to move out. And they think that little welfare check is going to get them somewhere. Being a mother you have to have patience with your child and that's something I do not have all the time. The least thing you need is getting up in the morning, getting her dressed and having to put up with all kinds of bullshit with a child not wanting to get her hair combed.

No one knew I was pregnant because I was scared at the time. But my mom finally found out when I was about six months. There was nothing she could do after that. I felt really bad that I couldn't just go up to tell her I was pregnant. That night they found out that I was pregnant my mother called the father of the baby and he tried to deny it. My family gave me a lot of pressure saying things like, "You should get an abortion." They would say things like I was a slut, etc.

Female, 17

I find that most students do not tell their parents that they are pregnant (often because they are denying it to themselves as well) and the subject is not discussed until the girl can no longer hide it. Most often this causes an ugly scene, but once the baby is born the grandparents usually change their attitude. Being a pregnant teen does not have the stigma it once did, in fact some teens feel it is a status symbol. Still, the situation can be extremely difficult—especially for a young woman who has to cope without support from her parents or boyfriend.

I don't really have any serious problems except that my menstruation is two and a half months late. I've been feeling sickly lately. Always hungry. I'm trying not to think that I'm pregnant, but I guess I really need to think about it. After all no female wants to be pregnant, at least not this female. I haven't told my boyfriend that my menstruation is late. Besides I don't think that he wants another child, he's 18 with two children and he doesn't need another.

Female, 15

There is a lot of reaction to this last entry. I ask the class what she should do. All those who respond say she should find out if she is pregnant. "Yes," I say, "but why?" "Well, if she is, then she needs to decide what to do." "Like what?" Silence.

It is very common for girls to put off having a pregnancy test out of fear, but, I state flatly, DENIAL is not a healthy way to cope with this situation. If she is pregnant, she needs to make some very important decisions right away. If she wants to have an abortion, the sooner she has it the safer it will be. If she chooses to have the baby, she should get prenatal care early, and learn about taking proper care of herself— eating right, not smoking or doing other drugs, and so on. If she is not pregnant, she no longer needs to worry, but if she plans to continue to be sexually active, she needs to use some method of birth control and use it correctly and faithfully.

> I found out that I was pregnant when I was 15 years old. For a long time I tried to deny it because I was scared. I couldn't tell my momma because she thought I was Little Miss Do-no-wrong. I delayed going to get a pregnancy test until near the end of my third month, the test came back POSITIVE!! I was not even hesitant to tell the clinic counselor that I wanted an abortion. It was like all the fear had drained out of me, and I became aware of the reality of carrying a child. After I had my abortion my boyfriend who got me pregnant tried to be really (in his words) supportive of me, I was feeling fine though. I still haven't told my momma about my abortion, but she does know that I'm not a virgin anymore. I'm proud of my decision to have an abortion, because I couldn't support a child.
>
> Female, 16

I ask why some girls do not tell their boyfriends they are pregnant. "They're scared they might get hit or he might want her to do something different than she wants." "Right," I say, "and what else might be going on?" One girl explains that a teenager who is pregnant does not even want to admit it to herself. To tell her boyfriend may be an added complication. I ask her if she thinks that most girls tell their parents. "Maybe some girls can talk to their mom but mine would yell and scream." Judging from the side comments of other girls, I suspect that few would seek out their mothers during this difficult time.

I tell a story that is still vivid in my mind although it happened many, many years ago. A young female in my class was looking very depressed and I walked over to her desk and asked her if she was okay. She said no, and extended her arm to reveal her wrist. "I tried to kill myself last night." We talked quietly and she told me that she found out she was pregnant and immediately told her boyfriend—of TWO YEARS—and his only response was, "Don't even talk to me until you have had an abortion."

This is not to say that the males never have an emotional involvement. I don't hear very often from males on this topic but when they

- Early, legal abortion is one of the safest medical procedures, safer than a penicillin injection. For adolescents, abortion at any stage of pregnancy is safer than childbirth.

- A 1992 study of women seeking pregnancy tests found those aged 14–17 to be as competent as adults to make informed and independent decisions about abortion and to understand the risks and benefits of abortion.

- 46% of teenage mothers do not receive prenatal care during their first trimester, 9% do not receive care until their third trimester, and 4% do not receive prenatal care at all.

do express themselves it is very powerful and moving. Too often we fail to realize the impact that an abortion can have on the life of the teenage male. The following letters poignantly describe the deep sadness that some have experienced:

Dear Baby That Never Had a Chance:

Baby I am really sorry for what we had to do and I'm sorry for not being there when everything happened. If we would have had you we would have never been good enough parents. Your mom has had a lot of problems in her life and is just now getting back to normal. We never gave you a chance but then again you would have never had a chance with us. I'll never forgive myself for what has happened and I can never apologize for what we did. I love you so much. I hope you understand why because I don't. I wanted you but then thought of what your life would be like. I think I sound like a person that doesn't care but I do. I just can't understand anything and I have a hard time expressing myself to you or anybody. I guess I'm just a punk. Now I wish I would have had you and not have been thinking of my life. Yours should have come first. I'm sorry. I really love you. And your mom is a great woman. We will never forget you. Words can't explain for what we did and there is no reason now for what we did. I'm so sorry.

   I don't think I will ever get over what has happened.

Male, 16½

....

I got this girl pregnant and she killed my baby!!! I mean she just took it into her own hands. She should've checked with me first because if she would've called me I would've said not to kill the baby.

Male, 17

....

About three months ago I went through a problem that scared me more than I had ever been scared in my life. My girlfriend got pregnant. It was my first time ever experiencing anything like this. I never talked about it, so when it came I did not know how to handle it when I found out how much money and all I had to pay. I was wondering how was I going to get the money. I never came to school. I nearly flunked but it seemed as if the world had already fallen in on me so I did not care.

Male, 15

The stereotype of a teenage girl nonchalantly saying, "Well, if I come up pregnant I'll just have an abortion" is a myth. I don't even know where it came from because I have never heard of anyone considering abortion as if it is no big deal. Both young men and women may be deeply affected and the support of a loving parent would be so welcome. It's a shame that so few teens feel that they can turn to their parents for advice, love, and support.

It was Friday night and I was at the clinic with two of my friends. I was about to do something which I would never forget for the rest of my life. I was about to get my very first pregnancy test. As I sat there with cold hands and a confused head, so many things crossed my mind. I really didn't think that the test would turn out positive but, to my surprise it did. At that point when the lady asked me what I was going to do I was sure that I couldn't keep it. So she gave me all the information and sent me on my way. When I went outside to face my friends I didn't know what to do and all of a sudden tears started to come down my cheeks. I don't think they expected it either and they just hugged me for awhile...but it was something I couldn't control....I called my boyfriend and told him. He asked me what I was going to do and I didn't know what to say. I was silent, just silent. That night I cried almost all night at least until I fell asleep. Then over the next couple of days I talked to my boyfriend about all our options and we decided that we weren't ready to have a baby. At first, I was sure that I couldn't keep it. But then I kept changing my mind. I kept trying to make excuses to keep it. And I said stuff like, "Oh, maybe Mom won't be that mad when she sees the baby." But, I realized that I was just not ready in many ways. So the next thing I knew, I was at Planned Parenthood....I was really glad my boyfriend came with me....It was pretty fast except I had some mild cramps for about 10 minutes afterwards. I felt a sense of relief and loss at the same time....Ever since then I've been trying to forget about it as much as possible but it keeps coming back every now and then and tears just take over. This whole thing took a very long time. Of couse there were things which I left out like the MediCal, transportation, cutting school, lying to my family etc. This whole thing was a lesson to me. I would advise anyone who is sexually active to take the best precautions they can because it's not very pleasant at all. It's hell to be quite honest. The worst thing is I keep seeing my baby's big brown eyes staring at me with this sorry look which makes me so guilty....I have so much more to say but I don't want to bore you and I don't feel like typing anymore so thanks for reading this Ms. Rubin.

Female, 15

I always make the point that abortion is legal in California and the girl does not have to tell her parents. Kids often hear that something is banned or required in another state and mistakenly think that the same is true of California, too. They also get a lot of misinformation from peers and family.

The next girl also describes what it was like for her to go through an abortion. Like many other girls, she got pregnant even though she was using some form of birth control. I repeat the litany that if one embarks on a sexual relationship it is extremely important to remember that birth control must be used *properly,* each and every time, *and* to realize that *nothing* is 100 percent effective.

I've been using a diaphragm for a year, but last summer I got pregnant. It obviously caused problems....I was trying to hold down two jobs and I was hassling with my mother too much. I started living at my boyfriend's house and that made my mother even sadder and angrier. Meanwhile, I was sick a lot. My stomach and head hurt and I threw up everything almost. My boyfriend didn't know what to do. I mean, he was only a boy, too, and here we were with only each other to hang on to. (We didn't tell our parents.) It made him grow up a hell of a lot faster. (Me too.)

Through Family Planning I got an abortion scheduled. When I went to the hospital I thought that all I had to do was sit on a table and somehow they would get the fetus out. Well, that wasn't true. I was first given this paper robe to wear after I had locked all my clothes in a locker. Then they put me in a recovery room and this woman gave me two shots. Right away I started to feel numb and in fifteen minutes I was dizzy. My doctor and my anesthesiologist came and talked to me about what was going to happen. Before I knew what was happening they wheeled me into a room with lights and equipment all around, and I breathed deeply and felt myself totally relax. I woke up and wondered where I was and whether anything had actually happened or not. I remembered then, and I felt so much relief! When I was fully conscious I wanted to get up and eat since I wasn't allowed to eat or drink the night before. I felt happy and proud of myself that I had gone through it myself....

I had no guilt feelings about my abortion. I knew there was no way I would be able to take the right kind of care for my baby. If I had been older and more secure, (I mean money, home and my boyfriend—if he would take the responsibility too) then I would have CONSIDERED having the baby. A person should be brought into the world loved, planned for, and WANTED. I didn't feel guilty about killing a person—I did almost feel guilty for not feeling guilty....

If you have any questions about almost anything about your body, contraceptives, abortion, infections, go to Family Planning. They can really, really help.

Female, 16

For some girls the experience of abortion lingers on long after the procedure. The following letter was given to me so that I could read it to my classes. As a result of this letter several girls exchanged phone numbers to talk with each other about their own feelings about their abortions.

Last October I had an abortion. It is not the fact that I had the abortion that bothers me. I know what I did was the best possible thing for me to do. I have no way to support myself let alone a baby also. For me there was no way I was going to have a baby brought into the world that I could not take care of and raise correctly.

Like I said before it is not the abortion that bothers me. It is the whole situation in general. I was stupid. I had unprotected sex. I used what is called the withdrawal method which in my case turned out to be the pregnancy method. Being pregnant was the worst experience in my life. I was sick all the time. I couldn't eat because I got sick after I would eat, yet I was starving because I couldn't eat. I did not treat my body the way I should have. I abused myself with food, drugs, and depression.

Now five months after the abortion (eight months since I was first pregnant) I am still dealing with the feelings that I don't understand. Why do I feel so different, I almost feel non-human. My life is so different from the lives of my friends....The thing about it is that much as I want to talk about it with my friends and much as they say they understand I know they can't and don't. Teenage pregnancy is something that is kept behind closed doors....I can't put into words exactly how I feel about the whole situation or even why I do.

Perhaps my situation will help you to never experience an unwanted pregnancy. All I can say is always use condoms. Without them there is never a safe time to have sex. Make your choices wisely.

Female, 18

Before going on, I comment that this young woman was wise to recommend condoms, but I warn the class that condoms are not 100 percent effective and should be used in combination with an additional form of birth control such as foam or a diaphragm.

In the next letter, a young woman who decided to have an abortion imagines that she has received a letter from her unborn child:

Dear Mommy,

I know you may find this very painful but I feel that you must know. I am not angry at you and you should not feel bad about your decision and what you had done. Any girl in your situation would have probably done the same. I know you made the right choice but you can't help but to think how I would of been or what I would of been. If I looked like my daddy or you. I would have been born sometime in this month. I'm really sorry I had to bring that up it only causes you pain. I'm sorry but you can't just forget about me you have to deal with the fact that you decided to get rid of me.

Love,
The daughter or son you'll never know
P.S. I love you Mommy!
Female, 16

Teenage fathers have the reputation of abandoning their babies. Sometimes it is their choice but other times the girl's mother does not want him around because "he got her pregnant"—as though he did it on his own! The following entries are from some teen fathers:

Well, Nancy it's like this. I did not plan on having a baby you know, but it just happened. See my girlfriend don't like condoms and her pill wasn't strong enough. So when we made love and it happened. We both don't believe in abortions or adoptions. So we had a girl. And now we're having another one and we're going to keep it. That's the main reason I sell dope. You had ask me how does it feel to be a teenage father. It's nice to have a baby and it's fun, you find out exciting things! Like when they learn how to walk, talk, their first tooth and everything. But it also has its bad times. Like sometimes we want to go places and we can't. But I'm getting me a 1976 Seville and her a convertible Mustang so we can move around easier. But Nancy that's it, the whole story.

Male, 15

....

I got a girl pregnant when I was 17. I asked her to get an abortion because I did not feel ready to be a father but she told me she had had an abortion. It turned out that she had not had it and she finally admitted to me that she was still pregnant. I waited for over a month before telling my father and he didn't take it too badly. I care a lot about the baby but because I go to school and work I don't get to spend as much time as I'd like with the mother and my son. We are planning to live together next year. I just hope things work out. I feel responsible for what happened so I would never have left her with the baby. My son is almost 4 mos. old now.

Male, 18

....

Being a teenage father sounds kind of odd huh? Yeah I bet your out there thinking to yourself, "it's never going to happen (to me)?" Believe me it could happen to anyone. My being a teenager and a father, has a lot of responsibilities. I'm on probation right now, and I'm paying restitution. I'm still paying it off, but now I got something else to pay for. I used to like going out to night clubs. Notice how I said used to. Being a teenage father also has its positive sides too. But when I find one I'll tell you. Maybe if we planned out all of this baby stuff it would of been better. I'm trying to find a job now, so I can support my daughter. I love her very much. She really means a lot to me because she reminds me of the one person I know very well, me. Right now I'm concentrating on getting out of high school. It's not so easy being a teenage father.

Male, 16

I am sure that I have had other students who have given their babies up for adoption but, with the exception of the case of incest *(see chapter 8)*, the following young man was the only one who ever wrote about this. When I read his letter, I asked him for permission to use it, but somehow it never happened. I contacted him a couple of years later, but by then he had lost his journal and the original letter. We decided to make a tape of him talking about his feelings, but instead he wrote another letter to me, which he dropped off at school. I didn't read it until I got home, where I sat at my desk and slowly absorbed what he had written. I am so touched by his willingness to reveal the burden he carries in his heart.

Today when you talked to me about wanting my journal and the letter it brought back memories that will always be inside of me. Sometimes I put those thoughts in the back of my mind; way back where I can almost get away from them, but there's no luck in doing so. Sometimes I'll even get the thoughts so far away that I won't think of them for a day or so but something or someone is always there to bring them back. A television commercial, someone with their baby, or even the worst, when someone actually asks me if I'm a father. When they ask me I sort of put myself out of it by just shying away, but I'm starting to learn that that is not the way to face up to something I did. I'll always be riddled with guilt and shame for what I put myself and my child through. When I found out that this girl was pregnant I really panicked. I totally denied it and really couldn't face up to it. Having a baby seemed to be the least of my concerns then. I was 15 years old and just beginning to understand the outskirts of life. I didn't need a baby to hold me back. But as the months went on I realized that I needed to live up to my problems and not hide behind my mother like I was doing. I tried to even get a look at the mother who was now about six months into pregnancy and for the first time I actually saw beauty in her. See when we had sex it was just sex and nothing more.

We were just two bored kids looking for something fun to do. I had had sex before that so it wasn't my first so I knew what to do and the ways to do it and thought of this girl as nothing but a thing. I really thought nothing for this girl but looking at her and seeing that glow she had made me want to love her. I still don't know what love is but at that moment I felt something beyond belief. As the days went on I tried to conjure up enough dauntlessness to at least talk to the girl but it was no use and I'll never forgive myself for that. I wish sometimes that I could at least listen to the baby to hear her kick or just catch a glimpse of her and compare her to myself. But I was just too much of a wimp and I'll never have any dignity for myself because of that. After the baby was born I didn't want to see her. The thought scared me so much that I nearly froze just thinking of it. But I often thought of her. Wondering if she received any characteristic from me like being a natural athlete or being able to spell with simplicity, if she was allergic to poison oak and if she loved nature like I do. After the adoption took place I grew even scareder because now I only had the thoughts with no memories. I still think of her and how she must change and grow physically and mentally each day. I often daydream and try to feel how it would have been if I were to take care of her. I know I'd be a good father and I know I'd put all my time and effort into taking the best possible care for her. Even though I haven't even seen her I still love her and always will. And even though I won't be a part in her upbringing I know that I will always be a part of her as she is a part of me.

Former Student
Male, 17

Over the years, many guest speakers have come to talk on the topic of teenage pregnancy, ranging from members of pro-life groups to representatives from adoption agencies to teen moms telling what their lives are like. Sometimes I feel that the teen mothers who speak tend to glamorize their situations, but their true feelings almost always come out in their private journal writing.

My advice to other teenagers: Stay in school and make something out of yourself and don't get pregnant and mess up your life (like I did) by having an unwanted child.

Female, 16

A few years ago, one of my students wrote about how she is handling her pregnancy. She volunteered to read this out loud to the class and instead of just sitting in her chair, she chose to come to the front of the room. In her overalls it was easy to tell that she was pregnant and proud of her decision to keep her baby:

I guess to be a teenage mother-to-be is kind of exciting. This is a totally new experience for me to go through. Of course, the morning sickness and tiredness I wish I could get rid of, but other than that I wouldn't change a thing. Everyone tells me that I'm not ready to have a child and I know that, but now I have to take a crash course and learn quick and fast. When I tell some people that I'm pregnant they don't get overexcited, they act "normal," and others act like it's a sin against God. I only say that because one of my teachers acted like I was a disease and she couldn't stand to be around me. Since I wasn't used to that kind of reaction I felt so bad that I almost cried. My mom told me that people aren't used to it and that they would come around sometime and she reassured me that this is my life and I chose to go through this and that I have her support in whatever I do.

When I found out that I was pregnant there was no way that I was getting an abortion. Everyone I knew said that I should get one, even my baby's father. I didn't listen to anyone. They opted for an adoption and I wouldn't go for that neither. This is what I wanted to do no matter who backed me up. The baby's father and I decided that since we wanted two different things that we should split up and that he would be there for the baby and all but not for me and I agreed. He had his life and I had mine and it just couldn't work between us because we had problems before I knew I was pregnant.

Female, 17

At Christmastime she was the only student to give me a card. She wrote on it: "Nancy, I know that we haven't known each other long. But you've made me feel comfortable being pregnant in your class. Anyway I just wanted to extend my gratitude."

Though the odds are stacked against them, some young women make the decision to keep their babies *and* stay in school. BHS has a special facility, the Vera Casey Center, to provide child care on campus for our students who are trying to juggle parenthood and study.

The program, the first of its kind in the United States, is almost twenty-five years old. While I am teaching about birth control and sexuality, my talks are often punctuated by the sounds of crying and screaming toddlers from the room next to mine! The infants have their own house across the street from BHS and it is required that the parent(s) take a parenting course, take the Infant-Toddler Lab course (spending time in the nursery), and at age sixteen become involved with the School to Work program. Other BHS students can earn credits by taking care of the babies. It is a highly successful program in terms of minimizing dropouts for teenage mothers and for preventing multiple pregnancies.

The Case for Sex Education

The preceding stories just give a glimpse at the consequences of this overwhelming statistic: over one million teenage girls become pregnant each year. Some of them will deal with the pregnancy completely alone, some will involve their partner, maybe their own family, and perhaps the partner's family. Many grandparents will once again be changing diapers as they become primary caregivers. So many lives are forever changed as we struggle to deal with this national crisis.

I don't think we need to look far to find the causes for this problem. Most Americans are very poorly informed about human sexuality, and we as a nation are paying a high price for the consequences of this ignorance. I think that misinformation about sex combined with a lack of love, support, or attention from one's family are the major causes of this epidemic of teen pregnancy.

It amazes me to think back on what I learned in school about human sexuality—or, more accurately, what I did not learn. From kindergarten through graduate school the extent of my entire in-school sex education totaled less than three minutes! In my eighth-grade science class the teacher held up an electrical plug and said, "This is like the male." Then he pointed to an electrical outlet in the wall and said, "This is like the female." He then took the plug and placed it in the outlet and said, "And this is sexual intercourse." For many years, I was sure I would get electrocuted if I engaged in sexual intercourse! Then again, what kind of sex education would you expect from a school whose dress code prohibited patent leather shoes because they reflected a girl's underwear?

I never even got to see the old film on the menstrual cycle that was fairly standard at all junior highs in the late fifties—of course the girls viewed it alone while the boys were shown their own film on sexual maturation in males. I would much rather have had some education regarding how my body worked and on the intricacies of human sexuality. We are all sexual beings with sexual feelings, and it seems so obvious to me that we should learn about this powerful force within us. Unfortunately, not much progress has been made since I was in junior high school. Too many school districts still have their heads in the sand: Classes like mine, which are open and honest about all aspects of sexuality, are still the exception. I suppose they think that if we don't talk about sex then the kids won't get the idea to "do it." Most parents never talk with their children about sex, and if they do, they usually wait until their kids are preteens. Sex education should evolve with the child's natural curiosity about the body and should continue with age-appropriate materials and information.

When I first started teaching Social Living, I asked my students if they thought that sex education led to sexual activity, and this is what they said:

No, I think sex activity leads to sex education.

Male, 17

....

Maybe, but it's better to know what to do if it does "come up." Pun intended.

Female, 15

....

Sex education might lead to it just because it gives them ideas but it might not because they would realize about VD or getting pregnant, etc.

Female, 15

- According to many studies analyzed by the World Health Organization, sex education led to a delay in starting sexual activity. Among those who were already sexually active, there was a decrease in overall sexual activity or increased use of safer sexual practices.

People can never be hurt by what they know: it's what they don't know that can hurt them.

Female, 17

....

NO, NO, NO!!! I'm still a virgin (yes, my choice) and I learned it all at 5½. I think the reverse is worse—curiosity and inaccurate knowledge leads to, in my opinion, pregnancy, VD, and unfulfilling sexual and emotional relationships. Okay—maybe they (a few kids) may start two or three years earlier than if they didn't know anything, but for the vast majority, knowledge is independence, and independence is the freedom to make the right choice for YOU (like me!).

Female, 16

For some students learning about sex is just a natural part of life and it has no specific beginning point. For others, a particular event, session with a parent, or a "new" word said at school may have triggered a curiosity about this new subject. This particular topic elicits some of the more lighthearted journal entries I see because they often have to do with innocent misunderstandings. Sometimes when I'm up late reading journals, beset by sad story after sad story, I'm grateful for the humor in entries like the ones that follow. Before reading this next one I always ask students to imagine this scenario taking place. Actually visualize guests coming over to this girl's house and seeing the dining room table elaborately set but with something a bit unusual!

This whole topic reminds me of the time my mother asked me to put the napkins on the dinner table (we were having guests)—and I went and got the box that said Stayfree Feminine Hygiene Napkins (or whatever you call them)—I had no idea—my mom just said, "Oh! Those are the wrong kind." To this day I can imagine the forks sitting on top of those Super Maxi Pads on the dining room table.

Female, 15

....

I learned about sex when I was four years old from my cousin and her friend. I thought it was boring although my cousin was 11 years old and knew what she was talking about—they used dolls to show me. The only thing I remember is that I asked them to show me with cars and trucks because I didn't like dolls. They said it has to be a boy and girl.

Male, 14

....

I don't remember when I first learned about sex, but I think I always had a knowledge of it. I never believed in the stork. (I'd never trust a bird with a baby.)

Male, 15

....

Sex—It's a vague memory, when I first learned of sex. Preschool I think. I had a friend who I grew up with. His older brother was a trip, many stories went from him, to my friend and on to me. There was this one story about how he screwed a girl. I figured that he did just that, screwed her. Then I wondered, screwed? How did he do that? He got out a screw from a tool box and screwed it into her. That didn't seem too nice. So my friend knowing what his brother is talking about (birds and bees) says let's go screw a girl. I thought that might hurt her, so I said no, I don't want to get in trouble. Anyway, that's my first knowledge of sex. Even though I didn't actually know it.

Male, 15

Last week we talked about orgasms and it got me to think I really didn't know what they were until I was 11. I've never seen or had one so I wondered what they looked like. Being myself, I asked my friends and they laughed, they thought I was just being funny but someone finally told me they said that it was medicine that made you feel happy so I went to Longs and went to the pharmacy and asked the man at the counter could I have an orgasm. He threw me out. I went home and told my mother. She told me. I felt really stupid.

Female, 15

The following young man was very lucky to have a father who knew a lot about sexuality and birth control, and who apparently felt very comfortable in sharing this knowledge with his son. I wonder how many parents are really knowledgeable about human sexuality, birth control, and sexually transmitted diseases. Just explaining the menstrual cycle, wet dreams, and stating "don't do it 'til you're married" leaves a lot of questions unanswered!

When I was in seventh grade, my parents separated and I spent one or two weekends a month with my dad. On one of these weekends my dad sat me down with a book titled <u>The Joy of Sex</u> and a tablet of paper with a pencil. He then proceeded to describe to me, step-by-step, the procedure of lovemaking (foreplay, intercourse, afterplay) using references from the book and writing diagrams.

About six or seven months later, my dad sat me down again with a number of objects to teach me about birth control. He showed me about five or six different items, describing how they work and how to use them. I am very thankful he went through all these steps, even though it wasn't for a couple more years before I could use all this information. It was really funny though because all I did was what my dad described to me and afterwards, V. (my girlfriend at the time, and my first experience), could not be convinced that I was a virgin prior to that evening. I guess my parents taught me well.

Male, 17

Because this young man's father was using a book with the word *joy* in the title, he was getting the subtle message that making love can be joyful. How many parents or teachers convey this message? Unfortunately, many of our young people—especially males—first see sexual images through X-rated films. Do these videos show relationships of mutual respect or realistic expressions of sex? TV—MTV in particular—is another "teacher" of sex education—showing females being pushed around, taken against their will, always being ready for sex, no relationship necessary, etc. With so many fathers absent from the home—or fathers who are present but are distant or abusive—where are the role models for our young males? I fear the Rambos far outnumber the Dr. Huxtables on TV and in the movies.

No parent or administrator has ever complained about my class being too open or having too hedonistic an outlook. However, I did have one parent ask me at a Back to School Night, "What ARE you teaching my daughter about sex?—she is terrified of it!" I certainly had not intended to promote the idea that sex equals death, but my warnings about the negative consequences of being sexually active certainly impressed this student!

Chuck the Diaphragm Man

Sometime during the weeks we are discussing sexuality, Chuck Small, "the Diaphragm Man," comes to talk about birth control. He has been coming to my classes longer than any other speaker. He has taken off from his job to entertain and educate my students all five periods four times a year, for an estimated total of 335 sessions—without remuneration. The kids love him because he is able to cover all of the basic information plus the seriousness of what it means to be sexually active while making the whole subject of birth control hysterically funny. Students have told Chuck that he should take his act on the "Tonight Show."

Chuck got his nickname from the huge ceramic diaphragm he made for my classroom. He holds up the heavy, foot-wide diaphragm and tells the students, "Nancy found this on an archaeological dig and she believes that the real reason that the dinosaurs died out was their consistent use of this ancient artifact." He has made such an impression on my students that when he's out and about in Berkeley, someone will usually spot him and shout out, "Hey, Diaphragm Man!"

Following is a condensed version of his chalk talk on human reproduction:

HOW TO GET PREGNANT

Okay—you take a male and a female. This is the female. She's got all the right parts. She's got a uterus, fallopian tubes, ovaries, and this little egg that has popped out of the ovary and is floating through the fallopian tube...a perfect place to get pregnant. Oh yeah, she's got a vagina, too. That'll come in handy later.

Anyway, she's walking down the street, minding her own business. But coming the other way—"Enter the Villain"—here comes the male. He's got all the right parts also. He's got testicles, or balls, where the sperm is produced. They're in this sack called a scrotum which kind of keeps them from getting tangled. Actually, it's kind of a temperature control thing—it's a long story. Anyway, the sperm travels out of the testicles through these tubes, up and over the bladder, meets with these various glands and continues out this penis thing which just hangs there. That'll come in handy later, too.

So, they're walking down the street. Their eyes meet. They fall madly in lust with one another. They start kissing and slobbering all over each other. She starts secreting fluids into her vagina so it's get-

ting all sloppy down there. The blood is rushing to his penis which makes it hard and it sticks out (it's hard to draw, but you get the idea). They run across the street to the motel, take off their clothes, lie down, put the penis in the vagina, move it in and out. [Draws in and out arrows.] (This way is "in," this way is "out," for you beginners out there.) Her vagina is secreting and contracting; his penis is pulsing and throbbing. In-out-in-out-secrete-contract-pulse-throb; in-out-in-out-throb-secrete-contract-pulse-throb-secrete, in-out....

All of a sudden he comes! The sperm goes flying up these tubes, mixes with this semen, and comes squirting out of the penis (splork!) right into the vagina! Millions and millions of sperm all looking for that one little egg. The first one there wins (yea!). The egg and sperm travel down to the uterus, implant on the wall, and develop into little "Junior." Nine months later (hopefully you've got this penis out of there by then 'cause...) out comes "Junior"!...Any questions?

Later in Chuck's presentation he demonstrates the correct way to put on a condom. He tells the class that you should not keep a condom in your glove compartment or your wallet for a couple of years waiting for just the right moment because it will deteriorate. He opens up a condom after first checking the expiration date. He places the condom over two of his fingers—"Pretend this is an erect penis. You can't put it on first thing in the morning hoping you will score later than night. Now you squeeze the tip to get rid of any air bubbles so that there is room for the ejaculate—the cum." A girl gasps and shouts out, "Oh, no! I've been doing it wrong." Chuck continues to explain and moves on to talk about all forms of birth control, including his "favorite" method—the rhythm method. His parents are Catholic and he says that if it wasn't for the rhythm method, he and his seven brothers and sisters would never have been born!

I first worked with Nancy in 1976, presenting Planned Parenthood's standard "Teen-Rap" to her classes. Over the years it has developed (mutated?) (abscessed?) into something more closely resembling a lounge act. Nancy has never tried to stifle my tendency (quest?) to get more outrageous as the years go by.

I talk about the mechanics of reproduction and the logic used in interrupting the process. We discuss the risks inherent in choosing various sexual practices (abstinence, heavy petting, intercourse, etc.). We

- A 1991 Roper poll found that 64% of adults say condoms should be available in high schools; 47% favor making condoms available in junior high schools.

- About 300–600 million sperm come out per ejaculation. Sperm die in the acid environment of the vagina within 2 to 6 hours; however, once they reach the cervix, they can live inside the woman's body for 4 to 11 days.

discuss the smell, taste, and feel of each method as well as the most appropriate attitude to adopt. And we talk about methods through history, from Egyptian alligator dung to female condoms...all in about forty-five minutes. Which is why I talk so fast; which is why they laugh at me.

I feel the most important thing to tell them is, "Look, I'm not saying, 'Have sex or don't have sex. Have babies or don't have babies.' Just realize that you are making a choice. If you choose to have sex and you choose insufficient protection, you are choosing to be pregnant. Both of you. Not good or bad. Just a choice you're making."

For speaking to her class, Nancy "pays" me with little pieces of paper. She asks the students to write me a short note of feedback. The responses are predominantly positive and completely devoid of "shock" (with a few snide cracks about my artistic ability). Nancy thinks I've saved the best one hundred or so but I've kept every single one from every year.

But there's a recurring theme to the notes that makes me come back for more. "I wish all my teachers were as casual about sex as you are." "I've heard about those methods a hundred times but laughing with you made them real." "I've never seen a guy actually touching birth control stuff." That's why I do it. That's what I get out of it. Confirmation of my own feelings that it's very important for people to put human sexuality right there on the table, accept sensuality as an everyday, everybody issue. If it's "right there," a comfortable friend, it's easier to apply common sense; from abstinence to birth control and STD prevention to tolerance of nontraditional lifestyles. Fear, folklore, and machismo are more easily confronted with the knowledge that comes with familiarity. I show them all sides of it. We joke about it and get serious, too. In order to remove the anxiety, first remove the mystery.

Chuck Small, Volunteer

Postponing Sex

Chuck's presentations are always energizing. In the days following his "performance" there is more than the usual student involvement in class discussion—more questions, more input, and, I would assume, more thinking going on. Because Chuck approaches the mechanics of sex and birth control in a matter-of-fact way and can actually get kids to laugh at it, he removes the aura of mystique that surrounds the whole subject and relieves the tension and the pressure to become sexually active that teens feel. This pressure, which is self-imposed as much as it is peer imposed, seems to be as big a factor in the decision to have sex as is the sex drive itself.

There are some things about sex which are still confusing to me. Although I think I am equipped with the most recent and fashionable knowledge in this field, I wonder how much I can really know without having experienced sex myself. I wonder, for instance, how difficult a sexual relationship really is to deal with. I have never even come close to a sexual encounter. The fact is I do feel pressure to have such a relationship. I have read much and heard much about the excellence of sex, that it is a supreme pleasure. And the views I've heard about how terrible casual sex relationships are, are contrasting and contradicting. I feel that society, or perhaps the society of my peers, expects me to be involved in relations with the opposite sex.

I've had good friends who were permitted to welcome their boyfriends overnight. A few of them developed serious sexual problems (probably due to monotony, i.e. "What are we doing tonight?" "Oh, I don't know, let's get a six-pack and fuck.") No, not for me. In this case Mama knows best.

Female, 17

....

I am not a virgin but in some ways I wish I still was. I wish my first time would have been with someone special, but it was with someone whom I did not care very much about. There is a lot of pressure for guys to have sex and a lot of times they are not having it for the right reasons. The next time I have sex it is going to be with someone special.

Male, 15

Many teens make a thoughtful and deliberate choice to postpone becoming sexually active. Some do this because of religious and moral values, others because they know they are not ready for it yet. Fear enters into it for some—and many hold off because the quality of the relationship means more to them and they are completely satisfied with a romantic but nonsexual partnership. I would like to think that some of the things Chuck and I have said in class have also had an impact.

> Right now sex is probably the last thing on my list. There are at least 100 things before it. I know right now I could not handle it mentally. It may ruin my life; I may get pregnant or get so involved that my grades drop. When I say I don't think I could handle [it] I also mean I don't WANT to deal with [it]. I am sure not going to let a guy give me the "if you care about me or love me at all" trip. Hopefully I will never be hung up with a creep like that. Sure there are times when I am a little curious about sex, but curiosity is not going to kill this cat for a couple more years.
>
> My mother has asked me to let her know when I do become sexually active so she can help me out in any way I need her. We have talked plenty about birth control…Well, I have a couple more years to decide. I have the rest of my life for sex.
>
> Female, 15

> I am one of the only virgin guys I know and I'm rather proud of it. From my first day of sex ed. I decided that I wanted to wait until I was old enough to handle the responsibilities of having sexual intercourse with someone and when I did I would wear a latex condom with nonoxynol-9 and a sperm reservoir tip because I wouldn't want to endanger myself but I especially could not do something so cruel to the woman as to put her at a risk of either getting pregnant or catching AIDS. From hearing what you read, I know that some girls are nervous about asking their boyfriends and/or lover to wear a condom and so I have decided well in advance that I am going to wear the right kind of condom.
>
> Male, 15

> I don't go around with a sexually active group, so there's not much peer pressure to be sexually active. I'm having too much fun. I don't visualize myself as "love relationship" material. If I asked a girl out, I'd

start laughing at myself. Again, let me reaffirm my feeling of security. I feel like a kid, not a "young adult."

Male, 15

....

I am a virgin and proud of it. It seems many people use sex wrong because they feel pressured....I used to feel pressured, like I shouldn't be a virgin. This class helped me to get in touch with my feelings and to do what's important for me. It helped me say no if I really wanted to. I learned that what's important is what I want, not what my friends want. I've got a long way to go—why hurry?

Female, 14

....

I am not sexually active, but every man I've had a relationship with has asked me to go to bed with him, and I've refused point blank. At times when a guy is not pressuring me I still feel pushed. I know they're sexually attracted to me and me to them, and by having sex I know I could bring initial pleasure to us both. But I always remind myself of the following day. Yes, even though I want to give my all to the relationship, the minor things such as pregnancy and guilt always stop me.

Female, 15

Someone yells out, "*Minor* things such as pregnancy?" Right, I don't think anyone looks at pregnancy as minor—no matter what their viewpoint.

I continue to read some general thoughts on sexuality:

What has sex become? Many years ago sex with someone you weren't married to was unheard of if you were a proper person. Now people seem to go out for a few days, not really knowing each other yet and do it. To me that seems a little bit ridiculous. How could people use a process for reproducing a race in such a manner. In a way, those who do just "pick someone up and have sex" are animals in the sense of dogs or rats. I wonder how something which used to be so sacred and important to people becomes "just another thing to do on a date." I don't know. Maybe I'm a little old-fashioned, but why people do something which could make you feel bad, lock you into something you don't want, or leave you with more responsibility than you might be able to handle is beyond me. Sex is natural, but without ourselves placing moral restraints upon ourselves, we become the animals we pride ourselves on being superior to.

Male, 18

....

Sex—I think that in general, sex is the most confusing thing that I've ever come across. I don't understand it! Why is one act so important? Why is it so different to make love with someone than just lie on a bed naked with them? It affects you in a lot of ways to think of your parents doing it. For them it's okay, acceptable. It's not for you though. If you do (as a girl) and your parents find out, you're a bad girl. You got into something they think you can't handle. But if they never did it 'til they were 23 and married, how do they know whether or not it's too much for you? What can be wrong with having sex when you're 15 if you truly care about the person, it's a wonderful experience for both of you, and you love each other before and after sex?

Everything must have been easier but duller 40 years ago when no one did it until they were married.

Female, 16

....

Sex seems great. I say seems great because I'm a virgin. Sex is like an ancient ritual to me. It is an act of great importance. It is an act that involves movement, visual stimulus, olfactory stimulus, and incorporation of other senses. But most importantly, sex is emotionally enriching, it strengthens bonds—it holds them in place as forces try to rip them apart. Sex is sacred. It fills my thoughts constantly. It is of utmost importance to me so that's why I'm still a virgin. When I finally perform the ritual—the ritual of sex, I will be sure that all of my conditions are fulfilled.

Male, 17

A few students remark that this seventeen-year-old will be highly disappointed because he has put so many expectations on sex. Others—girls—say that they would like a partner like him because he sounds like he would never use a girl but would respect her and be interested in her needs.

The Dating Game

In any given class there will be teens who have had a great deal of sexual experience, teens who have been pregnant, teens who identify as being gay or lesbian, and teens who have never formed a romantic attachment or even gone out on a date (often because the parents will not allow it). Students who have had a lot of experience sometimes forget what it was like, but the letters that follow generally strike a sympathetic chord in everyone:

> Every time I get close to a girl I feel like defecating or worse. I suppose it's nervousness that I am still a virgin but I am deteriorating. I keep having nightmares that I'm going to be the world's first 76-year-old virgin. Everyday I see girls I'd like to know better but I can't bring myself to talk to them.
>
> Male, 14

> I am a virgin. I haven't even been on a date. It's not that I don't like girls, but I just don't seem to get close to them sexually. It's not that I don't want to. I have definite urges in that direction, but I just can't seem to get anywhere. I feel positive about sex, and I feel that when I do have sex with someone it will be a beautiful experience.
>
> Male, 15

> Last year when I was 15½ this boy asked me out. I'd known him all year. He was older and very good-looking, and I'd had a crush on him off and on all year. But basically I thought of him as a friend or big brother. The first night I went out with him I was a little annoyed with him. He acted so ill at ease and unsure of himself. The next night I went out with him again, just because I liked the idea of having a boyfriend. Halfway through the movie he asked me if I wanted to go for a drive and talk or something. I knew just what he meant. I wanted to go. All my friends had made out with someone. They were always telling me what fun kissing was. I was curious. I didn't want to be left out. Before I had always thought I would never kiss someone I didn't really like, but now I was so curious I didn't care. We parked the car up

in the hills and talked for a minute or so and then he said something really dumb and put his arms around me and kissed me. It was so awful. I hated it. His mouth was open, but mine wasn't—no way! He got my chin all wet. I pulled away from him. I felt so confused! This wasn't fun at all. I told him to drive me home. He was very nice about it. He told me he wanted to stay friends. After I got home I felt so confused. What was wrong with me? Or was it him? I couldn't believe all kissing was like that. I hoped so much that it was his problem and not mine. It must have been that I didn't really like him too much. I thought of him as a friend. I hope that when I meet someone I really like it will all be different. (I'm still waiting.)

Female, 16

My heart always goes out to the guy in this last letter and those like him who are trying to make the moves that they have seen actors make on the screen, but who haven't quite developed the finesse to pull it off! I also empathize with the girl, but I remind the class that most of us go through awkward situations like this somewhere along the line because it is a learning experience—you're not expected to be an expert at the art of romance at fifteen or sixteen years of age.

My dates are usually nerve-wracking. I have a period before my dates where I put myself down and am incredibly nervous. Then I meet my date and mutter a lot. I sweat practically the whole time and almost never enjoy myself. I have a terrible time on most of my dates. I have girl friends but it's hard for me to have girlfriends because I'm so self-conscious.

Male, 15

I tell the class that I wrote a response in the last boy's journal suggesting that he wait until he felt more comfortable and confident about dating. A couple of years later I ran into him at the bank and he thanked me for the advice—as if I had said something quite brilliant. He said that he had waited several months and things had gone smoothly. It seems that teens and children keep pushing themselves to "grow up" earlier and earlier. Waiting for a little maturity can make all the difference in the world.

Alcohol and Sex

One thought I'd like to fix forever in my students' minds is that alcohol and hormones are an extremely dangerous combination and can be just as bad as alcohol and cars. When the brain becomes disengaged, biological urges become more powerful than one's moral values, and safer sex usually does not come into play.

> One time I went out with this guy. We got very high and drunk. We were parked in his car and we started making out. Things got to things and I had my clothes down and he had his down. He started to enter me but before he could I said NO! and pulled up my pants. It made me feel guilty at first that I had led him on so far, but he was also pushing me. Then I thought to myself, why should I feel guilty? The next night he called and apologized. I felt so good about myself, it was really great. That was about two months ago and he likes me twice as much as before. We still haven't had sexual intercourse and I don't plan to.
>
> Female, 14

I like to contrast the last entry with the next since both of them received phone calls the next day:

> I am no longer a virgin (physically). Last year I had a "relationship"—I wouldn't even call it a relationship. It was more really just to please him….He got me drunk and then fucked me. I say "fucked," not "made love," because there was not even a hint of love. It was the worst thing that has ever happened to me. It was even worse, though, because the next day he called me up and said, "Why did you give it up so easily?" Shit! What was I supposed to do? Now, I finally know. Although I am no longer a virgin physically I am a virgin mentally until I make love with someone who cares for me and I for him. You must have a good relationship, have the ability to communicate and love each other before you make love with a guy. Because sex is not a game; it is something which can hurt a person physically and mentally if it is used wrong!
>
> Female, 15

I tell the class that something always bothers me when I read the previous letter. They guess many different things and someone finally zeroes in on the line "He got me drunk." I picture the guy prying this girl's mouth open and pouring a bottle of booze down her throat. There might be some rare cases where a drink has been spiked, but most of the time we let ourselves get drunk. I think the girl should have said "I got drunk" instead of blaming it on someone else. So many sexual acts take place under the influence of alcohol and so often I hear that either the person regrets what they did or they don't recall if in fact they did do anything. Some girls have told me about going to a party, getting drunk, and waking up to find their panties down around their ankles. They want to know if they are still virgins if they do not remember what happened. This sort of thing can happen to guys, too.

One night I drank something...it was Coke and vodka, you see I hate BEER but I like rum and Coke. I gulped the whole thing down thinking it was just Coke. I woke up later lying on one of the girls' lap...later she asked me if I had fun. I didn't know what she was talking about and she said, last night. Well, I don't know what happened that night but I still consider myself ½ virgin.

Male, 14

....

The other night I went out with a girl who got pretty drunk. She is not the kind who would usually go all the way, but she wanted to just because she was drunk and could not help it. I said I wouldn't and just lay there with her and that made me feel so good about myself. Anyway I'd want her to remember what a great job I did.

Male, 15

I think the above young man's behavior was exemplary. Unfortunately, in such a situation, most males would have gone ahead and had sex.

Virginity

As much as we delve into the subject of human sexuality, at no time do I encourage my students to become sexually active before they are ready to do so. This readiness is a very individual and personal matter, certainly not something that can be legislated or defined in absolute terms. I think that far too many people—adults as well as teens—jump into sexual relationships before they are prepared for it emotionally, and without taking responsibility for safer sex and birth control. Consistently, I advise my students to postpone having sex—they have a whole lifetime ahead of them, so why rush? I also counsel them not to have sex just for the sake of having sex or to allow themselves to be pressured into it. If they do, it is probably not going to be a positive experience.

I am not a virgin but in some ways I wish I still was. The first time I had sex was with my girlfriend when our relationship was pretty much over. I don't know <u>exactly</u> why we did it but one of the main reasons was that I felt obligated. She was not a virgin and hadn't been one for a long time. She told me that she wanted to so I just went along. I was very nervous at first. It wasn't a bad experience, it just wasn't the right person.

The second time I had sex was really a mistake. I was very drunk and so was the girl. I am normally not attracted to her but at that point I was attracted to almost anyone.

Male, 15

I lost my virginity to someone I didn't really like or love and I regretted it afterwards. Since then I have had around ten chances to have sex. A couple of times I don't think I did because I was too drunk.
A couple of times I didn't want to because I didn't care about her enough. A couple of times I didn't want her to lose her virginity to me because I didn't care about her enough to have a relationship. One time I didn't have a rubber. One time I ejaculated prematurely. And one time I couldn't keep it up after applying the rubber. I don't think I'm in that bad of a situation. I'm just kind of having a complex with sex and I think/hope this will go away.

Male, 15

I am not a virgin and I feel bad that I first did it with someone I didn't care about. For virgins in the class: Don't do it if you don't feel comfortable about it. If you have to ask yourself about it, or you get pressured to do it—DON'T!

Male, 15

I ask the class if they think the author of this last entry was male or female. Many shout out that it was definitely a girl, but someone says, "You're asking us because you expect us to say it's a girl, so I think it's probably a guy." I tell her she's right, and I read several similar entries to emphasize a point that is seldom vocalized: some males wish that they had waited for the right person and the right time. It seems as if many girls want to lose their virginity either because they are curious or want to get it out of the way, whereas many guys say, through their writing, that they are in no hurry and are willing to wait.

I feel nothing about virginity. It's just something that's there. No, I'm not a virgin. I wish I had had sex with someone my age instead of the older man next door. I was 13, he was 19, almost 20. I feel good about the person I am presently having sex with. We use sex as an escape from relating with words to each other. We are planning to change that soon because we are both bored with just sex.

Female, 16

I warn the girls to be alert to the attention and the advances of older males. If they are going out with someone several years older than they are, they should ask themselves why these males choose them. Why would someone in their twenties or thirties be interested in a fifteen- or sixteen-year-old? I acknowledge that there are always exceptions, but most of the time these guys are just in it for the sex. Girls who have insisted that I'm wrong usually come back later on—even months later—and say, "You were right."

Yes, I have had sex when I didn't want to, once because I was told I wouldn't get a ride home...if I wouldn't have sex, once because I was drunk at a drive-in, and once because I thought the guy loved me.

Female, 17

I have had sex with many people I didn't love. I went through a difficult self-destructive phase in which it didn't matter to me if someone
thought me "fast" as long as I felt wanted or needed by someone. My
views have changed drastically now, and I realize you do not need to
be sexy to be loved.

Female, 17

What Makes a Relationship Work?

I state flatly that it is never acceptable to exploit another person, or to
manipulate or force them into having sex. We talk about ways that
females can clearly communicate their feelings so that they will be taken
seriously when they say no.

We get into a discussion on what constitutes a positive sexual relationship and I skip down to question #31 on the Sexuality Worksheet:

The most important attribute of a good sexual relationship is _____.

"Faithfulness," guesses one student. "Love." "Respect." "Honesty."
Rather than give the answer, I tell them to listen carefully to the next
few journal entries:

Having sex is a great feeling, BUT in contrast [to what] many people
think it's NOT the one and only purpose of going out with a girl. I think
sex is about five percent of the relationship. I really do like being with a
girl and just having a good time. In the eighth grade I had a relationship
with a girl where it was all sex, after awhile I felt kind of stupid. Now I
try not to have sex for a month or two. Those two months become
really special…you still have things to find out about each other.

Male, 16

The next two guys had initial experiences that were not great but
felt completely different about later relationships. The question is, what
made the difference?

I lost my virginity when I was 15 years old. I didn't love her, and I did-
n't respect her either. It was physically pleasing, but emotionally vacant.

Right now I'm with someone who I love very much and we've had a sexual relationship for over a year now. I was her first, and before we first made love we talked about our feelings about sex, the responsibility that comes with it, and the possible problems it could cause. But the most important thing to me was not pressuring her into it, I felt that sex would not be right, unless she was ready for it. Now we have a great sex life, safe and spontaneous, exciting and experimental. We've begun to eliminate all our inhibitions and worries, and replace them with romances and encounters. To me, she is everything, and when we make love, I want to please her more than anything else. I believe respect and being giving and relaxed are the keys to a wonderful, and loving sexual relationship.

Male, 18

....

I blew it (sort of). I lost my virginity in a bad way. It was a really uncomfortable, pressured situation—purely physical, although I fooled myself at the time. I wish I had waited but at the same time it prepared me for my next relationship and acquainted me with the logistics. I believe sex is good if there is communication between partners and both agree. Talking about it is very important.

My second encounter with sex was on my first night with a new girlfriend. We went on to fall in love (first and only real time for me) and go out for four months. Together we learned to enjoy sex more and more each time. Sex to me is not just intercourse, it is the sharing, loving and caring that goes along with it. It is an incredible feeling when all barriers are broken down. During sex is when I could best communicate my feelings. Some of the best talks of my life happened lying naked with my girlfriend. It's great to feel no inhibitions and dance naked and free to some of one's favorite music. It's great to make love, shower together and then eat a great meal.

Male, 15

I notice that some of the girls are looking a little a dreamy-eyed. Later several ask me for copies of this last letter because it expresses what they want from a partner—the romance, the communication (which happens to be the answer to the worksheet question), the comfort, and the sharing. It is more sensual than sexual. This tends to be more important to females than to males, but, as many of the journals reveal, it is not exclusively so.

The next few journal entries are about relationships where sex was added and both partners felt enriched and positive about it. Unfortunately these relationships are rare but I think it is what so many teens are searching for when they choose to become involved sexually at an early age.

I consider myself very lucky. My first time or what I consider my first time was an experience I will never forget. The person who it was with will remain in my heart always because of what he gave me. We went out for (off and on) six months. He was and still is a very special, warm, caring and very funny person. He was always very loving towards me but it took me that full six months to get to the point where I felt like I could make love to him. That feeling only was there once. It was the feeling of being completely comfortable with him. I felt like whatever I did was okay. By feeling all of this with him I was still able to feel (and he helped me) really good about myself. We were both comfortable enough to say—yea I like that—no I don't like that. That feeling of being your own person but also being part of someone else is a very powerful feeling. When it came down to the actual act of making love he was tender and gentle, knowing it would be physically painful for me. He asked me how I was feeling often and didn't expect much from me except love.

Female, 15

Making love to my girlfriend is the greatest experience that I have come across in my life. It's warm, wonderful and complete love. It feels good to know that she loves me enough to share her body and soul with me. It's magical and an experience I wish everyone else could do, not with my girlfriend of course, but with someone who they love and that loves them. I hope also that she doesn't feel like I'm using her because I'm not. Not at all, I would never intentionally force her to make love to me because then it's not making love its something else that disgusts me.

Male, 17

To me sex is something that has just become a more comfortable and open thing for me. I still am very confused, but now that I have had sex I feel different about the whole thing. My best friend used to sleep with her boyfriend. We used to make snide remarks and talk behind her back, because we were all very afraid. The most special part is being able to hold each other and physically show that we care about each other. Sex is too often used in our society to sell products, bring you to a movie, or to up the ratings of a television show. In the U.S. people are upset about how teenagers these days are too sexually active. We are products of their society. Each time we open a magazine or turn on the TV we get the message that it's okay to sleep with whoever, or if you're not sleeping with your boyfriend you're behind. Society has created an image and an example, but they don't want to deal with the problem they've created.

Female, 15

Lest I be accused of promoting sex among our young people, let me state my case. I am not blind to what it means to be a young adult in today's world and find it hard to believe that "Just Say No" would work for the average teenager with raging hormones. I was listening to National Public Radio recently and heard about a study in which fifteen-hundred Catholic priests were queried, and 40 percent admitted to being sexually active. If adult men who have taken a vow of celibacy cannot keep their promises, how can we expect our young people not to give in to the pressures? My purpose is to arm my students with the information they need so that they can act intelligently and responsibly when they do decide to become sexually active. The fact that I share this information with them now doesn't mean they have to use it now; it may not even be meaningful to them for years. In fact, no student has ever told me that they decided to have sex because of my class, but many have said that because of what they learned in Social Living, they have chosen to protect themselves or to postpone becoming sexually active.

The reality is that Mother Nature designed us perfectly for times past when people got married at a very young age and had babies immediately. Now couples are postponing marriage and children until they have established their careers, and many find it difficult to "wait until marriage," since it may be many, many years before they feel financially and emotionally ready to settle down. Then, too, many of my students are very fatalistic in their thinking, and it is easy to understand why. They have seen so much tragedy in their young lives—many have lost friends and siblings, or have even been shot at themselves—that they are not postponing anything that may give them an ounce of pleasure. Whatever the rationale, according to statistics, 77 percent of females and 86 percent of males are sexually active by the age of twenty, and one would assume the numbers are higher for those in their twenties and thirties. It would be hard to deny the need for more sex education.

> I have not "gotten down" with my girlfriend yet, but I'd like to this summer. I've been sexually responsible (I got my rubbers) for about two months. I can't imagine our relationship falling apart if we did. I think it would be great! I don't know how she feels about it, but I'd like to. I hate the pattern of masturbating on Sunday and Monday because I didn't get anywhere the previous weekend, and I've got to wait another week for another chance. Sex is great. I plan to do a lot of it this summer.
>
> Male, 16

After reading the above entry, I overhear some students making derogatory remarks about the guy masturbating. There is still a great deal of misinformation and mystery surrounding the practice of sexual self-stimulation. Some students feel that sexual feelings experienced during masturbation are inferior to those experienced with a partner, or equate it with the inability to get a partner. In other words, they look on it as a poor second, rather than an additional or alternative means of sexual gratification.

I tell the class that masturbation is a very common and very secretive practice, but it is possible to recognize someone who masturbates from certain characteristics:

- bad breath,
- hollow look in the eyes,
- pale skin,
- sweaty palms.

There is an awkward silence in the room, and a palpable increase in tension—then I add that this information is from a 1903 medical text, and everyone cracks up. I explain that for many years, people felt that masturbation was an illness, an emotional weakness, and was generally taboo. In reality, it is a common practice, and autoeroticism, or as one of my students once called it—making love to yourself—has many positive aspects: it's free, you can't get pregnant or get someone pregnant by it, you can't get or transmit an STD or HIV by it, it relieves sexual tension, and it's a way to discover your own body.

A number of journal entries have dealt with the subject:

I remember masturbating when I was a child. I did on and off throughout the years and I do occasionally now. I think it is perfectly fine. It is something you can do yourself although your lover may do the same thing to you, for stimulation. I don't see anything wrong with it, although most people, including myself, don't even tell their closest friends. I don't think kids should be embarrassed about it.

Female, 16

I think masturbation is for the virgins and not a great lover like me.

Male, 15

Yes, I do masturbate. I don't do it to relieve my sexual wants, but to get to know my body so I know what I like.

Female, 16

I have never masturbated before. I don't say it's wrong but I don't say it's right either. I feel it's kind of freaky touching your body.

Female, 17

I hate masturbation. I feel that it is very nasty.

Male, 16

I think masturbation is a good way to explore one's sexual feelings and desires without serious risks sometimes found in sexual relationships. I masturbate, but I wouldn't ever tell anyone.

Male, 16

....

There's too much of an attitude that since copulation is "better" (physically, emotionally, spiritually, or whatever) than masturbation, masturbation is not good. It has a number of advantages over copulation and each has its own appropriate time, place, and situation. I have been masturbating since I was eight. I have been told all the stories about going blind and/or growing hair on your chin as a result, but I haven't yet experienced either. I feel if I didn't release the sexual tensions inside, I would go crazy. It was a different story when I was eight. Back then I thought there was something wrong with me, until I talked to a Social Living teacher in the eighth grade.

Male, 15

When this young man notices the beginning of a beard, I hope he does not think it is a result of masturbating. I think he meant to say that he had heard stories of how it would make hair grow on the palms of your hands!

I go on to read some entries that have to do with the problem of managing sexual urges:

Sex?... I love sex. Actually, I've never had sex with a second party, but I love sex anyway. It seems to me that it's about time I satisfy these fucking raging hormones!!... I am probably the horniest person I know, but what's wrong with that? My friend and I talk about sex, exchange new ideas and forms of masturbation.... I don't see anything wrong with masturbation. I actually find it quite economical. No need for date money, no chance of disease, infection, etc. It would be nice if a couple of my fantasies could come to life, same-sex, opposite sex, both, who knows.... I see nothing wrong with sex. It should be fun, free, and available. If you ask me, the virginity thing is overrated. Of course, I can definitely respect those who value their virginity, or want to save themselves for marriage, or their one and only true love. It's just that I, personally, am not that way.

Female, 16

Sex seems like a very fun [thing] but not the epitome of life experience. Lots of it is in the head, too, because I'm really sexual even though I'm not sexually active. Some things will make me feel really sexy (not looking) but I won't have the urge to satisfy it physically. Our society has an awful attitude about it. It's something thin, confident, popular people do. Everybody wants to be a sex symbol. If somebody I'm kind of attracted to comes on to me, it'll get part of my mind really excited and another part will say, "He doesn't like you." That part will see it from his point of view, in which case I'm just another pussy. But sexual attention is nice in its own way.

I almost did it with my ex-boyfriend (when he wasn't ex) because I wanted to feel proud of something (my morale was below zero) and I wanted to do it because he'd feel macho, taking advantage of me when my self-image was bad, thanks to him. What complimenting things does it reveal about a person if he/she has put his penis into someone's vagina, or had a penis in her vagina? Big fucking deal. People are discouraged from being responsible about it. The media have made it into a fantasy thing to make it more appealing, and probably, most of the suckers are high schoolers because we're so insecure anyway, and we watch TV, and we're impressionable.

Female, 15

....

I have had oral sex since I was 13, but my virginity is important to me. I mean I'm a very horny person, but I have sort of mythical values just to maintain respect and pride for myself. So far it's worked.
I mean, I've enjoyed every sexual experience, some more than others, and I've never regretted anything. My stepmom says that as far as she's concerned, it's only on a piece of paper that I'm a virgin. As soon as I feel a certain level of stability in a relationship I will sleep with someone, and I really don't expect it to be any better than what I'm experiencing—probably only more painful.

Female, 15

At this point I ask how many have heard that "it hurts like hell the first time"? Most of the girls are nodding their heads "yes." I tell them it doesn't always hurt and that we will discuss this later.

I started going out with this guy—he's not a virgin, I am. I really do like him a lot, I think I love him, but I don't know too much about being in love or haven't had too many chances to be in love. I really think I'm going to lose my virginity with this guy, but I'm really scared. I came real close last weekend, but I said I wasn't quite ready yet. I asked my friends what they thought, and they have mixed feelings, too. Everyone's telling me to go to Planned Parenthood, which I'll do, I know, but I'm just hesitant because you're only a virgin once and I don't know if I'll be together with this guy very long. Is it worth it?

Female, 15

I ask the class what they would tell her to do. A few of the guys say, with a lot of bravado, "Yeah, go for it." The girls who speak all say to wait—that she will not have to doubt herself if it is the right person and the right time. She sounds too uncertain, and if she has to ask herself if she's ready, she's not. There is no harm in waiting.

I used to believe that I wasn't going to have sex until I could afford to get pregnant. I was going to wait until I had a job or was in college. But I got into a fantastic relationship. I went with this guy for a year and we were about as close as two people could get. After a year we broke up because it was our first year in high school and we needed space. We got back together after a month and were closer than ever. Not until the summer of the second year did we make love.

Female, 15

I tell the class the next one is bittersweet, which I'll explain later:

I first learned about sex (had sex) Christmas Eve at my house 2 years ago. We started kissing about 10 pm and she said at 11:30 she wanted me. I was scared. I had a rubber but I don't think I carried it for protection but just to look cool. Well, I put it on and was embarrassed because it was too big. I was only 13. I didn't say anything because I was too embarrassed. The rubber was too dry, I mean it wasn't a lubricated one, it was a regular one, so I got some Vaseline and put it on the rubber and stuck my dick in her. I pulled out and the rubber stayed in her. I was so scared she was going to laugh but she didn't. We did it again the next night. It was great. I didn't use a rubber. Since then I have had sex numerous times in all different ways in any place you can think of. I've had sex on campus, on the football field, here at school, in a Dead Head bus, in a Chinese restaurant bathroom, in a hotel, my ex-girlfriend's greenhouse, on a roof. Well, enough of that, I love sex. It's just great.

Male, 15

You can hear some of the guys saying, "Wow," and there are some envious comments. I remember the boy very clearly: he had a charming and infectious smile. The sad thing is that he died in a motorcycle accident a couple of years after he graduated. I was told that he had been drinking.

The Downside of Relationships

So often teens, girls especially, are envious of what appears to be the "perfect" couple. "If only I had a boyfriend" is a common statement, as if that would solve all of their problems. What they don't realize is that there are problems in almost any relationship.

I guess one of my biggest problems right now is that my boyfriend and I love each other, but he's so insecure that he won't express his feelings. He never tells me what's going on inside of his head. I'm dying to know how he feels when I say, "I love you" or how he feels after we've just made love. I always tell him how much I care—I love to talk to him, and tell him that I feel good about us being together. I love it when he holds me. I only wish he could explain how he feels—admit that he has problems just like all the rest of us, and cares about the way others feel. He doesn't realize how powerful our love is to me, and I only hope he feels the same way.

Female, 15

I can't tell if my girlfriend wants it too much, I mean she is always trying to provoke me to make love to her, and a problem is the fact that she wears me out. I usually tell her I don't want to if I don't want to, but that's rare. I would probably say something but I like it too!! It makes her feel good and secure and it makes me feel good 'cause I am getting as close as I can to her.

But the problem is I don't want our relationship based on lovemaking, so we go on stretches without any, right now it has been five days since we made love and we have two more days to go. I like the dry spells because I know I like her just as much without making love. And I think our lovemaking is our way of expressing our love and sometimes we will express it to each other as much as twice or three times a day (if I have the energy).

Male, 18

Just yesterday, a former student came running into my room looking for her best friend. I could see she was very upset and on the verge of crying. I asked her what was wrong and she said she just found out her boyfriend had cheated on her. I hear this same situation played over and over and it scares me when a girl or boy says, "I know they'll never cheat on me so we don't use condoms." Dealing with the emotional heartache is bad enough, but in this day and age one must think of exposure to disease, too. The next girl expresses it all too well:

The biggest disappointment I've ever had in my life is finding out that my boyfriend cheated on me. Not with one, two, three, or four girls but more. He had sex with all of these girls. When I write this I'm in shock. The person that I loved and trusted more than life. The person I dedicated everything to. The person that I was always there for and was always there for me. The person I believed loved me as much as I loved him. I was so faithful. It wasn't being faithful I just had no desire for anybody but him. He's so fucked up. What was he thinking. When I confronted him he just cried. He didn't know what to say. He was so scared. I've always been the one who has helped him through everything. I grasped on to him because I don't have too much else. He was the first person that I've fallen in love with and I still want him in my life. I know that that's wrong. I love him and can't let go of our friendship. He's my best friend. Disappointment is only one of the feelings towards this. Pain, hurt, humiliation are also what I have to deal with.

Female, 15½

I ask the class what they think about the statement "I still want him in my life." They are almost unanimous in saying she should let him go because he can't be trusted and will only hurt her again.

The next girl so clearly talks about the positive and negative feelings involved in a sexual relationship. If she could do it over again would she get involved? Is she able to "chalk it up to experience" and move on? Does she regret that she did it? Each person must make these choices for themselves and think not only of the immediate consequences, but of the long-term results of becoming sexually involved.

Dear Ex-Boyfriend,

So what's up with you? I wouldn't know. What happened? I'll never understand why it ended the way it did. We shared so much. I could never forget you, no matter how much I wish I could. There's so much to remember. Summer days at your house, going to the seashore, being by the stream at the campus. Maybe that's why it went wrong. All the good memories, or the best ones anyway, have to do with us making love. The best moment of my life was the first time I really enjoyed sex. We looked in each other's eyes and you saw me crying and you said, "God, I love you so much." I really loved you then. The problem with us was that we grew to love each other through sex. We had a lot without it but it wasn't enough.

I already wrote one letter, but I still hated you then. I guess I've forgiven you now. I don't want to be angry and hostile anymore, except in some ways it's better. Then I didn't idealize our relationship as much. It wasn't even close to perfect. All we ever did was make out and then make love. I guess I miss you because with you I was sure I was loved and it was pretty secure.

I forgive you for going out with S. so fast. That was shit. It was like you didn't give me one backward glance. But maybe you never actually loved me. I was more a steady person for you to anchor onto who would be there for you, when your mom never was. It didn't matter who it was...anybody would have done. That sounds awful. I hope it's just partly true.

I will never understand why you went out with me that one day when you knew you were going out with her that night. You could see I liked you again, you kissed me, held my hand and so on, yet you never

HOW CAN YOU TELL IF YOUR RELATIONSHIP IS ABUSIVE?

Barrie Levy, a Santa Monica therapist and abuse prevention specialist, offers this checklist
as a way to tell if your relationship is abusive.

Are You a Victim of Dating Violence?

- Are you frightened of your boyfriend or girlfriend's temper?

- Are you afraid to disagree with him or her?

- Do you find yourself apologizing to yourself or others for your boyfriend or girlfriend's behavior when you are treated badly?

- Have you been frightened by his or her violence toward you?

- Have you been hit, kicked, shoved or had things thrown at you?

- Do you not see friends or family because of his or her jealousy?

- Have you been forced to have sex?

- Have you been afraid to say no to sex?

- Have you been forced to justify everything you do, every place you go, and every person you see to avoid his or her temper?

- Have you been wrongly and repeatedly accused of flirting or having sex with others?

- Are you unable to go out, get a job, or go to school without his or her permission?

- Have you become secretive, ashamed, or hostile to your parents because of this relationship?

Are You an Abuser?

- Are you extremely jealous and possessive?

- Do you have an explosive temper?

- Do you consistently ridicule, criticize, or insult your girlfriend or boyfriend?

- Do you become violent when you drink and/or use drugs?

- Have you broken their things or thrown things at them?

- Have you hit, pushed, kicked, or otherwise injured them when you were angry?

- Have you threatened to hurt them or kill them or someone close to them?

- Have you forced them to have sex or intimidated them so they are afraid to say no?

- Have you threatened to kill yourself if they leave?

- Do you make them account for every moment they are away from you?

- Do you spy on them or call constantly to check up on them?

- Do you accuse them of seeing other guys or girls?

said a word. Then I find out two days later about your date. Why did you do that to me? You should have been honest. It caused three months of shit and I hated you for it. I've forgiven you now for everything but that day. I'm glad we went out and that you were "first" and so was I. I feel sorry for your insecurity and immaturity and I hope we get to be friends. I'll never forget you. I wish I could.

Female, 16

What I would do when my boyfriend starts showing a sign that he was going to abuse me constantly is tell him either he change or else you're gonna leave him. If he puts it off for awhile and starts throwing his physical anger at you again, break up with him. If he comes after you and threatens to kill you, talk to your parents if it gets much worse call the police. Girls, I know it's hard to let go of someone you love but don't make yourself miserable by going out with that kind of guy. There are other fishes in the sea. Think about school because school is very important. I have a friend she was killed by her boyfriend. So please think twice before you get yourself involved with someone because there's also so-called diseases going around.

Female, 17

Breaking up a relationship can be a devastating experience, but it can also be liberating. I was at a street festival in Berkeley, recently, when someone came up behind me, put their arms around me, and said, "This is a voice from your past, a former student." I didn't look at her but said, "I can't remember what your name is, but I recognize your voice, and I can quote something that you once wrote in your journal!" I remembered word for word her opening line—"Breaking up is such a return of energy...." Here is the whole journal entry:

Breaking up is such a return of energy after three years. It's almost too exciting. I'm really thankful. Suddenly I'm becoming aware of all these things that turn me on, all these things I, myself, alone, am naturally into when my space isn't being interrupted or intruded upon or fucked with in any way. Suddenly I'm remembering all those things I like to do, remembering new sensations of excitement, relief, deep relaxation, release ("It's over now, it's over, I can breathe"), and a life-loving, pervasive positiveness toward the whole experience—an attitude which may be connected to my love for life and all its facets and which feels sturdy and unshakeable at this time.

Female, 16

I tell the students a final story. One of my former students, an extremely bright young woman who went on to be Phi Beta Kappa at U.C., once told me that she had been lusting after this guy and they ended up drinking and making out in the bathroom during a party. They ended up in the bathtub and were getting very close to intercourse and she kept hearing this voice in the back of her head saying "Nancy Rubin wouldn't approve, we have no birth control." I wonder how many other times, in how many other places my name has come up, as a friendly reminder to just say no—or at least use condoms.

I hear the familiar sound of Velcro being unfastened and fastened, bags zipped, and papers being shuffled, and I know that the bell is about to ring. I tell everyone to have a great weekend, buckle up, just say no or use a condom, wear a helmet, wear sunscreen. Someone shouts back to me, "Nancy, use condoms, don't drink and drive." Most everyone leaves with a smile on their face. And so ends another week of school.

3 | Homosexuality and Bisexuality

To KICK OFF TODAY'S discussion, I have the following list on the board:

SOPHOCLES	JOHN MILTON
EURIPIDES	PETER THE GREAT
SOCRATES	FREDERICK THE GREAT
ARISTOTLE	HANS CHRISTIAN ANDERSEN
ALEXANDER THE GREAT	WALT WHITMAN
JULIUS CAESAR	HORATIO ALGER
HADRIAN	TCHAIKOVSKY
RICHARD THE LION-HEARTED	TIBERIUS
RICHARD II	CALIGULA
BOTTICELLI	NERO
LEONARDO DA VINCI	LOUIS XIII
FRANCIS BACON	HENRY DAVID THOREAU

I ask if anyone knows what these people have in common. Someone points out that they are all men, another that they are all dead, and another remarks that they all contributed something to history. Eventually someone asks if they are all gay. Yes, I say, all these people declared in their writings or in public statements that they were homosexual or bisexual. I ask if they know other people we could add to this list, and they shout out various names: Eleanor Roosevelt, Martina Navratilova, David Kopay, Rock Hudson, Leonard Bernstein, and James Baldwin. Someone asks about James Dean and Madonna. From what I've read, there is controversy as to whether or not James Dean was bisexual. As for Madonna? I don't think she wants to be labeled and is in a class by herself.

Before going any further, I acknowledge that many students may believe that homosexuality is evil, perverse, and immoral. I make it clear that my purpose is not to make any moral judgments, but to relate information that is based on what the scientific, medical, and mental health communities currently know about homosexuality—that it is part of human sexuality and is found in all societies and throughout history. I emphasize that we will be approaching the topic from a social perspective, not a religious or moral perspective, just as we did with the topic of heterosexuality. We'll be concentrating on what it is like to be gay in a straight society.

We'll spend one or two days on class discussion and journal writing and another day listening to a panel of gay and lesbian speakers. Beyond that, I feel it is very important to integrate the topic of same-sex relationships into other areas of the curriculum when it is natural to do so. For instance, if I am talking about sexual responses in the human body, I might say, "Let's imagine that George is lusting after Martha" (I always use George and Martha in my examples), "or perhaps he's attracted to Bob—his heart starts to beat faster, blood starts rushing…"

I have a short worksheet on homosexuality *(see Appendix)* that I use as a basis for discussion. I pass it out and we get started with the first question:

We know the causes of homosexuality. True or false?

The answer is False. Although there have been many studies, it has not yet been determined what causes homosexuality. Some feel that it is determined at birth, while others feel that it is set in the first few years of a child's life. There is an ongoing controversy of nature vs. nurture without any definitive answer as to why someone is gay. I personally know several sets of twins that were raised together where one of the pair identifies as straight and the other as gay. Some of them are identical twins! Additionally, some people find that their sexual orientation is fluid and changes over the course of their lives: in their twenties and thirties they may have identified as heterosexual, but that is not the case in their forties or fifties.

I tell the class that homosexuality, like left-handedness, appears randomly throughout the population. It has nothing to do with the parents' sexual orientation. We do not know what causes people to be left-handed any more than we know what causes people to be homosexual. In the past, being left-handed was considered abnormal. Children were scolded for not using their right hand for major tasks: teachers would hit them with a ruler, parents would tie up the left hand to force their children to write with the other hand. Lefties were more or less forced to adapt to a right-handed world, and unless they were truly ambidextrous, probably felt there was something wrong with them, and because of this, were probably never as effective as they could have been (imagine having to cut up an apple or throw a baseball with your nondominant hand). Similarly, many people who are homosexual feel pressured to appear "normal" to a straight world, to act as if they are heterosexual—even to the point of getting married and having children. They may accept the notion that there's something different about them or something wrong with them and do the best they can to fit into the system. "Coming out"—announcing to oneself, to one's family, and to the world that one is gay—takes a lot of courage.

I say all this to give my students some idea of the problems that homosexuals face, but there is more to it than that. I ask how many in the class plan on having children and all but two raise their hands. Based on what we now know, I tell them, both left-handedness and homosexuality are random occurrences: therefore, each person in the room who does have a child has an equal chance of having a child who is left-handed as every other person in the room, and the same chance as anyone else in the room of having a child who is gay, lesbian, or bisexual. This elicits a response—often heated, mostly from the males— "I'd kick my kid out of the house!" or "Not my kid. My son is going to be straight!"—and some of the guys do high-fives or applaud these outbursts.

When order is restored, I add that my gay friends and almost all of the gay speakers who have come to BHS over the years came from straight parents, most of whom had a difficult time accepting the fact that their son or daughter was homosexual. Many were ostracized from family events, were told to lie about or cover up who they were, or were not allowed to bring their partners home. Almost all of these parents wished that their children were straight. Common reactions that parents have are rage, denial, and guilt—what did we do wrong in bringing up our child? Sometimes a parent will send the child to a psychiatrist to "fix" the "problem." One can only imagine the shame, self-hatred, and pain that so many young gay people have endured. On the other hand, some parents have responded to their child's declaration of homosexual orientation by saying, "I was wondering when you were going to tell me!" I tell the students about PFLAG (Parents, Families and Friends of Lesbians and Gays), an organization that helps parents come to terms with having a gay child.

Getting back to the original question of what causes homosexuality, I emphasize that, since we don't know what causes it, there is no way to prevent it or "cure" it. Right now, there is nothing that can be done to change a person's sexual orientation. Most gay and lesbian people do not want to be "cured," for they feel there is nothing to change—their sexual orientation is natural for them. They would just like society to be cured of its intolerance for people who are different. Most of all, they would like to be accepted by their families and friends. This is how one girl expressed it in a letter to her mother:

Dear Mom,

You don't like the fact that I'm bisexual. You can't accept the fact that your daughter whom you raised in a very good and respectful way likes men and women. First of all I thought that it was a stage I was going through but it wasn't. I went through the stage when I got in touch with myself and my feelings. I'm sorry you are hurt, you hurt more than a little and I know it. But there isn't anything I can do about it. That's the way I feel, what brought these feelings to my attention is unknown to me and anyone else I know.

You want me to be straight and I am, I still like men and I enjoy being around them. I enjoy all that they can give me and I can give them. With guys I have found out what relationships lacked. It was a really tight closeness. With men you are as two, a him and a she. But with a woman it's not two, instead you are as one, a whole human being instead of two. It's her and you together close and caring. A closeness that is not in a woman-and-man relationship. That sounds nasty to you and at one time I was saying, "I could never do that," but

I have because it was something that I needed to get out to make my life whole, to make me whole.

I don't know what more to say. But I'm sorry I have brought sorrow to you. I do wish you would accept me as a person and not as your freaky daughter, I'm not a freak. All I can say is please accept me and how I happen to be. I'm happy as a child can be, I'm healthy. It's not going to bring harm to me. I thought that is what parents wanted for their children, to be happy. I'm happy so that's all that matters. All I want right now is for you to still love me and let me live and learn right now.

I love you more than you will ever know, sometimes I may not show it in a positive way. But I love you. If you don't accept me as what I am now how are you going to accept me two years from now when I leave home? And to leave home and know you don't approve of what I'm doing is a heartbreaker, you can't live my life, I have to live my own.

Female, 16

This young woman was on the BHS basketball team many years ago and was very open about being bisexual. I asked her how her teammates handled it and she said that they were all accepting except for two of them. After she graduated she told me that she ran into the same two at a lesbian bar in Oakland! I have heard many times that those who are most openly homophobic sometimes end up being gay themselves.

When I first started feeling sexual confusions, I actually wasn't confused at all about my own feelings. What the only confusion was was the confusion society put on me telling me that my true feelings were wrong. I only wish people could understand homosexuality. I think that if everyone could feel it for just a day, they would understand that it's not a choice you make, it's just something you have to accept. I know some of you are probably thinking, "I've heard all this crying bullshit before!" But have you ever considered that it just might be true? And with just the possibility being there, of this being true, do you think it's cool to condemn or fag-bash an entire race of people you know nothing about?

Male, 16

- 1 in 4 gay or bisexual males is forced out of the parental home prematurely due to issues surrounding sexual orientation. Up to half resort to prostitution in order to support themselves, thereby dramatically increasing their risk of HIV infection.

- Of 289 secondary school counselors surveyed, 1 in 6 thought there were no gay students in their school. 20% believed they were not very competent at counseling gay students.

- Gay and lesbian youth are 2 to 3 times more likely to attempt suicide than their heterosexual peers and may comprise 30% of suicides among youth annually.

I identify myself as being gay or as some people say, "dyke." The only people who know I'm gay are gay themselves. I haven't told my mother because she's the type who'd say, "I'll get you some help." Like, she would want to change me. Some people will bring up the subject to see my reaction. They may say, "I don't see anything wrong with it," while others may say, "Yuck, I would never do THAT." It's been difficult for me to have people change their minds about me. They are going by what they have heard but they have never seen me doing anything, but to me it seems too late to change their minds so I guess I have to go on with my life. My advice to other gay teens is to COVER UP YOUR TRACKS. If you have questions about being gay, go to someone you know is gay and ask them any type of question you want and nine times out of ten they can help you. I don't feel special being gay, I feel like anyone else except I feel different in my own way—like, I have a secret—and it feels great!

Female, 16

....

Even though I have never actually had sex with anyone of either sex, I know that I am bisexual and I am very happy about it. I think hetero-sexuality is boring. It's been DONE. I know that I am not exclusively a lesbian because I have loved and do love many men, but there are also many women I have been attracted to. If I could choose in some won-derful fantasy realm, I would most want to be a gay man. All my favorite books, movies, and people are [by] or are about gay men....
The only person that I have really talked to about all this is my cousin who is bisexual and I am the only one in the family who knows it. We talked about how awful it would be if our family couldn't accept us. I am proud of the way I am, but I am hesitant to tell my family and friends because I would not want them to make me hate them. I am very sensitive about homophobia and the rampant amount of it at high school terrifies me. I would really hate anybody that was ashamed of me for being how I am.

Female, 17

....

The best thing that is happening to me is also the worst—I've finally got it out of me that I'm gay. I feel this is really good for me because I now know that I've repressed this for a long time, and this gave me a lot of anger inside, anger at myself, depression, and made me sort of closed up! So now that it's finally out in the open I feel much better but...I also feel right now really insecure. I've only told it to one person and I'm not sure to whom I should tell it. I'm in a position where I don't know what direction to take or what to do and I hate this insecurity.

Male, 16

It's hard for most teens to come to grips with their new powerful sexual feelings, bodily changes, and general confusion about identity—"who am I?" The possibility that they may have homosexual or bisexual leanings sometimes adds to anxieties and fears that already exist and brings up a whole new set of questions that must be answered. Sometimes this amounts to a fear of being gay.

I've never had sex before because I haven't found the right person. I guess I'm looking for the perfect person! I say "person" because I've felt for years that I was probably bisexual. It's something I've learned to live with in my life. I used to try to ignore it but lately I've been trying to think about it and who I want to be. I want to be comfortable with myself before I get involved with anyone. I want to know that I can tell my family and friends about how I feel. Most of all I don't want to have to feel ashamed for who I am.

Female, 16

I want to be a normal, typical, regular teenager, become an actress, etc. I'm scared I might be gay. I don't really think I'd be able to tell because I've never had a relationship with a girl and I have had a few with guys. My parents are all into accepting everything and that being gay is great. I know someone who died of AIDS and I babysit for gay couples. So I feel bad for <u>not</u> wanting to be gay. But I <u>don't.</u> I really don't. It's fine for other people but...it scares me. I love hugging my friends, when I see a girl I automatically think is she pretty or not. I want to stop. I <u>don't</u> want to be gay. How do I know?

Female, 15

- Approximately 33% of all males have had at least 1 same-sex experience leading to orgasm since puberty.

- In 1973, the American Psychiatric Association removed homosexuality from its official *Diagnostic and Statistical Manual*, signifying that it no longer considered homosexuality a disease.

> Sometimes I get really scared I'm homosexual. I've never really had an experience except once or twice when I was four and five, but I didn't really know what I was doing. I got scared because I've never had a boyfriend. I'm already 15 and I've never gone with anyone. What's wrong with me?
>
> Female, 15

One girl offers that there is nothing wrong with not having a boyfriend. "Lots of girls don't have boyfriends," she says. The last two writers shouldn't try to decide what they are, they should just wait and see who they fall in love with. They should take plenty of time to figure it out rather than jumping into something that they will feel guilty about later. Another girl offers that "there is no hurry—like you said, Nancy, they have the rest of their lives for sex—I think they should just relax and let nature take its course."

> I'm unsure of my sexual orientation and it is very frustrating. I can't tell if I'm bi or gay. I can't stand the stereotype gay. I want to have a relationship, but can't find anyone to have one with. It is very hard and lonely to grow up not doing what society generally expects of your sexuality.
>
> Male, 15

This example illustrates that some gay people also do not like the "stereotypical" gay. Students are often surprised that there is such diversity among gays and not every gay person is attracted to every other gay person. Most gay people also grew up with the same belief as straight people—that being gay was wrong—so there are many gays who have a lot of self-hatred.

The worksheet has other questions, such as "Homosexuality is not found in the animal world" (False), and "You can always tell if a person is gay" (also False). At the end of the worksheet, students are asked to complete the following statement:

If I found out my best friend was gay, I would _____.

In general, their responses reflect a high tolerance and a supportive attitude:

If my best friend turned out to be gay, I would let him be gay, and treat him the same way as always. If he is my best friend, he's been gay all the while, and whether I know what his sexual preference is or not shouldn't make any difference at all.

Male, 16

....

If I found out my best friend was gay, she would still be my friend like she always was, but I would not be the one she wants to like for a lover. We will just be friends like always. It won't really bother me that much and if someone was talking about her, I wouldn't like that because she's my friend. We will always stick together.

Female, 15

....

If I found out my best friend was gay, he won't be my best friend anymore.

Male, 17

....

If I found out my best friend was gay, I wouldn't be surprised about it, because I know a lot of gay people, and I also work with one. So as long as we have an understanding that they are gay and I am not, everything is cool. I am the kind of person, whereas I don't put you down because you would like to be something different, that's what God made you. Because I wouldn't like anyone to put me down for being a lady. So I feel whatever a person would like to be, be it.

Female, 17

For students who want to talk about issues concerning homosexuality—no matter what their sexual orientation—we have had a gay, lesbian, and bisexual support group at our school for many years. One of my students who attended the group wrote this:

I'm gay. I know it. All 2,500 students that attend Berkeley High School know that I'm gay. I came out at a Women's Day school-wide assembly. I'm a strong believer in the slogan "Silence equals death." Gay people must speak out and tell people that gays are everywhere. I came out to not only accomplish this, but for one other reason. I did it also to show younger, confused homosexuals that attend Berkeley High that it is okay to be gay and that there are places that will accept you such as Berkeley High's gay, lesbian, and bisexual support group.

Now it's been two months since I came out and I have received only positive feedback. People have stopped me in the hall and said what a great job I did, and how courageous I must be.

Male, 17

He is very courageous indeed and fortunate, too, that there is a high acceptance at BHS. I wonder in how many other schools could someone come out and receive this kind of support. Some studies have shown that 30 percent of teenagers who commit suicide are gay. In fact, according to a 1989 study commissioned by the U.S. Department of Health and Human Services, suicide is the leading cause of death among gay male, lesbian, bisexual, and transsexual youth. It is hard enough to grow up in this day and age, but the added impact of being gay or bisexual and dealing with the negative reactions of peers and family can be a burden that is too heavy for some to bear. Some of the previous letters express fears about status and gay-bashing, but, perhaps due to the general tolerance at BHS, most of the gay students I have known have felt quite comfortable.

This is how the BHS support group was described in the "Clubs and Activities" section of the 1990–91 yearbook:

Project 10 is a student-run gay, lesbian and bisexual social support group at Berkeley High School. It was founded by Mary Griffith, a fundamentalist housewife living in Walnut Creek. Her son Bobby was a homosexual, and she could not accept this. Feeling alone and hated by the world, Bobby committed suicide. In the face and world of "homophobia and ignorance" Bobby could not accept who he really was—a gay person. From that point on, Bobby's mother, Mary, went on a crusade to educate herself and others about homosexuality. Since gay high school students are often isolated and misunderstood, Mary set out to reach these students by starting a high school support group. Thus giving birth to Project 10. The "10" refers to a study indicating that about 10 percent of the world's population has homosexual tendencies. Although Los Angeles schools were the first to begin their own Project 10 and to receive national attention in the 1980s, Berkeley High has had its own support group during the 1970s. San Francisco has just started a group as well in the recent years. It is Mary's hope that such a group will prevent any other "Bobby's" from taking their own lives. They are here to break the grip of shame, to support gay, lesbian and bisexual students so that they are not alone and may walk with pride knowing that they are in good company.

Since this yearbook came out, there has been further controversy as to what percent of the population is gay. Because we do know that many teens are concerned about their sexual orientation, I think it is positive to have this kind of support in a school—no matter what the actual numbers are in the general population.

The following letter was in a journal that was turned in over eight years ago:

I'd like to talk about the best relationship, best thing going on in my life. I've known R. since seventh grade. We went through two years of private school together—if that doesn't make you kill each other you're gonna come out best friends! We understand each other perfectly (but there's always mystery...). We're both obscure, music-loving Cancers, with divorced, whacked-out parents and new, big ideas. My family's notably better off than hers and we were raised very differently (economically and emotionally)—while her mother clings to her and suffocates her, I'm lucky if I can get mine to pay attention to me. She's also more artistic in taste while I'll tend to lean to more rock 'n roll raunch.... I'm more of a leader and she's slightly more subjective...but our differences complement each other beautifully and although I trust her completely with my heart and soul I've never ceased to be fascinated and impressed by her. Even amazed. It's so wonderful to love someone and really like them, too.

We're both very serious about sexuality and wouldn't screw around with it if we weren't deeply attracted to each other. It's hot and heavy but it's innocent and tender. And although it brings up some serious issues about homosexuality I feel confident and safe in our relationship—

Ann Landers...

Readers answer the poll: Are you happy to be gay?

Dear Friends: A while back I asked my homosexual readers to respond to the question, "Are you glad you are gay, or would you rather be straight?" I was not surprised that the yeses won, but the volume of mail was astonishing. The last count was 75,875 responses, with 30-to-1 saying, "Yes, I'm glad I'm gay."

I asked for postcards only, but thousands of gays and lesbians wrote letters. It has been a busy time—and an enlightening one. Here are some sample responses:

From San Francisco: What a question! If I had a choice I'd be straight, white, possibly Swedish, 6-feet-1-inch tall and Protestant. My life would be easier, but I am not sure that an easy life is always the best life.

Chicago: We have four children. One of our sons is gay. He is the brightest and most sensitive, caring and thoughtful of the four. We have often wondered if being gay made the difference and have concluded that it did.

Upland, San Bernardino County: Are there any studies on what causes heterosexuality? Are people born straight or do they choose it? The straight folks I know seem perfectly normal to me. How about another poll?

Detroit: Am I glad I'm gay? You've got to be crazy. I've been beaten up, spat on and discriminated against in the job market. Who would choose this?

Columbus, Ohio: Yes, I'm glad I'm gay, but I regret it took me 20 years to admit it to myself and 45 years to open up about it.

Oakland: Actually, I'm bisexual and I choose to be so. When lucky enough to be presented by nature with two options, why not take both?

Harrisburg, Pa.: I have known since I was 7 years of age that I was different. I'm an adult now and have been in a rewarding relationship for five years. I do not push my preference on anyone and ask only that people not persecute me for being who I am. God alone is my judge.

Portland: For the first 36 years of my life I wanted desperately to be straight. I married and became the father of two beautiful children. I am a successful attorney. When I turned 40, four years after my divorce, I tried to straddle the fence—straight by day and gay by night. It didn't work. Finally, I met a terrific man and we are extremely happy. So, Ann, to answer your question, "Yes, I'm glad I'm gay," because that's who I am.

Yonkers, N.Y.: I am a straight female who wishes she were a lesbian. Why? Because women are much more intelligent, caring, sensitive, generous, honest and decent than men. My girlfriends are fabulous. The men I know are vain, exploitive, painfully self-absorbed and boring.

Charleston, S.C.: Everyone knows black people don't choose to be black but that doesn't prevent discrimination. Do you *honestly* believe if people accepted the fact that homosexuals were born that way, it would make a difference? I don't.

Lexington, Ky.: Am I glad I'm gay? My response is an unqualified yes. It's thrilling to know that there are people out there who would happily kill me because of my sexual orientation. I am delighted that the government discriminates against me at tax time and I can't file jointly. I'm ecstatic that I'm barred from serving my country in time of war. I'm overjoyed that all major religions reject my lifestyle. I love it that I could lose my job if the truth were known. Best of all, it's great to be viewed as an outcast by one's own family. This is what it means to be gay.

the sex is wonderfully exciting, the love seems to me very real, and we still know how to have oh-god-let's-not-be-so-serious-for-awhile-and-go-throw-socks-out-the-window-fun. (I'd worry if we lost that.)

I have a therapist and we've been to see her a couple of times together and she says we're one of the healthiest couples she knows! I'm actually very proud of us. I think R. is beautiful and I'm interesting when I'm with her and together—look out world! We're quite a team.

Our parents know now but that was a tough one. My dad uh— "walked in" on us. They're less than crazy about the sexual aspects of it but they do seem to respect our friendship. My dad had an absolute fit at first but he's calmed down a lot now as he's growing used to her ever-present energy.

I don't, and I seriously doubt she does, consider myself "gay." Any-one with as many pictures of men on their walls as me! My mom's been married three times and dated a lot and I'm probably a little threatened by men and doubtful of their consistency. But I do love them. And they do turn me on. For some reason I always seem to end up with male friends who're gay—they're the most attractive to me as people somehow…. I don't think teenagers really know <u>what</u> they are!

Female, 15

Recently she sent me another letter. I like to read this one because it is a thoughtful reflection on bisexuality. It also puts the high school years into perspective:

Although, believing as I do that human sexuality inherently supports a wide range of possibilities, I resist labels—for the sake of clarity I'll begrudgingly tolerate the classification "bisexual." I don't think my views on the matter have changed very much since high school—the idiocy of judging people on the basis of whom they fall in love with has been apparent to me pretty much from the sandbox on.

I didn't stay with the girl I was in love with in my sophomore year, but I doubt that anything I wrote about her was exaggerated or untrue. It was a wonderful relationship, and even though it ended badly (and honestly, how many of us didn't somehow blossom in that gloriously intense pain of adolescent heartbreak?), it was a very real, very com-plete, very important event in my life. If it is true that we become the sum of our experiences then we owe the greater part of our passion and yearning to those first hurried grabs at companionship.

I don't think about her often. I don't miss her. But I still live by many of the tenets established then, the ideas I whispered in the dark, grinning as she emphatically agreed. And I'm glad I had that company then. In the end she seemed a different person, and I mourned the loss of my friend even more than the loss of my lover. Hell—it was high school. Not like it was hard to get laid. I was disappointed that the "happy ever after" alluded us, but I also saw the possibilities in moving on. And it was inevitable. From beginning to end—inevitable. The end was every bit as devastating as the beginning was elating—I don't know that I'd choose that pace now, but then it was perfect.

For the record—I never found it difficult being "bisexual" in high school. I had the same relationship problems as the "heterosexual" kids I knew: what, if anything, do I tell my parents? where can we go to be alone? why does she ignore me when her friends are around? Did she get that note I left in her locker? I didn't have to worry about pregnancy or overnights and I could have cared less what people thought. I realized something early on, that most of the time people are way too preoccupied with their own angst to give a damn about what you're doing. There isn't much you can do to be any weirder than anyone else.

After sophomore year I tried out some different relationships: one man, a few boys, and one girl. I stayed with the girl. We've been together for six years now and if life has gotten a little less exciting, love certainly hasn't.

Last I heard, her high school partner has been involved with a man for many years.

Like most kids at the start of puberty I had homosexual experiences. They were nice. I didn't feel any pressure which made me feel better about it. I still have experiences. A person can love someone of the opposite sex just as much as someone of the same. It wouldn't disturb me to have a lover who is bisexual, considering I may turn onto the same road.

Female, 16

....

Lately I really feel the need for affection. Not just sex but affection. I need a boyfriend sometimes, but I have had a girlfriend. It was my first gay affair, and I loved it. We really liked each other. But now that we don't see each other anymore, I want someone else. I like this one girl who is also gay, but she's so afraid to be discovered at school that she won't even touch me. I'm a very open person and I like to touch, all my close friends know this. So when she doesn't respond to me I feel hurt inside. This whole situation is so painful sometimes, and scary, too. My question isn't "What should I do?" [but] "Why does it always happen to me?"

Female, 16

I ask the class what they think and one girl quickly offers that it is exactly the same way a girl would feel when a guy does not return her affection—the feeling of rejection. She should just continue to be herself and the right person will come along. She added that it is understandable that some students would not want to be out of the closet in high school and therefore not be as open to touching as this girl seems to be. Another girl adds that it is easier for girls to hold hands and hug and kiss each other in public, but guys can only hug on the football field or after some athletic event. One openly gay student told me that she has seen some of our male students going into gay clubs in Oakland but at school they would have girlfriends. She called it "straight by day and gay by night."

In the past few years, I have found that more and more students are willing to reveal in class that a friend, relative, or parent is gay. Many years ago, one guy accidentally let it out that his mother was a lesbian, and within minutes, about eight of his classmates talked about having a gay sister, gay father, and so on. At the time, this openness surprised me, but it would not today. Following are some of the journal entries in which students talk about having a gay parent:

My father is a professor at Cal, he's very smart, he's a great athlete, he's an author, an inventor, a well-off man—and he's gay. I found out he was gay when I discovered the key that unlocked the locked drawer on his desk. The chances of me finding that key were a million to one, but I did. I had suspected he was gay because he started having a friend over for dinner quite often. Sometimes the next morning I'd see them driving down the street. This meant they'd spent the night together, and when this happened 12 or 13 times I put two and two together. I've only known for about six months and when I found out I didn't feel any different towards him. I love him for his intelligence and his ability to understand. He doesn't know I know and I won't ever tell him I do. He's a great parent and he wants the best for me. I'll always love him and I don't care who he loves.

Male, 16

....

Homosexuality doesn't make too much difference to me because I have a parent that is gay, and she doesn't try and force her sexuality upon me. We both live different lives, but her sexuality doesn't really stand out all that much, at least not with me.

Female, 17

....

Dear Mom,

I wish I could forgive you for what you're doing to your life but it's just too hard on me to even think that you are even gay. I care about you that's why I moved in with my father. I didn't want to explode on you. You know I don't even like to visit you because when I see you I feel like I don't even know how I feel. I know it's your life but it affects me. I don't agree on your new kind of sex act.

Love
Your son (I think)
Male, 15

....

Letter to Mom

(Re: the divorce) I realize that it was not only your fault but was Dad's fault and the fault that both of you—you and Dad had to work in the night time or we would not have enough money. These are areas which you were not totally in control of. I love you and I need you not to feel bad because although it hurts when I think of it I am able to know why it happened and I do not blame you. I think you also feel sometimes that you have made life hard for me because you're gay. I admit that sometimes it was hard for me but that's my problem. I've never had a problem with your homosexuality, it has always been I was afraid of what my friends would think and that they wouldn't like me. The fact that other people cannot accept it makes my life hard. But no friend is worth having if he or she won't be friends with me because of my mother. I do wish people would not be homophobic for the sake of the other kids who are growing up. What I'm really trying to say is that I wish other people would just accept homosexuality, and for the people who make it difficult for the children of gay people I would just like to say take a look at yourself, you look like a fool and you're acting unnecessarily mean and causing little kids who can't help what their parents do pain and isolation. I really love the fact that you're gay because I love N. and I think she's wonderful and if you were together with a man I probably wouldn't like him. I love you more than the sky, the earth, the sun, the moon, the universe, doubled, tripled, more than any amount imaginable. You're my best friend and I love you forever.

Female, 15

....

I recently started living with my dad, after living my whole life with my mother. My mother and me never got along and I've always been able to talk to my dad. But there's a problem. My dad is gay. I knew that when I moved in, but I didn't think it would bother me. I'm not gay and have had enough girlfriends, but since I've moved in with him and his gay roommate, I feel weird every time I bring friends over, and my confidence with girls is totally gone. Am I being naive or does nobody care?

Male, 15

In the following letter a girl proudly talks about her father's sex change. I include it here because so often you hear people say that a gay parent ("Terry" is essentially a lesbian) will make their kid gay or be a total embarrassment to the child. In this unusual example we can see that *love* is the most important factor:

Dear Nancy,

Well let's start from the beginning. My biological father is a transsexual. It may seem to others that because I am writing this letter that I am ashamed of her but that is not how it is. I would love nothing more than to tell the world "the story" but I have to respect my sister's wishes and maintain her anonymity. This is not only my story to tell.

Terry has known throughout her whole life that she was not meant to be a man, she was a woman trapped in a man's body. She had the opportunity to marry two different women, one would have stayed with her through the surgery and one thought she could change "him." For my sake I am glad she chose my mother but for her own things could have been better. My parents loved each other and still do but Mom wasn't able to handle her husband changing his sex. Terry began cross-dressing when I was about four years old. This was because, to be eligible for surgery, you have to live as the opposite sex for at least one year. At this time she was still living with my mother, but as soon as she found an apartment she moved out. During this time I was much more involved in Terry's metamorphosis than my sister. In fact I gave her her name and helped her with her voice training, we would sing the ABC's together. I was still too young to understand how much she was hurting emotionally. As I have seen to be very common among post-op TS's there is a <u>long</u> period of fear and self-hate where you think that everyone can read you and you don't pass or fit in anywhere in society. This seems kind of like a carryover from the common pre-op hatred of themselves. Anyway, the only way this really affected me was that all our activities with Terry were pretty asocial. We used to go to matinee movies every Sunday. She also wouldn't go to parents' meetings often. It has been 10 years since Terry's surgery and, through a lot of hard times, we two have managed to stay together. Because my sister wasn't as much a part of her metamorphosis, and because she has always had a huge need for social acceptance, she feels a lot of resentment towards both of our parents and some shame over the "abnormality" that Terry represents. For my part, I would rather have Terry than no one, because if Terry hadn't had the surgery she would have killed herself and I would resent that loss far more. I am also thankful that my parents had the sense to maintain joint custody because it is very uncommon for a transsexual to retain a relationship with their children. I feel honored to have had the opportunity to grow in this environment and most of my friends have thanked me for enlightening them. I mean when all the information you are getting is from Geraldo, even with Tula [a famous transsexual] as a guest (mild sarcasm), you don't usually get an unbiased viewpoint.

I can't wait for the day I go on Donahue in Sweeps Week and am finally able to get back at the woman who said that a transsexual who brings a child in the world is disgusting and immoral, and that no kid can grow up with the knowledge of such a parent and not go crazy. I may not be perfect but I'm also not that fucked up. Any family where you are getting the love you need can't be all bad.

Female, 16

As I've said, on the whole, BHS students are very accepting of people who are not heterosexual, and there is a general atmosphere of openness at our school, but that is not to say that intolerance and hatred do not exist. In fact, a couple of unfortunate incidents have occurred in my own classroom. Last quarter we were discussing some of the issues on the Homosexuality Worksheet in one of my classes when everything exploded.

It started off innocently enough. Erika asked me, "Where do you get your statistics?" I explained that they come from many different sources—Children's Defense Fund, Planned Parenthood, governmental and university studies, medical journals, and so on. "How do we know that your information is accurate? I don't believe you." I complimented her for challenging me, saying that it is always good to establish whether so-called facts are valid or not. She ignored what I said and continued to badger me and several other students joined in on this attack. I invited Erika to bring in *her* statistics and resources to share with the class. She declined the offer.

I explained that I attempt to bring in the most up-to-date information available, but that at any time, new research might prove that information incorrect. In addition, even the researchers do not always agree. For example, today most experts agree that AIDS is caused by a virus—but there are others who still believe that it is not a virus at all. "I will always try to give you the current prevailing opinion and let you know that there are other viewpoints. I encourage you to look into any of these topics further," I said. "Let me know what you find out!" The shouting did not subside and I firmly said, "Enough—we are moving on." Someone yelled, "There you go again, cutting me off just because I disagree with you." I was overwhelmed. To my relief, the bell rang and we all escaped.

Over the weekend, I went back to the mountains to relax and think, hoping to gain some insight as I replayed the drama of fourth period over and over. I tried to think of a way to get into a win/win situation with Erika. I put the incident behind me and enjoyed the rest of the weekend.

On Sunday, I returned to Berkeley and stopped off for a burrito at a local taqueria. I was standing in line and from behind me I heard, "Nancy Rubin?" I turned around and there was a young man who looked somewhat familiar. "It's Jesse. Remember me?" I did, and he told me that he was rereading his journal recently—he had been in my class some five years ago, and we shared some positive memories from the class. His remarks felt especially good after last Friday's turmoil. It is rare for me to go anywhere in Berkeley without running into at least two or three of my former students. Most of the time they bring me up-to-date on what they are doing. They usually comment about a speaker they remember from class or how they just ran across their journal. Very often they will tell me how much the class meant to them.

Monday arrived, and we had gay and lesbian speakers that day. They came from the Pacific Center for Human Growth, a local organization which serves the needs of sexual minorities in the community. Over the years they have sent speakers to all my classes every quarter, all for free, and all with the approval of my administrators. I am proud to say that our school has always been open to speakers and topics that some schools consider too controversial. That day the panel was composed of a woman lawyer who is a Latina, a Mexican male who owns his own company, and a black male who is a nurse.

The first two classes went smoothly; after the presentations, the students asked great questions and there was an interesting exchange of information and opinions. In fourth period, things got off to a smooth start, but quickly fell apart. Sergio, who is very proud of his Mexican background, arrived after I had introduced the speakers and sat down next to me in the back of the room. He quietly whispered, "Why are they here? Who is that white woman?" I tell him she's not white, she is Mexican, and she's here to talk about the fact that she is a lesbian. Evidently he found this extremely disturbing. He jumped up on his chair and screamed, "You fuckin' sellout!" I tried to calm him down and gave him a choice of being respectful or leaving the classroom. He elected to stay. The speakers kept their cool and continued on until another student spoke out, saying that he was from Africa and that there are no homosexuals there. He got a lot of support for this statement, with some students even clapping.

Odell, the black speaker, asked, "Young man, where are you from?" "Eritrea," he replied. Odell said, "I have neighbors who are from Eritrea and they are both gay." The young man declared, "*America* made them gay."

Again, there were cheers of support. Odell explained that people often come here to escape persecution. The student from Eritrea calmly declared, "In our country, we kill homosexuals." I think to myself that that is good reason for not admitting that you are gay and perhaps that is why it appears there are no gays in Eritrea. It is also a good reason to come to this country. But many in the class do not see it this way.

A black girl said that she resents it when gays compare themselves to blacks. Odell attempted to address her statement, saying that of course there are differences, but both groups are oppressed and have experienced violence. She cut him off, leaning forward and spitting out, "You aren't a black man, you ain't nothing!" The class exploded but the speakers continued to keep their cool. Fortunately, once again, the bell saves the day.

As the class noisily exited, I managed to keep myself together until a young counselor from the Health Center came over and innocently asked me, "How are you doing, Nancy?" I hugged her and started to cry. She is a mental health counselor, a former student, and the twin sister of a lesbian: the perfect person to listen to my story! The guest speakers were less shook up than I was because they have experienced all this before. I apologized to them profusely.

Later, Odell sent me a note expressing concern over the incident:

As you know, I have had the pleasure of speaking to many of your students over the past five years as an invited member of the Pacific

Center Speaker's Bureau. But I have never in all that time encountered a group of them as hostile and poorly behaved as the ones I met recently. It was a real shock, and after doing as many speaking engagements like this as I have, I don't shock easily. That this episode occurred in one of your classes was especially surprising to me. Everyone in the Bureau knows the class discipline and courtesy that are so characteristic of your students in general—not even chewing gum is allowed. But this was like a walk through a war zone or a three-ring circus.

This is not the kind of classroom I remember from my own days as a student at Berkeley High, more than thirty years ago.... I felt embarrassed and sorry for you, knowing how seriously you take your duties as a teacher of young minds. I could see embarrassment in the faces of other kids in the class. One of them walked past us on the school lot outside as we were leaving. She thanked us for coming, but she was too ashamed even to look at us, and she just kept walking with her head lowered.

I know you prepared the students for our arrival, and you gave them the option of not attending the presentation, or even of leaving the classroom if they found it too upsetting. One of the disruptive [students] said she had no intention of leaving the room, since her parents paid taxes for her to attend public schools. Of course, I pay taxes for her to attend public schools, too.

I am very unhappy and worried, as a black man, when I see black children (and unfortunately, many adults as well) who seem to be unaware of any similarities between the oppression they experienced growing up as black in America and the oppression sexual minorities live with everyday in this country.

Odell Taylor, 61, L.V.N.

Sergio and I have had several long private talks since his outburst in class and we have become good friends. I found out that, at the time, he believed homosexuality was morally wrong. He was upset with the speakers, and he was angry with me. He thought I was prejudiced, since all the gay and lesbian speakers were people of color; in particular, he thought I was making some kind of statement about Latinos. Of course I explained to him that the speakers were selected by Pacific Center and not by me. Interestingly enough, he has since changed his mind about gay people and has decided that this is not a fair basis on which to judge people. It is amazing to see how quickly perceptions can change.

Erika, however, has yet to speak to me and avoids eye contact whenever we happen to pass in the hall. I wrote her a long letter in her journal but she never came to pick it up. I hope someday we can talk and I can find out what was really bothering her. I don't think it was me, the topic, or the speakers.

One speaker explains her reason for speaking to high school students:

I have done many things in my life. I have literally sailed the seas, fought forest fires, been a chef for American royalty (the denizens of Hollywood, that is), performed at Kennedy Center, danced wildly in remote villages in Bulgaria and was a substitute teacher for a few years. But none of these things has been as important or challenging as my work as a volunteer lesbian speaker for the Pacific Center for Human Growth.

I recall an occasion in one of Nancy's classes—a young woman looked me straight in the eye and said, "Aren't you scared? You know, people hate you." At the time I kind of glossed over it and waxed rhapsodic about the strength of community or some equally abstract thing, but in my bones I knew that she had asked a question of tremendous consequence and followed it with a statement of laser accuracy. The question hadn't been asked in a sarcastic or mean way. If anything she seemed just a little incredulous that I wasn't cowering as a matter of course. It has given me something to gnaw on for years.

The answer is yes, sometimes I am scared, and the knowledge that the mere concept of homosexuality turns some humans into snarling, frothy-mouthed pit bulls is not exactly cheery. I grew up thinking that I was some kind of disgusting pervert. Nothing could be further from the truth (well, okay...I do play the Bulgarian bagpipes which is an acquired taste and might be considered "perverted" by the uninitiated). After much wasted worry that there was something wrong with me I find out that I am a very normal loving person. That is why I keep speaking. I know that there is nothing about me that should warrant such hatred. If that hatred is hurtful to me, a fairly self-actualized thirty-five-year-old, what must it do to people half my age?

Everyone is negatively affected by homophobia. Homosexual kids have to grapple with self-esteem issues for years to get over feeling like a pervert, and a fair number of them never make it. Drug and alcohol abuse and suicide is rampant among lesbian/gay youth and that is largely due to the pervasive homophobic attitudes they grow up with. Heterosexual kids grow up afraid and hating a whole group of people with whom they usually have very little personal contact....

So, I speak, despite my fear of being hated, to show my audience (and myself) that the stereotypes are easily blown.... It's time that this nutzo homophobia stuff dries up and blows away so that we can all get on with our lives. I thank Nancy and her students for playing their part in this effort.

Jhos Ceapach Choinn
Musician/Artist/Public Speaker

I always have my students write thank-you notes to our speakers. We never pay any speakers and I think this is the least we can do. I try to instill in my students the idea that it's important to let people know that you appreciate their time and effort. So many people nowadays fail to RSVP, or send thank-yous for special gifts, or return phone calls, and I want my students to learn some proper etiquette. The speakers appreciate this gesture, and the feedback they get helps them improve their presentations. I never read the thank-you notes unless asked to, and students do not have to sign their names. The following represent the wide responses to various panels of gay and lesbian speakers that I have had over the years. These notes were shared with me either by the Pacific Center speakers or the students themselves:

> Thank you very much for coming in the other day. It's such a lovely feeling to be part of a small subculture that is growing up learning to accept and respect everyone. It was wonderful to hear my peers asking intelligent, respectful questions—and how kind and brave of you to share yourselves and answer them. I really think your time made a difference. Be proud of who you are and we will be too. The world is changing. I hope to God that my generation will see past the blind fear that has caused so much pain. Well, anyway—we <u>are</u> everywhere!
>
> Take care.
> Female, 15

....

Thank you so much for coming to speak yesterday. I really liked hearing what you had to say. You seem so intelligent and together. I'm bisexual, and I felt that the things you had to say were true of me, also. (Right now I'm in a really wonderful relationship with a girl in Nancy's eighth period class.) Anyway, thank you so much for your time. Good luck.

Female, 15

....

Dear Speakers,

Your visit to our class opened up many minds and I'm sure it made a lot of people realize that lesbians and gays are normal people that live much like straight people do. I thought that I was open-minded, but your talk made me realize that I had a lot of false information and ideas about gays. Thank you for coming.

Female, 16

....

Dear Speakers,

I enjoyed your presentation on homosexuality. I really hated gays before because they seemed to pose a threat to me. Once a gay woman approached me and after that I was really close-minded about gays. All the speakers said that gays don't approach straight people. I finally accepted that that gay woman was an exception and I am more open-minded now. Thanks.

Female, 15

....

Dear Speakers:

Thank you for coming and speaking. It was interesting. It's important to point out to people and that people realize that gay people are perfectly normal. My father is gay so I thought it was strange when somebody asked if it was weird for kids to grow up with gay parents. I'm glad you could straighten him out (no pun intended). Thanks again.

Female, 17

Dear Speakers,

Thank you for telling me a lot of things. In my country, this kind of speaking will not be so public.

Male, 16

Sometimes the letters to the speakers are brutally honest and the letters that follow show the other side of the coin:

I hate you guys, you fucking fags. You guys think you run the world, well, you fags brought out that gay disease (AIDS). You ever come here again and I'll personally kick your asses.

Male, 15

....

To speakers:

That is sick because God didn't want the same sex to be with each other. He meant for the opposite sex.

Female, 16

....

Dear Speakers,

Well you express yourselves good. It's good to know that you are proud of what you are and stand on your beliefs.
Signed,
Don't Understand
P.S. God doesn't approve of gays and lesbians! So may God Bless You.

Male, 16

....

Dear Speakers,

That kind of stuff is nasty and unclean and unnatural and I don't like to be around people like you guys. You should be ashamed of yourselves, really you should—you're nasty fags and lezzies. I admire you though for having the guts to come in class and talk about it.

Female, 16

A.J. Williams was one of the few speakers who ever wrote back to the students. He was a very intelligent man who had maintained a 4.0 grade point average in math at U.C. Berkeley and had many interests, one of which was the environment. He had come to my classes to describe what it was like to live with AIDS, and in his presentation he talked openly about his homosexuality. This is what he asked me to read to all of my classes:

To Nancy's Students:

I thank all of you for the permission you gave me to enter your lives as much as you allowed that to happen. Sitting there, listening and asking questions in the way that you did, touched me and filled my heart in ways that allows me to know why it is I want to live. I came to your class to warn you, to tell you before it becomes too late that there is a life worth living, that unless you're careful, you may fall victim to all the subtle messages being given to you constantly that would have you self-destruct, that would have you kill yourself in a thousand little ways without your ever knowing that you were doing it. I wanted you to know that what lies ahead for you is a matter of your choice, and that how things turn out for you is up to you more than you may realize; that self-love and wisdom may indeed be the only way remaining by which we can save our own life, and the life of the planet.

I felt sad and hurt that a few of you felt it was necessary to write notes telling me that you felt by having AIDS I was getting what I deserved for being a "fucking fag." One person expressed how she had no sympathy at all for me, because I am gay. Well, everyone is entitled to their opinion, and I respect the right of each of those who wrote those kinds of notes to say what they did. I feel sorry for them, and I wonder if it's already too late; could it be that they are already dead? That, unable to think for themselves, they live life reacting to things they don't really understand, thinking what they've been told to think, destroying their lives and the world we live in. The same mindless ignorance that generates racism is the same mindless ignorance that motivates the sexual bigotry that compels people to hate "fags." Why does anyone bother to do it? I mean, what is there to get out of hating gay people? Does it make you feel like you're more of a man, or woman? Does someone pay you money for hating the way you do? Honestly, what is there for you to get out of it? I would understand it if gay people were running around trying to force you to have sex with them, or if they tried to kill you, or steal from you—but they don't. I must ask you, the ones of you who feel you can't feel any sympathy for a gay person, and the ones of you who feel justified in hating "fags," I want you to consider the question: do you really hate gay people, or have you become one of those people who have been so successfully brainwashed that you don't realize that what you feel about gays isn't actually what you really feel as much as it's what you've been very subtly taught to feel. You see, as long as we keep hating each other and fighting amongst ourselves, we are kept in control and we stay blind to who and what the real enemy is. Some time I would love to come back and talk to you just about life itself, and what it means for us all to live on the same planet together. I'd love to hear your ideas on what you think it's going to take to make it better; to end racism; to end war, etc.

The behavior you act out in school is scarcely more than a death dance as you blindly cut out the heart of your own life by sleeping it away, drinking it away, drugging it away, TV-ing it away, reckless-driving it away, f—king it away...it doesn't matter, call it what you like. I just wanted to warn you, before it's too late. But maybe I'm already too late.

Thank you,
A.J. Williams

His comment about "sleeping it away" had to do with the fact that some of my students were sleeping in class (I usually wake students up and make them sit up, but sometimes I don't notice). A.J. worked at the University of California Greek Theatre where BHS has its graduation. The year he wrote this letter, Bobby McFerrin gave a great commencement speech and sang, and A.J. took a photo of me with Bobby. It turned out to be the last time I saw A.J. That summer, he died after a long battle with AIDS. Now I can only share him with my students through a video and his letter to my class.

I love the next poem and read it to all my classes. One time I read it at a meeting of the Human Rights Foundation, a primarily gay and lesbian group. I got very choked up as I read it, realizing that many of those who were listening had lived this message. The young man who wrote it was from a foreign country; although English was not his native tongue, he expressed himself beautifully.

I AM

I did not make the choice
Yet I suffer the consequences.
You built the prison,
My self-consciousness is the jailer.
I am gay.

You question my manhood
And I question your ignorance,
Which surrounds me tightly.
Your swords of prejudice poise ready
To wound my self-confidence.
I am gay.

The direction has been set, the course written,
And yet I question the authors of my destiny.
You can change it, if you just
Let me be
What I have to be.
I am gay.

I cannot live in a lie or illusion.
I cannot live in the loveless bounds of a closet.
I cannot live as you want me to live.
Tell me I'm normal,
Let me live as the human being
I am.

Male, 16

4 | STDs and AIDS

Sexually Transmitted Diseases

Facts, humor, worksheets, guest speakers, scare tactics, journal entries—I use all these methods to try to get the message across that there can be major consequences if one chooses to be sexually active. When it comes to teaching about sexually transmitted diseases (STDs), though, some students (and parents) might accuse me of going in too heavily for terror.

Every nine-week session, Lisa Sterner, our health educator, comes across the hall from the Health Center to show slides of STDs to each class. These slides are very graphic and have a reputation for being "gross." Lisa has a beautiful way of interacting with students and she tells them that they do not have to look at the slides and that she will warn them before any of the particularly "nasty" slides are shown. Most students have heard of herpes, syphilis, and gonorrhea but are unaware of two of the most prevalent STDs, chlamydia and the human papillomavirus (HPV), more commonly known as WARTS! Even though the slides are repugnant, most of the students want to see more of them, but some of the kids fall apart and run out of the classroom screaming. Few will ever forget the slides. As students leave I can hear them saying, "I will never have sex." "That was soooooo nasty." "I'm going to get me hundreds of condoms." "We would have to see these right before lunch."

I'm glad that Lisa's presentations make such a strong impression because even though STDs are very common among teens, they rarely talk or write about dealing with them. Either they are uncomfortable about it or it's another case of denial. The following journal is one of the few I have read on this topic over the years. In it, the young woman sadly describes the anguish that she will have to live with forever:

Genital warts. Genital warts, genital warts. GENITAL WARTS. These clinical words turn stale on my tongue. I've always felt that in some sense I was immune to all those multiple-syllable venereal diseases, chlamydia, gonorrhea, syphilis, genital warts. Of course, that was before last Wednesday when I found out I have (ouch) genital warts. (I cringe to write or say the word aloud).

I went into Kaiser last Wednesday for a very painful bladder infection. I left Kaiser last Wednesday with the knowledge that I had (yes, the dreaded word) genital warts. My doctor told me in such a stoic way that I felt I had no right to feel pain about this news, that I was just another body to examine—diagnose—and go on my way.

I contracted this venereal disease from my current boyfriend. He had told me of his previous bout with warts, but he had them burned off. The doctor told him his case was very mild and if it didn't come back in six months he was pretty safe in thinking he'd never see warts again. Little did he know that a year later he would give them to the girl he loves.

From the STD video that I viewed at home I discovered many painful facts. I learned that genital warts, along with herpes, are incurable viruses that live in your body forever…(forever is such a heavy, bleak word). Comparatively, syphilis, gonorrhea, and chlamydia are all bacteria that can be cured with antibiotics. While a curable disease seems much more appealing than my affliction, I realize that untreated syphilis can attack one's central nervous system causing blindness, craziness and death. Chlamydia can attack a woman's fallopian tubes and both chlamydia and gonorrhea very seldom have symptoms, so often go untreated.

The fact that hit me the hardest was that pregnant women with intact warts can transmit the warts to the baby during birth, affecting the baby's thin membranes: eyes (causing blindness), ears, and nose. Most women with genital warts opt for a Caesarian section but I have always, always, always dreamed about giving birth to my future baby normally (obviously many years from now). My mom and many other

- Each year, roughly 1 in 4 of those teenagers who have had sexual intercourse acquire an STD.

- Chlamydia has more new cases each year of any STD. In women it can lead to infertility, ectopic pregnancy, and chronic pelvic pain; in men, if untreated, it can result in infertility.

- STDs are less likely to produce symptoms in women and therefore are more difficult to diagnose until serious problems develop. Up to 75% of chlamydial infections in women are asymptomatic, compared to 25% in men.

women I know say that giving birth is the highlight of their lives. But now, my biggest dream could be shattered. I realize that as a pregnant woman I might not necessarily have the warts, but the chance is still there.

The movie definitely gave me the perspective of the magnitude of how bad genital warts can get. But even though my warts don't look like cauliflower or coral growing out of my body, I still feel disgusted with myself.

My boyfriend is being very supportive of me right now and is feeling properly guilty for what he has given me. I feel very angry at him for not being more informed on warts and not taking the initiative and responsibility for being safe. I'm also so angry at myself for being such an irresponsible person when I knew better. I knew the magnitude of consequences for unsafe sex intellectually, but somehow I thought they would never affect me. In some ways, this is the perfect lesson for me. I've had unsafe sex with four other people, but why did I have to contract disease from someone I love? I think sometimes that it would be so much easier to just hate the guy who gave me something. But that's not the way it is....

I promise myself that I will never have unsafe sex again. I could never live with myself if I ever gave this awful never-ending disease to anyone, especially someone I care about. All I ask for is the assurance that I will be able to give birth to a healthy baby....

Female, 16

....

- Risk of pelvic inflammatory disease (PID), associated with chronic pelvic pain, infertility, and increased risk of ectopic pregnancy, is estimated at 1 in 8 for sexually active 15-year-olds compared to 1 in 80 for sexually active women age twenty-four and older.

Talking about STDs is difficult; it requires speaking about bodies and symptoms in very graphic terms. It is often assumed that the information is too explicit for youth, so the topic is covered in general, sweeping terms, ending with statements such as "there are diseases that you can get that are serious, so be careful or don't have sex." But I have spent enough time with young people to know that many of them are having sexual relationships, and that they are doing so in ignorance. They have very little REAL understanding of the various hazards to which they are exposing themselves, and yet it becomes clear through the detailed questions that students raise, that many of them have already been exposed to an STD. They have an endless supply of questions that they obviously have never had the opportunity to ask.

Therefore I use my position to present to students the information that they want and need to hear; it isn't couched in a cloud of judgment and it is concrete enough that it addresses their true concerns, moving beyond the generalities and being specific. I talk about the different diseases, how they are transmitted, what the symptoms look like and feel like. An important part of the educational process involves dispelling popular myths that give people a false sense of security. For example, many students believe that a person can tell if a woman has gonorrhea by putting a finger in her vagina and then sticking it in her ear to see if it gives an electrical shock. They feel that if a partner passes that "test," then they can proceed to have unprotected sexual relations without worrying about contracting an infection. Hearing beliefs such as these motivate me to continue educating students about STDs; to hide from giving them accurate and complete information that they need to protect themselves from serious infection is to do them a disservice.

The primary message behind my presentation focuses on both helping students realize that they are the only ones who can be held responsible for their bodies and their health, while also giving them some basic information and skills to do so. I tell the students that I am not trying to scare them into celibacy, but rather that I want to give them the information that they need to make healthy, informed decisions about their own lives. I emphasize that they can't rely on their partners or fate to protect them from a serious STD, but that THEY have the power to protect themselves. Students often get a helpless, fatalistic attitude that because a person can't entirely eliminate the risk of STD, there is little point in even trying. By becoming aware of the specific symptoms, the modes of transmission, and the consequences of living with various STDs, the students are empowered and motivated to accept the responsibility of protecting their own health. I work to overcome the students' sense of invulnerability; I tell stories that come out of my experiences in the high school health clinic, and I let them know that the examples I give are coming from their own peers' lives. Finally, I remind students that making good decisions is a process that everyone needs to learn how to do, and that instead of being discouraged by mistakes, they can learn from them. I emphasize that if they have made unhealthy decisions in the past, there is no reason that they can't work towards changing their behavior in the future.

Lisa Sterner, Health Educator, M.P.H.

AIDS

Of all the sexually transmitted diseases there are, clearly AIDS is the most dangerous. Until a cure or preventative is discovered, the presence of this killer disease demands that we teach our children how to protect themselves from contracting it. I also cover AIDS when we discuss drugs, as sharing needles has been targeted as a way of transmitting HIV. But since more kids are sexually active than are intravenous drug users, this is a good place for this information.

There is a part of me that still feels like AIDS is a new subject, but most of my students were four or five years old when the term AIDS was introduced. For them it is a fact of life and, unfortunately, a very grim one. I consider myself and my students very lucky because our school district has allowed me to talk openly and graphically about this health crisis from the very beginning. I remember telling my classes in the early '80s that HIV, the virus that causes AIDS, was infecting gay white males and Haitians. When I realized that this information was no longer adequate I called for a special assembly to disseminate current knowledge of prevention to the senior class. I didn't want any of my students to graduate thinking that they were safe as long as they were not gay or Haitian! Intellectually most kids know that it is not who you are but what you do that puts you at risk, but it is always easier to believe that disaster only descends on "other" people—and it's even easier when those others are unlike ourselves.

At our school we have always been permitted to talk about vaginal fluids and semen. I was shocked to learn that in many other districts, teachers are not permitted to use these words. Instead, they would have to use more sanitized (and less precise) terms like "bodily fluids." I was a member of a committee, sponsored by Kaiser Permanente Medical Center, that produced a powerful educational play about AIDS called *Secrets*. We had to write two scripts so that the more conservative districts could use less "offensive" language—as though vaginal fluids or semen were somehow disgusting. To me, there is nothing obscene about the physiological workings of the human body. I think it is nothing short of miraculous. On the other hand, I find the idea of a teenager not being taught honestly about the possibility of contracting this horrible disease an offense of the highest order.

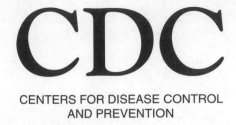
CDC

CENTERS FOR DISEASE CONTROL
AND PREVENTION

HIV / AIDS
PREVENTION

Facts about

Adolescents and HIV/AIDS

The behaviors of young people, particularly adolescents, can make them vulnerable to HIV infection and AIDS. The number of cases reported annually among U.S. adolescents (13–19 years of age) has increased, from 1 in 1981 to 159 cases in 1992 . Through September 1993, a total of 1,412 cases of AIDS among adolescents has been reported. In 1991, HIV infection/AIDS was the sixth leading cause of death among 15- to 24-year olds in the United States.

Although the number of adolescents with AIDS is relatively small, we know many more young people are infected with HIV. Since 1 in 5 reported AIDS cases is diagnosed in the 20–29 year age group, and the median incubation period between HIV infection and AIDS diagnosis is about 10 years, it is clear that many people who were diagnosed with AIDS in their 20s became infected as teenagers.

Among adolescents reported with AIDS, older teens, males, and racial and ethnic minorities are disproportionately affected. However, the proportion of females among U.S. adolescent AIDS cases has more than doubled, from 14 percent in 1987 to 38 percent in 1992.

AIDS Cases Among U.S. Adolescents
(13–19 Years) Through September 1993,
By Exposure Category

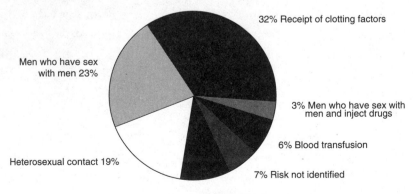

32% Receipt of clotting factors

Men who have sex
with men 23%

3% Men who have sex with
men and inject drugs

6% Blood transfusion

Heterosexual contact 19%

7% Risk not identified

10% Injecting drug use

ASK ME IF I CARE

In 1987, I was involved with UREP (University Research Expeditions Program), where I assisted U.C. Berkeley researchers with a study of the social and psychological aspects of HIV/AIDS. Part of my job was to interview people in London about AIDS. It quickly became very clear that the English were far more aware of how HIV was transmitted than people in the U.S. were at that time. This was due to a massive media campaign sponsored by the government with the support of the BBC. I spoke with illiterate Londoners who knew more than many college-educated Americans. Such a lack of knowledge was disgraceful as well as tragic, because AIDS is preventable. It was not until that same year that then-president Ronald Reagan addressed the issue in a speech. By then, over twenty thousand Americans had died of AIDS, and untold numbers had been infected.

Yet, here we are, over a decade since the first cases of AIDS were reported in this country, and some parents still don't want their children to know about sex, birth control, and HIV prevention. Nor are there enough school programs set up to address the issue. The Center for Population Options (CPO), reported that in 1993, only two-thirds of the fifty states (34 states) required HIV/AIDS education through law or policy. (The state of California did not require its schools to provide AIDS education until *1992*—a bit late, I think!)

Back in the early days of the epidemic, I surveyed the teachers in the science department to find out what they were teaching about AIDS and HIV. I was dismayed that a few of the teachers refused to talk about it in their classes. Some of my students told me they were learning about other viruses, but not about HIV. Fortunately this has changed. Not only are the science teachers discussing it in their classes, but many teachers in other subject areas are incorporating HIV/AIDS information into their curriculum. In addition, the Health Center has trained students as peer educators to go into many different classes and talk about AIDS, so our students are getting information on prevention from many different sources and at different times during their years at BHS.

The only 100 percent effective way to prevent HIV is never to come in contact with tainted blood in any way or to have sex at all. Realistically speaking, few people are going to opt for celibacy, therefore, we need to teach everyone about how the disease is spread, and how they can protect themselves from contracting it, and we need to do this *before* they become sexually active, not after.

We tell young kids not to play with matches, but I don't think you could say there has been an increase in children setting fires because of this. Similarly, demonstrating how to use a condom properly does not give the message to have intercourse. I maintain that ignorance is *not* bliss. In fact, when it comes to AIDS, ignorance can equal death. Anyone who is sexually active, or is going to be, needs to know the proper way to use a condom and the risks involved—condoms *can* break.

When people walk into my classroom they are visually bombarded by a wall-to-wall-to-ceiling collage of posters, banners, bumper stickers, quotes, and photos. Of all the hundreds of items in my room, the thing that stops everyone in their tracks are the photos of Matt, one

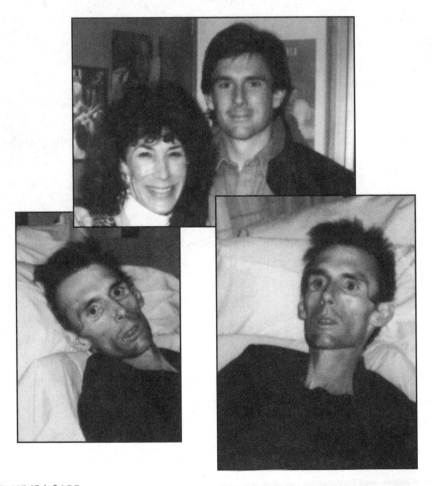

ASK ME IF I CARE

of my first AIDS speakers. In the top panel, one photo shows the two of us together in my classroom and one is of Matt speaking to my students. In these pictures he looks healthy, handsome, and charming, even though he had full-blown AIDS at the time. Below these are photos of Matt in the hospital, taken less than a year later. Twenty-nine years old and the flirtatious grin and playful eyes are replaced by a hollow, gaunt look and a stare so vacant and lifeless that people ask me if this is the same person and what happened to him. Yes, I tell them, this is Matt, and this is where life in the fast lane took him.

These photos of Matt speak volumes about what the AIDS virus can do to the human body and about the speed of the deterioration. I often wish I could blow them up and put them on billboards, or show them on MTV, or "90210," or "Saturday Night Live," along with ads for condoms. I ask my students if they ever see condom commercials on TV and they say rarely. Early on in the AIDS epidemic, I wrote all of the major networks asking them to accept condom ads. It seems to me that showing commercial or public service messages about condoms would make them more familiar and therefore more acceptable for teenagers to use, and would hopefully cut down on STDs and pregnancy. American teens see nearly 14,000 instances of sexual material on television each year, and only 165 of these refer to sex education, sexually transmitted disease, birth control, or abortion. I wonder what changes might have taken place had this nation not been afraid to openly discuss condoms and AIDS ten years ago.

Matt was a regular speaker in my classes, and often, he and A.J. Williams would come on the same day. I would tell my students that two PWAs (Persons With AIDS) would be coming to talk, and most of them would assume that this meant two gay white men would be speaking. They'd be surprised to learn that Matt was white and straight and A.J. was black and gay. Many students have told me that these two men really changed their views on who can get AIDS.

Like many of the other speakers with HIV/AIDS, A.J. talked far more about how to live life, and learning to love yourself, than about the disease process. He talked about the negative messages that society gave him about being gay. Internalizing these messages had made him feel like a second-class citizen who didn't deserve to be loved.

Because he was black, he was made to feel that he was even less worthy. His acceptance of these messages led him into self-destructive behavior—seeking refuge in dark bars, drinking, and having one-night stands. He urged students not to allow this to happen to them because he feared that many of them were already caught up in this same type of behavior.

Here are some reactions to A.J.'s presentation:

To me AIDS means a slow and painful death. You know I used to be like hundreds of people that would think that AIDS can be caught by doorknobs and toilet seats. But until that day when A.J....came to our class and spoke about AIDS, that is when I opened my eyes and realized that we must help these people. Not only that but they should be more afraid of us than us of them. You know I really get mad at anyone who would talk bad or make fun of AIDS. Because frankly I feel that if I ever got AIDS I would want love not laughter, a home not the streets. And last but not least, a companion not an enemy.

Male, 16

Before I start writing on this subject [What person has had the greatest impact on your life?] I have to tell you something Nancy. When I first wrote this paper I wrote about my brother, but someone has came along and influenced me more. This person is A.J. Williams.

As soon as I seen A.J. in our classroom I knew there was something special about him. I didn't even know he had AIDS when I saw him. A.J. is a fighter. That's something I never was. I give up too easy. I have always been a loser or quitter. I admire A.J. because he does everything we do. He's not going to give up just because he has AIDS. He's going to school and barely gets enough money to live but he's fighting. I think he's going to beat the disease AIDS. He will live as long as it takes to find a cure for AIDS. See that's why I admire A.J. so much and that's why I came to see him three times while he was here.

Female, 15

Matt always made a big impression, too. He was charismatic—a natural speaker—and could reach each student in a very personal way. He had contracted the virus by having unprotected heterosexual sex. He was not bitter about it and told my classes that his AIDS diagnosis had "saved my life." He had given up alcohol and drugs and had stopped being, as he put it, "an arrogant asshole." Once diagnosed, Matt was always completely open about his health status, but by then he had infected his girlfriend and no one knows how many others. When he told people he had AIDS, few would believe that anyone who looked as healthy as he did could be carrying the deadly virus. To make the point, he would walk up close to a girl in class and say, "What if I came up to you at a party and said, 'Would you like to go for a ride?'" and usually, before he could even finish the sentence the girl would say yes because Matt was an irresistible flirt. Keeping eye contact with the young woman he would ask, "Do I look like I have AIDS? How would you know? You can't see this virus and this virus doesn't know who you are—it does not care."

Both Matt and A.J. are dead now, two more lives cut short by the AIDS virus. Before they passed away, I was able to capture one of their presentations on videotape. I still show parts of the tape to my classes because their message is so important.

I feel that the best teaching tools in my classroom are the speakers who come to talk about their personal journeys. There is no comparison between listening to a health expert talk about the AIDS epidemic and listening to a person who is actually living with the virus or is caring for someone who is infected. These firsthand accounts seem to stay with students the longest. We are so lucky to have had these speakers share their lives so openly with all of us.

Christian Haren, who was one of the original Marlboro men, is an extremely popular and dynamic speaker. I arrange for him to come whenever possible, but he is not always available as he has been devoting himself to speaking to students all across the country. He has won many awards for his outstanding volunteer work and community service. In 1989, *Newsweek* honored him as one of fifty "American Heroes."

Gregg Cassin, who is HIV positive, has spoken to my classes many times, and we have become good friends. When he comes to my room, he often picks up the photos of Matt and says that it really scares him. Gregg is a model and admits that it is very difficult to think that some day he may look as emaciated as Matt.

Today, Gregg enters the room and we hug and kiss each other. Kids are settling into their seats, the bulletin is read, and I introduce Gregg. He loves interacting with teens and his ready smile and confidence put everyone at ease. He begins to talk.

Gregg is thirty-four years old and grew up in a strict Catholic family (he describes his father as an Archie Bunker/Al Bundy type). As a child, he wanted to become a priest. He came out in his senior year of college, at which time he sought counseling from a priest to help him deal with being gay. The priest suggested that Gregg focus on learning to love himself and also advised him to move to a community where he could get the support and acceptance he needed. So Gregg moved to San Francisco and later to Paris. He lived in Paris for several years, during which time he had a two-year relationship with a man named Xavier. Gregg has always had a close relationship with his own parents, but when Xavier was hospitalized with AIDS, *Xavier's* mother refused to have any further contact with her son, and cut him off from the rest of his family. A student interrupts to ask if this was because he had AIDS or was it because he was gay? Gregg said he really did not know because at that time, the two issues were so connected in people's minds. Another student asks how Gregg's parents responded to his being gay when they first learned about it. Gregg says that when he decided to come out to his parents, he feared rejection from his father and prepared for the worst. He gathered together some photos of himself from infancy through childhood and adolescence and into manhood. He showed these to his folks and said, "I want you to know that I am a gay man and I am still the person you see in these photographs." His father immediately said, "I love you son," gave him a big hug, and added, "I wish you could have told us sooner." His mom, who had sat in silence, said, "I always knew."

Gregg continues to talk about his work in "the healing circle" where people get together to discuss being HIV positive and having AIDS. He describes his work at a camp for people with AIDS. He talks about some of the people he has worked with, like the young man who got infected from his very first sexual experience with a teenage girl. Mostly he talks about the importance of love. He looks at each student and quietly says, "I know a secret about you." I sense a bit of discomfort among the students. "I know a secret about each and every one of you. You know what each of us wants? We all want to be loved unconditionally. **If love isn't the most important thing in your life— what is?"**

The bell rings and no one moves. This is in sharp contrast to a typical day where many kids are packed up and halfway out of their seats ten minutes before the end of the period! Gregg thanks the students for their attentiveness. Several go up to shake his hand or hug him. Some are in tears and he says, "You're so beautiful." Out of the corner of my eye, I see Matt's photo and his haunting and vacant look, then I glance at Gregg, who looks so attractive and vigorous, and try not to think of the future.

IF LOVE ISN'T THE MOST IMPORTANT THING IN YOUR LIFE—WHAT IS?

I believe love is the most powerful healing force on the planet. And that the sharing of love is where we find fulfillment as human beings. For me, speaking is both prayer and therapy.

I believe in my fellow human beings and our inner need to acknowledge this love power. I come in as an alien to many of the students as a gay man that is HIV positive. It is my belief that all people want to be free from their prejudice and fear. I do too. So I go to schools and places where I may feel most afraid and least welcomed so that I can heal. So that I can remember as the Dalai Lama has said "All men want what I want." We are the same. I come to schools to see the eyes that look so distant, separate, or afraid transform to eyes of love and compassion. We need one another. More profoundly than we need food or air, we need one another. We really do. I'm honored to be a part of this fragile human race, that so intensely fears one another yet whose existence is reliant upon it. That is the beautiful mystery of the universe. That is our challenge.

I see the schools as the greenhouse of our children and yet they seem so cold and devoid of love. I've never found someone who I didn't feel respond to love. I used to come to the schools thinking I had cornered the market on pain being HIV positive and having 60 percent of my friends either dead or HIV positive. But I have found this pain to be a part of all life. These young people taught me this as they hug me with tears in their eyes and tell me of their drug addiction, bulimia, mother's suicide, parents' divorce, etc. They have taught me that we can't escape or run from this pain we can only hold one another's hands through it and see it as the incredible heart-breaking, heart-opening miracle worker that it is.

Gregg Cassin
Founder and Director, San Francisco Center for Living

Sometimes I find speakers in unexpected ways. Last year I learned that one of our staff members was taking care of his son who had AIDS, and I invited him to listen to Gregg speak. Later this man offered to talk, too, from the point of view of a parent of someone with AIDS. Due to his work schedule he was only able to speak to one class, and it happened to be one of my most difficult classes—almost two-thirds male and generally a very boisterous group. He began by saying that he had never spoken about this publicly and it might be rather emotional for him, but one thing his son had taught him was that it was okay to cry. The students were suddenly quiet, giving their complete attention and total respect to the speaker. He read part of a letter that his son had written to him recently, warning us first that the letter was somewhat confusing because AIDS had affected his son's mind:

Mom and Dad,

I'm truly embarrassed about the last few days, I truly don't understand any of it! The phone calls, the crawling, the whole shitty thing! Is this it? Why do I get these bouts of sickness? Who knows—only God. I guess that's it, God....

I'm embarrassed about all of it, being gay, where the hell did that come from! Being stupid sexually? But you know what when I was 17 to 24 (or so) we didn't know about AIDS....

I'm so frustrated! What in the world would I have done if I didn't live here? Thanks! Crawling, falling—I would of been a mess.

When you say your prayers at night pray people with AIDS will have some peace because there is so much frustration and anger that comes along with it, so much! It's such a sad thing.

Thanks for all of your help.
Sorry for this whole damn thing.
I love you both.
Male, 28

Two months later the son passed away. Shortly after his death the father came to speak again, and the mother joined him, too. They talked about having raised their children in a Christian home and how they all attended church together as a family. Although it wasn't easy for them, they always accepted their son's homosexuality and loved him unconditionally. I was so touched that they came to speak, knowing how very difficult it was for both of them. Later, they each wrote a letter to me.

The father wrote:

I chose to come speak in Social Living to make students aware of the danger of AIDS. Anyone can get it no matter what race or religion. [I want you] to be careful in [your] sexual attitudes and actions, to be kind and gentle to anyone you know that has AIDS. Love that person as they are, and who they are. Give time and energy to that person. That person is someone's brother, sister, son, daughter, aunt, uncle, etc. Offer to help in the home of an AIDS person. Do dishes, vacuum, make beds, mow lawns, or any other way. People that are taking care of an AIDS person lose sleep and get tired.

The mother wrote:

I chose to come because our son wanted us to tell others, so maybe it won't be late for them to find out all there is to know about being a homosexual. "Tell others what the dangers are," said our son as he was dying. "I didn't know."

I believe it is a very difficult thing to realize you are HIV positive. The struggle within you must be one of the worst things to know, knowing, as of now, it could turn into AIDS. It can be prevented. My prayer would be—you would make a different choice than my son did, you have that choice. Make a wise decision, it could affect your life forever. There is no turning back once you have AIDS.

My son said, "Mom if you know anyone who has AIDS, be good to them." My heart goes out to other moms [and] dads...experiencing this disease with a son or daughter. It is a disease and they need tender loving care, just like a person with any other disease.

We spend some time discussing the latest facts and statistics on AIDS, such as which bodily fluids have the highest concentration of

HIV (blood is first, followed by semen and vaginal fluids). We talk about how it can be spread through the use of infected hypodermic needles and why it is more likely for a female to get it from a male

than vice versa. Someone asks about kissing. I reply that the concentration in saliva is so minute that no case has been documented of anyone becoming infected just through kissing. Some experts estimate that one would have to take in several quarts of saliva in order for HIV to be transmitted through kissing—choruses of "yuck," "ugh," and "gross" echo throughout the room!

When I am satisfied that everyone is clear on how the virus is spread and on the best protective measures they can take, we move on to the journal assignment on AIDS:

AIDS—how has AIDS changed your view on intimacy? Do you know anyone who is HIV positive or who has AIDS? Has this changed your relationships? Has this epidemic changed your life in any way?

Before they start writing about AIDS, I read some of the journal entries I've collected on this question, stopping now and then for further discussion:

> AIDS is one of the few things that <u>really</u> scares me. To think that you can now die from one of the most pleasurable experiences in the world is sad. To me AIDS is like a plague. I mean it'll probably end up "getting" everybody. I wish it would just disappear, but that's highly unlikely. I've really changed my sexual "habits"—because Lord knows that this shit, literally, scares the fuck outta me.
>
> Female, 15

> AIDS—one of my best friends is HIV+. It hasn't changed my view of her at all. I still love her and support her now more than ever. The only

thing is sometimes I get upset because she is still having sex with this one boy who she has been with about five months but she still hasn't told him that she is HIV+.

Female, 16

I tell the class that all of my speakers have said that they would always be honest with their partners and let them know that they were HIV positive. I want my students to know that some people are *not* honest and that most teens have not been tested. They are at risk if they are having unprotected sex and they are at risk even with condoms since condoms are not 100 percent effective.

AIDS is so scary. Of all of my fears AIDS is one of the worst. By me being sexually active I am scared to death of AIDS. I always always use condoms thanks to my dear mother who educated me about sex. I hope someone finds a cure for AIDS fast. I pray every day that no one I love will get AIDS. I would probably cry forever.

Male, 15

....

AIDS really scares me, I'm not sexually active presently, but AIDS makes me scared to start. Knowing my luck, a condom would break and I would be infected. You always hear stories of people who contract the virus on his/her first sexual experience and that, in particular, scares the s t out of me. It really angers me to have to grow up in a world infected by AIDS.

I think the worst thing about AIDS is all the homophobia that is developing. This virus has lengthened the already great distance between heterosexual and homosexual people. This has separated people to a point that is absolutely absurd. People are scared out of their minds. AIDS is scary enough without the separations it imposes on families as well as societies.

Female, 15

....

Ever since I've decided to follow Christianity, sexual diseases such as AIDS have been the least of my worries. Since my conversion I am no longer sexually active so such diseases aren't a worry to me. As for others who, for whatever reasons, do not share my views on sexual immorality I think that protection such as condoms should be a high priority. I can't see how someone could be so embarrassed that they would risk AIDS or even pregnancy.

Male, 16

....

How do I feel about AIDS? AIDS is really, really, really shitty. I mean, it has taken away a lot of this generation's sexual freedom. It's like, if I want to sleep with a guy, I have to put him through the third degree about his sexual history. None of us have the freedom of casual sex anymore, and it's just not fair. It seems like the choice is virginity, condoms, marriage, or death, and none of these are very acceptable to me (my favorite form of birth control is the pill.) GRRRRRR. It's also killed many, many innocent people and babies. It's almost as bad as the Black Plague was.

Female, 15

....

AIDS scares the shit out of me. I have many friends with AIDS. I don't like being paranoid about it, considering one of my best friends had sex with a girl who had three tests out of five come out positive for AIDS, and my friend hasn't had a blood test yet. I'm afraid to be around him, knowing he might have it. I'm afraid he might bleed all over me or something. It pisses me off. I will always wear rubbers, I think, unless I'm sure, if not only for birth control. I think it's a plague. I'm heterosexual, but have many gay friends. It sucks.

Male, 15

....

I don't ever want to catch AIDS in a sexual relationship. My lover and I have talked about catching AIDS by having more than one sex partner and we have come to an agreement not to fool around. This gives us more time to enjoy the art of making love. If my lover caught AIDS I would bear with her until her time is up on earth. I will make her life as comfortable as possible and show her that I love her deeply.

Male, 17

AIDS doesn't frighten me. I know how I can get it, and how I can't. I will always use a rubber, even though I have not yet become sexually active. Of course, I can't see all the sexual situations I'll be in, but I think that I will be adamant about the use of a rubber. I think about many different situations, and place myself in them, and plan my reactions.

I should say that AIDS doesn't frighten me for myself, but I am very frightened for other people. There are people who think you can get AIDS from a public toilet—do these same people know how you can really get it? From unsafe sex? That is what frightens me. For I am under the impression that where people are misinformed (or uninformed) about one thing, they are often uninformed about others. Teenagers who know about AIDS and birth control, etc., should travel and tell other teens—if your health teacher is 105 years old and has 4 months on the 4 food groups, are you going to listen when she talks about sex (if she talks about sex?)

Female, 16

....

AIDS doesn't affect me now, but I do think about it. I don't worry about getting it because I have a monogamous relationship with a girl who was a virgin when we met. I do think about it though.... My father is a homosexual. I have never talked to him about it. He knows that I know but I don't think he has admitted it to himself. I don't really worry about him because he has a "wife." Sometimes though I don't like say sharing a Coke with him. I know it's dumb, but the fear involved is too great to overcome. I guess that's why so many people don't get tested. We need to overcome our fear.

Male, 17

....

Dear Dad,

It's really a horrible tragedy that something like this would happen to you. Why didn't you just tell me how you were. It's really a shame that I had to find out like this. I mean it's bad enough just to know you are gay but what really takes the cake is that you weren't even careful. Now we all have to pay and suffer, why couldn't you of just told me before. Think of how my brother will take it when he hears his father is gay and has AIDS. Tisk, tisk, dude.

Confused son,
Male, 16

After reading the above entry, I point out that it was one of the earliest journal entries on AIDS. The father may not have been careful, as the son assumed, but it is more likely that the father contracted the virus before he knew anything about AIDS and how it is transmitted. The virus lives in the body on average from seven to eleven years before the onset of the disease; he could have become infected in the early '80s when not that much was known about the disease.

AIDS hasn't really affected my life at all, although I know quite a bit about it—my biology class participated in the AIDS education program a few weeks ago and I read about it in the paper. I do know that my father is very prejudiced against people with AIDS. We were talking about it one day and I asked him if he knew anyone who had AIDS. He said he didn't hang out with those kinds of people. I got very angry. Then he said he wasn't prejudiced, but I know he is. I really worry for people with AIDS because I know there are a lot of people like my father, and worse.

Female, 15

....

Phew? Heavy subject! I think AIDS to most of today's teenagers is like the Vietnam War. You hear about it, and you feel bad for the people who have it (or went through it, fought in it, in the case of Vietnam War), but you don't think of it in relevance to you. People in general tend to feel like disasters such as AIDS, happen to [other] people, but could never happen to them. I think people better start trying to change their attitude.

Myself, it has relevance to me for a few reasons. I know two people, one of whom graduated from high school last year, and one of whom still goes here, who both have AIDS. (My mom has a friend who has AIDS, who is dying in the hospital, right now, but I've never met him.)

At this point in my life, I am not able to be attracted to anyone, and do not feel casual about sex. However, I did have a boyfriend last year, and we made love. I'd never had sex before, but he'd been having sex for two and a half years, sometimes every day with different partners who were strangers, sometimes with a few steady people. At the time I didn't know as much about AIDS as I know now, and I didn't even entertain the idea that my partner could have it and not know it. Sometimes we'd use rubbers, but not always.

It's now possible that I could have contracted it from him. I'm not saying that he has it, but considering the facts, I wouldn't be surprised. I brought this issue up one night, about three days after it had occurred to me. We were talking on the phone. He didn't even want to acknowledge the idea. Full of denial, he didn't want to discuss it as a realistic idea. However, the more I think about it, the more possible I realize the idea is, but I too can't help feeling it couldn't happen to me. I think I better start acting as though the idea is possible though, because if I'm carrying the virus I should know, and if I make love to someone he could contract it from me.

I should get a blood test, but for one thing I'm not sure how to go about it. I'm not sure if I would need parental permission. Besides, if I went to my doctor for the test without her knowledge, I would have to pay the fee which I'm not sure I could afford. And last, but not least, I don't know how I would handle it if I found out I did have AIDS.

Female, 15

I ask students what she should do and they say she should get tested so that if she is HIV positive she can get medical treatment and learn how not to transmit the virus. Most students are aware that there are many places to be tested anonymously or confidentially. I make sure everyone knows that they can go directly across the hall to the Health Center where testing is offered free to all students. I pass out a list of clinics in the area.

I have been sexually active for three years, and I always use condoms. Even before the issue of AIDS was a big deal I was using condoms. My main concerns when having sex is contracting an STD or getting pregnant.

Last night I had sex with a new person, and... I told him before we get intimate I'd stress that we use a condom, because we don't know who we have slept with, and who they have slept with. He was very mature, and in agreement about the whole situation.

One concern that I have right now is that my brother is gay, has been gay for years. This is the brother that used to molest me. I have a fear that he has AIDS or the virus. I'm too embarrassed to ask him, but I hope I don't have it. I would like to go and have a test, but am insecure about what the results would be. I'm not afraid of people who have AIDS, but sometimes I think about what a woman said on a talk show, how "this is God's punishment for gay people." She is entitled to her own opinion. Just as I have mine. The best way to be protected is either abstinence, or the use of a condom EVERY TIME.

Female, 18

AIDS—this is one of the many reasons I've delayed becoming sexually active. I'm a junior now and frankly I'm surprised I'm still a virgin. I used to think that sex would be a semi-casual thing for me. But now that there are so many dangers involved, I've had to stop and think. Lord only knows what I might catch from some of the gorgeous men out there. Maybe this is better and I'll lose my virginity to someone I really love. Maybe not. One thing I can say—AIDS has certainly made monogamy stylish again.

Female, 15½

ASK ME IF I CARE

I didn't see the video (was absent) but I think I know a lot about AIDS. My parents talk pretty openly about it and I've seen other things on it. I know that at all times I should make the guys I have sex with use rubbers but I don't. My boyfriend and I have sex pretty regularly— once or twice a week. He deals drugs and he's around a lot of nasty broads but I never make him use a rubber. I think I should. Once I asked him to and he got mad. I often worry. I encourage my friends to use rubbers because of AIDS but I'm always so afraid to make the guys use them. Another guy I had sex with used a rubber the first but not the second time. He has a reputation for being one with the ladies. I should of but he conned me out of it. I always say I'll make them use one but once they say no I meekly agree. I suppose I better start being more afraid of AIDS than of the guys.

Female, 15

I ask how many students know someone like this young woman and far too many students raise their hands. I wonder how many of them recognize themselves or are just too far into denial—"this couldn't happen to me—not with my friends."

I recently spoke with the woman who wrote the preceding letter. She is currently a senior at a university in Washington, D.C. She said that all through the years since taking my class, she had *always* intended to take the AIDS test and came closest to it after Magic Johnson spoke out. It took a tragic event for her to decide to be tested. She was a victim of date rape. She sought out therapy through a counselor at her college and finally chose to be tested. Fortunately, she is negative.

She recalled being more concerned about STDs such as chlamydia and herpes than AIDS when she was in high school. But that was in 1989, and now AIDS has become of primary concern. She asked me if I still told the story about the cruise ship (it was what she remembered most about the class). I said that I hadn't for awhile, but this jogged my memory.

One summer I worked on a cruise ship that made the Love Boat seem tame by comparison. One of my assignments was to keep the underage kids from drinking. While the parents were off dancing in one of the lounges and indulging in the incredible spread of food at the

- At most, 60% of the estimated 1,000,000 HIV-infected Americans know they are infected.

- In 1993, the rate of increase in cases of AIDS reported was greatest for women, racial and ethnic minorities, adolescents, intravenous drug users, and persons infected through heterosexual contact.

- Lesions from STDs, such as syphilis and genital herpes, facilitate transmission of HIV.

- Estimates of the number of children who will have lost a mother to AIDS by the year 2000 range from 80,000 to 125,000.

midnight buffet, the teens had their own disco. The young females from thirteen to seventeen years of age, but looking much older in their high heels, party dresses, and makeup, were left to their own devices—and the parents did not have to worry about them drinking and driving! I based my fictitious scenario on this experience.

Let's say that Jennifer goes on a Caribbean cruise and has a romantic and sexual affair with one of the guys on the crew. He promises to write and to see her the next time the ship is in San Francisco. She is unaware that he has done basically the same thing every week for the three years that he has been working on the ship. How many women has he slept with and how many partners did each of them have? I draw a diagram on the board of the potential partners and the risk involved.

Jennifer returns to school. Months pass, he never responds to her letters, and she falls madly in love with a guy a year older than she is. She tells him she's a virgin. He trusts her. He remembers her from the year before and "knew" that she had not been involved with anyone. He doesn't use a condom because she's a "virgin."

The point of the story is that people don't always tell the truth or know the truth, and what if—? As the saying goes, when you have sex with someone, you are having sex with everyone they ever had sex with, whether you realize it or not.

The girl who wrote the next letter says essentially the same thing. She left it on my desk last spring:

Dear Ms. Rubin,

I don't know where to begin. I had my first experience with sex this past June. I was only fifteen. The reason I say only is because of the limit it has put on the rest of my life. He (my first) was a virgin too and I still insisted on him using protection. Except for a couple of times when I first started birth control pills. I trusted him and my only concerns and beliefs were that I could only get pregnant. Heaven forbid a disease. Towards the end of our relationship I met someone new. This new guy impressed me. He was a big-time dealer, had tons of girls and enough money to be content and unemployed for the rest of his life. He knew about me and my boyfriend and said it didn't matter and that we can be on the under. When we had sex for the first time I didn't make him use protection. I thought it would have killed the moment and besides I was on the pill. I wish more then anything that I had not thought like that. So eventually me and him begin to spend a lot of time together and he tells me that he wants me to be his. So in an overwhelmed state I broke up with my [first] boyfriend. Everything between us was fine. I would go to his hotel room every morning before school, we would have protected sex, he would give me a bath and ten dollars for my lunch. I began to trust him and would even do favors for him like holding some rocks or even his gun. Eventually I was known as his woman and all his little sellers would always have an eye out for me.

Then one night we got into a fight, he was mad because he had given me some money to buy some clothes and he didn't like what I bought. He began to accuse me of things, like hugging too close to my male patnas and not giving him enough of my time. He left me in the hotel room crying, promising to do better. The next morning when I went to the hotel room like I did every morning, I arrived to find him having sex with some dirty ho'. I was hurt and most of all scared—just the day before we had unprotected sex and he was still sleeping around. I decided it would be best if I stayed away from him for awhile, until I wasn't so hurt. A week later I was in the hospital. I had chlamydia and PID [pelvic inflammatory disease]. Today those are the least of my problems. Six months have passed since I was in the hospital and I have to get an AIDS test. I feared this test because a tiny part of me knew it was going to be positive. Two weeks later after taking the test I went to the clinic to get my results. I sat in the room with the health advisor talking about what I would do if my test was positive, all I could think is kill myself. She asks to see my paper to match the codes. I see a little red stamp that says ok on the results sheet and I feel a small sigh of relief, then she turned to me and says "Your test results are...positive". My exact thoughts at that moment weren't anger or thinking I wasted my life, but my thoughts were that my mom was going to lose her baby girl.

A new level of quiet descends on the class—you can feel the intensity as students listen to every word. This is real. This is the AIDS epidemic at our school. This young woman has made it very clear that this disease is not "out there" but far closer to home. I continue to read:

The point to this letter Ms. Rubin is that I was hoping that you could read this to your classes. I hope I can help people understand that there is plenty of time to wait and there are plenty of guys out there so if it doesn't feel right don't do it. Also no matter what you should always use protection, AIDS is a disease that anyone can get. I am an average teenager that goes to school, parties and may have even been kickin' it with you. I am in no way a lesbian or have I ever shot up. I get approached by guys all the time who want to have sex and they don't have a clue to the fact that I am HIV positive and the sad thing is that maybe one out of twenty would use protection and probably eighteen out of twenty are promiscuous....

I face this struggle of being HIV positive every day, but I have no anger or regrets anymore. I know this happened to me for a reason, maybe to warn and educate others or maybe so I can move on to my next life. Either way I am going to stay strong and I have the support of my friends and family. Please understand one thing. You never know how important your life is until you are about to lose it. If you aren't happy with your life change it while you still have the power to do so.

You never know where your sex partners have been or where their partners have been, whether it is being promiscuous, shooting up, getting high and having sex with girls or guys they don't know, or just plain having unprotected sex, it only takes one time to get the virus. I went seven months not knowing I had the virus, what if I was promiscuous or had unprotected sex during that time? Please be careful because this is the plague that can and will wipe out everyone if it is permitted to. Remember to get tested for everything if you are intimate. An HIV test won't offer you a cure but it will save someone else's life.

Thank you,
An average high school girl

Not too long ago, she wrote me another letter to tell me that she was getting along very well. I really admire her for her resilience. She reminds me of so many of the AIDS speakers who would not just give up on their lives, but turned their diagnosis into something positive—and she has managed to do this at the young age of seventeen.

It's been about a year and a half since I've written to you last regarding my being HIV+. In this short time the world has changed for me and only for the better. I have become a lot more responsible. It is almost as if my situation has given me a fork in the road and I have two options. One to learn to value what is left of my life or to give up and slowly self-destruct. I have chosen to value my life and live each day like there is no tomorrow. I have now come to realize that god has given me a gift. You may hear this and say that I am crazy and looking at being HIV+ through dreamy eyes but I have thought long and hard about it and realize that life is all mind over matter and if you have a strong mind you will live a strong healthy life. I have strong proof of this because at almost two or three years of being HIV+ I am one hundred percent healthy and have the T-Cell count of an average healthy teenager, if not higher. I have learned self-pride. I have also learned to be myself and that includes not being pressured into having sex with anyone.

With the changes of my views, I have changed myself, which has attracted different friends, none of which know I am HIV+ and probably never will until I choose to publicly announce it and that will only be to educate others and help stop this disease. Because I now have the knowledge, experience and, most important—concern, I will use this tragedy to turn it into an opportunity to help others....

It is sad that I have to share my life right now in paper only and not in person with you guys, but there is too much ignorance, fear, and lack of knowledge to expose my name or face. Please, however, take what I am sharing seriously and think what you value more—a night of risk that can limit your life, or open[ing] doors all through your life, knowing you can live each day for the next if you so choose to do. My life is not over, actually it has started over and is much better for me, but it is limited and there are fears that I must face. I know that these fears I must face are not going to keep me down and that is why I can face life to the fullest for me.

I tell my students that I have stopped crossing out the names in my address book of friends who have died from AIDS—the boy who sat next to me in Latin class in eighth grade, two teachers from this school, the anesthesiologist who used to give Christmas parties to collect toys for charity, Jim H., Gary, Jim F., Pete D., A.J., and Matt.

I give the students time to write their journal entries, and as they are working, my mind drifts back to Matt. The last time I visited Matt in the hospital—the time I took the last photos of him—he was so weak he could barely talk. I had to strain to catch his words as he told me he wanted me to have his sheepskin-lined leather gloves which were on his hospital bedstand. I keep them in my car now, and wear them on chilly mornings. They give me a special warmth as they remind me of the happy times we spent together.

SOMEONE DIED TODAY

Someone died today.
My brother died today.
He died of AIDS.
People do die, you know.
It wasn't nothing.
It wasn't a mere
blip on the screen.

It was a gruesome,
horrific death.
Painful and shocking
to witness.
Skin drawn so tight
over his skeleton
that his eyes
would not shut.
And then there was
the aspect of dementia.
Was that Matt or
was that some distortion?
I never knew.

He said he was lost.
He asked if he were
alive or dead?
Where is the white
light, I wondered?
Please, God, he
needs YOUR help!

He was 29.
Handsome once.

An athlete once.
A fisherman once.
An alcoholic.
A human being.
A teacher of harsh
realities.
An inspiration.
A hero for many.

I shed tears today.
My heart was
broken today.
It shall mend,
but it wasn't
nothing that
my brother died today.

For Matt 2/24/61–2/1/91
Elizabeth Kuykendall, mother of two daughters

5 | Etcetera Letters

IT IS A TUESDAY after a four-day weekend, and once again I come back from the pure beauty of the mountains to the chaos and stress that descends upon me the minute I set foot on campus. I stop by the mail room first, and in my box is an announcement that one of my colleagues has died of cancer. Jeff had been a teacher, our former principal, and a union leader. He had written a wonderful letter of recommendation for me when I applied for a Fulbright Scholarship. Even though I didn't get the grant, I treasure the letter he wrote on my behalf. The last conversation I had with him was just a few months ago: at my request, he had come to my room to talk with me about some problems I was having with one of my classes. As always, he was caring, humorous, and supportive.

I love long weekends, but it takes an amazing amount of energy to get everyone back in a work mode—myself included. After this bad news, it's going to be even more difficult. I decide that this is a good day for the "etcetera" letter assignment:

> **Write a letter to anyone else: sister/brother, relative, pet, friend (imaginary or real), stepparent, God, romantic interest, drug, skateboard, musical instrument, body part, music, hormones, ETCETERA.**

This journal assignment is one of my favorites because it allows my students to use their imagination, to be creative and playful, to have a little fun. They are allowed to write to any person, living, dead, or imaginary—or to a place or thing, fanciful or real. The only restriction is that they cannot write a letter to themselves or to their parents because those are topics for future assignments.

Some of the most interesting and amusing journal entries come out of this assignment: since there is no topic imposed, the letters generally reflect what's uppermost in the writer's mind, and this runs the gamut from the trivial to the tragic. I use many of the "etcetera" letters to provide background for other parts of the course, but today I read a random sampling to give the students some idea of what they might write in their own journals:

Dear School:

I know you are preparing me for my life ahead, but I don't see how geometry or badminton can do this. Yes, maybe in 30 years from now some one will say "Gee, how would you like to play a fun game of badminton," and I'll say "Okay, I'm really good 'cause I played badminton when I was 15."

I'm thankful to you for my good teachers, but the rest of them, where do they come from? Are you trying purposely to torture us kids? Maybe it's useful for us to learn to deal with people you don't like or don't get along with. Boy, I've heard that before!!

I really thank you for all of my friends—guys and girls—that's the best. So much fun!! Although some awful stuff too—fights, break-ups, etc. Well School, you definitely got your ups and you definitely have your DOWNS! But you're one peachy keen invention!

Thanx, yet Fuck You
Female, 15

To the Adults of America,

Sometimes I feel uncomfortable, or should I say less knowledgeable when I walk into a roomful of grown-ups, well you may call yourselves grown-ups but are you? Are you really mature? When 51 percent of your marriages fail and you kill 150 wildlife species everyday, does that seem sensible?

You may say, "Everyone makes mistakes." Well then excuse us, the teenagers of America, when there are one million girls impregnated every year, and young boys are shot down in our streets everyday. Please, don't stare when you begin to realize that the rehab centers are starting to fill with teenagers, and about a quarter of every teen's allowance is spent on drugs and/or alcohol. Don't let us get in the way when we stand in line at the grocery store, shopping for our drunk mothers, or praying at church for our fathers to come home.

"The only way out is through"—Robert Frost

Well, it seems we can go through almost everything, but it will never end. Our society will only become deeper into debt, into destruction, and deeper into depression. Ending only in having we the children turn on the adults and the world that neglected us—"the forgotten generation."

And that anger will show when today's children and teens are old enough to realize how horrifically our needs have been ignored. We will see that our parents and grandparents have left us enormous debts and a filthy environment. We will realize that no one had the compassion and no one was willing to make the investments of time and love necessary to ensure that our generation can enjoy the same blessings, and actual necessities that will soon become indulgences.

Male, 15

....

Dear Tae Kwan Do Belt,

You are only about two years old, but you symbolize a great thing in my life. I used to be concerned about your color, but now I realize it doesn't really matter, except in a technical way. What you symbolize is the confidence, ability and power I've gained while studying with you. It's incredible how much I've grown physically, mentally, spiritually, and emotionally since I've been wearing you. I hope to continue with that practice for a very long time, so you will continue to enrich me.

Thank you,
Male, 16

....

Dear Past Life,

Are you real? Did you really exist? Or is it just my imagination? I have had flashbacks after I saw my friend's earrings to when you came home from war and saw your wife and child again. I even remember every detail including your son's sand pail and yellow shovel. When I see films of The Battle of Dunkirk, D-Day, and the liberation of Paris, I have a very strange feeling that I was there. These are my favorite parts of history. Why? Was I there? Is that why I'm so interested in France? And is that why I take French? What was in those earrings that made me flashback? Please find a way to tell me. A way where I know it is not my creative mind.

Female, 15

....

To the fairies, druids, elves, hobbits, wizards, and jesters, forests, sunsets, rivers, aspens, snow, moon, adventure, and mystery: You are my world. In some distant past life I was one of you and I wish for you to know that you are still within me wherever I go. You are my inspirations and many of my fantasies. You make life a little lighter and create a world of perfection that I can relate and escape to anytime I wish. You are my childhood and child memories that I often miss so much. You teach me always ways to stay happy: your music and dance a release. You remind me constantly to be free, open, sensitive and energetic and I cherish this.

Stay with me always.
Female, 17

....

Dear Parents' Divorce,

FUCK OFF! You never seem to go away. Whenever I'm feeling fine you seem to come back to me. I know it's been 8 years but you still won't go away. Why won't you go away? Fuck you. What did I do to deserve you? I wish you never existed. Go to hell!

Male, 15

....

Dear Vietnam Wall,

You are so covered in sorrow that anyone can feel it by a mere glimpse of you. When I saw you I felt so much misery for those who died or are missing, and for those who lost the men engraved in you, that I sat down by your side, and wept quietly for those who cannot. I could not take a single picture of you, because nothing imaginable can capture the incredible emotional experience one experiences at your side. Your picture would have been on the same roll as happy times. You would have made me associate death with cheer and with my friends. You made me think about how insignificant it is to be rich or popular, and to cherish the fact that I am alive. I pray that you remain there for centuries to come, to touch other people's souls as you did mine.

Female, 15

The next group of "etcetera" letters all have something to do with different parts of the body or things that happen to them. I can hardly think of any part that has escaped the students' pens. I preface the first two letters with the explanation that very few women are satisfied with their breast size, and even though there is a lot of humor in these entries, one can sense the frustration and mental anguish that these two women feel. I also mention that we will talk about penis size later on. Males generally only worry when they are too small but females worry about being too big as well. Some are concerned that others will notice that one breast is bigger than the other!

To My Dearest Tits:

Fuck You! I am so sick of you guys it's unbelievable! Do you know how much hurt you cause me? People I don't know and who don't know my name identify me by sticking their hands in front of their chests to say that I have big tits. Someone else told me that my tits naturally show themselves off. Can't you shrink or something? I've tried everything, exercise, vitamins, diets but you just insist on being so goddamn perky I can't take it anymore. I swear to god, you've got minds of your own. If I was a guy I wouldn't have to worry about this. But nooooo... I've tried every bra: wire, wireless, cotton, satin, lace, sports, polyester, strapless, cross-in-the-back, cross-your-heart, bras too tight, and bras too big. What am I going to do with you!?

Ungratefully yours,
The Rest of Your Body
Female, 16

Dear Tits (Breasts),

I know this is quite strange. But, I'm writing you to ask you please, please, please grow!! I feel so uncomfortable because you're so fucking small. My little sister has bigger ones than I do!! Do you know how fucking frustrating that is??! I hate it! My friends, guys, always say "Oh! I didn't know you had an older sister!! Can you believe it!? The little fuckers!!!! My sister is in 8th grade! God, I'm so mad at you! What is your problem? Why aren't you growing? If you're planning on staying this size, I'm gonna have a fit!!! You're big enough so that when I run you hell-of-hurt but if I wear a bra I feel so weird. What if someone sees the strap? I worry about it constantly!! I wear about two tanks over it plus a T-shirt!! Also when guys hug me I freak out they'll feel I'm wearing a bra! I know this sounds funny, but really it isn't. I'm constantly scared about it, and I hate it! So of course I hardly ever wear bras!!! Why are you doing this to me?!

Still Waiting.
Female, 15½

P.S. You must...you must...you must increase my BUST!!
ARE YOU LISTENING??

There is much laughter, mainly from the females—a kind of sigh of relief that others know just how it feels. Sometimes girls will talk in class about how much negative attention they get because of their breasts. They talk candidly and I am always impressed with their openness and that the boys are respectful. At this point I sometimes mention that half of all males between the ages of eleven and seventeen experience gynecomastia—enlargement of the breasts which will decrease within a year or two. It always helps to know that you are not abnormal and that your problems are not unique.

With the next journal entry we move from tits to zits. It's a problem that affects both sexes equally:

Dear Pimple On My Face:

Oh, pimple, yes, I did address you as "Dear Pimple" but I sure the hell didn't mean it. I HATE YOU. You just happen to be as big as a volcano, and you are erupting, getting bigger and bigger and bigger and bigger. Soon, because of you I will end up just one big walking pimple. Thanks a lot. Oh pimple, please just go away. Leave me alone. I have enough problems without you. You make me so self-conscious about you and all your little kids that are also growing up. The least you could do is use some birth control to stop all the other zits from popping up.

I hate you so much you couldn't believe it.
Female, 15

I ask how many students know someone who sucks his or her thumb and almost every hand goes up. I realize I need to rephrase the question. "How many of you know someone *your age* who does this?" About one-third of the hands remain raised. I had never noticed the phenomenon until I had one class with four girls who all sucked their thumbs!

Dear Thumb,

I was born with you in my mouth, and I bet you are tired of me constantly sucking you, aren't you?! You know, the only reason why I suck you so much is because of my own insecurities. People talk about how ugly and bruised you are, but I don't care because you are my very own, and I love you. It's about time that I stop sucking you because I'm way too old. I bet you are cold a lot because you are always wet and hangin' around in the air. I'm sorry.

Love, Thumbsucker
Female, 16

I have had students say that they will not wear sandals because their toes are so ugly—one sticks way out or they are all covered with corn-like things. So many secrets hidden beneath bras, makeup, and shoes!

Dear Foot:

Why the hell are you so goddamn huge!? Jesus, 12 inches of this huge, long mass of flesh. Do you know how many companies make a size 15? No wait, let me rephrase that; do you know how many companies don't make a size 15, or how few stores sell them!? For god's sake, take a breather, take five, take anything, except more room in my shoe. Do you know how hard it is to keep from tripping on every stairway? Do you know how many people have asked me, "Damn boy, how big are those things?!" No, let me rephrase that, do you know how many people haven't asked me that?! Geez, stop growing!

Male, 15

Dear Feet,

Thanks for everything you have let me experience! Without you I would never be able to feel the movement of dance, I would never be able to feel the freedom walking on the beach gives me. I know you hate me when I stuff you into those little tiny toe shoes and dance upon your little toes 'til they bleed but I guess you know the joy it gives me. If only you could feel the freedom my soul finds when you're helping me turn and whirl around. I think you do know otherwise you would not let me be as coordinated as I am. You have managed to put me in some kind of funny places though. But that's okay. I've gotten out of them all with your help. As little as you are I trust you with all my weight.

Your Thankful Keeper
Female, 15

Whenever I think of ballet dancers, the same humorous image always comes to mind. I once had a student who was very serious about dance. She was not sexually active because she could not risk getting pregnant: she said she would look very unusual in a tutu if she were to get pregnant. To this day, when someone mentions ballet, I picture this girl, eight months pregnant and on point!

Dear Dick,

How's it hanging. I hope to the good side. You just happened to be my best friend. You are the right size for me to handle. When we go inside a girl you make me feel so good. I'm sorry that I put a rubber on you before sex, but I don't want you to catch any diseases and we are not ready for children. I'm just writing you, because you are my pal.

Male, 17

When you have a broken arm or foot everyone notices and sympathizes. But living with diabetes, back injuries, or other chronic or "invisible" problems can be very difficult.

Dear Back:

Everyone tells me that I'm too young to have problems with you, only older people or people with bad posture are affected. Well, they're wrong. I'm 15 with great posture and you don't care. I can no longer sit through movies or a long class. I'm not allowed to play any sports for the time being, that was a major part of my life. I play violin but I had to quit the orchestra because I could not sit for the required amount of time. I have been to so many doctors, specialists, and physical therapists that I can't count them anymore. I have had (it seems like) thousands of tests ranging from painless blood tests to hours of sitting absolutely still on a table with injected radium dye for two hours while they take pictures of me. Every doctor says there is nothing wrong with you, well there is, but they don't know what it is. You're always with me and probably will be for another two or three years. No one in my family has this problem. Why did you have to choose me?

Female, 15

....

Dear Allergies,

I hate you! I hate you! Please, oh please go away. I don't want to put up with you anymore, I am so sick of sneezing and wheezing.... Another thing. Those allergy shots don't do shit! They hurt and cause my arm to itch, they're a pain to get, I hate them too!!! I just want to tell that I am so happy that that arctic weather killed all you fucking pollens. And you can't make me sneeze anymore. I don't mean to be rude but just want you to go away. Please, oh, please, oh please! Just go away! You drive me crazy.

I see a guy I like, I go talk to him and what is the first thing I do? Sneeze and sneeze and sneeze. Oh my goodness, I have made quite a first impression!

Just go away!
Your loyal customer,
Female, 15

....

Dear Hearing Aid,

I'm glad to have you. If I didn't my lifestyle would be so different. I might not be at BHS, I might not have so many friends, and I might not be at the same emotional level I am at now. And I certainly wouldn't interest very many guys.

Together we have accomplished many things. I can lip-read but that's not enough. I can hear a little but that's not enough. The two together is what benefits me the most. If I didn't have you, so many people would grow irritated, angry, and insensitive. Like some friends who used to mumble and when I asked them to repeat, they'd say, "Oh never mind." In time, however, they began to slow down and it grew natural for them to speak clearly. But adults can be very insensitive too. They say something and do not wish to repeat. But when I tell them I have an aid, they instantly change their attitudes. But I don't like those kinds of people; they feel sorry for me.

I hate people who feel sorry for me. The person(s) I'd really feel sorry for would be my future husband and my children. He'll have to live with the fact that all his children will have some degree of hearing loss. And that'll be hard to deal with because he won't know what it's like, he won't have lived with it all his life, and so when his children come home, humiliated by all, he won't know how to comfort them.

But for now, I'm very grateful to have you. My life would be so different without you. I'd probably be more dependent on others, more pitied, and having less fun. Thank God I came along this decade. (Otherwise I wouldn't have you.)

Female, 15

....

Dear Period:

I hate you, I hate you and yet I suppose I love you. You make me feel dirty and insecure always looking back and wondering whether or not you've messed up my clothes again, but at the same time you make me feel like a woman, you let me know that I am very capable of producing human life. Sometimes I really wish you were gone since I don't plan on producing anything soon, maybe not ever. But when you finally are gone I know that I will miss you very, very much because it will signal another drastic change in my life.

Female, 16

....

Dear Hormones:

You are the most confusing thing in my entire life. I can't understand why you won't coordinate with the rest of me. You're way ahead of my brain and my heart. You want to have a sexual relationship, I can tell, but you'll have to wait until the rest of me is ready. You see my brain's worried about the commitment and the effect of having sex. It ponders being caught or known to be having sex. My heart needs to be sure of this guy, that he is loved and the one to lose my virginity to. So hormones, for Godsake slow down, wait up for the rest of me. Let me be ready at the right time.

Love, your body.
Female, 16

Music plays a big role in the life of most teenagers. I feel that everyone in the room will relate to this next entry:

Dear Music:

There are so many times when I have been filled with anger and frustration and the minute I turn you on it all somehow drains. You help psych me up for cross-country and track races, you give me that anger I need to be the very best I can be when I run.

Sometimes when the world is full of problems you have tantalized me and given me that natural high, taken me into the clouds so that I might get away for awhile. Your words have been consolation to me when I am upset. Your lyrics let me know that I'm not alone out here. You give me the energy to get up in the morning and help the sleep come faster at night. Nature and the trees seem more beautiful with you playing melodies through my ears. Thank you for concerts, that fill stadiums with glorious music. Mesmerizing, intensely, flowing through me. Thank you so much for always being there ready to play at any hour of the night or day. I hope you continue to play for me forever.

Love always,
Female, 15

....

Dear Guitar:

I am so glad to know you. All the things I can create with you make me feel magic. A way to channel my imagination. The sound a reflection of me through you. You are a philosopher showing me many new things, making me aware of the subtleties in life. You are my love, always there, and giving me only and all that I can put into you myself. You are a mystery, a secret, but you will only give me hints. You are a relationship which becomes more meaningful and close with time. As much time as I spend with you, I still want more. I want to go deep into sound as I go deeper into myself. Keep in touch with me.

LOVE,
Male, 17

The next letter is always a crowd pleaser:

Dear Toilet,

A few weeks ago, I flushed a rubber down you. I know I'm not supposed to do that, but Mom checks all the garbage cans and burns all the papers and throws out anything else. It just would not do to have her find a rubber wrapped up in a Kleenex. Remember—I'm not supposed to lose my virginity until I'm engaged or married. Whoops! Really, though, T. is my best friend; we went out for four months before we did [it].

Anyway, I was so worried that you might get stopped up and explode, or worst of all, backfire and end up downstairs in Mom's toilet. But you didn't, so I thank you, very much.

Sincerely,
Female, 15

"By the way," I ask, "what is the best way to dispose of a condom?" "Don't put it in the toilet because it could stop it up—I think you should just throw it in the garbage," suggests a lanky male student. One of the peer health educators says that she learned that you should tie them up so that children do not think they are balloons and play with them. There are some kids laughing—and grossed out—at the possibility of this happening.

We have students from all over the world and I often think of how difficult it must be for them to adjust to a completely new culture, a new language—and to Berkeley High. The attachment to the home country is often very strong and remains in their hearts even as they become "Americanized" and form new friendships.

My Dear City [Puerto la Livertad, El Salvador],

I hope that my people take care of you. My beautiful city, you don't know how much I miss you, but one day I will return and walk in your streets. I recall my memories of you. I am very far away from you, but you are in my heart like the blood that keeps me alive. Trust me, the one thing that I most want is to be there with you and to do the same things that I did as a child. Now I just want to tell you to wait for me. Adios for now. I love you.

Male, 16

Dear Graffiti:

Wassup? Well, I just want to thank you for a couple of things that you have done for me. First of all thanks for making me feel like I am really, really doing something, making me feel fresh, cuz hella people say that what I do is hecka "fresh, cool, and funky."

Second of all thanks for giving me respect. Since people know I'm raw, they give me respect in a funny kind of way.

Third, thanx for all the attention. Girls like me more since I'm talented at something that most people don't know how to do. You just bring me happiness!!!!

Male, 15

I had a long talk with this young man. I told him that I wanted to learn about his love of this art. He explained that he didn't tag buildings and public property but he designed things on paper that people admired and would make into T-shirts. I felt I understood him better after our talk. I no longer put him in the same group as those who put up the ugly (in my opinion) graffiti that is so prevalent around our school. However, a few days later I found his name etched into the back of one of the classroom chairs!

Whenever I watch the Olympics I get caught up in the thrill of victory and the beauty, strength, and perfection of the human body. I often think of what it takes to get to that level. All of the sacrifice, lonely hours, and endless workouts. The following students know the agony of injuries and the punishment to the body and soul—and the love of competition and satisfaction of knowing you have done your best:

Dear LaCrosse:

If there has ever been something that calls for so much sacrifice and so much pain and gives so little in return it must be you. I dedicate every day after school, Saturday and a good part of the summer to you and what do I get in return? A stinking letter and arthritic knees. Some deal. Why anyone would want to play sports is beyond me. You go out and give 110% and the coach still yells at you. You get banged up, bruised, and battered and people still call you "garbage." If I came to school with as many bruises and cuts as I have after a game people would be sending me to counselors and arresting my parents for battery. In 2½ years of serious sports I have lost two teeth and sprained ankles, torn cartilage in both knees, taken so many hits to the head that I wonder how much longer I will be able to talk straight, and had more bruises, bumps, and pulled muscles than I care to remember. This makes me wonder, are you worth it? Unfortunately I am hooked and I've got to have more.

Male, 16

Dear Gymnastics:

I really don't know what to say to you. I love you and I can't stand you. I'm not in you any more thank God, if I was I'd go crazy. You were my only life from 4th to 8th grade. I lived my life around you. I missed so many childhood experiences because of you. At the same time I learned many things like dealing with complete and utter fear and major accomplishment and major defeats or losses. Thanks to you I'm very sure of my body and its capabilities but I also now have ankle, knee, hip, back, shin, and wrist problems because of you. When I was in gym, I saw children the age of four and younger in the sport with me and I genuinely felt sorry for them because they're gonna go through the stress, pressure, and hardships of competition, and everyday training trying to give your all, knowing that the coaches expect more than that. You can't say "I'll try" to a coach, you have to say "I will." I knew a girl who was ten years old and a great gymnast but before every competition she'd cry herself to sleep at night. That's no way to live your life. I was at the gym six days a week four hours a day. My life revolved around gym 'til I was 13. At the age of 13 you shouldn't be looked down upon because you're old and washed up. 13 for Christ's sake you still have your whole life ahead of you. I practically killed myself a dozen times for you and I don't really know why. It gave me a sense of accomplishment, I kept in shape, and it's very hard to give up your first love. If I had a kid though I wouldn't let them take gymnastics and go through what I did.

Female, 15

One of the most often repeated complaints in the journals is that "all of my friends have boyfriends and I feel like I will never get one." Many of the boys desperately want a girlfriend, too, but are too shy to make the first move. Almost everyone wants to be in love. That is why I love the next two letters, and so do my students:

Dear Romeo,

Where art thou Romeo? Shit, if you can appear in Shakespeare's plays, why can't you appear in the halls of BHS? I need you. This is such a difficult and stressful time in my life, I need someone to love me and support me and give me strength. I promise I will do the same for you. I have always dreamed of the day when you will appear in my life. I don't expect you to be perfect, and I know our relationship won't be perfect, but I know I am ready to try and give and work at it. I've never had anyone hold me in his arms or kiss me and I yearn for that kind of affection. So if you feel the same way as I do, knock on my door, give me a ring, write me a note, or just say "hi." Let me know you are there, because I am ready and waiting.

Love,
Female, 15

One time after I had read the letter to Romeo, I found the following entry in a young man's journal, together with a note to explain it:

(Note: This is not a response to the Dear Romeo letter and though it may sound like a disguised version of that letter, it is only because I share some of the same feelings. Please do not mark me off for plagiarism as this letter contains my own feelings, not someone else's.)

Dearest Juliet,

Wherefore art thou dammit? I know you're out there somewhere so why in all my life have you never shown yourself before me? All that I desire is someone with a female perspective who also understands me and knows me well. I will trust you more than anyone else and I know I'll be able to talk to you about anything. All my life I have dealt with people, most of them male, who thrive—or at least enjoy—taking my thoughts, words, or emotions and turning them into jokes or just not caring at all—as if everything important to me is just bullshit and a waste of their time to even listen to. But you, my love, you will not do that. You will listen and care, and in turn I will do the same for you.

But, for right now, since I have no clue as to who you are, I have to just go on searching, hoping that one day you will appear and free me of my total silence of inner thought and deep emotions.

With love and desire I take my leave,
Forever Hoping,
Male, 14

The next few letters are all addressed to siblings:

Dear N.,

I think you're a rad sister. You seem to be following the path a whole bunch of people I know followed. When they got out of sixth grade and went to seventh (like you) they wanted to be all popular and everything. They got fucked up. They all had to do drugs or drink to be part of the "popular" group. Don't do it. You seem to want to be "popular"—hella bad. It's a totally warped idea. To me, doing drugs is the stupidest, most fucked-up thing anyone could ever do to themselves. N., that shit ruins lives. Just be a good student and your time will come. That's what happened to me. I made non-drug friends and eventually I knew everyone at King (Jr. High) and they all knew me—

not because I did drugs, but because I was friendly to people. Don't fuck up. You're the only sister I have.

Love,
Male, 15

I ask if anyone in the class is an only child and several hands go up. I tell them that I am the "baby" of my family and always enjoyed being the youngest. I was called "TAT" by my older brother and sister, which stood for "Tag-Along-Tattletale." Even though I was excluded from many of their activities, I could never imagine life without them. I love the next letter because it makes me think of the impact my brother and sister had on my life:

Dear Brother or Sister I Never Had:

During my life my feelings about you keep changing. When I was younger I always wanted a baby sister, but that was probably just to be a doll-figure for me—I didn't realize there was more to having a sister than a baby to hold. When I was in junior high it was a big brother. I was jealous of my friends who got along with their cute older brothers, and since I was relatively isolated from teenage boys, that seemed a fun way to change that.

I wonder if you would look like me? Would we get along? Would I get jealous of our parents' attention to you (or vice versa)? Would you be attractive? Would we keep in touch as adults? Would my relationships with my parents be different? Would you like our stepmother? Would you get along with our parents? And especially, would I be a different person from the experience of having you as part of my life—however great or however insignificant that part might be.

The answers to these questions will never be more than guesses, but I'm satisfied with being an only child. I know that the choice my parents made about having children was the right one for them, and although it will probably be different from the one I make with my kids, I respect it.

Regards,
Female, 15

Sister,

Hey baby girl. You are the spark of my life. You can't even talk and yet you bring in more love…. You are joy itself. One made from love. I had no doubts about you. I knew I would love you—boy or girl. Only a year. Ever since you were born, my life has seemed complete. And besides, now my children will have an aunt. You're my pride and joy even if you're not my own baby. I still feel the love as both a father and a mother. Love. You make it all possible.

Male, 15

And we mustn't forget our four-legged friends:

Dear Dusty,

Even though you are only about two feet tall, and have grey hair, and bad breath, you are the BEST doggie any boy could want! You are always loving, never mean, polite, always smiling, never complaining, and much, much more. You are getting old, but I hope you live as long as I do. You are the best Norwegian elkhound ever! Ever since we've had you, we've never had any problems with elk in the area.

Love ya,
P.S. Woof, woof.
Male, 15

I give the class time to write their own "etcetera" letters. Then, in the few remaining minutes of the period, I explain the "time capsule" letter that has to go into each journal, too. It isn't due for several weeks, but I like to give them plenty of warning. The directions are all on the Journal Assignments worksheet (see Appendix), but there are always questions to be answered.

Write a letter to yourself. Say anything you want and enclose anything you want as long as it weighs under half an ounce. You might want to write about your feelings regarding your family, self-image, friends, dreams, fantasies, fears, etc. Think of it in terms of a time capsule of your life

right now. You may want to have your friends write something inside or on the envelope. Place this letter in an envelope and seal it. Put the following items on the envelope:

1. Address the letter to yourself.

2. Put a different return address in the upper left-hand corner as a backup to your current address.

3. Put the date you wrote it AND the date you wish it to be sent on the BACK of the envelope.

4. Put $$$ or postage on the envelope—29 cents for the next couple years and figure 5 cents more for every two years thereafter. Please do NOT lick the stamps but paper-clip them to the envelope. ENJOY!! ENJOY!!

Students can have the letter sent back to them whenever they wish: one, ten, fifteen, or even twenty years from now—on their birthday, on graduation day, or any other day they choose. The most popular date is graduation day—last June I sent out 127 letters, of which 50 were mailed on graduation day.

They can also write as many letters as they want. So far, the record is seven letters, written by a former student body president—one was to be sent the day she graduated from BHS, another on the day she planned to enter Harvard, another the day she hoped to graduate from Harvard, and one each on her twenty-fifth and thirtieth birthdays! I can't remember the other two dates she picked.

I have thousands of letters waiting to be mailed, all stored at my home in pizza boxes. Almost every day I mail a couple of letters, but many are filed away waiting to be sent in the year 2010 and beyond. One student who wrote his letter in March of 1990 wrote this on the back of his letter:

Send

a) When postage for this letter is 50 cents, or

b) On my 50th birthday 2-25-2023.

Quite a few letters have gone out that I had kept for ten years. Whenever I explain this assignment, someone always asks what will happen to the letters if I die (I *do* seem old to them). I reply that my grandfather lived to be 102 years old and I am taking good care of myself, but in the case of my sudden demise, my sister Helen has promised to take over the project. (Of course she agreed to do this when there were only a few hundred letters.) She has already taken over for me on several occasions—like when I went rafting down the Colorado River or took trips to foreign countries. So barring a fire or earthquake—I live almost directly on a major fault—the mail will go through!

Many of the students decorate their envelopes with stickers, drawings, or notes from friends. I love looking at them and wondering where the students are and where their lives have taken them. I rarely find out if students receive their letters. One student wrote to thank me for mailing his letter and sent me a large black-and-white photo of himself, telling me to look for him in TV ads, and now and then I'll run into former students and they'll say, "You really did send the letter!" (Do they think I use them to start fires in my fireplace? Of course I send them!)

6 | Racial Identity

WE'RE FIVE WEEKS INTO THIS SESSION, and we've already lost nine instructional days—seven to school holidays, and two more to "staff development days," and in addition, several days have been shortened for various reasons. Often it feels like I am squeezing in a few moments of teaching between holidays, assemblies, rallies, schoolwide testing, etc!

I am not aware of any other school district that celebrates International Women's Day, but we have been doing it since the early '70s! This year, we had an assembly for the first time, and it was initiated and organized by a sophomore student. I must say that I was extremely apprehensive as I walked into the Berkeley Community Theatre. (It is not unusual at our assemblies for some students to be very disrespectful, yelling rude comments and walking out in the middle of their peers' performances.) My class was assigned to a section at the back, and I had the worst seat in the whole auditorium—the last row, last seat on the far left side—but I could feel that this assembly was being well received. The program featured performances by the Afro-Haitian Dance class, a skit by the BHS chapter of NOW (National Organization of Women), a slide show by the Asian Student Union, a poem by La Raza Unida, a poem entitled "B.I.T.C.H." and one called "Double-Dip Chocolate," and an incredible dance performance by a young man who combined his traditional East Indian dance with current hip-hop moves, all done to classical Indian music. It was a beautiful cross-section of BHS students, showing their talent and pride in their race, gender, and sexual orientation. One teacher, while introducing one of the performers, mentioned that she herself was a lesbian, and a senior male student "came out" and then proceeded to read a poem about women.

I left the assembly with a renewed spirit and a feeling of connectedness. I had especially enjoyed the rich diversity of the performances. We have so much to learn from one another's cultures, ethnic backgrounds, and different life experiences. This was one shortened school day that I felt was worthwhile.

Berkeley High School is fortunate to have such a wonderful mix of students and teachers. We have quite a few ethnic clubs, including the African Student Organization, Asian Student Union, Spanish for Spanish Speakers Club, International Ambassadors Club, Vietnamese Student Association, Native American Student Organization, Kiswahili Club, and Multicultural Coalition. The African-American Studies Department has been in existence for years, and now there is an Ethnic Studies Department.

Since 1991, BHS has required all ninth-graders to take a class called Ethnic Studies, the goal being to promote better understanding among students and foster racial harmony. Reaction to the program has been mixed. Some of my students think it has been beneficial, others think it's a waste of time—similar to the comments I hear about Social Living! I tell them that all new programs need to go through a developmental stage in order to find out what is most effective, and this class is still in its infancy. I think it is very important to have this course because our school has such a racially mixed student body, and I don't have enough time to deal with racial issues in depth in my own curriculum.

When the subject of race is brought up in my room, I always ask how many students have friends of other races and it seems like every hand goes up. I rephrase the question to ask if these are friends that you bring to your house and spend time with outside of school and again the hands go up. But always it is followed by "but the school is so segregated." It is immediately apparent to anyone who walks on the campus that groups of students voluntarily segregate themselves by race in certain areas of the campus.

Today our college advisor spoke to my morning classes. Before she left, she commented on how wonderful it was that my classes reflect the racial makeup of the school. Too few classes are so integrated. I wish we had more time to get to know one another in Social Living and explore the myriad of backgrounds that comprise each one of my classes. I look around and see a girl who was born in France, of mixed parents, sitting next to a boy from Eritrea. In front of him is a young man from Brazil. Across the room is a boy from Poland sitting next to a girl from Tibet. And so on! I always encourage these students to share what is similar and different in their native lands regarding the topics we discuss. We all learn a lot from this, and it keeps us all from letting our perspectives narrow down to what goes on in our own little worlds.

I walk around the room, stopping to ask students if they would be willing to read someone else's journal entry out loud. When I have enough volunteers I hand out entries written by males to females and vice versa, and attempt to give each reader a passage written by someone of a race different from their own. I say attempt because it is often difficult to know the race of many students. All these journal entries were written in response to the following question:

Racial identity/feelings about race relations: How do you feel about your race/ethnic background? Have you ever experienced any racist attitudes?

I love watching the faces of the students as they read another person's thoughts as if they were their own. I like them to just read and let the powerful feelings expressed sink in, hoping that a few moments of "walking in someone else's shoes" will make everyone more sensitive.

An Asian male reads an entry written by a young woman who is racially mixed:

My mother is American and my father is Ethiopian. I look Ethiopian. I live with a white family—my father still lives in Africa. I have a white stepfather who's like my real father. I think of myself as mixed or brown, not black. I can't tell if I'm racist or not. I'm the only brown person in my family. I know that there is racism in my family. Yes it's hard for me. It's hard for me to feel like I fit in. I'm always afraid a white boy won't like me because I'm mixed. And it always seems like black boys like me 'cause I am. I mean they're always shouting at me or talking to me. I am very confused about me and how my color reflects on my life.

A Mexican girl reads what a male of mixed race wrote:

Being interracial has been very confusing. Through the public eye I'm considered black, but through mine I'm mixed. I've been called names like zebra, piss-colored, yellow, Oreo, half-n-half, corn bread, and nigger. I find these names to be offensive, but I don't really trip unless called "nigger." The confusing part is not knowing if whites accept me or if they feel threatened by my presence. As well, vice versa, sometimes I'm not sure if blacks think of me as white or as black. I feel very comfortable around either race, I'm just not sure if they are comfortable.

I wish there was no racism and it never existed. Of course I know that will most likely never come true because you will be amazed at how much ignorant people are still keeping racism alive.

A white girl reads a long entry from an Asian-American boy:

I hate racism, I hate stereotypes! I hate apartheid, and I hate racist people! Although I've been a little more sheltered than others, time and time after time I have felt the bitterness of bigotry. Yes, I am a person of color and I'm damn proud of it! <u>Asian</u>-American, both from Chinese and Japanese ancestry.

My great-grandparents were the first in my family to face the discrimination in the so-called "Land of the Free." They were put into Angel Island in San Francisco before they could enter the U.S. and they were victims of the Japanese-American concentration camps during WWII.

Did you know that Chinese coolies were brought over to America in the same ships that were used for the enslaved Africans a hundred years earlier? It's true.

I don't mean to contradict myself, but most of the racial attacks made at me have been done by white people. This is no doubt [true] for all people of color and that's a fact! This does not mean I hate white people. I merely am saying this is the case from my personal experience. A racist is a racist regardless of skin color.

Fuck! Ever since childhood I've endured hundreds of racial slurs, discriminations, and accusations not to mention almost becoming whitewashed. Whitewashed is a state of mind which makes a person of color feel ashamed of their skin color, native language, and true cultural identity, making them want to become as Caucasian as possible! Hell I've been called everything from nip to nigger and nearly beaten up three times. Fuck'n'shit! I'm just as fucking American as anyone else! And quite frankly I am tired of being fucked over!

Even though I'm a fifth-generation American I have encountered numerous occasions of discrimination, accusations, etc. Just a few for example:

1. I have been called a Nip, Jap, gook, Chink, Chinaman, oriental, Flip, tight-eyes, Fu Manchu, 24-hour rice-eater, etc., etc., even a wetback and nigger!
2. Asked ignorant questions like:
   a. Do you speaky English?
   b. Are you related to Bruce Lee? (or another Asian person in the area)
   c. Is it true that Chinese are smart cuz they eat a lotta fish?
   d. Why do you all look alike?
   e. Is it true Oriental chicks have slanted vaginas?
   f. How come your people eat rice all the time?
   And a lotta other bullshit questions!

3. Placed in situations like:
   a. Waiting for hours to be seated in a restaurant and when you are finally seated the waitress and the other people give you the look like you don't belong there and then you gotta wait two more hours to be served.
   b. Go back to China! Ya goddamn foreigner!
   c. Open yer eyes!
   d. When I was six a redneck around thirteen started making racist remarks at me in a YMCA summer day camp. In return I called him a "honky." He tried to strangle me. Luckily a counselor pulled him off of me.

I turned to the martial arts because of a lot of racial violence that happened to me and because I wanted something to boost my Asian pride. I think the reason why people of color give in to racism and are ashamed of their skin color is because of the vicious stereotypes in society.

There are many giggles and gasps of disbelief during this reading. Most kids are familiar with racist comments about blacks, whites, and Latinos, but many are surprised at the ignorant and racist remarks aimed toward Asians. They just didn't think it existed.

A natural (I think!) blonde reads how a black male feels:

> It gets me very upset when I walk down the halls and people of other nationalities start to hold on tight to their valuables, or ask me if I have anything (drugs). Just because I'm a young black male, people think I'm involved with crime, or am very violent. Also just because I come to school dressed good they think I sell dope. I really don't appreciate it, and I know people of other nationalities wouldn't if I assumed something bad about them. To be honest, I feel like hitting people because of it—male or female—and in some cases have, and still will. I know it doesn't help but that's how I feel at that time.

I wake up the young white student who had volunteered to read this from a Mexican-American's journal:

> If I were to fill out an application for a scholarship, or something that required the distinction of my race, I would check the box that said, Hispanic, or Mexican-American. But in all honesty and reality—I know next to nothing about the Mexican way of life—and culture. My father never taught me to speak Spanish and I wish he had—because then I would at least have that. However, I don't feel deprived, because I wasn't reared toward any particular culture by my parents, so that left vast options open for me. I have the power to experience all types of cultures with an open mind. I think the culture I know the most about is the Native Americans, because although the bad experiences bordered equally with the good ones, I stayed with Indians for a large part of my childhood. I feel like a neutral being of no certain breed, able to experience the richness in all the many cultures in the world.

A male, possibly mixed, reads what this black female wrote:

> At times I regret being black—or should I say African-American (yes, I should). This is because of the social ridicule and deprivation (aside from discrimination) that comes with my background.
>
> When in public places, I often feel insecure around non-colored peo-

ple. I feel I always have to <u>prove</u> myself—my respect, my intelligence, my pride. It often feels like people are watching me, almost surveying me—waiting for me to make a mistake! And when I do make a mistake it seems like all the non-colored people are laughing in their heads saying, "Ha! Ha! Such a silly negro. I knew she'd fuck up sooner or later—they <u>always</u> do."

I try very hard to step away from the racial stereotypes that come along with my ethnicity. It makes me mad and ashamed to see other blacks being loud and obnoxious and acting rude and disrespectful in public. They are representing us as a people when in public, and society looks upon these people as dumb, ignorant and "uncivilized" and that gives the whole of us a bad rap!

It's sad and it's difficult to read, hear, and see things that clearly point out that blacks aren't doing anything for themselves. We have one of the largest populations and the only thing we can match with those high numbers are our unemployment rate, teenage pregnancy, crime rate, and illiteracy! It's sad and shameful.

Although I have strong feelings on the negative views of blacks I am also PROUD to be an African-American. We have come a <u>long</u> way—we still have quite a ways to go—but we HAVE come a long way!

I'm BLACK and I'm PROUD and I know I wouldn't be the person I am today if I were of any other racial or ethnic background.

A black female reads from the journal entry of a young man from Central America:

I'm from El Salvador; but I have been mistaken as a Japanese, Chinese, Hawaiian, and Peruvian. Well, it pisses me off because I think it is very improper to call somebody another name without asking where are you from. Ignorant people that can't think just love to fuck around with other cultures. So for best results, next time, if you don't know where your new friend comes from, ask.

A black male reads a journal entry of a young woman from Iran:

Yes, I have experienced racism. But it's funny (not literally) that people don't know what to call me when they get down to it. I've been called an Arabian bitch, and a fucking Indian, and a Mexican, and all sorts of other names.

Actually, what I am is different from what race I am. My race or nationality, if you will, is Iranian. Persian. In other words, I come from Iran. I speak Persian. Yeah, yeah, I also eat Persian food—lots of rice. I also eat steaks, linguini, Chinese, and everything else. What I am is a human being. Well, most of the time, anyway.

The funny thing is that I never even think about race at all. It's like, with the problems I have, I'm beyond that. It always takes me by surprise when someone, my father or mother, reminds me that we're ethnically different. I stare at them for a few seconds, and then like—ohhhh, yeah, now I remember that I'm technically Iranian.

I always specify my ethnic background as a human being, if I can get away with it. If people are really serious about ending racism, I think it's one small way of contributing.

A black male reads about a Native American girl:

People just see me as a privileged white girl. My mother was on welfare when she was a kid and her father escaped from his life of sharecropping on the reservation to get me where I am today. My mother worked hard to become the top person in her field and it was hard. Everyone says "you don't look Indian." Well, I'm not, I'm Native American and my people were oppressed worse than black people were. My people were purposely massacred by chicken pox-infected blankets donated to us for help. I hate racism! I hate people who think that all Native Americans look the same, in fact, the Choctaw are sometimes lighter than the Irish or English!

I think the next journal entry is charming, and I usually read it aloud myself just because I love the innocence and the beauty of the child's perspective:

All my life I've lived in a neighborhood in which my family is the only white family. I grew up playing on the block with black children until I was at least eleven, all my best friends were black except for one who was Hispanic. With such a background, it's literally impossible for me to feel racist. As a child, my mom once came to my school to give a lecture on Black History (though she's white) and when she asked the black children to raise their hands, I was among them raising my hand cuz I thought my freckles qualified me to be black. My grandmother after bearing nine healthy children, adopted six more (who I never knew were adopted until I was old enough to figure it out) two of which were black, one Asian, and one Hispanic, one Italian, and one white. When I came to Malcolm X and Willard, and finally Berkeley High, I was bewildered by racism and prejudice. It was an unknown concept to me. Now, I can feel racism around me constantly and it makes me sad. I wonder why [people] who are supposedly maturing with age, aren't as mature as children who are able to disregard color, race, and style.

P.S. I never did figure out why freckles didn't qualify me as being black, I mean, the color just didn't mix?

This brings up the question of how one learns to dislike another group of people and of where stereotypes originate and what reinforces them. Students offer a number of answers: TV, advertising, the government, family, peers, religions, and school (citing both teachers and textbooks). A few students say they think there is more conflict at school over class and economic barriers than there is over race. I say that we all tend to judge people initially by appearances—the clothes they wear, the way they walk or talk or wear their hair, the kind of music they like to listen to, the fact that they're fat or short, etc., etc.—mainly because these are things you can tell at a glance. It is much more difficult to find out what a person is really like inside—often we do not have the opportunity, and sometimes people put up so many barriers that it would be almost impossible to get to know them even if we wanted to. I tell the class about a former

> In Germany they came first for the Communists, and I didn't speak up because I wasn't a Communist. Then they came for the Jews, and I didn't speak up because I wasn't a Jew. Then they came for the trade unionists, and I didn't speak up because I wasn't a trade unionist. Then they came for the Catholics, and I didn't speak up because I was a Protestant. Then they came for me, and by that time no one was left to speak up.
>
> —MARTIN NIEMOELLER

student, a young man who often sported a colorful Mohawk and made quite a statement with his personal style of dress (he always wore all black, with lots of leather and metal, and a pair of handcuffs dangling from his waist). My first impression of him—based solely on his "looks"—was that he was very threatening. When I got to know him, I found out that he was extremely sensitive, compassionate, and articulate. This was his response to the question on racism and prejudice:

Racism? How ironic a question to put to me. Racism is the most irrational form of hate. To me hate is hate, prejudice is prejudice. It is almost always based on fear, fear of that which is different, that which one doesn't understand and isn't willing to put forth the energy to try to understand. It is sad that this attitude, inherent in the mind, perpetuates itself, feeds on itself and becomes self-fulfilling, a vicious cycle.

How could one look at me and imagine I could be racist? My dress and hairstyle is contrary to what society has deemed "normal"; most look at me and see a punk, nothing else. I have suffered the same attitudes present in racism from <u>all</u> walks of life, all sections of society. It's nice to know that hate is not a commodity monopolized by any particular race, color, creed, or religion. In my case the irony is that the attitudes that victimize me are not by virtue of birth but by an action of my own free will (I really don't think I have to explain that to you). The people that tell me it's my own fault should examine their own values and prejudices. I am perhaps more frequently and completely stereotyped than victims of actual racism. So few actually see the connection.

How then could I be racist? I know only all too well how it feels.... I empathize for all as much as myself, that we stand in judgment of that which is our ignorance.

Male, 18

Most of my students will say something like "we all have a little prejudice within us," but rarely has anyone acknowledged being a racist like the following young man did:

WHEN I STOPPED BEING A BIGOT

I was very much a serious, hate-mongering bigot.... I knew a lot of racism was complete bullshit, but practiced it in thought and word, but at least not in deed....

This racism I practiced was anti-social, immoral, and unexcusable, I knew that subconsciously, but did not realize it 'til about two months ago. At least I have an explanation for my behavior. As I saw it, the hick racist Confederate-flag-waver shitheads were racist bullies, they lived in mainly white controlled towns, with unpowerful minorities within it who usually were untroubling to the whites. A far cry from Berkeley, a town that was new and bewildering to me, since I moved here only two years earlier.

The hick racists had no reason to fuck with the black folks in their areas because blacks there were mostly not full of black pride. I saw black pride as threatening. I heard of "the master plan" where there was supposed to be a conspiracy among whites against blacks to destroy them. I know that most blacks in this city think such an outrageous suspicion is bullshit, but many believe it in places like East Oakland and Richmond. I hear it in black pride music, especially "Public Enemy Number One." For awhile I thought that many blacks had suspicions against whites like myself. My racist thoughts were not caused by "blind hatred" but by racial tension. This is an explanation of my past behavior not an excuse for it.

This racist phase lasted for the first twenty months since I've been in Berkeley. But it became painful as soon as I realized that I was wrong, and needed to change. It was my New Year's resolution to cleanse my mind of my racist feelings. I tried and tried. I talked with my best friend, and with another close friend. I soon had greater understanding of the world around me and I developed tolerance and became a better character—the person I'd wanted to be. I had a lot of problems. Being racist was one; another was low self-esteem, not liking yourself. I've solved one problem. I must now have better self-esteem. I never knew a bigot who liked himself or had good self-esteem.

Maybe I can talk about my difficulties with my change. I still feel like a racist shit.

Male, 16

I reread the part where he says, "I never knew a bigot who liked himself or had good self-esteem," and tell the class how true this is. If someone calls you fat, ugly, a nigger, fag, bitch, whatever, they are saying more about who they are themselves—and their insecurities—than they are about you. Our halls and classrooms reverberate with racial slurs and endless put-downs. Maybe that's because there is a lot of insecurity in being a teen. It is sometimes easier to put someone else down than to look at your own "stuff."

Many students complain about the uphill battle of fighting off racial stereotypes. One of my Chinese students described his frustration like this:

> What really bothers me is the stereotyping by other races about Asians. Everyone in this American society expects me to be smart and every Asian to be smart. Yes, I am smart, but not every Asian is smart. Not every Chinese kid at BHS is going to Cal or some other big-name school. Everybody thinks you know kung-fu like Bruce Lee. I know nothing about kung-fu....
>
> Male, 15

One young woman described how she felt as the only person of her race in her classes:

> I don't have a problem being black. I do have a problem with black attitudes. I speak correctly or "proper" as my friends call it. I get so much grief from them because of the way I act and speak, supposedly "white." I really could care less. The only thing I have a problem with are my classes. With the exception of two, I am basically the only negro in my classes. This makes me feel awkward because my classmates of other persuasions stare. I get the feeling that they are waiting for me to transfer. But I'm not. (smile!) Most of my friends have dropped the classes they had that were predominantly white for that reason. Dumb, dumb, dumb. Another thing I don't like is that most colleges now want to "feed in" so-called minorities. I get the feeling that they look more at your race and less at your grades.
>
> Female, 18

When I read the next letter it brings on a few smiles even though it brings up the sensitive topic of reverse discrimination:

> Most of the racism that I have encountered has been from African-American males. I hate to say it, but many of them view all white people as ugly-looking, rhythmically challenged, over-privileged racists who look down on all other races. Two things that have disturbed me the most

are being called a white boy (how would a black teenager feel if he was called "black boy"?) and being told that white people can't dance and don't have rhythm. (I am a drummer so I cannot stress how much I really, really, really hate hearing that.) I also hate how some minority groups look down on and exclude white people. In conclusion I would like to say death to all fucking racists, Nazis, and anti-Semitic, homophobic, gay-bashing, xenophobic mother-fuckers!!

Male, 15

Many of my nonblack students have complained of this reverse discrimination. From someone who is half Italian and half Indian:

It's hard for people to be white at this school. In my entire career at BHS I've never heard any white person make a racial comment towards a black person but I've heard lots of blacks say: "white this, white that." And it's very frustrating 'cause whites are the ones known as being racist.

Female, 15

And from another student:

All the stories you just told seemed to put racial discrimination on whites. Well to tell you the truth I think that's bullshit. I admit there is a lot of racism around but whites are not the only bigots. I am not racist and never have been and a lot of my friends are minorities, but I'm sick of being messed with just 'cause I'm white. It doesn't happen so much anymore but when I was younger it was much more apparent. I used to live and still do where there is a large community of African-Americans. And when I was in junior high I was harassed constantly. I can recall many times being called a "honky" or a "little white boy"; that really pisses me off. If I had responded "what, nigger" or "what, black girl" it would have been considered racist as hell.... Singling out any race and harassing them seems very wrong to me.

Male, 15

Children who are the product of an interracial marriage have a different set of problems. Many face the serious situation of prejudice coming from multiple sources, sometimes from within the family itself. Others experience difficulty in establishing their identity. Many are offended that, when they fill out forms, there is no box for them to mark that accurately reflects their racial background.

I am one of the most confused persons racially on this planet. My mom goes by "Hispanic." She is Spanish, Indian, Greek, North African, Turkish, plus she considers herself Jewish. My dad is white, Polish 'n' Lithuanian, but there's some Mongolian blood not too far back that gives everyone slanty eyes on my grandma's side. He goes by Jewish too. But it's sort of like, when you take on too much school work everything sort of gets done half-assed. When I was five or younger I remember watching those TV ads on Channel 2—"I'm proud to be an African-American," "I'm proud to be a Mexican-American," "I'm proud to be an Asian-American." What the hell was I? "I'm proud to be a mixed-up American." I went to an all-white school, spoke Spanish at home, and ate couscous for dinner. I never went to religious school but always took off of normal school for "High Holidays" and had the Jewish grandma from hell (Dad's side). None of the white kids had the same culture as me, none of the Hispanic kids looked like me and most were Mexican, which I'm not. I mostly stuck with white kids because it was easier. As I have grown older, I have wished more to make my racial identity more a part of my life. I enjoy sharing my cultures through dance and seek more activities that are considered "Hispanic." But I don't know what I am yet.

Female, 18

I have six very different nationalities in me. I am Native American, from the Sioux and Choctaw tribes, Mexican, Italian, Spanish, Portuguese and Japanese. If I tell someone what I am, they can usually pick out some features from most of these nationalities, but…most people just think that I am white. I really don't care that much though, I know what I am. It is just very hard sometimes, I never know what people think that I am. I experience a lot of racism. When people think that am white they treat me one way, good or bad as it may be. But when they find out that I am part Mexican or Japanese I usually get treated with more respect by ethnic minorities and some whites too, but sometimes people look down upon me, and think of me as a "no breed." Being thought of this way does offend me. I just don't think that it should matter what you are, and what I have found to be true is that it doesn't. People shouldn't just be looking on the outside because it really does not matter, and anyways, it is all about who you are perceived to be, not what you really are.

Female, 15

In the past couple of years I have had more students than ever before write in their journals that they hate white people. I have talked with some of these students privately to try to get at the reasons behind their feelings. Many of the students who have expressed antiwhite sentiments have one parent who is white and one who is black, and they feel they have to choose one group over another. They say that, since society generally will see them as black, it is easier for them to associate with and identify as being black. In some cases, this has meant a total denial of their white blood. I do know that tensions often run high. In some classes we talk very candidly and seriously about racial problems, while in others, discussion becomes too heated and volatile. Entries like the following two would initiate a wonderful exchange of viewpoints in some classes, while in others they could not safely be read:

> I hold many of the stereotypical ideals about what makes a woman look sexy, so I often don't find myself as attracted to minorities as Caucasians (except there is a really good-looking young, Afro-American girl in your sixth period class; I don't know her name (for some reason it seems hard to approach her—I think it's partly because I'm not sure if she'll relate to me, and partly because she sits across the room). However, I have absolutely no problems making friends with anyone, regardless of race or sex or physical disadvantage, as long as they aren't assholes.

> One of my oldest best friends is mixed (black/white) and many people would probably say that he "acts white" because most of his friends aren't black. I think that many blacks, because they are raised in a lower social class than the average white, tend to act differently (less prudish). My friend doesn't act white, he merely acts like he lives in a middle-class family, which he does. I think many blacks are also pressured into "acting black" because it is politically correct and they don't want to be outcast or insulted. One acts the way one does because of who their parents and friends are not because of their race.

> I also disagree with the present movement to "go back to your roots." This is America—not China, Mexico, Africa, India, Great Britain,

Italy, Greece, or any other fuckin' country. Every color and country is represented in American history. Be proud of the contribution that each and every one of them made. Do not base your pride on a few specific people whose only link is the color of their skin. And instead of shouting and angrily stating your message, correct people. It's true that there are a lot of assholes out there of every race that will act like shit-heads, but they aren't usually important anyway. Don't give the assholes any excuses, your anger at them will only incite more attention from them. Instead, racial relations should be improved between people of open minds. We exist. Approach us friendly-like and we'll probably return the favor. Then hopefully, the idiots will follow those of us who've already figured out how to correctly treat our fellow humans, and in a few generations, racial tensions can be eased off a bit.

Male, 15

This topic comes up every week in one of my classes. I feel happy being African-American or whatever people call it these days. I would not change or trade my color for anything. Being a minority is alright. I have no problems. Racism is something that I personally have never felt.

I hear a lot of African-Americans blame white people for everything. I think that it is time for them to start putting the blame on themselves not whites. I feel that interracial relationships are fine, it's not like you can stop your feelings for someone because they are not the same color that you are. People need to wake up and see that the world will always be like this and that America is the melting pot of the world so there will never be one color as a color that is superior to anyone.

Female, 15

It is not uncommon for students who are foreign-born, or whose parents are, to reject their native culture in a desire to become completely Americanized. They may feel embarrassed that their parents speak poor English or stick to their old country ways. I think we all need to feel proud of our heritage, whatever it is, instead of fighting against it. Some students have found that becoming active in an ethnic group can be helpful.

Up until this year, there was not a single second of my life that I was proud to be Asian. My parents have always said to me, ever since I was a little girl, that I must speak more Chinese because otherwise I would forget it all. Part of me wanted to live my life eating pizza with a fork instead of rice with chopsticks. I thought it was because we were Asian that my parents were so different from other parents; not allowing me to go to other people's houses or letting them come to my house, not letting me talk on the phone, expecting me to do well in school and in playing piano and violin. I saw the Asian Student Union assembly last spring and it really struck something inside me that I had never felt before. The people who spoke were voicing the pride I'd never heard in myself and it really touched me. I guess it made me realize a little more who I really was and who I could really be. I was what they considered whitewashed and I realized for the first time that that wasn't what I wanted to be. I wanted to be proud of who I was, I wanted to know what was inside me.

I joined ASU this year and I find myself looking forward to the weekly meetings. I've met many people through ASU and I look forward to meeting many more. It feels sort of like that is the only time I can really feel like myself; where I'm comfortable and proud of who I really am. So tell all those Asians out there, have pride in who you are and what culture is in your blood. Knowing your own identity will mean more than wanting someone else's.

Female, 15

It seems to me that instead of wasting energy battling over the differences among us we should work to understand our differences and, hopefully, to celebrate our diversity. I keep looking for the positive signs, and they are there. It is true that some students state that negative racial comments are aimed at them daily, but a surprising number report that they have never experienced any prejudice. I've been the target of slurs myself (I have been called a white supremacist bitch and once found swastikas on the door to my room). But the following letter makes me believe that it is possible to break down barriers and make changes:

I admire you Miss Rubin! You are the only white person I ever liked. I thought no white person could teach me anything I don't already know. In fact it's so strange that I realized that I respect you. I just thought I admired you because you were trying to make a difference. But now I know I also respect you as a person.

You consistently are having problems with our class and you never gave up. I guess because you thought it was worth it. It was, Miss Rubin, because I'll never forget you. You just don't understand how much change you have created in my life.... I thank you.

Male, 17

The following information was gathered as part of a study on adoption. The 136 survey participants were from five Social Living classes during the fall of 1992. In addition to illustrating the diversity of our school population, the responses to the question of ethnic identity demonstrate the inadequacy of the customary racial categorizations (e.g., white, black, Asian, Hispanic).

Ethnic identity as defined by survey participants:

Asian-American	5	German-Ukrainian	1
Eastern Indian	3	Finnish/Irish/European	1
Chinese	4	Russian/Scottish/Irish	1
Filipino	3	Irish/Scottish/English/Swedish	1
		Irish/Russian/Swedish/Hungarian/	
Chicana/Chicano	3	French/Italian	1
Mexican	1	Czechoslovakian/English/Greek	1
Hispanic	1		
		Japanese/Scottish	1
African	5	Indian/Irish/Black	1
African-American	18	Italian/Indian	1
Black African	1	Iranian/Native American	1
Black	10	African/German	1
Eritrean	1	Argentine/Arabic	1
Afro-American/Black/Negro	1	Chilean/European	1
		Irish/Black	1
Jewish-American	4	Black/White	2
Jewish-White	3	Black/Chocktaw	1
Italian-Jewish	2	Black/White/Asian	1
German/French/Jewish	1	African-American/Cherokee	1
Eastern European Jewish	2	Russian/Greek/West Indian	1
Danish-Jewish	1	Asian/White	1
Hungarian Jewish	1	Russian/Jewish/English/Irish/Native	
		American-Osage	1
White/Caucasian	16	Polish/Italian/African-American/Russian/	
European	7	Czechoslovakian/Seminole/Jewish	1
Italian-American	3	East Indian/German/French/Russian/	
Irish-American	1	Swiss/Vietnamese	1
New Zealander-American	1	Black/Cherokee/Irish/	
German	2	White-Spanish/French-Creole/	
Eastern European	1	Chiricahua-Blackfoot-Apache	1

Note: Of the students surveyed, 3 were adoptees, 1 was an offspring of anonymous artificial insemination. Survey data gathered by Johanna Metzgar.

7 | Letters to Moms and Dads

Write a letter to your mother.

Write a letter to your father.

These letters should express both your positive and negative FEELINGS about the person, and any suggestions for improving the relationship.

I SPEND VERY LITTLE actual class time on this assignment. I just read a few letters of the dozens that I've collected over the years, remind the students that they need to include one letter to their father and one to their mother in their journals, and pretty much let it go at that.

In spite of this minimal input on my part, these two letters tend to be the most personal and emotional of all the writings my students include in their journals. Whether it is an outpouring of love or a diatribe, kids tend to get more involved with these letters than they do with any other journal entry. This is one reason I assign them as homework. I think they need the extra time and the privacy to gather their thoughts together and get them down on paper.

Since they have so much to say, the letters to parents are usually the longest entries in the journals. It is not unusual for students to complete the other assignments in a very brief paragraph or two but to go on for four or five pages in these letters, putting down on paper the frustrations, fears, hatred, and love they've kept hidden inside for years. Some letters are very short with intense feelings summed up in just a few powerful sentences, but those are the exception.

I realize that this assignment can really push a lot of buttons. One young man wrote in his evaluation of my class: "So many times I felt like writing what I really felt, but it was just so painful, I didn't write very much. Especially the letter to your parents. I wanted to write to my real father but I didn't because I prefer to shut him out. If I were to do it again I would surely have handled it better. You can't believe what a tremendous block I have over my emotions. I have conditioned myself to have almost no emotions. I was scared. I mean really scared. I'm sorry. I gave it a real effort. However I'm sorry I didn't handle it all better." I tell my students that if any particular assignment is too painful for them, they should see me and we can substitute another one. I always encourage them to try, but I certainly do not want them to deal with any feelings they are not ready to handle.

For years, sociologists have been warning us about the decline of the American family as a viable social unit. After reading an especially gloomy set of letters, I'm ready to pronounce it all but dead. It is rare to read of what was once thought of as the typical American family— where both parents live together and the young person feels safe, loved, and validated. There are many single-parent families, some of which are functioning very well, and others not so well. Some kids live with siblings or an aunt or often a grandmother. We have kids living in foster homes and others with no homes at all.

The configuration of the American family has changed so much that I'm not even sure what "normal" is any longer. I know that many of my female students intend to have a baby without ever marrying or living with the father, and to them, that is a perfectly normal family.

Because my students generally have little or no control over their family situation, I make a conscious effort not to dwell on the negative aspects of family life. I don't read too many letters, and when the few I read prompt discussion, I try to put the emphasis on looking for ways to improve family relationships. I also try to make my students aware of what good parenting is so that when they start families of their own they will not repeat their own parents' mistakes.

There are mom-and-dad letters that touch on every segment of the Social Living course, so they appear in other sections of the book, wherever they are appropriate. The ones in this chapter have to do with family relationships, primarily. I hope they will give my adult readers

According to 1992 Bureau of Census Statistics:

- There were 9.7 million married-couple families with 2 children present in the home. This mythical or idealized traditional family represented 10% of all households in the nation.

- 10.5 million families were headed by a single parent.

- 36% of black children lived with 2 parents, compared with 77% of white children and 65% of Hispanic children.

- 5% of all children under 18 years lived in a home maintained by their grandparents.

- 442,000 children were in foster care.

ASK ME IF I CARE

a good understanding of what family life looks like from the teenagers' point of view. I would not read this many letters to my students; I read just enough to show them a diversity of opinions.

Some students use this assignment to vent pent-up anger and to express hatred for a parent they can't get along with or who is absent:

To my father,

I know you never hear me when I speak, so I thought (yes, I can do that) that maybe if I wrote to you my feelings you might take the time to think about what you've read. You know I'm very unhappy at home and it's not because I'm crazy or because I'm wild. I'm not wild. You've just never raised a teenage girl before and you don't know how. Whether a parent can accept it or not, at sixteen a person needs their freedom—freedom to make their own choices, freedom to decide their way of life, freedom to be their own person. I'm not getting that freedom I need.

Being a girl has nothing to do with it. I have a functioning body and a functioning mind just like you or any other "normal" person. That is a fact you have to accept because my being won't go away, but instead will grow bigger and stronger with time. That is one reason I'm not happy. I don't feel you treat me as an equal, as a human being. I feel I'm someone you use your "authoritative" position on—someone to manipulate and control. Look at the birds. A parent is to give guidance, not to oppress or deny one of her own life. The parents push them out of the nest—but do they know how to fly? They <u>learn</u>, and by their own experience. No one can tell them how to do it.

Lack of communication: Not only between you and me. What about between you and your wife? In your parenthood, how many times have you fought in front of your kids? How many times have you hugged and kissed in front of them? Not counting the past year, I'd say next to none.

Everything emotional is always hidden. Why? I grew up thinking you never fought and never made love. You've always been reserved and self-contained. You know, I can't even remember when the last time you kissed me was. Did you ever? You claim you love me, but I don't feel any love. I only feel oppressed. Tied down. An eager dog on a leash. The only reaction I get from you is when I threaten your position, challenge your immortality. That reaction is violent. Slap me, crack me, hit me, beat me—does it help? You try to scare me into silence because you know it works. It's a cop-out. Instead of facing the problem you shut me up, and thus ends the problem—everything all peaches and cream.

Are you aware that if I got pregnant there's a way I could legally emancipate myself from both of you? Did you know that if it's legal you have no control over what I do, who I'm with or where I go? Also, why is sex such an evil subject to you? How come when I was little I never got any books with pictures showing how different boys and girls are. Do you really think you can control at what age I'm going to have sex?

…I'm not a ball of clay for you to mold into a being as close to yourselves as possible. In blood and in flesh you're closer than anyone can get, but in mind and soul you are at this point farthest away. Think, realize, believe, admit. It's all there….

I haven't said half the things I would've liked to but it can't all be said at once, and anyway you probably won't listen again.

Not always yours,
Female, 16

....

Dear Dad

It's been a long time. I haven't seen you for over three years, it seems like a lifetime. For the longest time I wanted to see you, but now, I hope you're dead. You're such an idiot. You're so irresponsible, and a hypocrite. You are a liar. I don't really have anything to say to you, I've said it over and over a million times. So why should I say it again. I miss the guidance a father would give me, something that you could never give me. All the things you stood for in my life are useless to me now. So for what you took from my mother; her love, trust, and some part of her soul, and for what you could never give me: Because of these things for your sake, I hope you're dead.

Regrettably, unfortunately, embarrassed of, and always reminded of,
Your son
Male, 16

Dear Dad,

I know that you have worked hard all your life to support us kids and of course Mom's antics (alcoholic) but that is all you did. You never showed that you cared about anything I did, you never said that you loved me. I resented it when you spanked me and when I remind you of it you deny every bit of it! Also when I remind you of hitting Mom you do the same exact thing, and yet I have seen you do it! I can't talk to you at all because you are just a god damn asshole!!!!!!

You don't want to be close to me because I am just like your daughter of your first marriage. I don't see why you hold that against me. I have tried talking to you, writing to you, and no matter what you give me one big intellectual speech (which I don't understand) and then everything is supposed to be alright. To me you haven't been a father and there is no way you ever can be! You have loused up my life just like everyone else and you don't even care what is happening. All you do is bitch bitch bitch that I don't do anything!

Shit, Dad, I have done everything and I get no confidence for myself from you or anyone else! I have tried everything to gain your love and I give up! You really don't give a shit about me or what I do, all you do is tell me what to do and you don't bother to show me how. Now how am I supposed to turn out "right" if you don't bother to help me! I am just sick of our family and I am going to leave this family for good! I have lost my love for you and there is no way you can make it up!

Your daughter
Female, 15

The next girl addressed her letter to both parents. It was not exactly what the assignment called for, but the letter is very telling:

Dear Mom and Dad,

I wonder what it would be like to see you together. What would it be like to have a normal family, to have a whole family? Mom, I worry about you. Your job is so stressful that I can see it changing you. It makes you angrier and easily agitated. I see those obnoxious students draining the love out of you.

• Children of divorce make up the largest share of children living with 1 parent (37%), followed closely by children born to a parent who never married (34%).

• More than 80% of adolescents have parents who are employed outside the home. The percentage is even higher for those in 2-parent families.

• 11% of black 15- to 17-year-olds live with neither parent.

And Dad, I don't know what to wonder about you. I guess that is the whole point. I remember your bald head, but that is about it. Everything else comes from pictures and a few stories. I am angry at you. Angry for the insecurities your absence has caused in me. For the way you just left. For the ways you have said you don't love me and my sister. I'm angry for the financial hardship you have put into my mother's life and mine and my sister. I'm angry at the amount of control you have in our (non-existent) relationship. You left me without giving me a chance. Hell, I don't want a fucking chance to prove that I am a good daughter. I know I'm a good daughter. You couldn't have better. I was going to call you a loser, but we are both losers here. You and I, at least we share that.

Female, 16

....

Dear Dad,

I shouldn't waste my time writing you because you never spent any time with me. You have even denied me over the phone to your wife. Sometimes I wish that I could see you and tell you how much I hate you. You cheated on my mother and even told her that you weren't the father of her child. DAD, I HATE YOU.

Love
HATING DAUGHTER
Female, 15

....

Dear Dad:

It's too bad you waited so long to rebel. Fifty-year-old teenagers are rare so you should feel out of place. It wouldn't be so bad if you hadn't already committed yourself to a family. I don't want to make this too long and drawn out but I just can't have much respect for someone who would walk out on me and those close to me. Maybe it's a blessing in disguise because I've learned to be independent—I have to be because if I start depending on someone, they might just dump me as easily as you did. I hope you're enjoying your hot tub...and snobby friends and rich wife. It would be nice of you to share with your family living off unemployment and your petty child support.

Forever, your daughter
Female, 16

....

My Loving Father:

I don't really know you, but I would like to see you some day. I don't know how I would react to it, but I would most likely be cool. I have met a lot of people who have the same last name. I will never know if they are related. Because you left just as I was coming on the scene. I really don't care to see you, the more I think about it.

Your illegitimate son.
Male, 17

The next girl addressed her mother by name, then very formally signed the letter with her own full name:

Dear _____,

How are you doing? Terrible I hope. I can't even begin to express how much I hate you. You blame me for everything that went wrong in your life. You told me that my father (whoever that may be) tried to talk you into getting an abortion but you refused. After you gave birth, you said he tried to talk you into putting me up for adoption, but again you refused. After three short months my father left you. I wish now that you had listened to him and either aborted me or put me up for adoption, because anything would be better then torturing me for 16 years for a mistake your stupid ass made. I'm glad I don't live with you anymore and believe me you don't ever have to worry about me, or ever seeing me again because I don't ever want to see you. In fact as far as that's concerned I don't even have a mother.

Uncaringly Yours,

_____

Female, 16

Dear My Mother's Ex-Husband,

I hate your stupid ass.... You call about every six months or so. I could be dead for all you know. You don't know how old I am or when my birthday is, because whenever you do talk to me you always ask me, So how old are you now? or When is your birthday again? That's shit you should already know.... I sometimes wish that you would die. Well, actually you are killing yourself slowly by using crack.... I don't want to ever see you again. You don't have to worry about coming to my graduation or anything because you are not invited.

Your ex-daughter
Female, 15

Many letters seek connection, and offer love and forgiveness, even to a father or mother who has not shown they care at all. These letters are probably the saddest of all the ones I read.

Dear Dad,

You probably haven't thought of me or don't think of me at all, but I think of you a lot even though I can't remember your voice or what you look like. I know you have a wife now and two other kids but it hurts me to know that you know you also have another daughter out there and that you're not taking any effort out to find me even if it were just to say hi or just to see what I look like. I may not know you but there's a space in my heart for you waiting to let all my feelings for you out and I just want to see you so I can tell you how much I love and miss you.

Love, your daughter
Female, 15

Dear Father:

How are you? I hope you are fine. I have never heard or seen you. I wish you hadn't did what you did, leaving mother two years after I was born. I don't know too much about you but I still love you.

Male, 15

Dear Daddy:

I'm mainly writing this letter to you because I don't have the courage to tell you personally. I'm really sorry that things turned out so bad for us. Daddy, you know that I really do love you, but it's hard for me to love you when we are always arguing. For some unknown reason you can't meet me halfway when it comes to forgiving. Daddy, you always ask me why I'm so mean to you. When I try to answer you honestly, you interrupt. The truth is, for fourteen years of my life I've seen you beat and emotionally kill my mother. You drove me to a psychiatrist and turned my sister into an identical you. But I still found a way to forgive you. Now that you two are divorced you are still finding ways to hurt my mother. When you hurt my mother you hurt me. I have to find ways to hurt you back, that's why I do and say the things I do. Daddy, Mama has a new life and she is living out her dreams, dreams you always destroyed. I'm telling you I'll do anything to help make those dreams come true. I've never told you I loved you because I always built a wall of hatred between us. I hope that someday we can knock that wall down together.

Hoping,
Your loving daughter
Female, 16

....

Dear Dad,

I wish I could be closer to you. Why won't you listen when I talk to you? I want to get to know you inside and out. I know you love me, because you show it in every way, except just telling me you love me. I'd tell you I love you—it's just that I feel afraid because I don't know what your reaction will be. Sometimes I cry when I'm in bed at night. I feel so lost because I can't talk to you.... Dad, you're like snow. You come and stay for a while and then you melt away and don't come back for weeks, even months. Even though you live nearby you don't visit me enough. When I call you at work, you're too busy to talk to me. When I call you at home, you're always out. I wish you weren't so busy all the time. I know you don't have much money, but you don't have to spend a lot on me. All I want is to be with you, to walk in the park with you. I liked it when you came by every Sunday, and we went for walks. Some Sunday soon we should go on a picnic. Then we could <u>really</u> talk together. I love you, Dad. Please, let me show it.

Love,
Female, 15

....

Dear Dad,

I do love you and that's why our relationship is so hard on me. I know time and distance is a factor but there is something missing. Somehow you don't let me grow up. You still treat me as though I was your 8-year-old baby that you can take fishing. Dad I hate to break it to you but I hate worms now! It goes deeper than you not letting me grow up. It goes down to the fact that you can't relate to me…. I know you feel cheated and hurt that mom took me away from you but she had to do what was right for her.

You know it's kind of funny, sometimes I take a step outside of a situation I'm in and look in. So often what I see is me trying to find the love I never got from you. Me looking towards people hoping they will understand me and I guess give me kind of a fatherly love. You were never around to give me that kind of masculine love. I don't really even know what it is but I guess it's kind of the feeling of being protected and cared for.

Even so Dad there is something I admire in you. Sometimes it's the thing that keeps me going. Your music. I think it's wonderful. I love just sitting in a room watching and listening to you play your cello. That sound is love, Dad. You may not be able to share it any other way but the love you share with your music is incredible. That's really when I feel closest to you….

Oh God, Dad, don't you see I'm a person with feelings? Don't you see that I love you and want you to accept me for who I am? You just don't try. I've asked you and asked you to try but you don't. All it takes is letters, phone calls. You won't even call.

I love you dearly,
Female, 15

Dear Mom,

…You've supported me through my whole life (16 years) and you've been a good mother. God, we've had some really bad times though and sometimes when you yell at me for doing something which you considered "wrong," I hate you so much! Then you can turn around and be sooo nice and say how sweet I am; I love you! At the present time I like our relationship and I hope it keeps going in this positive direction but I'll never be able to forget that time at the old house when I was about eight, and I didn't want to cuddle with you and how you hit me and then you hit me again and the whole time you were yelling at me and that one shove that brought me into the wall. That's when you stopped, but you were still yelling at me and screaming at me to "get out of the house!" Well fuck, you don't fucking say that to a crying and hurt eight-year-old girl…. God you've hurt me so much in so many ways. But you know what? I still love you. All the times you've grounded me, all the times you've called me an "idiot," a "bastard," an "asshole," "stupid," and god knows what else, I still love you. And all the times you've let your bad feelings for someone out on me and put me down and made me cry, I still love you. I've never said anything about this, but I used to wish that every time you left in the car and were late coming back you had had a car accident and died, but then it scared me, because I still loved you. I hope our relationship keeps on getting better as the years go on because I love you mom! Just do me one favor—don't start getting into those heavy drugs that some of your friends take once in a while at parties. And, don't get stoned so often….

I love you.
Female, 16

....

Dear Mother (whoever you are),

Someday I want to meet you. Someday when I'm old enough and I feel that meeting you won't tear me apart. I think about you a lot—what you look like, how you act, how you smile, if you are married and have other children. I wonder what our meeting would be like. Do you think about me? Sometimes my adoptive mother tells me that you must have been very young when you had me and you probably were not married to my father. My adoptive father thinks you must have loved me very much to know that you couldn't take proper care of me and to put me up for adoption. I thank you for doing so, because my parents are two of the most wonderful people in the world and one day I want you to meet them. I think I would like to be friends with you. I love you even though I've never met you.

Love,
Female, 16

....

Daddy—

I have so many questions for you—Where are you? Why did you leave? Do you still love me? I'm almost sixteen, did you know that? Sometimes I hate you, I curse your name—other times I miss you and wish you were here. I remember you—at least a little bit. It's been almost seven years since I've seen you. I've changed daddy—I'm almost a woman now, not the little tomboy that you remember. You do remember— don't you? Who's gonna give me away at my wedding? My life is so different without a father....

My God, I don't even know if you're alive!!! Please come and find your daughter, she still loves you.

Love,
Female, 16

Money crops up as an issue frequently. Most of the time the situation involves a father who is not paying child support, but sometimes it has to do with material goods being given as a substitute for love.

Dear Dad,

Why do you have to be such a temperamental asshole?!? You complain about everything. You fly off the handle at the slightest fuck-up. And some of the things you say really hurt. Why do you treat me like a reject—because of the way I dress?!? Let me be me. And could you please, maybe, talk to me sometimes, instead of just always giving money. I don't really think I know you.

Male, 16

Daddy:

I really don't know what to say to you. I feel as if you've deserted me. Don't you know I need you? I know I still see you and you send me money for bikes and stuff, but it doesn't mean anything if you aren't here.

I seem to be always getting myself into these strange situations and don't know how to handle them. I don't want to burden Mommy with them 'cause she already has enough problems. The only two people I could ever talk to or get advice from have left me.

Female, 15

....

To Daddy:

I hope right now wherever you are that you're not in the best of health. You aren't shit, you never helped me out, you always tried to play like you were trying but you didn't give a f—k. All you cared about was selling your drugs and smoking it too. You are nothing but a big letdown on yourself, you should be ashamed of what you are. I almost fell for your little scheme pretending like you cared but you don't. You really hurt me a lot and I'll never forgive you for it. I bet right now you're living in your big condominium selling your dope and throwing your life away in Manhattan, sending us dirty money. Well, I don't want the shit, so keep your dirty ass money you bitch!!!

Your supposable daughter
Female, 16

....

Dear Pops:

I used to love you, but all those years with no man in the house, all those years with rats and roaches, ghetto life was not fun, and you were living high on the hog.

You not loving your children enough to pay child support and trying to be half-ass slick about not paying it too. Have you ever heard of a father changing his name in order to keep a little money from his kids and family? Furthermore, he just gives half of his money away to those

• A National Research Council report found that fully ¼ of all children between the ages of 10 and 17 (a total of at least 7 million nationwide) are growing up in circumstances that limit their development, compromise their health, impair their sense of self, and thereby restrict their futures.

ugly bitches and/or drinks and fucks it off. I think you're nothing more than a sucker.

Male, 16

....

Dear Dad,

I'm still not quite sure if you don't care or if you're just plain stupid. You cry to Mom that your relationship towards "the boys" isn't good, yet the only time I've seen you in the last ten years is when I call you. I used to call you faithfully every Sunday just to hear you say, "I'm busy." And you're so damn shallow that you only relate to me, my older brother, and the rest of the family as "financial dependents." Maybe someday you'll realize that you divorced Mom, not your kids.

Male, 16

....

Mom…

You're such a selfish bitch! I hate you! You make life miserable for everyone. You don't deserve to be a part of this family. All you ever care about is your little store/restaurant and money! You greedy pig! I'm sorry to disappoint you but money can't buy happiness….

I guess I'm glad that you're a workaholic. I don't have to stay home with you and your big mouth.

I don't even know why I'm bothering with this letter. You don't even know most of what I've written 'cause you don't understand it even though you've been in the U.S. for thirteen fucken years!!!

Your daughter—
P.S. Thanks for <u>NOTHING</u>!
Female, 15

Many teens talk about the frustration of dealing with parents who can't seem to get their lives together:

Dear Mom,

Why can't you face all the facts? You need to go on welfare and get food stamps. You need a job. You can't come by my house every day asking for food. You desperately need money and a place to live, so try and get a job. Don't count on others to help you all the time. People have other things to do! You are not my first priority. I have my own life. It's not that I don't love you, it's just that I have no idea how to handle you. I really wish you'd go away and give me a chance to do what I want to do for a change and not get mad when I can't see you when you want to see me. I have too much to do. I have my own life to handle and I can't handle yours along with mine. I'm not God. So give me a chance to do a good job on my life and once I get that straightened out, maybe I can help you.

Your son,
Male, 15

....

Dear Mom:

Writing this letter brings out a lot of hate, grief, disappointment, and love. It's easier for me to write you instead of telling you in person because I know you wouldn't take it into consideration. You know, Mom, it hurts not having you in my life like a real mother as you were many years ago and lately I've just come to terms with that. I feel like you don't exist. You seclude yourself in your room mostly all day doing cocaine, sometimes I get scared that you're gonna have a stroke or heart attack over something as deadly as cocaine. I can't help but hate you for not [taking] how I feel into consideration, you always make fun of your cocaine habit, you try and justify your reason for doing it and that's not fair to me or you.

I grieve over you as if you were being burned alive.... Drugs are controlling you. They've taken over the way you speak, your health, personality, etc.... I never believe anything you say and I don't trust you. This is hard for me to deal with because you're my mom. Why do you get paranoid and your eyes get so big as if you're a monster within yourself.

On the other hand I love you. You have given me so much love, care and happiness that no one else ever has, you've taught me all I need to know, to deal with practically any obstacle that may enter my life, you were my super mom, no one could come close to you,

and then, your love was true.... I just hope one day you'll be able
to overcome this drastic period in your life.

Love always,
Female, 18

....

Dear Mom,

That is what I call you though I often forget that that is what you are
to me. Sometimes we are more like sisters and oftentimes I play the role
of the adult while you drink through life. I don't remember a time in
my life when there was no alcohol. I think it probably all began when
Dad left. I remember you used to lock yourself in the kitchen every
night and I would sit outside of the door. I know that you cried while
you were on that side of the door but I cried on the other side, the side
you never cared about. Life goes on—forgive and forget. That's a great
view. You think you have control over my life and that what you say
has an impact on my ideas. I gave up thinking about pleasing you
awhile ago. You tell me that I don't understand your problems and that
I just haven't lived through enough to, but that is not an excuse for
you to ruin both of our lives.

Nancy said that in alcoholic families it is often the child putting the
alcoholic to bed, feeding, taking care of, watching out for. The reason I
get so upset when you tell me no, I can't do this, I just am not responsible enough, is because from my point of view I am the responsible
one. I am the one who watches you going up the stairs at night, I am
the one who puts you to bed when you can't do it, I am the one who
says you can't come to the phone when I know that you'd say something that you'd regret. I don't know why I do it, I just always have
and probably always will.

When you drink you say it doesn't affect me, that it is your life.
Why is it then that my grades go way down during your heavy drinking
times? That I cry constantly and refuse to eat with you? Why is it then
that I tell you suicide is okay? You never stop to think that taking care
of you is hard on a fifteen-year-old girl....

Despite everything you've done I still love you. I can no longer trust
you enough to be around you and get attached again, because I love
who you are when you are sober, and I can't stand to see that person
lost every night to alcohol....

Sometimes I like the freedom your alcoholism gives me. We have a sort of unspoken rule that I can say whatever I want to you when you are drunk and not have to face the consequences. I figure this is because you don't want to deal with me saying that you were drunk therefore you never mention it again. I do say horrible things, but I mean them and have never regretted saying them. You probably regret some of the things that you said, at least I hope you feel horrible for ever saying them. Like "I aborted the wrong child, I should have aborted you," and saying that your true feelings come out when you drink because you are just a screwed-up bitch when you drink.

I say I love you, and I do, because of the fact that I have lived with you for a lot of my life and my life would change if you died, but I can't deny that I have wanted you dead many a time. I am sure you feel similarly, but in the end we have to live with each other and I'm gone in three years forever so have a nice life if you live. And I'll see you around…maybe.

Love,
Female, 15

To My Father:

I wish I had gotten to know you better before you died. Why didn't you spend any time with me and my sister unless Mom nagged you to? You were my father and I loved you. There's not a whole lot to say. Didn't you love me? I'm sorry I'm not a boy, but it wasn't my fault. I feel like I missed out knowing you—being with you. It makes me angry when I think about how you didn't even eat dinner with us. Sure we were screaming, fighting little kids. But everyone needs to feel wanted. That was missing in our family. I don't understand why things were like that and I'll never know why—since I can't ask you now. I wanted to be with you, share things with you. I wish I had told you how much I loved you. When you died I was so angry. I didn't think of the fact that you died young and missed out on a lot of your life. You were only 37. I could only think of how you left me with my insane mother with her drugged-out boyfriends and my vicious sister. When you and mom got divorced I was so hurt. Didn't you care about the fact that I had to live with her crazy boyfriend? Didn't you care about me at all?! I never got to know you and be a part of your life. That's what hurts me most of all now.

Female, 15

After I had read a batch of horrendous letters one day, a male student came up to my desk and said, "My letter is going to seem so boring after the ones you read. My family is so normal." I said, "Great! I'll look forward to reading it." I also told him he was very lucky. Since then, I've taken care to read more positive sounding letters so everyone does not get totally depressed. I let my students know that what I am doing is reading them letters that reflect the reality of how parents are perceived. Unfortunately, many, many letters are extremely negative—especially to fathers. Fathers seem to receive the most vicious and angry attacks. It is extremely rare to hear about a father who is concerned, loving, and available. Sadly, an overwhelming number of fathers fall into one of the following categories: workaholic, alcoholic, absent with no connection to family, lives in another state, doesn't send child support or keep in touch, father unknown, or mother won't talk about him. The Brady-Bunch, Father-Knows-Best, Bill-Cosby kind of dad is pretty rare.

> *ONE NUCLEAR FAMILY CAN RUIN YOUR WHOLE LIFE*
> *(seen on a bumper sticker)*

One of my students wrote in his letter "Life is <u>not</u> 'The Cosby Show.'" The world would be a better place if everyone communicated with love and humor like the Huxtables—and all major problems were solved in thirty minutes. However, the families on the average TV show and my students' families are worlds apart.

I do hear about some of the happier families out there, families where there is a loving bond, mutual respect, and plenty of give and take. When the nine-week course falls at the end of the school year, I suggest that my students might like to give their letters to their parents as a Mother's Day or Father's Day gift. One of my students did this one year, and his mom was so pleased, she framed it and put it up in their home! This was his letter:

Dear Mama—

For Social Living we've been asked to write our parents a letter. Some will praise, others condemn their parents, most tell them things that they've never before told them. I, myself, would like to address the issue of the hiemerschmidt of the panzey times.

Ha-Ha, you say. But I think that below our joking around is a real lesson that you've taught me. You epitomize the ancient Taoist virtue of "being," Mama. You go through life with an air of contentedness and happiness, which radiates to those around you. Not to say that you haven't been heaped with bring-downers many times throughout your life. Somehow, however, you manage to keep this attitude of...I don't know, words don't really do it justice. It's deeper than optimism, beyond contentment, more than just an "attitude." Zen. Sometimes when you are doing the things that you do best: caring, laughing, listening and learning, explaining. I think to myself, I could learn more from this person than any book in the world.

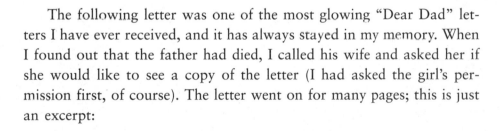

Sometimes I worry that I don't express this enough. If I don't then Mama, I'm telling you now—there's not a day goes by that I don't, at least twice, actually stop what I'm doing and go, "What an incredible Mama I have." Sounds great, eh? I love you at least twice a day! But I think you know what I mean.

Words just don't do it, I think....

I love you, Mama
Male, 15

The following letter was one of the most glowing "Dear Dad" letters I have ever received, and it has always stayed in my memory. When I found out that the father had died, I called his wife and asked her if she would like to see a copy of the letter (I had asked the girl's permission first, of course). The letter went on for many pages; this is just an excerpt:

Dear Dad:

I'm beginning to appreciate what a great person you are. For me, the things that stand out in you are integrity, dignity, outspokenness. You are not afraid to stand up for what you believe in and you do what you feel is right. I admire you for that. You have always shown me a lot of love and made a lot of sacrifices for me. You are really a neat person with a great many talents and abilities. I know you care and you've always treated me like a human being. You made me feel that you valued my ideas. Suddenly I see you not as my father, but as a person. You are a person whose friendship I would feel proud to have if you were not my father and I feel lucky to be your daughter. You don't always understand children and I think you relate better to adults—but that makes you talk to me as an equal.

Female, 15

....

Dear Mother:

This is your son writing you to let you know how I really feel. Sometimes I know it's hard for you to cope with being a mother and at the same time being a father too. I love you with all my heart, soul and mind. I know it's not easy for you to come home from a long hard day at work and the house being unclean, food not cooked. You work weekdays and weekends just to make ends meet. You are a hard-working, warm, loving person, and I would like to let you know that I understand and I love you for loving me all these and those years.

Male, 16

....

Dear Mom:

I love you! You are one of those rare mothers who are never afraid to show your feelings towards me or anyone else. You are open and curious but never nosy. I know at times I hurt you when I criticize your appearance or weight…but I don't mean it. It's just me and my insecurities which have nothing to do with you. I'm proud of you, no matter where we are you manage to turn heads and make people smile. You have a gift of happiness which always brings out the best in those around you. The encouragement you constantly give me, the rewarding praise, and the never-ending support all make me a better person. You make me feel special, and in your eyes I am. Although I rarely share my in-depth emotions with you, I know that you are and will always be there when I want to talk. Often I take my luck for granted, having a mother and sharing my life with a person as marvelous as you is far too wonderful to be taken casually. Our fights and my complaints are normal in families and are insignificant when compared to our love. I'll always love you.

Female, 15

Dear Mom,

For all the times you've held me up

And for all the times you've let me go

For the times we laughed so hard that tears came to our eyes

And for the times we cried and then realized how silly we looked sniffling and started to laugh

For the times you've hugged me and told me you loved me

And for the times you've told me that it looked like a tornado blew through my room

For taking my cracks about your clothes

And for letting me borrow your shirts

For showing me how to use the potty-seat

And for telling me not to flush mini-pads down the toilet

For being so determined and thinking you could hang-glide (and belly dance, and sail, and play jazz piano, and live in a camper for a year, and build a greenhouse)

And for being so supportive of my dreams

I'd like to tell you how much I love you and how special you are to me. I don't think I could ever want anything more in a mother than what I have every day with you.

Love,
Female, 15

....

Dear Papa,

Dear me, I could go on for pages about how wonderful you've been and always will be. I must say I've been extremely lucky in the parents area. Just lately your taking me in was a lifesaver, I don't know how long I could have lasted with B. and especially when your place is so tiny. But it's neat. I love being with you. I don't think I could live with anyone else and be with anyone else so much like this, except for you. I think we fit together. We're a good pair like Sherlock Holmes and Watson no not really we're both like Watson. Hee hee. But as I've said before you really aren't a father any more you've graduated to a

friend.... It's nice to have a parent you can talk to about anything....
I've really enjoyed all the hysterical laughs you've given me...we do
have fun together, don't we? It's really neat to have a dad that goes to
rock concerts with you. Can you imagine, how many fathers like rock
concerts? None that's how many. I also like picking out your clothes for
parties.... I greatly appreciate all the papers you have helped me on.
The things you typed at 12:00. Thanks. Oh you are such a good person
and father....

Bye, love
Female, 16

Dear Pop:

I just wrote Mom, so I'm out of all the compliments I can write about
you two as parents. As much as I love Mom, there is something you
and I have that is so deep and so special to me. I used to make myself
cry thinking about you dying when you'd be late from work. You are so
much of an inspiration to me.

My eighteenth birthday was so wonderful. The two memories I have
both are connected to you and you alone. When I woke up and saw
you I felt so good about myself. Your smile and hug (your shy, awkward hug) made me feel special. At dinner with my friends, when you
toasted me, rarely have I felt so much love in any situation. It wasn't
the toast, because the toast was awkward and embarrassed. But it
touched me very deep. I could feel that under your shy toast, that
couldn't be said in front of my friends, you saying "I love you." I wish
you could know that I got the message.

This letter can't do justice to how much I love you. I want to say I'll
make you proud, but I already know you are proud of me.

Thank you. I love you
Male, 18

In the typical scenario of family life after divorce, custody of the
children goes to the mother, and the relationship between the father
and his offspring tends to weaken. This is not always so, however, as
the following letters reveal:

Dad,

I love you, I love you, I love you a million times I love you. You are so
unusual in such a special way, a way that I don't think I can express in
words. I love being with you; your sense of humor, the things we
share—things I couldn't share with anyone else. Sailing, tennis, volley-
ball, books, people—just things in general. You're a beautiful human
being…. You're one of the very few men I've ever seen be able to cry
and I think that's beautiful to have that ability.

   Don't ever feel guilty about being divorced—don't ever feel it has
harmed me. I think divorcing was the best thing you and Mom could
have done. I feel very lucky that you and Mom are still such close
friends. Also I doubt we'd be as close as we are now because we can
have a separate relationship in a way that I think children whose parents are married miss out on…. You're so strong and sensitive at the
same time.

XXOXOXOOXX
Female, 16

....

Dear Daddy:

Most people change the way they feel about their parents after they
divorce and resent the one they don't live with bitterly. But even
though I don't see you very often, I've never resented you, and I've
always felt a closeness to you different from another person. I hope that
our wonderful relationship won't change.

Female, 15

....

Dear Dad;

Thanks for being the most chillin' force in my life. Whenever I'm ready
to crack under the pressure of whatever, it's your voice in my head
that's always bringing me back to sanity. Thanks for teaching me to
laugh at what's going on around me. Thanks for helping me to ignore
the bad parts and take pleasure in the spoils of life. It's a skill (or set of
skills) I'm far from mastering, but I think I'm on the right track.

Thanks for being one of the few people I know whose intelligence and mental health I can really admire, and for combining this with a love of humanity. My admiration of that love is often the only thing that counteracts my antisocial tendencies. Your intellect challenges and stimulates mine in the most delightful ways.

Thanks for providing me with some of the best times of my life. Thanks for really caring; for doing or saying things which may have seemed unpleasant and uncalled for to me at the time, but which have helped me in unexpected and later appreciated ways.

It's unfortunate that we haven't had a real father-son relationship, because 95 percent of the time we've been half a world away, but I know that you've been here with me, in person and in spirit, for the worst and the best times of my life.

You're one of a very few people who I really and deeply love. You mean a lot to me. Thanks, Dad, I'm truly indebted. I only wish I could somehow return the favor.

Love,
Male, 17

Adolescence is usually a period when the parent-child conflict over dependence vs. independence, restriction vs. freedom comes to a head. In some families, the issue becomes a battleground. In others, it is worked out with a little compromise. I like to read the following letters to my classes, hoping to give them some insight into this ongoing struggle:

Dear Mom,

Thanks, Mom, for everything. But, Mom, there is one thing I would like to say. I do feel that I have been through a lot. And I also feel that I'm very mature for my age. I can't understand why I can't be a little free. I am 16 years old and I know right from wrong. I have never tried to hide anything from you. I have always expressed my feelings to you. I don't know if you can't accept the fact that your little girl is growing up, but I feel that I need a little time to grow by myself and sometimes just to go out to see what things are really about. But, see, the way things are now, I can't go out places. I can't go over to my friends' houses. I can't have my friends over. In all these things I'm trying to understand why I cannot. Mom, times have changed, and I feel I am responsible and mature enough to know not to get into something that

I think I can't get out of. Mom, I feel I shouldn't have to go through this because you did. Well! Maybe it's for the best. But no matter what I don't understand, I will always still love you Mom, because you are my one and only.

Love always,
Your daughter
Female, 16

....

Dear Mom,

I love you. I feel very lucky to have such a wonderful person as a mother. You have done all the traditional mother jobs; taking care of me when I was sick, comforting me when I was upset, making sure I got to school when I was little, helping me deal with school, and you have done these so well. But you have been oh so much more to me; a loving companion, advisor. You have instilled in me morals and an ability to be an independent human being. Many people say that their mother is their best friend, but you are not my best friend. You see, there are some things that I do that I don't tell you and I feel that best friends usually confide completely in each other. I know that there are some things you don't tell me and this is OK because mothers and daughters aren't best friends. You have guided/helped me to become a complete independent human being and still allowed me to be dependent on you. Of course I have my complaints. My brother, for example, I think he probably got the benefit of being your second child because you figured out what you had done wrong in raising me. Sometimes you fly off the handle and yell at me because you're mad at him and this makes me so angry. I know our political views sometimes clash and I appreciate the fact that you have tried to be supportive of my actions. Sometimes you are too protective and old-fashioned, but that is part of being a mother. Anyway, we all have our faults and for fifteen years we have been living with each other's. Thank you for always being there (here) for me and for giving birth to me (which I understand wasn't exactly a party) and for raising me with as much love and understanding as humanly possible. You are the person I can hate, be angry with, curse, and turn to in the end. Someday I won't be a teenager anymore and hopefully it will get easier. Keep up the good work.

Love always,
Female, 15

Dear Dad:

I thank you so much for the freedom you give me. You don't have a special mold that I'm to fit into when I grow older. I don't have to conform to sex roles or teenage roles. I can be myself. I thank you for being so open with me, trusting me with things that are important to you, even asking my opinion. I thank you for listening and trying to understand and helping me with my problems when I bring them to you, but not before. Some things I can't tell you—trying to discover my identity and my feelings and how to handle them. But I guess those have to be discovered by myself. And I don't think I'd want you to read a lot of things written in my diary or my assorted collec-tion of essays. I don't know how you'd take knowing the intensity of my struggles and feelings. But I enjoy talking to you so much. Our family couldn't possibly exist as it is without you. You are its mainstay.

Some things I disagree on, especially on some aspects of raising us kids, but I guess I can raise my own kids the way I want to.

Your affectionate daughter
Female, 15

....

Dear Mom:

Above all, the most important thing that you do is that the whole family spends time together—on vacations, out of doors, on hikes, etc. Our togetherness is a big part of our lives and makes our relationship much stronger. All my friends are happy to have you around, <u>if you don't stay too long</u>—and you show your respect for them, and you learn from each other.

Of course, you make me mad a lot. But that is only because you're pointing out something to me that I don't want to have pointed out. Usually such a thing is for my safety, or because I was wrong, or you don't agree with me. And sometimes I know you get mad at me, but how can you not get mad at someone you love?

I guess what I conclude is that in our family the generation gap is small and quite bridgeable. My relationship with you and Daddy is so important to me and is different from so many others'. Most of it I can't explain, but I know that it is built on love and respect. I love you for sharing with me such a relationship and experience. I hope to be able to give someone else such a relationship too someday. Thank you.

Love,
Female, 15

The previous entry always reminds me of the time I was in junior high and my parents had picked me and a friend up from a co-ed ballroom dance class. My friend and I got into the backseat and my parents began an endless inquiry in to the events of the evening. I felt embarrassed that I was being asked all these questions until I got out of the car with my friend and she said, "You are so lucky that your parents care about you—my parents never ask me anything."

I tell my students that often it is difficult for parents to find the right balance between showing their concern and respecting your privacy, laying down rules and allowing freedom. Some students complain that their parents are too strict but most realize that this comes from caring and most appreciate it deep down. Many students want more guidelines and I hear more from them than I do from kids who feel that their parents are too strict. In the interest of being liberal and "with it," some parents have given their children too much freedom too early.

Dear Mom,

You're a flake. You're naive. You're stupid. You never do anything when I fuck up. I could kill the mayor, rape his wife, and rob a bank and you'd just sit there and call me a naughty boy. Damn! You are so fucking lucky that I don't take drugs, or cut school and stay out all night. I could and get away with it but I don't. Why not, I wouldn't get punished. I guess you guys are busy with my scrub sister but I still need some guidance. I do love you and I'm sure you love me, so show it, okay. Oh, hell. Never mind. Maybe it's too late.

Love,
Male, 15

....

Dear Mom;

Well, damn it! A mother and son aren't supposed to have a "relationship." A mother is supposed to be there to help her son through the moments of doubt and loneliness and despair and darkness. Oh yeah. You helped me when I was little and I still love you for that. But now that you're a high-paid lawyer, where are you? I realize you need personal growth too, but children aren't a part-time deal! Life is <u>not</u> "The Cosby Show." I need you. I need somebody. Dad can't be it. Besides every day I grow more horrified the more I realize how much we are alike.

Male, 15

To me, this last line speaks volumes, and after I read it, I ask the students if any of them have found themselves doing something that they despise in their parents. Many immediately raise their hands. I tell them it is very common for people to copy patterns of behavior that they have grown up with, even if the behavior was once repugnant to them. They end up doing things they once vowed they'd never do, like yelling at their children, refusing to listen, or saying "Because I said so." Most abusive parents, for instance, were abused themselves as children.

This is one reason I urge my students to keep their journals. Years from now, when they are raising their own children, they can reread the letters they just wrote for this assignment. Reflecting back on their own problems as adolescents may help to make them more understanding as parents and keep them from repeating the mistakes their parents made with them.

I always take time out to play "parent license," a game I made up to get my students thinking about what it takes to be a good parent. In this fantasy game, I make myself the absolute ruler of California, and I have placed something in the drinking water that makes it impossible for women to get pregnant without a pill to counteract the sterility. I have done this to cut back on teen pregnancy, parents who are unfit to raise a child, and unwanted children (I heard on NPR that 22,000 babies were abandoned in U.S. hospitals in 1992). I make my students the legislators, and it is their difficult task to devise a set of standards that one must pass in order to obtain the antisterility pill. After all, we have minimum requirements to drive a car, get a loan, or become a cosmetologist, but to do the most important job in the world we do not have to pass any test!!! I ask them to break up into small groups and come up with a set of standards, and I put some ideas on the board for them to consider:

MINIMUM OR MAXIMUM AGE TO BEGIN FAMILY?

SINGLE PARENT OKAY?
(ARTIFICIAL INSEMINATION? ADOPTION?)

INTERRACIAL OR MIXED FAITH OKAY?

DISABLED OKAY? (TOTALLY BLIND? WHEELCHAIR-BOUND?
MENTALLY RETARDED?)

HOMOSEXUAL OKAY?

IS IT OKAY IF THE COUPLE USES DRUGS? ALCOHOL?
SMOKES?—HOW MUCH?

SHOULD AT LEAST ONE OF THE PARTNERS HAVE
A HIGH SCHOOL DIPLOMA? A COLLEGE DEGREE?

SHOULD THEY HAVE HEALTH INSURANCE?

IS IT OKAY IF THEY ARE HOMELESS?

SHOULD THEY BE REQUIRED TO TAKE AN HIV TEST?

DO THEY NEED TO HAVE MONEY IN THE BANK?
IF SO, HOW MUCH?

SHOULD THEY BE REQUIRED TO TAKE A COURSE
ON CHILD DEVELOPMENT?

The small group discussions get very heated as each question is addressed. They usually decide that eighteen is the minimum age—which I think is far too young—and they usually say absolutely no drugs—no alcohol, smoking, or "harder" drugs. There is always someone who says this scheme will not work—there will be a black market for the antisterility drug! I ask them to just PRETEND that this is a possibility and go along with the activity!

The point of the "parent license" exercise is to make them aware of some of the difficulties in parenting that they might not have thought of and to get them to consider the enormous responsibility that comes with raising a child.

Young women who find out they are pregnant often seem very casual about it. "Oops, I'm pregnant and I'm against abortion and I could never give up my baby." Teens often visualize an adorable infant without thinking through what it will be like to have a toddler—or a teen!—of their own. Having a child means a minimum commitment of eighteen years, I tell them, and there are no guarantees. For instance, students frequently say they want to have a child so there will be someone to take care of them in their old age—but it's possible they might outlive the child, or the child might move far away, or might not want to have anything to do with them. Would they be willing to raise a child with a disability, birth defect, or disease? What if they have twins? I want them to think through the what-ifs ahead of time.

The reason why I chose to speak to Ms. Rubin's class about my teen pregnancy was to let teenagers know that being pregnant, having a baby, is not cute or easy. I think a lot of people get too hung up on what someone else is doing so they follow that trend, but having a child that you have to take care for X amount of years is no trend or fad. IT'S REALITY.

Lethea Hale, 17
Mother of Charnaye Lenice McCowan, 16 months

Considering how fragmented family life has become, it surprises me that nine out of ten of my students say they want to have children. Each one of them is physically capable of becoming a parent right now—all it takes is a penis inserted into a vagina. But I want them to *choose* to have a child when they are emotionally and financially ready—after they have really thought through the impact this will have on their lives and understand the responsibilities that go along with producing and raising a child.

Our future depends on the parenting skills of this generation. I try to be optimistic, but being realistic, it is not a pretty picture. Our young people have few good role models, few resources for learning how to be good parents. I can only point out the pitfalls that they may encounter.

I like to close the discussion on a positive note by reading the following letter. After reading it, I usually comment that it makes a good argument for postponing having children:

Dear Mommy:

I feel special about our relationship because our relationship is much different from most kids my age. Both you and Daddy are so much different from the parents of my friends. You trust me so much more, accept the behavior of all my different friends, and you do so many things with me.

I guess it's because it is the second marriage for both of you, and that you are both older than most parents, that you can treat me like an individual and let me be who I want to be. You trust me to do things I want to do, and by advising me on values—but not forcing them on me, my morals turn out to be much like yours. You trust me to stay home on long weekends by myself when you go on a trip. You trust me to keep myself healthy and in good company—and not to screw up my life. And because I never go against your teachings too much, you'll trust me forever.

Female, 15

- A majority of teens have parents who are 35 to 49 years old. However, more than 25% of teens in families headed by mothers live with a parent younger than 35. Many of these young parents were themselves teens when they became parents.

- When Ann Landers asked her readers if they would have children again, knowing what they know now, 70% of those who responded said No!

8 | Sexual Abuse

WHEN WE ARE ON THE SUBJECT of human sexuality and relationships, there is always so much playfulness and student input about personal experiences that it is difficult to close down discussions and move on. On the topic of sexual abuse, though, the whole tone changes. Students generally have little to say about it, except to ask, "How can anyone do that to another person?" Only a couple of times have students shared their experiences in class, although some girls have reported that their mothers, sisters, or friends have been sexually assaulted. However, I have received so many anonymous letters and notes from students who have been molested that I know it happens all too frequently, and this is why I cover the topic in my course.

All abuse is painful and remains a part of a person's personality—whether they are conscious of it or not. It is important for individuals who have been abused to work through the pain and damage and begin to heal, and to break the cycle of abuse which is so often passed on from generation to generation. For some, confronting the abuser is part of the healing process, but this is not always possible. Many of my students have used their journals as a stand-in, and I think this has been helpful for them.

There is no journal assignment that specifically asks the students to write about sexual abuse, but I do take time to talk about it in class so that they will be aware of the problem and learn how they might avoid it, how to support others who have suffered from abuse, and, for those who have survived, where to go for help. I show videos on sexual abuse and domestic violence, and as always, I read from student writings to help make certain points (plenty of journal entries on sexual abuse have come out of other assignments).

In delving into this subject, I know that I may open up many wounds and unearth secrets that have been long buried. I can only hope that people will find comfort in knowing that they are not alone and that there is help for them at school and in the community. I tell my students that they can find a support group for almost everything: "If you are a vegetarian, bisexual person of color who is allergic to cats, there is probably a group for you!" "Really?" shouts a boy in the back. No, I'm exaggerating, but there is a group equipped to deal with almost any special situation or problem.

One of the agencies I always talk about is Bay Area Women Against Rape (BAWAR), an excellent crisis service that was started because of an incident that took place at BHS in 1971. One of our students was raped in a stairwell on campus, and she was treated so poorly by the police and hospital personnel that her foster mother organized the group. One of the initial goals was to educate police and emergency room workers to be sensitive to the issue of rape and abuse. In addition to this, BAWAR now provides counseling and advocacy for survivors of sexual abuse. The sensitivity training has been beneficial, as many of my students have subsequently told me that the Berkeley police have been very understanding and supportive.

When I tell this story, someone speaks up: A girl was raped *on campus?* Yes, I say, I know of several cases, and I am sure that more have taken place that I haven't heard about or that have gone unreported. Then I tell them about one of my male students who left BHS with a friend right after school. He was just a half block from campus when a man asked him to help lift something heavy from a van. The student told his friend he'd meet him at the bus stop and went to give the man a hand. When he got into the van, the man closed the door and attempted to assault him. Luckily this student didn't panic. Not only was he able to talk the man out of it, but he remembered enough details to give the police an excellent description and the man was later apprehended! I don't want my students to feel paranoid, but there is always the potential for danger. I think it is smart to carry yourself in a manner that shows you're alert and aware of your surroundings.

Who Are the Victims?

- Approximately 20% of children are sexually abused before they reach adulthood.

- 29% of rape victims were under 11 years old.

- 32% of rape victims were between the ages of 11 and 17.

- 1 out of 8 adult women has been the victim of forcible rape.

- Teenage girls are the most likely victims of sexual abuse.

I ask what a person should do if he or she has been sexually assaulted. A boy shouts out, "Report it." A girl counteracts by saying she might not want to report it, and that the last thing she'd feel like doing would be to talk to the police. Finally someone says that the person should go to the hospital to be checked for bruises and injuries and to be tested for STDs. I say yes, getting medical attention comes first. It is important not only for the medical attention, but to gather any evidence in case you wish to report the crime. Too often a person will want to shower and wash away any reminders of the awful incident, but this may also eliminate any evidence.

I tell my class that I would always encourage a person to report the incident, but that it is a very personal choice. I once did volunteer work at a local hospital emergency room. I would sit with the survivors of sex crimes while they awaited treatment, so I understand how difficult the situation can be. Besides coping with the physical shock of the assault, most victims suffer from deep emotional stress. They may have guilt feelings, as if they were somehow responsible for the attack, or fears of reprisal if they do file a report. If family and friends are not supportive, the reluctance to report will be even greater.

I try to impress upon my students that most acts of sexual assault are committed by people we know and trust. We usually connect sexual assault with a newspaper article about some woman who was walking alone in a deserted area or forced into a car and then brutally raped at gunpoint. This happens, but not nearly to the extent that acquaintance rape occurs. Of all of the many journal entries or anonymous surveys where abuse is mentioned, I can only recall a few incidents that involved a stranger—the rest were about a friend or relative, or a friend of a friend or relative.

The two letters that follow were written by the same student. They illustrate how disorienting the experience can be and how important it is to seek counseling:

> Well, this is going to be very difficult for me to discuss, but I'll do the best I can. Last month I had a terrifying experience. I was raped by an old friend. We were friends for four years but he seemed to think that he deserved something in return. I said "NO" several times but he forced himself upon myself. It was horrible for me. It took me five days to report

- 84% of rapes go unreported. The reasons most often given by victims is the desire for privacy and the fear of stigmatization.

- Fear of having their name made public is second to the fear of contracting HIV/AIDS.

Who Are the Rapists?

- 39% are acquaintances.

- 36% are relatives (husband or ex-husband, father, stepfather, brother, cousin, uncle).

- 22% are strangers.

- 3% victims declined to answer.

this experience to the police, because I spent three of those five days over at my boyfriend's house. He was very supportive towards me.

Now, I'm getting ready to go to counseling for this because it scares me from time to time.

Five days later, she dropped by my classroom and handed me this note:

Nancy—

Right now there isn't a change in my situation. It seems that since this horrible incident occurred I've just been going extremely wild for the last two weeks. I've been drinking heavily and smoking weed. I'm very scared of what's happening to me. I've gotten to the point of sleeping with my ex-boyfriend's friend. Nancy this is getting the best of me. I don't know what I'm going to do. Me and my present boyfriend are having problems, my mother is very disappointed in me too.

I'll write soon.
Female, 17

This girl was obviously very frightened and confused. I ask the class what additional feelings she might have been experiencing. We talk about betrayal and how difficult it is to trust again. I tell the class that I never heard from her again, but I suspect that without counseling and without the support of her boyfriend and mother she would have a difficult time recovering.

The next letters show how deep and long lasting the psychological damage can be, and how difficult the healing process is, even with the help of counseling:

I was molested when I was four by my baby-sitter's husband. I told my baby-sitter (not snitching) and she hit me and told me I shouldn't say things like that. It happened over and over it seemed like fifty times. Then other people started doing it to me. My uncles (three of them to be exact), my best friend's father and two other guys. From age four to fifteen I never told. Now I have admitted it and I don't feel guilty. I am seeing a psychiatrist. My mother is supportive. So what is my problem? I can't have normal sex with men. I fear some, I hate some. Sex to me is meaningless. I could make it with anybody and the next day hate him. I have dreams about girls, I think having sex with one would be great and maybe even fulfilling for me but I still like men. I used to be a prostitute, not off of the street but $200–$500 tricks.

Female, 16

....

Dear _____

God only knows what your name is. You. The man who raped me. Well, I've given you a lot of thought since you raped me, at four. I've examined and tried to analyze my feelings towards you, many a time. I think I know, to a certain degree how I feel.

Of course you've caused me an incredible amount of pain. More than I'd think anything that took fifteen minutes could cause. You've screwed my feelings up about many things. Love, sex, myself, men, relationships, are probably the main ones. No matter how much therapy I go through it will never rid me of the problems you've given me.

However, I understand you, and the act, as much as I know how. I know someone who has raped once, and have learned from his first-hand experience exactly how he felt. I've read many books written by rapists, watched many shows and live discussions where rapists have talked. I don't blame you, I blame society and whatever or whoever in your background caused you to rape. I'm not angry at you, I don't even know you, I'm angry at your actions. And yet, I still don't know if I can forgive you.

Female, 15

I feel that this last young woman was quite unusual in that she sought to understand the reasons that men rape. She saw that it was his problem not hers. She didn't blame herself nor did she blame him—she understands that it is far more complicated than that.

The event that had the greatest impact on my life was when I was sexually assaulted. It happened when I was fourteen. A stranger came up to me while I was walking dogs through a park. He began talking to me and he made me feel uncomfortable, he was standing too close. When I tried to leave he grabbed me, spun me around and fell on top of me. He put his hand down my underwear and began groping. At first I froze but then I could remember my mum's voice "scream and kick him in the nuts." I began to scream. This freaked him out. He tried to put his hand over my mouth but I kept moving my head so I could scream more. Then I tried kicking him in the nuts but my leg was pinned down. The thing that got me out of that situation was the fact that I got angry. I lost my temper. I went psycho. I was determined to get him off me. I pulled my arm out from under me, determined to keep hitting him until he got off. The dog chains were still in my hand and I kept whipping him across the face until he got off me. I was so fired up. I stood up and screamed after him "You bastard, don't you ever do that to anyone again." I wanted to run after him and kill him, I was so mad.

He turned himself in about a month later. He got four months. It took me a year to get over it, another year to be back to myself. For five months afterwards I tried to carry on as if nothing happened. I felt that if I let it get me down I would be letting him get to me. On my fifteenth birthday I went to the doctor with some mysterious illness. I ended up crying in his office. I cut school after my appointment and drank a bottle of brandy. I was lucky that my doctor organized counseling for me. It was the best thing that could've happened. Trying to forget it ever happened just made it worse. It wasn't until I got counseling that I dealt with my feelings on the attack and finally got over it.

I've forgiven him. I've let it go. It doesn't hurt me anymore but I'll never forget. It has been the most powerful influence in my life ever.

Female, 18

We talk a little about how to defend oneself. I can remember one speaker on rape prevention saying that if we knew how to prevent rape, we would put it on every billboard available. People of all ages have tried different methods with varying success. For this young woman, fighting and screaming prevented further assault. Others have used whistles, said they had herpes, HIV, or were pregnant. I have known women who have thrown up, pretended to faint, or acted severly retarded and were able to get out of a threatening situation. But none of these defenses is guaranteed to work. Within the first few seconds, one must try to determine what strategy might prevent harm—but not everyone can think so quickly when taken by surprise. Our school offers classes where students can learn basic techniques of self-defense, as does the local Y.

Then the discussion shifts to providing support for a friend or relative who has been sexually abused. I direct what I have to say particularly to the males in my class, telling them that it is likely they will someday form a relationship with a female who will at some point confide in them that they had been molested or raped. Women will often keep the secret to themselves for years and some trusted male will be the first person to hear of it. "How will you respond?" I ask. "Let her know you believe her and it wasn't her fault," offers one guy. "Never push her into sex because she may need to really trust you and it may remind her of what happened to her." I tell them they need to be very understanding; they may not even have to say anything—just be there to hug her and listen.

I read some advice from some former students. I point out to the girls that the situation may be reversed since males are also victimized:

> I have never personally been molested. I went out with a girl who had been molested and told me about it. This has caused me to almost never be sexually aggressive. I wait until I am absolutely certain, meaning she has to tell me, that she is interested.
>
> Male, 17

When I look up from reading I can tell that other male students agree with the last writer. They would never force themselves on a female. I go on to the next letter, from a student who used to play football at BHS then went on to the University of California at Davis:

> Dear Nancy:
>
> I'm sorry to say this, but the reason I'm writing you at this instant is because I can relate to something you always used to say to me. I've thought about you a great deal since school started, but do you remember when you used to get bogged down by all the problems people would come to you with?
>
> Well...how did you ever deal with it? I have a friend—are you sitting down?—who was raped this summer! I only found out about it two weeks ago and it has hit pretty hard. When it happened she had two

very close friends to turn to, but after several months they can only carry so much. Now she has turned to me (and me to her) and it is a heavy responsibility. I'm so very glad that I can help.

Two weeks ago I didn't know that I knew anyone who had been raped. Now I know three! I wonder how many other people I know but am clueless about? Rape, now, seems like such a reality! It never did before. Life is so scary! I just got back from a workshop for the friends of victims, and from what I can tell, she is in the "Outward Adjustment" stage of "recovery." I'm not sure if you are familiar with these stages, but that means the incident is in the center of her conscious and her life basically revolves around it. I'm sorry to lay all this on you, but I had to get it out. I'm dealing with it pretty well.

Male, 18

I feel that these young women were very lucky to have such a supportive friend. I am sure that his willingness to attend the workshop and be there for these women meant a great deal to them.

How should you comfort someone upon learning that they have been abused? Not everyone will want the same treatment, but I feel that this next young woman gives some very good advice—based on her own painful experience:

When I was about eight and a half, my stepfather started having me give him massages. At first it was a normal shoulder massage, but one day my mom was gone and he made me jack him off. Then he took off my clothes and he tried to fuck me, but it hurt, so I started crying so he stopped. Then a couple days later I told my mom, only about the massage, and she got real mad and said she was gonna leave him, but he talked her out of it. Then sometimes he would like to look at me nude and stuff—and he'd walked around nude, too, but I hated it. He always made me touch him—and he said if I told anyone he would do "something bad" and he said <u>nobody would ever believe me if I told them</u> what he did. So, I never said anything for three years, until I told my friend after my mom finally left him. My friend started crying along with me and said her landlord used to fuck her, but she thought she was the only one it ever happened to. Now I feel sick whenever I think about him. I wish my mom hated him. She doesn't though—she acts like it's really not a big deal, because she thinks it only happened once.

He still calls us, and my mom makes me be polite to him and it makes me want to scream. I hate him and I wish he would go away or die or something. I never want to see him again, but I know I will, and every time I do I want to kick him in his pants.... Girls—if this happened to you be careful about who you go out with, because I finally realized I was going out with guys who were just using me for sex, because I thought all guys were like that. Or at least I didn't want to believe there were guys that aren't like that because that would mean my step-daddy was a freak and I didn't want to believe that then, because I loved him. Also—guys—if a girl tells you she doesn't want to have sex that might be why, so don't <u>push her</u> or she might <u>never</u> feel comfortable enough with you to have a good time. Also, if a girl tells you she was abused I think the best thing to do is hug her—<u>nothing more</u>—and <u>show her that all guys aren't like her daddy</u> (or whoever). After a while she will probably trust you more and more. Last word to the girls (and any guys who have been abused also) if you are being abused or have been abused—<u>tell someone you can trust</u>—believe me—you will feel <u>so much better</u>—and do whatever you can to get out of that situation (if it's still going on) because the longer it happens <u>the worse it gets</u>.

Female, 16

There is an awkward silence as I finish this last letter. I know it has made an impact on the class even though I read it quickly and without much emotion. I have been accused before of reading these letters as if I didn't care; but the truth is that if I remember the person who wrote it, dwell on the pain they were communicating, and try to imagine the impact it has had on their lives, I would be too choked up to continue. So I tell the class this and ask them to understand that this is my way of coping with all this misery. I would be a total basket case if I read these letters with all the emotion they deserve.

Many students have described situations in which they told their mother that the father, stepfather, or mother's boyfriend has molested them, and the mother either did not believe it could have happened or was unable to face the truth. It is hard to imagine the pain of confiding in someone you trust only to be rejected in this manner. Not only is it a blow to one's self-esteem, but in effect it cuts you off from the help you need. After all, if your own mother, father, or best friend doesn't believe you, who will?

> I was sexually molested. I was in the fourth grade and the molester was my mother's boyfriend. I told my mother. She paid little or no attention to me. She broke my heart when she acted as if she didn't believe me. He is still around and still tries, and it still tears me apart.
>
> Female, 16

....

> When I was 13, I was molested by my mother's husband. At the time he was my mother's live-in fiancé! I guess that just shows you how much my mom was affected by this incident. You're probably thinking, "Well maybe she just didn't tell her mom and that's why they got married!" But I told my mom EVERYTHING no more than one hour later! I was "fondled" by my mother's fiancé in my bathroom while I was curling my hair.... No one took me seriously!! I still remember how scared I was—how sick he was! I can still see the way he looked at me—I can practically feel the way he touched me! I remember every last word he said to me before and after the incident!!
>
> The real SHOCKER was when he SWORE to my mother that he didn't mean it the way I took it—that he was just trying to show me he cared for me in a fatherly way!! FATHERLY WAY?? BULLSHIT! You don't feel on and around a girl's breasts and waist while breathing heavily and erotically and call it a fatherly gesture!
>
> I guess if he had raped me (sexually) he would have told her he was just trying to show me he loved me!
>
> PLEASE! GIVE ME A BREAK!
>
> Female, 15

The following letter is from a young man whose mother handled things quite differently. Instead of putting him down, she accepted his account and took action. How different an experience to be believed by a parent than to suffer not only from the abuse, but from the lack of parental support and involvement:

> When I was in the fourth grade, me and some of my friends were in the environmental park at the back of Washington School. A man was

sitting there. We were running around and he told us to come over to him. He pulled out his penis and began to fondle it. He asked us if we wanted to. Some of my friends played with it and so did I. After they left I stayed, being a naturally curious person and played with it some more. He put it back and said he was going to go get some of his many girlfriends. He left and I told my friends and we all thought "Oh boy, we're going to get laid." He never came back. When I got home, I told my mother. She got a little hysterical and called all of the parents of my friends and the police.

After all of that was over, I realized that what had happened was a bad thing and that I should never let it happen to me again. Later that evening, my mother told me of an experience she had with a man in a car playing with himself.

Male, 15

In the next entries the girls do their best to be assertive and to recognize an abusive situation, but they are overpowered by men who are physically stronger and able to play with the girls' feelings:

I was molested about three weeks ago. By a man I knew—I baby-sat his son. Before I started baby-sitting for him he was always making passes at me so I told him to stop it. I was not interested in him or any man. He stopped and we were still friends. One night I went over to his house to sit for his kid. His wife was somewhere—not at home. He took off my clothes, not violently, but forcefully, and started massaging me, except I don't really recognize it as a massage. He kept sticking his fingers in my vagina, asking me if it felt good. I kept saying, "No, it doesn't, why are you doing this? Please stop!" And he answered my question. He said that he was a friend of mine and friends are supposed to make other friends feel good. I said it didn't feel good, would he stop. He didn't. The whole time he was doing stuff to me he was doing it in such a friendly, nonchalant way, it scared me. I felt immobilized. He didn't penetrate me. It didn't get quite that far. I finally broke down and started crying. It stopped there. He left. I felt horrible. I wasn't going to tell anyone. Fortunately I'm a pretty strong person and I thought about it and decided that it just isn't fair for one person to force themselves on another person in a violent manner or just "fucking with the mind" manner, so I told my parents. When I say "fucking with the mind" I mean to say that when I was with that guy he was working on my mind trying to get me to believe that what was happening was all right for various reasons. Let me tell you something (especially those of you who are thinking why didn't I run from the guy or get a butcher knife and cut him into little pieces), when you've got a 35-year-old man talking to a 15-year-old girl the way he was talking to me, it's easy for that guy to play head games with the girl. I'm 15. I've been aware of men's attractions to me or any other girl for, at the very most, two years. How can anyone have the guts to ask me, "Why didn't you do this or why didn't you do that?" Two years can't give a girl lifetime experience on how to handle rape situations, or if not rape, simple come-ons from men. I think this is a side of rape that most of you haven't heard. I've gotten through this situation pretty well. Well enough to press charges against this guy....

Female, 15

....

I looked up to him because he was older, someone who seemed to care, and always seemed to bring out my smile and make me laugh in my time of need. We were pretty close to the point where he was calling me his niece. I was also in fact, fourteen and still a virgin at the time and still very innocent and he was nineteen with a lot of experience.

It happened so fast we were no sooner talking and then...I didn't know what had happen. Like I said I was very innocent I didn't know what exactly to expect but that sex really scared me and that bad girls did and good girls didn't. I asked was I still a virgin and he said no. I started to get hysterical and crying shouting, "Why?" and "You spoiled me now!"

I nearly died. I never felt so cheap, so dirty, so horrible in all my...life. I was so scared and worried that my family would find out I wasn't a virgin by my physical appearance.

I was heartbroken badly. I attempted suicide. I felt I was no good. Then I started turning to alcohol and drugs (this is what started my drug abuse and alcohol abuse) to take away that pain, something to fuck me up so bad I'd forget! Then I started to feel "Well since it's gone I might as well go all the way and go to bed with anyone else." By this time he started to brag to a lot more people saying how he had me and how I wanted it.

It hurt so bad to hear those lies...I wanted to wait until it was right, when I got married that's how I was brought up, that's how I wanted it to be.

How can you want something when you're fighting to get away from it? And why is it everyone (majority) blames the women more than the male, knowing that we are powerless when it comes to physical strength and especially when she's saying "NO" and he's saying "YES!" Most importantly why is it other females will tend to side with the male and say it was her fault, especially teenage girls and that she's making it up because she's jealous, etc., etc. Instead of supporting our sex and sticking together despite no matter how it may seem and to take into consideration that the girl may be right and the only jealousy that is there is within themselves!?

My embarrassment and disgrace kept me silent for a year and a half and letting him get away with it. And later on him trying to tell me he always loved me and that I'm special—God, he's UGLY, I HATE HIM, I HATE EVERYTHING ABOUT HIM!!!!!!!!!!!!!!!!!!! I still see him; he is always trying to say hi. It's over and done with I know but I have a lot of regrets...pain and disappointment inside.

Female, 16

Some experts feel that males are victims almost as often as females but are less likely to report it. In addition to all of the negative consequences that sexual abuse has on females, there are two additional issues that males must confront. First, if the perpetrator was a male (and the majority are), the young boy or adolescent typically wonders if the incident means that he is now homosexual. Secondly, the young male can feel overwhelming shame if he was unable to fight off the attack. In our society, where males are supposed to be strong and inviolable, being a victim amounts to feelings of loss of power and control. I talk about this a little and also point out that it is just as true for males as it is for females: the perpetrator is usually an older acquaintance.

Dear T:

You really must be a fucked-up man. You sure did fuck me and my family up. I really thought you cared, but how could you prey on little boys, that are only looking for that father or friend to look up to. I trusted you, you were my idol, and then you molested me. I was only eleven, I didn't ask for that. I put you in jail, and I hope you die there, because that's what you deserve. You deserve to die in jail, where you can never touch anyone again.

I didn't believe that that could ever happen to me and I didn't believe that it was happening, but you made it all come true, and it will be with me for the rest of my life.

Thank you. I hate you.
Male, 17

....

I was a victim who got molested. It was a long time ago but anyway it happened one day when my stepsister's father molested me. I remember when he used to get me out of my bunk bed and take me into the bathroom and would tell me to suck his dick. I was really mixed up and he would tell me if I didn't something bad would happen so I didn't know what to do. He told me never to tell. So after that night he came and he would take me out of my bunk bed and take me to the bathroom and pull down my pants and take his dick out and rub it up on top of me or something cuz I didn't feel it on me. After that it happened a few more times so one day me and my cousin went...told...what happened.

Male, 18

I warn the class that this next entry has some very graphic descriptions but to listen carefully and see if they can determine what is behind this incredibly forceful language:

This is an act that really disgusts the hell out of me and I would love it to stop completely. I wish I could become a masked avenger and go out and kill all of these sons-of-bitches that do these terrible things. I want to grab them by the throat and throw them around the room a couple of times. Then beat and POUND the living SHIT OUT OF THEM. Depending on if they were male or female. For males I would grab their scrotum, penis, and up that fucker off. For women, I'd take a drill and just drill, drill, drill, drill. I was molested as a child but I don't have time to tell. But I just want to say that I caught myself almost molesting my little cousin and I hate myself. I didn't do anything but put her on my lap and was reaching around to her front. I stopped, put her down, and almost jumped off a balcony. I hate myself for this and I'm not ever ever going to do this to anyone ever. And if I do, then let my soul burn in hell for all eternity.

Male, 17

I point out the statement "I was molested as a child but I don't have time to tell," and that most likely the anger he is expressing is tied up with his own sexual abuse. I ask the class what they would say to him. A student suggests that he must get some help to deal with his own victimization or he is likely to repeat the cycle. She notes that he "almost" did something to his cousin but stopped but maybe next time he would not be able to stop himself.

This boy certainly needs to learn to control his feelings. I have spent much time on the phone trying to find groups for teenage boys to learn how to control their anger. They are extremely rare.

Over the years I have received a number of letters dealing with incest:

Dear Cousin,

I'm not going to ask you how you are doing because I don't care, I don't care if you didn't want to know how I was doing.

What on earth possessed you to do something so stupid and sickening to me. You must have been sick in the head or something when you molested me. Everyone acts like nothing ever happened, they just go on with their lives and forget about my feelings.

I will never forget what you did to me for three of the most worst fucking years of my life. I have tried to forgive you for our families' religious belief, but it is very hard, you have changed my life completely.

Female, 15

....

Nobody knows this but I was molested when I was about five by my uncle. I hate him. Someday I'll face him with it and he will be fucking sorry he ever did it to me. I'd kill him I swear I would. I hate him more than anything. My parents know I hate him—they don't know why. How can someone do that to a little five-year-old girl?? Someday I'll ask him—he'll be sorry he did it.

Female, 15

The next two letters are from the same girl. The first is a letter to her brother and is followed by her response to some questions I had written in her journal:

Dear Brother,

So are you happy? I hope not! You deserve everything that is happening to you. I hope you get beat everyday. I hope you get butt-fucked by every nasty creepy, vulgar guy in this world. You deserve it you son of a bitch. Well get used to it, I put you away for years, years! That's what you get. I told you, you wouldn't get away with it and you were so sure Mom and Dad would just hush the incident. Well wrong! They didn't! How does it feel to be locked up? They don't let you have any freedom—huh—. Well you took my freedom away. When other guys beat you up, and mess with your mind, do you remember beating me up and messing with my mind? When other guys who are stronger than you rape you, do you remember the anguish you put me through when you raped me. You bastard! I hope you rot in hell! You're never gonna get out! NEVER! This is what you deserve, I don't care what kind of prestigious life you could have lived, but what about the life I have to live knowing how dirty I feel inside, thanks to you. By telling on you, I can make you see what terror you put me through. Think about it every time I go out on dates I wonder would this guy be dating me if he knew my dark secret. I wonder if he will be evil like you and take advantage of me. See what you've done to me, I'm paranoid of anything like it happening again. I HATE YOU!!!! You've ruined my life. So I hope you're getting some of the same tragedies.

....

Ms. Rubin,

My brother B. beat me and my family mentally and physically. He made most of us feel like shit. He took a tiny barely grown child and transformed it into someone who was horrified to be at home. This definitely was not a good growing up experience. Today B. is in a jail where hopefully he will stay for awhile. He is 18 and possibly will be eligible for parole. I had to see many psychologists to finally realize that he did the wrong and I was just another unfortunate victim of incest.

Female, 15

Sometimes I have my classes fill out an anonymous survey (the only identification they give is their age, gender, and class period). I use it to keep me in touch with my students' needs and to give them a chance to ask questions they might not want to bring up in person. There are only three parts to the survey:

1. **Describe a situation, problem, experience, or feeling;**

2. **Questions for me or the class;**

3. **Current feelings about the class.**

On the bottom of the sheet they can indicate whether or not it is all right for me to use their material. It is through this activity that many of the incidents of rape, incest, and other sexual abuse have been shared. The following story was from an anonymous survey:

Last year my Dad got laid off his job. After that he started drinking heavily. When he comes home he beats up my Mother then he comes into my room and forces me to have sex with him. The first time I told him to get the hell out of here then he threw me against the wall and gave me two black eyes. Now I am carrying his baby and am thinking about killing myself. Help.

Female, 15

After reading this to the class, I ask them what they would tell this young lady. "Call Children's Protective Services," "See a counselor," "Tell Nancy," "Move out of the house—get out of the situation" are some of the many suggestions. I never found out who wrote the letter. I would look around the room at each of the young women and wonder if they were the one harboring this terrible secret, but I think the person who wrote it never came to class again. The distinctive script never appeared in any of the journals. I hope she got the help she so desperately needed.

When I was 12 years old I had a sexual relationship with my father. At the time I felt there was nothing wrong with it. But as I've gotten older I've come to resent him. I felt he knew what he was doing and since I trusted him I let him. But now when I see him I can never really talk to him. I feel very uncomfortable with him. I hope this doesn't affect my relationships with other guys in the future.

Female, 16

I tell the class that it is not unusual that some girls have thought that "doing things with daddy" was normal—that all little girls did them with their fathers. Many times they do not find out until they are

teenagers that what was done to them was wrong. They may have felt sexual pleasure, and then, when they find out that they were tricked, manipulated, and used, they may experience tremendous shame, guilt, and distrust. Other emotions that a survivor may experience are depression, shock, numbness, disbelief, and feelings of powerlessness, fear, and anger.

I ask the class what they think about her statement "I hope this doesn't affect my relationships with other guys in the future." One girl says, "Of course it will—she must get some counseling." I agree and again remind them that we have free counseling at school, and the community has many places that are also free. Again, I repeat, something a speaker quoted, "Do not keep your feelings buried deep inside of you. Remember, you're only as sick as your secrets."

The following letter illustrates once again the conflicting emotions in a case of incest. What is rare about this example is that the girl has come to an understanding and *forgiven* her father:

Dad,

This is such a hard letter to write because my feelings are mixed. You did a great job of bringing me up to be a smart, intelligent, well-groomed (etc.!) young girl. I thank you for that. I also thank you for giving me all the wonderful material possessions that I have. But frankly dad, YOU FUCKED IT UP! You molested me! How could you do that?! You must have some serious problems. In fact, I now realize that the reason why you never allowed me to do anything was because you thought I'd go out, meet a guy and have sex. You were paranoid I'd be like my mom and meet someone like you and get pregnant. And you were also jealous! The things you've deprived me of, and the sexual, physical, and emotional damage you have caused me are inexcusable. But I have forgiven you. Yes, I have. You have a problem and you need help. But I still love you, dad.

Always yours,
Female, 16

The next letter was written by another girl whose father had an incestuous relationship with her and got her pregnant. Her letter illustrates so clearly the mixed emotions that many survivors feel—the love and hate towards the perpetrator. All I know is that this man was convicted and sent to jail; and the girl gave the baby up for adoption.

Dear Daddy,

I really don't know what to say to you. I put so much trust in you and you betrayed me. All those times you told me you would stop and you never did. I never understood how you could do that to me. I thought you loved me. All those times you said that you loved me and I was your baby girl. We did so much together. You always took me to the movies. You took me to the hottest concerts. I could talk to you. I could tell you when I thought you were wrong and when you were right. I loved you and you betrayed my trust. How could you hurt me? You were my daddy. You raised me from the time I was two or three years old. You were the only daddy I ever knew, and now my father and I have a child. Because of you I had a baby of my own only to have to give her away. I feel guilty at times but then I think about the times you hurt me so bad. I cried all night. The most terrible secret I ever had. You never loved my mother and you never loved me. But that doesn't change the fact that I still love you and I don't know why. We had fun together and now it's gone and I have no more Daddy to love. Maybe one day you will think about how terrible this experience was for me. You are such a sick man. That's real funny because I remember when you used to say "Yeah, I know I'm sick," but you thought it was funny. It's not, it's crazy. You ruined it for me, and you ruined it for yourself also. You were a wonderful Daddy, but you were a terrible man. I'm not sure how I feel about you anymore. It's really hard to hate someone you once loved so much.

Female, 15

Most often I do not know the rest of a story. What is special about the next letter is that Mercedes, the woman who wrote it, sent me another letter many years later to let me know how things were going with her. The second letter was addressed to my students—she wanted to reach out to any of them who might be in similar situations—and is rather long. The first time I read it to a class, I asked the students what I should cut out of it, and the overwhelming response was "nothing." So I left it as it was.

Dear Dad:

I hated our "exercises," as you called it. Once I told you, straight out I didn't like the "exercises." Again it was "too bad, you have no choice." You would tell me that there were people out there who would hurt me if I wasn't stretched out, etc. Every chance you got, you'd tell me it was time for our "exercises." I'd go upstairs, get undressed and wait then you'd come up and sometimes you'd ask what I wanted to do first. I'd usually say our "breathing exercises" (your name for a blow job). I thought that was the most disgusting, but it hurt the least. I used to dread when Mom would have to go on a business trip. I'd wake up and find myself in your bed! I started a fake cry so that you put me back in my bed. In the mornings, I had four hours between the time Mom went to work and I went to school. I used to want to set the clock ahead so I could leave. Once, I even asked to be changed from a ten o'clocker to a nine o'clocker, but the teacher wouldn't let me because I had to be in a certain reading group; I wished I had been dumber.

I'm not sure exactly how you said it but you told me not to tell anyone. It was "our secret." I'm not sure why I never told—maybe I was embarrassed or afraid. I don't know. I do know that it wasn't like in "Something About Amelia" [a TV movie about incest] where they said she was afraid "Daddy wouldn't love her anymore." I hated you. I was so glad when you moved out. I had to deal with your "desires" from five and a half years old to eleven years old. I never told anyone 'til [I was] 15½ years old. After you and Mom broke up.

Female, 15

....

To Nancy Rubin's Class,

About seven years ago, when I was in Nancy's class, I wrote a letter to my ex-stepfather. It was a letter I never sent to him but one that Nancy reads to her class each semester. It was about incest.

My mother and stepfather broke up when I was in fifth grade. He was out of my life, and I was safe. I didn't have to think about him anymore. I never forgot what he did to me but I tried never to think about it, and gradually the memories faded.

It had never occurred to me that what happened to me happened to other kids. "It" had no name to me. It was just part of growing up. An unpleasant part, yes, but I didn't know any different. It wasn't until I was in Nancy's class that I learned that what happened to me was common enough to have a name—incest. That was the year I finally told someone. I told my best friend and she said that she had kind of thought so. I couldn't believe it! I thought I'd done such a good job keeping it a secret. I had in a way been very proud of keeping it a secret. Also proud of being tough, strong. My brother and sister had both been to see counselors, but I hadn't. I thought that I didn't need to, that I was strong enough to pull everything together all by myself.

When I was a senior in high school, I told my mom about what had happened. She was so upset. I felt horrible. For two years after, I felt that if there was one thing in my life I could take back it would be telling my mom. After all, what happened was part of the past, there was nothing she could do about it, so why tell her and make her feel bad? I know now that it was a good thing for me to tell her even though it was so painful. For two reasons. One, it would be hard to have any sort of close relationship with her if there was such a big secret I was hiding. Two, there was something she could do about it. My mom was the one along with my best friend who persuaded me to see a counselor. I finally did when I was 20 (2½ years ago).

It was a scary thing to see the counselor. I mean, I had told people before that this stuff had happened, but I had never <u>really</u> talked about it. It was hard to talk about this stuff that I'd pushed way back in my head for ten years. I knew that if I talked about this stuff it would hurt. So it was really hard to make myself think about it. I mean I wouldn't hit my hand with a hammer cause it would hurt, so why should I think about this stuff from my past when it's gonna hurt? Right?

But after I'd gone to see the counselor once, I couldn't stop going. It was like I wanted to just get it all out. Even if it hurt a lot at least I'd let it out and then it would be over and I'd be relieved. I knew that I wanted to take care of this stuff while I was young. Try and get it out of my system rather than just keep it inside all my life. Because if it's inside, it's there and it's gonna mess with your life. Even if you don't really think about it, it's still there. I wanted to get it out before I became like other women I knew who were alcoholics or who couldn't deal with their feelings and be close with people. I didn't want to be like that, so I kept going. And it did hurt, it hurt a lot.

I got really depressed and angry, and I stayed that way for a few months. I couldn't concentrate. I didn't feel like hanging out with my friends. I was barely able to finish that semester of college, and I decided to take the next semester off. I didn't want to go anywhere. I couldn't eat much. I felt pretty shitty. There were times when I was so angry I wanted to throw things, break things, hit things. I was so pissed that this man had fucked with my life and ten years later, even though he was gone, he was still fucking with it. I hated him.

I used to be afraid of him, but I'm not anymore. I used to see him sometimes walking down the street in Berkeley and I'd be really scared and feel sick. I'd turn away so he wouldn't recognize me. I was afraid that if he saw me, he'd get all angry again and come back and hurt my family, hurt my mom. When I saw him up on Telegraph one day after I'd been seeing the counselor, I still felt scared but for some reason I followed him. At one point, I walked ahead of him and waited at the next corner. When he got to where I was, he said "Hi," like I was a stranger. I realized he didn't even know who I was! As he walked past me I yelled out his name and walked right up to him. (It's weird because he seemed smaller than I remembered him.) I looked him right in the face and said, "I hate you. I hate you for what you did to me."

He looked at me like I was crazy and said, "I didn't do nothin' to you!" I said, "You don't know who I am?" I told him my name. I wasn't afraid. I'm not sure if he figured it out right then, but he looked disturbed. Then I said, "I may not be able to do anything, but you're evil and it will get back at you." He still said, "Nah, I didn't do nothin' to you!" real defensive like. I just said, "Whatever," and walked away.

Even though I was a little scared at the time and it was real weird to talk to him, it made me feel good that I had confronted him and made him feel intimidated. And, I realized that he's sick and he's mean, but he's just a bully who picks on people weaker than him. Once someone stands up to him, he leaves them alone. When my mom had stood up to him and told him to get out of her house, he hit her and threatened to kill her, but she didn't back down, and he left. Now that I've said something to him, I don't feel scared inside anymore.

I'm almost 23 now. I moved to San Francisco. I like where I live. I have a job that's okay. I haven't finished college yet, but I will someday. I'm doing things that make me feel good like trying to help people, or protesting things in our society that seemed fucked up, or just doing things that are fun for me. I'm in a relationship now that makes me feel pretty good. Better than I used to. I still see a counselor sometimes cause I don't have all my shit together. But hey, I'm working on it.

Take care. —The Ten O'Clocker

Note: When I first went to a counselor, I went to Bay Area Women Against Rape. They offer free confidential counseling sessions with someone who specializes in sexual abuse counseling. I found it very helpful.

Mercedes called me recently and said that she was thinking about coming to school and speaking to my classes about what had happened to her. I could tell that she was hesitant to speak publicly about such a personal issue. I told her that I would love to have her come and felt the students would be very respectful and would greatly benefit—but I wanted her to come only when she felt it would be the right time. A few days later, she called to say that she wanted to do it, and we set it up for Friday morning. Like most of my speakers, she had to take time off from work and she appeared for free.

Friday morning arrives and I walk into my classroom which is used by another teacher first period. Her students are exiting as I attempt to slip into the room to set it up for my classes. She is erasing the board as I begin to put the chairs in order. I find it very frustrating not to have any time to prepare my room in advance as I would like to so that I can have as much time with my students as the five-minute break between classes allows! Before I can get everything organized, students start wandering in and begin to ask questions—"Are we having a speaker today?" "Do we need our journals?" "When is Chuck the Diaphragm Man coming to speak?" "Is there a new journal question?"

In my first class, the Daily Bulletin is read. This is the main means of communication within the school. Everything from tickets to the girls' basketball play-off games to visiting college recruiters, bake sales, and meetings of clubs as diverse as La Raza, Scuba Diving, Gay and Lesbian Support Group, and Poetry Magazine are announced. Amy reads the bulletin while I take roll and students wander in late. I tell the class that Mercedes will be speaking today and read them her two letters. Mercedes arrives just as I finish. I welcome her and give her a hug. I can feel everyone looking at her: they have just heard two powerful, disturbing letters on incest and here is the woman who wrote them. I ask Mercedes how she is feeling and she shows me her hands and says, "I'm shaking." I ask her if she wants to relax for a few minutes before she speaks, but she says she's ready.

She relates her story, much of which was in her letters. You can tell that the memories are still painful, but she seems poised and confident and answers questions openly and honestly when she is done.

Male 1: Did you use drugs to escape?

Mercedes: No, I was too scared of getting addicted. I know that drugs enhance one's mood so I would only want to use a drug when I was happy. However I know many women who turned to alcohol and drugs because they were sexually abused.

Male 2: What kind of relationship did your mom and your stepdad have?

Mercedes: Abusive. Like, at dinner, if we made too much noise or held our fork the wrong way he would yell at all of us. He threatened to kill my mom—after my mom broke up with him, he came back to our house one night. They were arguing in the kitchen, I went in to see if things were allright, and he had a knife at her throat. He had a horrible temper. In separate incidents he hit me with a belt, choked me, and hit me in the face.

Female 1: Weren't you really angry?

Mercedes: At the time I didn't feel anything—I just shut down. I had fantasies of doing all sorts of things to him—even killing him.

Male 3: You could arrange to have an accident happen to him.

Mercedes: No, I don't want this man to be the focus of my life and I wouldn't want that on my conscience.

Female 2: Did you tell your mother?

Mercedes: Yes, and she believed me—she was upset. She made a sound that is impossible to describe. It wasn't a scream or cry, it was this wrenching and agonizing sound. At the time I wished I had not told her. You don't want to have people hurt for you because you don't want to feel more hurt.

Female 3: Did it affect school?

Mercedes: It happened regularly—I don't think I thought about it in class. Because I didn't allow myself to think about it—it came out through my body—I had migraines and weird rashes.

(I nudge the girl sitting next to me as I know that she has migraines and was sexually abused by her stepfather.)

Nancy: What advice would you give to anyone in here who might have experienced sexual abuse?

Mercedes: That's hard to answer. I was ashamed. I was just glad it was over. If you don't deal with it, it is something that will be festering inside of you—it won't go away. Don't try to just ignore it.

There are only a few minutes of the period left and I ask Mercedes how she feels about having spoken here this morning. She says, "I felt that I couldn't do any more on an individual basis and that maybe by speaking I could help more people. I'm glad that I came." The bell rings and all of the students applaud. I feel so proud of Mercedes—I know this was not easy for her to do—and feel sure she has indeed done what she set out to do.

In the past two years I have had three former students volunteer to share their stories of incest with my classes. Besides Mercedes, I had a male who was molested by his father and his Boy Scout leader, and a professional athlete who was molested by her cousins and her father's business partners. I have been deeply moved by their struggle to heal and their willingness to reveal their past to 175 strangers.

I think they prove that, as terrible as the experiences of rape and sexual molestation are, there is hope. Although it is not the only answer, therapy can help tremendously with feelings of shame, anger, guilt, self-blame, and depression that these experiences bring. Though it can be difficult, it is so important to reach out, find help, and use it. One must learn how to get past the physical and psychological victimization—and begin to feel good about oneself again.

The evening after Mercedes spoke, I got a phone call from the girl I had nudged when Mercedes mentioned migraines. We talked about other things for awhile and then she asked, "Why did you touch me when Mercedes was talking about migraines?" I said, "It's unusual for young people to have migraines and since both of you had been molested I thought maybe there was a connection. Do you remember when you started to get migraines?" She said they began when she was kicked out of her house. "So then the headaches are due to stress?" "No, I think it is what you said," she replied, and then she asked for a referral to our Health Center.

I feel that Mercedes was the main inspiration for getting this young woman into counseling. I had been trying for many months, but not until she heard Mercedes speak that morning was she ready to go for help.

I guess there are two reasons I spoke and will continue to speak in Nancy's class about the sexual abuse that I experienced as a child: to help others and to help myself.

On a personal level, speaking to the class was a big step for me. It was something I hadn't thought I'd be able to do. Even though I felt it was very important, I thought it would be too hard, too painful. But

I finally felt strong enough to do it. I find that as I deal with things and talk about it more, it becomes less painful for me....

There may be a student in the class who is currently experiencing abuse and needs to hear someone else talk about it to know that there are people who can help stop the abuse. There will probably be a few students who have experienced sexual abuse in the past and are now trying to forget about it and ignore it as I had done in high school. But I think it is important to not forget, to deal with what happened. It is something that will be with you the rest of your life, but you do have some control over the way it affects you. And for those students who have not experienced any abuse, they may have a friend one day who needs help dealing with past abuse. Also, in general, I think that as people become more aware of sexual abuse it will be harder for abusers to get away with it.

Mercedes

9 | Alcohol, Tobacco, and Drugs

MY STUDENTS ARE sometimes surprised that I share something in common with a more famous Nancy regarding drugs. Nancy Reagan and I both believe in the catchy phrase she made so popular, except that I choose to spell it and interpret it differently. Instead of *Just Say No,* I tell them, my motto is *Just Say Know.* Obviously, by saying no to drugs one can avoid many problems, but the fact is that most high school students will experiment with drugs. Those who avoid them during their high school years often find themselves facing new pressures and endless opportunities to party when they leave home for college or to go off on their own. I want my students to be armed with the information they need in order to make intelligent choices based on facts, now and in the future. They need to know the physical and emotional risks involved with drug experimentation and to understand the consequences of the choices they make.

Many teens have told me that, because they have been told Just Say No too many times, such remarks just make them want to do the opposite. Therefore, I have chosen not to take the authoritarian approach or the stance of a preacher. But before I can teach about drugs effectively, I know I must earn my students' trust. I have to demonstrate to them that I will be open and honest, and that I will base what I say on reliable, up-to-date information. Otherwise, most of what I say will fall on deaf ears. I try to establish this trust by handling the topic of sex candidly on the very first day of class and maintaining this level of honesty from that day on.

Even when I have established this rapport, I find that teaching about substance abuse can be very tricky because the topic is a highly complex one. For one thing, a bewildering number of substances come under the heading of drugs: marijuana, cocaine/crack, heroin, PCP (angel dust), MDMA (rave, ecstasy, XTC), LSD (acid), amphetamines (speed, meth, crank), steroids (rhoids), prescribed medicines, etc., etc.

ALCOHOL, TOBACCO, AND DRUG USE IN PRECEDING 30 DAYS

As part of their annual study of drug use among American young people, University of Michigan researchers surveyed in 1993 17,000 high school seniors in 139 public and private high schools nationwide, 15,500 10th-graders in 128 schools, and 18,800 8th-graders in 159 schools. The numbers in this table represent the percentage of students reporting alcohol, tobacco, and drug usage in the 30 days preceding the survey. Most percentages reveal a slight increase from 1992 levels.

	8th Gr.	10th Gr.	12th Gr.
Alcohol	26.2	41.5	51.0
Been Drunk	7.8	19.8	28.9
Cigarettes	16.7	24.7	29.9
SmokelessTobacco	6.6	10.4	10.7
Marijuana	5.1	10.9	15.5
Stimulants	3.6	4.3	3.7
Inhalants	5.4	3.3	2.5
Tranquilizers	0.9	1.1	1.2
Cocaine	0.7	0.9	1.3
Heroin	0.4	0.3	0.2

Then there are all the alcohol and nicotine products: beer, wine, malt liquor, coolers, hard liquor, cigarettes and cigars, chewing and pipe tobacco, and snuff. I need to have a huge store of information at my fingertips in order to answer all the questions that come up. Is marijuana addictive? Which is worse for you—marijuana or cigarettes? How can you cure a hangover? A student says she heard that XTC causes the fluid in the spinal cord to be damaged—she wants to know if this is true.

It is even more difficult to explain the mixed messages our society sends out about drug use. Why is marijuana illegal, but not alcohol and nicotine? If cigarettes are hazardous to your health, why are they allowed to be sold? These are complex questions to answer when you consider that well over 500,000 deaths are directly attributed each year to alcohol and tobacco, which are both legal drugs. By comparison, an estimated 5,000 to 6,000 deaths each year are due to cocaine (including crack) and heroin use.

All eighth-grade students in the Berkeley school system are required to take a semester-long Social Living course in which they spend approximately five weeks studying substance use and substance abuse. What I present in my course is an extension of that program. Because I can only spend a week to ten days on this topic, I try to focus on three main issues: the facts and myths about the different drugs—especially alcohol, marijuana, and tobacco; the consequences of occasional or even one-time use; and the problems that attend growing up in a family where someone is a drug abuser.

Rather than begin with the journal assignment itself, I use a special worksheet to get us started. The worksheet contains questions such as these:

What kills more people in the United States than alcohol, illegal drugs, homicide, suicide, car accidents, fires, and AIDS combined? (Answer: Nicotine)

50% of all Asians do not produce the liver enzyme that metabolizes alcohol and therefore they become seriously ill if they drink. True or False? (Answer: True)

Which of the following can help you sober up? a. drinking strong coffee; b. taking a cold shower; c. walking in the fresh air; d. sweating it

**out in a sauna/hot tub; e. letting time pass; f. all of the above;
g. none of the above. (Answer: e. letting time pass)**

**Ms. Rubin says that one of the most dangerous combinations involves
drug/alcohol use and _____ ! (Students often say automobiles, which is
a good answer, but the answer I am looking for is hormones.)**

As I expected, the questionnaire triggers a lively classroom discussion. Someone has a story to tell about blacking out, and we talk about the difference between passing out and blacking out. I say that, to an observer, a person who has passed out will look as if they are asleep—whereas a person who is blacked out will remain conscious and may drive, talk, dance, etc., but will not remember anything upon coming out of it. I emphasize that blackouts are your body's way of telling you that it cannot handle alcohol—something like an early warning system.

This leads us into a discussion on alcohol poisoning and alcoholism, and I find myself fielding tough questions already. Someone wants to know if her parents are alcoholics if they have a few cocktails every night. I tell her that studies have shown that if *adults* elect to drink, it is okay for men to have two alcoholic beverages a day, and women should limit their drinking to one alcoholic drink. Within these guidelines, there are additional warnings, such as one should not mix drinking with driving or operating machinery, and pregnant women should not drink at all. In other words, there are so many variables that I can't give her a definitive answer. We talk a little about the difference between moderate and heavy drinking, and about how people absorb alcohol differently (depending on weight, gender, what they've eaten, type of alcohol, etc.), and then I read them one current definition for alcoholism:

> Alcoholism is a primary, chronic disease with genetic, psychosocial, and environmental factors influencing its development and manifestations. The disease is often progressive and fatal. It is characterized by continuous or periodic impaired control over drinking, preoccupation with the drug alcohol, use of alcohol despite adverse consequences, and distortions in thinking, most notably denial.

In general, teens who drink are not drinking for the wonderful bouquet and flavor of the wine but to get drunk. Many are binging: according to the University of Michigan study cited earlier, 27.5 percent of the seniors had ingested five or more drinks in a row at least once in the preceding two weeks.

Alcohol can be used moderately and responsibly by many people, but it can become dangerous, even lethal, when used in large quantities or in combination with other drugs or activities (driving, swimming, etc.). It does not take a lifetime of abuse to have deadly consequences. A few beers and an automobile can be a very unfortunate match. A few drinks and raging hormones can lower inhibitions and good judgment—often resulting in unsafe sex or remorseful feelings the morning after. As one sixteen-year-old girl succinctly put it, "Alcohol took away all of my boundaries and morals."

I want all my students to know the physical and emotional risks involved with alcohol abuse, but I also want them to get home safely if they do decide to drink. As one of their journal assignments, I require that all of my students sign the Contract for Life put out by Students Against Drunk Driving and have a parent or guardian sign it too. By signing it, the teenager agrees to call the parent or guardian for transportation if they have had too much to drink or if their driver has had too much drink. The parent or guardian agrees to come and get the teen at any hour, any place, with no questions asked. The parent or guardian also promises not to drive under the influence, or to accept a ride from a driver who is drunk.

If students are unhappy with the wording of the contract, they can change it. They can also make a contract with themselves, but they must write out the terms of this agreement. Some of my students tell me that in their circle of friends they always have a designated driver. One student wrote:

> I totally agree with this contract. But the only difference in my case is that my friends and I work it out that someone's the designated driver. That's one of the first things we clear up before going to a party or whatever. I remember one time, my friend and I were at a party and I drove there. As I started to get into it, I decided to have a few beers. The point I'm getting at is that my friend came up to me and said let me have the keys so I can drive home. Who knows, maybe he had a few drinks also, but I trust him that he didn't or else [we] would have both been walking home.

Male, 17

- Researchers estimate that alcohol use is implicated in 1/3 to 2/3 of sexual assault and "date" rape cases among teens and college students.

- In one survey of high school students, 18% of females and 39% of males said it is acceptable for a male to force sex if the female is stoned or drunk.

A few students are concerned that if they show this contract to their parents, the parents will assume they are using alcohol and/or other drugs. Additionally, a couple of students insist that they never drink or use other drugs due to religious or moral reasons and therefore they don't need to sign it. I tell them that it is great that they feel it is unnecessary, but I point out that, since we are surrounded by drugs, some day they may find themselves in a position where their driver is under the influence. (At least half of every class always admit they have been a passenger in a car when the driver was drunk or high.) I make up a scenario that puts them at a family wedding, and their favorite cousin or uncle is to give them a ride home—but he's had a few glasses of champagne in a short period of time. How will they handle this situation? Hopefully, they will remember that they have signed the Contract for Life and will abide by its terms instead of putting themselves at risk.

One student asks, "But what if I live with my mom and she's an alcoholic? What do I do when *she's* my ride home?" She described how, as a child, she would duck down in the backseat of the car and try to sleep because she was so frightened—thinking that they would crash. She asks what can she do in a situation like this? Someone suggests that she could take a taxi or take the keys away, but she replies that this could have very serious consequences—like a severe beating. All I can do is suggest that she try to avoid these situations and talk to her mother about it when her mom is sober. For her there will be no easy solutions.

When Parents Are Substance Abusers

Whenever I'm asked what the major drug problem is at our school, I always reply that, without a doubt, it's alcoholic and drug-addicted parents. Many of my students have written about the disruption it has caused in their lives, both in letters to their mothers or fathers or in response to the journal question on drugs:

> **How do you feel about drug use/abuse? What experiences have you had or been around? Do peers influence your behavior? Is there a history of drug use in your family?**

Dad:

I should look up to you, and I guess I do, but you have a bad drinking problem. So how can I? I know all you have is me and then the fateful liquor store. You know I care for you very much, but it's really hard to love you when you are drunk all the time. You always have beer in the 'frig. Your friend is drinking all the time too, except she doesn't drink until she's drunk and she doesn't drive when she has been drinking.

I know I'm hardly ever there, but when I'm there you're drunk, or you're not at home. I can't really get to know you if that's the case. I care for you very much, but I don't think of you as my father. Hope you stop drinking.

Female, 16

....

I hate alcohol, alcoholics, people who don't understand alcoholism. I guess that's a lot of hate, but that is what alcohol does. My father's an alcoholic, so is my grandfather and stepfather. Some families have traditions—we have alcohol, alcoholism, and alcoholics.... My sister is really nice to him. She thinks that if she's nice, then he won't get drunk. I worry about her because she is with a group of friends who drink. I told my neighbor that I was never going to drink and she said that that was a little extreme because drinking is fun. Well living with an alcoholic is not fun. It's the furthest thing from fun and fun is not a good enough reason for what I've been through.

Female, 15

Some would describe her sister's behavior as being codependent; and the neighbor apparently needs to be educated about alcoholism. The writer is wise to realize that she is at risk, and for her, choosing not to drink is a smart decision.

I hate drugs more than I have hated anything else in my life. They're killers and all they do is ruin lives. My mother and stepfather are very heavily into drugs and they are really messed up. Me and my sister have been living with our grandparents for the past four years because my mom was using all the rent money for dope and we got kicked out. They still haven't found a place, maybe they're not even looking anymore. They move around all the time, staying with their "friends" and caring about nothing. They have taken my grandparents for every cent that they have and many relationships have been hurt, and the thing that pisses me off is that they don't even care! My grandma has had to go back to work to pay back all of their debts and my mom still takes her money. I think my grandma knows what she's doing with it but she just can't admit it to herself.... Everyone hates each other and nobody trusts. I used to have to sleep on my money in order to prevent it from being stolen. They used all my money out of my bank account, now I have nothing to go to college with.

Female, 15

The following student called his mother by her first name when he wrote this letter. He was an extremely bright young man:

Dear M:

I'm not quite sure what to say to you. I don't hate you; I don't care enough about you to hate you. I should thank you for the mother you've been to me: a pathetic whining alcoholic with a martyr complex. You're too ludicrous to take seriously. One of the most completely irrational people I've ever met.

I'm sorry I can't love you like the son's love you want, but you never taught me to love or feel, just to mix drinks. Perhaps this I should thank you for. If I felt anything at all I wouldn't have been able to survive through the things that have happened to me in this life, but then again, you've never known anything about your son's life. Probably would have horrified you if you had.

One last thing, mother. Take care of my little sister. Learn how for her sake, because someday I'm coming back for her to take her away from all the damage you've done. And if you hurt her, I'll kill you.

Your son,
Male, 18

I ask the class what he means about not being taught to love or feel. A girl says that since he was never shown love he doesn't know how to love. Another student says, "He is numb because he must bury his pain from having lived with this kind of a mother."

What I remember of my parents' divorce is a blur of screaming and broken dishes. Both of my parents are alcoholics—well, were at that point in time. F. [her mother] was a binging alcoholic and may still be. The most recent memory is as follows: her being drunk for weeks on end, functioning somewhat at first then lying in bed drinking or unconscious, occasionally getting up to wander around the house, babbling incoherently, wearing a filthy, malodorous, blue bathrobe that hadn't left her body in way too long. Finally spending a couple days drinking, retching, and crying—in bed—then at long last sleeping for a couple days. This particular recollection was two years ago. I was living with her and J. (her husband, who happened to be at least five years younger than some of the guys I've dated) at the time. I do have some less tame and equally disgusting memories of her on a binge. However, I do not resent her for exposing me to this at such impressionable ages. I love my mother with all her past and present defects, and now more than ever I understand why she chose to deal with her problems & depression in that manner.

Female, 15

I ask the class if they think this young woman may be at risk to use alcohol or other drugs. Several students are aware that alcoholism can run in families; I offer some facts and figures to underscore their comments:

If one parent is alcoholic, the child is 34% more likely to be an alcoholic than children of nonalcoholics. If both parents are alcoholic, the child is 400% more likely to be alcoholic. If the child is a male with both parents and a grandfather being alcoholic, that child is 900% more likely to develop alcoholism. About 28 million Americans have at least one alcoholic parent.

As a matter of fact, the above young woman ended up using many drugs—including crack and heroin. I urged her to attend a drug rehab program for adolescents that had just started in Berkeley. The last time I saw her she was no longer using heroin or crack, but she said that when she saw heroin being used in a movie, it took every ounce of her strength—and her boyfriend's support—to resist going out and using again.

The next writer expressed happier memories, but is still aware that she has inherited alcoholic tendencies:

Dear Dad,

You are the most wonderful father in the world, did you know that? You must know, for I have told you several times. You're lovable, caring, helpful, and support my interests and future plans—and I respect that so much! You and mom have brought me up to be a pretty neat gal. Boy did you spoil me! I remember how you'd take me out to 31 Flavors at least two times a week and you would buy me the best toys in the world! But not only did you give me things, you gave me a lot of love and brought me (and still do) a lot of joy.

I am so proud to be your daughter and I'm not at all ashamed of your alcoholism now. I used to hate you when you drank, that's for sure. You did cause me and Mom some pain, emotional and a little physical, too. But I still love you. I know you cared and you hated yourself then. I could tell, because <u>after</u> you were drunk—you would always break down in tears in front of us—and tell us you would never touch liquor again. But you couldn't help it if you <u>did</u> drink. It wasn't <u>your</u> fault—it was an uncontrollable force taking you over and <u>making</u> you drink.

Daddy, I think I've inherited a little of your alcoholism—but I'm going to do something about it before it gets serious. Don't feel guilty please! You are so wonderful. I could never stop loving you even though you drank! Actually I think your alcoholism brought us closer together. We understand each other better. And every time we argue, no matter what it's about, it <u>always</u> brings us closer together. Anyway, you mean the world to me—I'm extremely lucky to have you as a dad. Thanks, Pop.

Love forever,
Female, 17

She came to talk to me one day about an older guy she was dating. In our conversation, she talked about seeing him over the weekend and also said she had been drinking. I told her that this really concerned me since there was such a history of abuse in her family. I asked her when she planned to quit and she said something like, "I know I will but it's not really a problem right now." Her brother had spoken in my classes as a recovered alcoholic, and of course she was well aware of her father's problem, but at the time her attitude seemed to be "it will never happen to me." Happily, time and distance have given her a different perspective. This is what she wrote years later:

> It's hard to believe that the person who wrote that was me, seven years ago. I recently saw Nancy Rubin during a vacation back to California, and she read this entry to me. I was surprised by its forgiving tone, and found it interesting that I feared alcoholic addiction. Firstly my addictions toward money and relationships is where I would probably feel most concerned. Secondly I feel that my forgiving attitude toward my father was only a way of denying my pain and excusing him from his addiction. I know now that regardless of his helplessness over alcohol it was not okay that he hurt me and others while intoxicated, and nothing will erase the memories of such dreadful and regular occasions. I also know that I have no control over the addiction of others. At the time, I felt I had so much control, that forgiving him (he was constantly apologizing after drinking) would make him never drink again. (Live and learn!)
>
> My father (and entire family), has been in recovery for two years now, and miraculously after a multitude of hardships which preceded this letter we've all gone on to live very healthy, happy, and successful lives. I now look back on my memories and attitudes of such a time as difficult learning experiences, without which my life would not be as rich and colorful as it is today.
>
> Female, 23

I ask if anyone is familiar with Alateen. A few students raise their hands and one of them says it's a group for teens who care about someone who uses—a family member or boyfriend or girlfriend. I add that the name may sound as if the teens who attend have a problem with alcohol, but the purpose of the group is to provide support to those who are living with or dealing with someone else's use. Many of my students have greatly benefited from attending these meetings. Alateen teaches that you can't change the alcoholic's behavior but you can learn how to react to their behavior; you can't stop them from drinking but you can learn to stop being codependent.

One of the common characteristics of growing up in an alcoholic family is that of role reversal, where the child becomes the protector and parent. I recall one Alateen speaker describing how fearful she used to be that her mother would set her hair on fire when she lit her cigarettes over a burner on a gas stove. Instead of the parent teaching the young child, now the child must keep the parent out of danger. A lot of anger and resentment can build up from having to be a caretaker at an early age and those who have been forced into that role often feel as if they've been deprived of their childhood.

Dear Mom,

I love you a lot, but there are other feelings that I have for you. Well here goes.

You have totally ruined my life, and I don't think that I will ever recover totally. You kept me up 'til all hours of the night with all your crying and screaming. I had to take care of you because no one else would. My brothers were much older than me so they would stay out until they decided to come home. Dad was always at meetings, but could I do school work? No. I had to tend to you when you should have been tending to me. Shit Mom I was only five! Then as I got older all you did was yell at me because I got bad grades! What do you expect? I had to stay up at night with you so you wouldn't hurt yourself. Then I had to rush home every day after school! Your drinking was absurd! You drink too much over nothing.

You have lost all of your moral standards and you have embarrassed me once too many times. I am just sick of caring for you! To me you have done the worst damage! I lost the experience of growing up from a child. I had to grow up at the age of five! You don't care what people are trying to do for you and I think that that is just pitiful! You can ruin your life because I don't care anymore! One thing more—just stay out of my life FOREVER!

Your daughter
Female, 15

....

My main problem right now is my mother. She is supposedly a recovered alcoholic. I say supposedly because although she no longer drinks, she has many other problems. I no longer live with her. After the years of pain while she was drinking I decided that I could no longer live with her, so now I live 500 miles away with my father. But she is still my mother, and the pain is continuing each time I call her. One time she was practically hysterical because she hadn't eaten for four days. She has no job, takes medication for her "nerves," which I think that she is addicted to, and is basically very mentally unstable. She has numerous relationships with men, upon whom she becomes totally dependent. She has friends who would be willing to help her, but she is too proud, I suppose, and ends up finding things wrong with them and breaking off. It is so painful for me to call her up and hear that she is extremely depressed (I can tell by her voice) or that she has received an eviction notice or that she hasn't eaten. I feel like it's my responsibility to help her out, (going back to the old "children of alcoholics accept parent responsibility," I suppose) but my father says that she is the one who must ask for help. I feel guilty that I live my relatively happy life here while she suffers through each day down there. It also makes me angry because she is an extremely talented writer, and her downfall is a waste of that talent. I rarely discuss this, I suppose I just try to ignore it. I used to think that if she would just stop drinking, everything would be okay, but I now know that that is not true. I am resentful that I can't have a wonderful mother the way I would like her to be. Lately I've been thinking about attending an Alateen meeting, even though she hasn't had anything to drink in two years.

Female, 16

Playing with Fire

It is common for students whose parents or friends are substance abusers to deny the risk and become users, too. It's a recurring theme in the journal entries. So often I will read in someone's journal that they are disgusted by their mom's or dad's alcoholism or drug use, and then I realize that several times throughout their journal they have talked about getting high and/or drunk. Their journal cover is often a collage of alcoholic beverages, marijuana plants, and cigarette ads. Either they don't get the connection, or they think, "I'm stronger than that weak alcoholic. I can stop whenever I want." Some will say that they "only use weed" and therefore won't end up like their mom or dad who is an alcoholic.

I use statistics, facts, videos, speakers who are recovering addicts and alcoholics, and speakers from Alateen, but it is hard to compete with the drug culture in which we live. Some students get very offended when I point out that their behavior is risky. It is not their fault that they may have inherited a predisposition but I do think it is my responsibility to let them know that they are playing with fire. I worry about the following student, for instance, because, although she says she is scared, the bulk of the letter suggests that she does not feel she has a problem:

> I guess you could say that I'm the typical American girl. I live in the hills, my parents are divorced, I have a great boyfriend, I have a cat, etc. You know all of that other shit that goes with the typical white girl. I hate that fucking stereotype. Oh, you're rich, you live in the hills. Fuck that. Most people don't know half of my problems.
>
> When I was a little girl my father would drink, beat up my mom, throw her down cement stairs, steal money from my brother. It was to the extent that my brother would fight him off with a baseball bat. My dad was an alcoholic. But I never thought I would have a problem with drugs or alcohol because I'm adopted. But then when I found out my birth mother gave me up because she was a crack fiend and an alcoholic, I started to get worried. Maybe that's the reason I have a high ass tolerance. I only weigh 105 lbs. and it takes at least a 40 [forty ounces of beer] or two and some hard alcohol. Weed is cool too. It makes me feel good and relaxed. I'm not an addict either but I'm scared. But I can handle it. I am a varsity soccer player, get good grades, and have a pretty good relationship with my parents. So fuck all that shit, about I'm gonna be addicted. I can handle it.
>
> Female, 15

I tell the class that I have had many speakers who, like the previous young woman, used drugs when they were in high school and still managed to do well academically and in sports. The stumbling drunk with slurred speech or the wino with a brown bag sitting in the park represent only a small fraction of the addicts in our country. Some of their classmates who are model students may be heavy users—as may some of their teachers, doctors, bus drivers, and religious leaders.

Being able to hold down a job, play sports, or keep up one's grades in school makes it easier to convince oneself that the drug use is under control when it really isn't. The problem is that drugs are sneaky and play with one's mind.

> I feel that if you can control your drug habits and don't let them take over your life and one just uses occasionally, they're fine. I have done many drugs including LSD, alcohol, marijuana, cocaine, tobacco, and hash. I still smoke a pack a day and drink almost every weekend but I have quit smoking marijuana and have quit using LSD but still use cocaine on occasion (very rarely). I come from a family which has a history of alcoholism and tobacco use on both sides of my family. That really scares me because I don't want to end up an alcoholic like my two grandmas, my grandfather, and my father, or die from emphysema like my grandfather.
>
> Male, 15

This young man was charming, playful, and bright. He regularly participated in class and never appeared depressed or high. But I told him I was very concerned about his use. Often students feel they have nothing to worry about when they give up the so-called hard drugs, or cut back their use, or switch to a different drug. I agreed with him that he *should* be scared because he was still using, plus there was a history of drug abuse in his family. As one of my speakers put it, it is best to have a healthy respect for the power of drugs.

> Drugs are something that are very much a part in my life. However, I don't like alcohol that much. An occasional wine cooler, beer, or mixed drink is my limit. Both of my parents don't drink. They're just like me, they drink an occasional wine cooler or beer. Weed I feel is not a bad drug. It could be a bad drug if you abuse it though. My whole family smokes weed including my grandparents! My parents also smoke weed with me sometimes. They say they'd rather me smoke weed with them than with some stranger. Last semester I got high more than twice a day, EVERYDAY!!!!!!! But my boyfriend was really on my case so now I don't smoke weed at all during the week. I might get high after school one day, if I don't have any homework. But I don't buy weed at all anymore. Not even on the weekends. People just get me high. I love

weed!! I've experimented with almost every drug. I took Ecstasy for the first time last weekend. It was really fun. I like taking acid a lot also. I've snorted and based cocaine. I've based about five times and it's something I wouldn't do again. Cocaine doesn't give me the satisfactory high that I like. I've tried crank, 'ludes, 'shrooms, hash, and of course nicotine! I have not tried PCP and I don't ever plan to.

I know my drug use has been cut down. I don't feel dependent at all. And for once in my life I feel I have my drug use under control. Because for a long time it was out of control. I really doubt I'll ever stop using drugs. Especially weed. But I'd rather smoke a joint than do any other drug ever.

Female, 15½

There is laughter when I read the part about her grandparents smoking weed, but by the time I finish reading the whole entry, most of the students agree that this girl has a major problem with drugs and that she is in denial. No one ever fantasizes "I want to be a drug addict when I grow up." It just happens, often very slowly: you're convinced there's no problem, you have everything "under control," but before you're aware of it, you've fallen into a lifestyle that may be extremely difficult to change.

At the beginning of class today, I put on the board information from a book called *Uppers, Downers, All Arounders* which spells out the five stages of drug use:

1. experimentation
2. social
3. habituation
4. abuse
5. addiction

I remind the class of these categories and ask them to think about which one the next writer might fit in:

My relationship with drugs is pretty well balanced. I think I've tried some drugs indeed a lot if you count everything in food nowadays but drugs in the usual sense anyway I've tried LSD, pot, mushrooms, alcohol, opium. But back to the balanced part. I've tried all these and don't feel that they're part of my life. I mean my favorite drug is mushrooms and I only take those when I really want to get in touch with myself say in the mountains on a full moon alone with good friends the occasion has to be very special or sometimes rarely something spontaneous, mushrooms are pretty sacred to me and if I never took them again that would be okay I know where I'm coming from and where I'm going to and I don't need to.

Male, 16

We talk a little about what he says and come to the conclusion that he's probably in Stage 2. Someone says, "At this point he seems to be in control, but then again, all people who use say this." I acknowledge that many drug users who are in Stages 3, 4, or even 5 still feel they are in control. I also mention that many people do not go beyond the first two stages. Once again I emphasize that anyone who buys drugs on the street is taking a chance. The LSD, for instance, could be anything from pure acid to toxic amounts of a look-alike drug to something that contains no drugs at all.

On Being Addicted

We talk about what constitutes true addiction, about why people use drugs and how they get started, whether all drug use is bad, and how people know whether they are in control or not. There are so many questions to answer, and so many issues to address, that once again I regret how little time we have to cover this major problem. I read some more journal entries and we talk about which of these writers might have a problem:

Dear Needle—

I'm so glad I haven't used you more than just a couple times but God how I want you every second of every day. Its been a long time—I know and you know—but no one else had a clue. Innocent, wholesome-looking blond teenager—maybe even virginal at times but no—no one would ever guess that I could've been a junkie, injecting ludicrous amounts of freebased white-powder drugs into my veins. The greatest rush I've ever had. Your relatives don't even compare—and I've tried all of them in almost every way possible, (save crack). The first thing my eyes went to, Nancy, when I walked into your class was the poster "One prick could kill you"—true in more than one way. Anyway hopefully my yearnings for you will end one day but I doubt it. At least I'm strong enough to resist your beckoning. I've seen what you do to people. Hookers putting you into veins in their feet desperate to get high, smoking speed, heroin and cocaine through glass pipes. You couldn't get me high enough to make me unable to see myself, and that's not me.

Female, 15

Above the words "save crack" she later wrote "I lied." The next letter is her imagined response from the needle:

Dearest F.

I love you. Don't you know that? Don't I make you feel better than you've ever felt? I mean come on, let's look at reality: your father's an asshole and your stepmother's a bitch. When you go inside their house you sneak around to do your laundry and grab some grub. Your mother lives two blocks away and never, ever fuckin' calls. Your brother is an ass-kisser and on his way to becoming an alcoholic. Your best friend is a little self-absorbed and your boyfriend gives you attitude. Me? All I want to do is take your mind off your problems, the only harm I do is leaving a little mark on your arm. Your veins feel nice and you use me like an expert. When are we gonna party together? I hope you do me soon.

Love, your friend,
Needle

I often wondered what I would do if I were in her shoes. Where does one get the inner strength to resist? I felt such heartache when I thought of all the problems she had experienced by the tender age of fifteen. I talked with her and suggested a couple of resources—drug counseling through our Health Center and a new adolescent drug treatment program not too far away from the high school.

Dear Alcohol,

How do I love thee? You make me feel so bad, so sick. I only drink you when I'm depressed. I don't like being depressed, but when I drink you, you make me more depressed. I can't stop. You make all my problems

• Youth are more susceptible to the toxic and adverse side effects of drugs and can more readily progress to substance abuse problems.

• Adolescents have immature levels of sex hormones which are quite susceptible to drug disruption.

• Many current drugs of abuse like marijuana, the opiates/opioids, and the new rage, anabolic steroids (rhoids) can potentially alter sexual development or function.

go away, that is, for awhile, then you leave me at the worst time. Why? So then I want more of you. You are so cruel, yet I love you. I could not live without you. You are my best friend.

P.S. See you tonight.
Male, 15½

When I told this young man I was very concerned about him and asked him if he was open to any help, he said no.

The next journal entry was written by a young man who proudly wore his BHS letter jacket. By all outward appearances, he had everything going for him, and you never would have guessed that the entry was his. When I talked to him about his drinking problem, he said that his mom was going to get him into a rehab center. After he finished my course, I sent him a note through his history teacher, but I never heard from him. I hope he did seek help:

Dear Beer:

I think I use you too much. You've become a growing part of my life. I drink you at dinner, all night on Friday, and all night on Saturday. Sometimes I even enjoy your company in the morning. Shit, I'm fucking up.

I never used to like you. My first taste was bitter and vulgar. But now, the bad things about you have disappeared. I don't seem to mind anymore. Sometimes, I think I enjoy your taste. I know I really don't.

But, beer, you were the beginning. No offense, but you introduced me to your relatives—the whole family. I don't think I haven't missed trying one of the family. To tell the truth, I've spent most nights with many of your family. I know you don't mind.

Every weekend, I get fucked up. My parents complain, my friends complain, my non-friends complain about me and you. They don't understand. I look forward to the weekends—me and you. Sometimes, I can't wait.

Yet, I think I might use you a little bit too much. I know you help release me from my problems, fears, and life. But more and more problems are occurring. Shit, I have too many of them. I can't handle them any more. But you help me out. I'm thankful for your help. But everyone says I don't need your help. I know I do.

- The psychological and emotional growth of youth can also be affected by psychoactive drugs during the critical years of maturation.

- The adolescent years are critical to the development of learning and the acquisition of academic skills. Depressant drugs, marijuana, and psychedelics all impair learning to some degree.

I got my report card. I'm fucking up. I'm even fucking up in swimming. I'm also losing friends. None of them call. You give comfort, but what really scares me is that you don't care about my problems. I mean you take 'em away for a while, but that's it. You gotta do more than that. You gotta help me some fucking more.

Somebody told me I drink a bit too much. I don't know if I do. Last I had you beer, I had a lot of you. You didn't get me real drunk—you let me down. You got me depressed. I saw what a fuck-up I really am. I don't even deserve to live sometimes. I'm given too many opportunities which I throw away.

I hope this weekend we'll get back together and have some real fun. I need to release and relax. I need to get away. I don't think I use you too much. I use you just enough. I thank you for helping me get away from it all.

Your user,
Male, 15

....

• 3 million students reported binging at least once in the previous month (binging is defined as drinking 5 or more drinks in a row).

• Junior and senior high school students drink 35% of all wine coolers sold in the U.S. and 1.1 billion cans of beer each year.

• A 12-ounce can of beer has the same amount of alcohol as 1 shot of whiskey or a 5-ounce glass of wine.

I am 15 years old. Recently I've begun drinking a lot on weekends. When I first got drunk I hated the taste of the alcohol but I loved the feeling. Now, unfortunately, I love the taste as well. Pressures from school, mainly school work, have gotten me to the point where I feel I need to get drunk each weekend just to forget about my responsibilities. I'm not feeling any peer pressure to drink, but, in a way that bothers me. I have to face that I'm doing this to myself by choice. Alcohol has become too important in my life, I hope I can help myself get over the thrill before it's necessary due to my health. I don't know if someone can help this problem. In fact, I'm not even sure if I want to stop drinking but I'm open to and appreciate any suggestions.

Female, 15

I comment that it is very difficult—if not impossible—to help someone who isn't ready to change and once again talk about resources for support both at school and within the community. Then I continue to read.

Drugs aren't completely foreign to me either. I love getting drunk or stoned occasionally at parties or with friends—just for recreation. Right now I have a joint in my dresser drawer that I am waiting for the right moment to use. Since I don't do it very often, each time for me is special. It bothers me to think of some teenagers (a group of people I hang out with occasionally, for instance) that base their whole life around "being fucked up," who need to "get ripped" to have fun. I don't deny that being drunk or stoned is fun, but if people can't realize the fun things <u>besides</u> that, they're <u>missing</u> out.

My friend and I have talked about trying stronger drugs together—acid or cocaine, but for now I'm quite satisfied with things the way they are.

Female, 15

Marijuana

Many students assume that because marijuana is an herb—and is natural—that it is harmless. I point out that there are between four hundred and five hundred chemicals in a cannabis plant, of which thirty have been studied for their psychoactive effects. Most students would agree that smoking cigarettes is harmful to the delicate tissue in the lungs and throat and are aware of the damage that heavy drinking can do to a person, but the subtle psychological changes that marijuana use can bring about and the problems that habitual use can cause are not so obvious. Kids see their friends giggling and having fun while high on weed; they don't see anything to cause alarm. As far as I know no one has ever died from smoking marijuana. (Last year a student at another high school died almost instantly after taking a hit from a joint that had been laced with some other chemical, but technically, the death was not directly caused by marijuana.) That does not mean that there are no harmful aspects to using it. The problem is getting this message across.

Fact sheets I compile are helpful. They relieve me of the pressure of being the only authority, and they provide material for discussion. We go over the one I've brought in for today:

- Tolerance to marijuana occurs in a rapid and dramatic fashion.

- Current street marijuana is 3 to 7 times more potent than the marijuana of the '60s and early '70s.

- All available research on marijuana was based on a THC calculation of 20 mg per marijuana cigarette (considered in the 1960s to be a high-dose exposure). Current street "joints" are routinely analyzed to contain 40 mg or more of THC [tetra hydrocannabinol, a pschyoactive chemical]. Thus, researchers really aren't sure what they're dealing with in the marijuana of the 1990s.

- Chronic marijuana users show a certain apathy, a tendency to neglect life's problems.

- Some of the negative effects of marijuana are lowered testosterone levels, a decrease in the ability to do complicated tasks, a temporary disruption of short-term memory, decreased tracking ability, an impairment of eye-hand coordination, and a loss of the sense of time.

Then I read more of my students' personal experiences to illustrate the potential consequences of smoking weed—or ganja, dank, chronic, pot, or bomb. (These are all slang terms for marijuana. New names are constantly being thrown into classroom discussions and often I ask students to "translate" them for me.)

I think that lately the biggest problem I've been having is that I smoke too much weed. I smoke it at least once a day and sometimes maybe two or three times a day. I've tried to just say no but I always end up doing it anyway. Most of the time at least one of my friends will offer to get me stoned. I am noticing that I am slowly getting a worse memory and that affects me in school a lot. I really don't know what to do.

Female, 15

Drugs, I hate them, I wish they weren't around. They influence people in a weird way! The drug I hate the most is weed! Both my parents smoke and I hate it. I hate the way it changes them. They become slow and when you try to explain things they take a really long time to comprehend. I hate it when my boyfriends get high because they don't act normally! You can't get close or talk about anything serious with someone who is zonked. I hate the way their mouth gets dry and their eyes looked glazed. I just hate it. I used to get high a lot about a year ago and at first I really liked it. I would laugh a lot and fit in with all my friends! But soon I wasn't laughing as much and I was doing stupid things because I didn't have as much control over myself. Then I hated it, I hated the way it made me feel. I didn't have a good time and I thought everybody looked stupid zonked. That's when I got into stealing my parents' weed and giving it to my boyfriend who would sell it and give me the money. I loved that because I always had money but I didn't like it because my boyfriend was getting zonked all the time due to my weed! Also I was getting a lot of nasty people approaching me. So I stopped! That pissed my boyfriend off [and] it pissed the guys he was selling to. I lost pretty much the whole crowd of people I was hanging out with. My boyfriend was my only friend but he kept using and it was getting worse! I got mad at him and I hated being with him. I threatened to leave him and he cut back but then he got back into it! I hated the fact that his using weed and alcohol was getting bad, but I loved him and I wanted to help him so I stayed with him. He got really bad and I was the only time when he wouldn't use. I was the break in the cycle. Then he started stealing things. He stole his father's girlfriend's car. His father took him away the next day! He spent 15 weeks in rehab! I cried and cried. I denied the fact that he had a drug problem to his parents and friends! It wasn't 'til I spoke to his mother one day when I finally told someone everything I knew about him. She loved him and I loved him and we wanted to help him. He came out of rehab a different person. Trusting, loving, caring! He was my best friend and even though we have broken up I would have to say he is the closest person I've ever gotten to know.

Female, 17

My high school grades have not been good enough for a University of California. I plan to attend a junior college, most likely Santa Barbara City College and then look at my options. It kind of saddens me to watch many of my friends being accepted to good universities and colleges around the country. But then again, many of my friends are in the same boat, so I guess I'll just have to be happy with what I've got.

I can blame much of my problems (reinforcing your views I'm sure) on my marijuana use during the eleventh grade. I kind of gave up on classes and became friends with people who shared my dislike of school, and desired the same escape from our structured lifestyle and the problems and pressures that came with it. My abuse became so bad that there were stretches when I was smoking just about every day. There are some good things about marijuana. It makes you relax and you can learn a lot about your true self from your thoughts while under the drug. But when you let it control you like I did, weed has only negative effects. My short-term memory was atrocious. It brought my motivation down to an almost complete standstill. I didn't have the will to exercise, it gave me a terrible complexion because of all of the junk food I ate when I had the munchies, and worst of all it created a vicious cycle. If you smoke enough weed it will make you very self-conscious, and because of all those other effects mentioned above, I didn't feel good about myself. I thought everyone was talking about what a big drug addict I was, and to escape all those negative feelings, I'd get stoned again, thus completing the circle and starting the next one. I had no desire to work in school, no desire to get a job, no desire to improve my health. I mean last year alone I must have contributed several hundred dollars to marijuana dealers. It all ended when my parents and I agreed on a pact of not smoking weed for two months in exchange for more personal benefits. I was amazed at how much better I felt. I started making new friends, got healthier, got a job and had a lot of extra money since I wasn't buying ganja anymore, and in general just felt like a better person.

So, there it is in a nutshell. The reason behind my J.C.-headedness instead of a real college. I mean there are other things that contributed to my failure in school, junior year, but marijuana was by far the biggest factor. I guess I'm telling you this because I'm really angry at myself for letting this happen. Maybe you can tell your students that if it wasn't for weed, an otherwise bright and intelligent kid would be headed for college. It's kind of a shame.

Male, 17

I point out after reading this that I see nothing wrong with attending a junior college—for many students this is an excellent choice. Talking about college reminds me of some of the advice I got when I was in high school, and I end up telling the class two stories from my past.

One day, for no apparent reason, my Latin teacher called me out of the classroom and we had the following conversation:

Miss Clark: Where do you plan to go to college?

Nancy: U.C. Berkeley, like my brother and sister [they had both been students of hers] and the rest of my family.

Miss Clark: Nancy, you're not college material!

I must admit I was not much of a Latin scholar but I didn't think much of her skills as a predictor of my future either!—maybe she should have stuck to her singing of "Gaudeamus Igitur," which she banged out on the piano and forced on us each Friday!

Some time later my counselor asked me the same question:

Mr. Pollard: Nancy, where do you plan to go to college?

Nancy: U.C. Berkeley, like the rest of my family.

Mr. Pollard: Nancy, 43 percent of the freshmen class flunk out and you'll be one of them!

I think Mr. Pollard should have stuck to coaching basketball! (For the record, I graduated in four years from Berkeley and did over three years of graduate work, too!)

The kids seemed surprised at all this and then tell their own stories about being put into lower-track classes, counselors who are rude, counselors who are never in their offices, and so on. I explained that each counselor has some four hundred students. Most of them would love to get to know each counselee but the situation generally does not allow it. Scheduling, college recommendations, the constant influx of new students midsemester—the demands are just too great to allow for adequate counseling.

Each topic is linked to so many others and it is very easy to get sidetracked in a positive way. I love how the different mix and chemistry of each particular class can take us off on tangents and into new areas, but it also makes it difficult for me to keep all five classes in more or less the same place! Before we get too far afield, I pull the discussion back to marijuana use, and read a pair of letters from the same boy:

Dear "Weed"

Weed, I'm not going to lie about you and I love you and I don't think I could stop using you. You scare me sometimes but other times I just say what the hell, you are a big part of my life right now. Some people tell me I should stop using you because "it fucks up your life." Then I think about it and say I smoke everyday more than once but I still play football, go to every practice, go to my classes and get good grades and I still have a great social life with everyone, so why stop. I have a great life. Sometimes I think weed makes me think a lot broader about things. I figure things out, why this happened, why she's like that and I realize things. You make me feel so good. I'm glad I met you, please don't leave me.

Love,
Weed Lover
Male, 16

....

Dear Weed Lover,

I'm writing this letter to you because I think you need to hear this. You need to stop using me. I am bad for you. I'm killing your brain cells, making you forget things and I'm making you lose all commitment. You are losing friends over me and also investing a lot of money in me. I have screwed up a lot of people's lives and I don't want to screw up your life, so stop using me.

Love,
Mary G. Juana

I ask the class if they recall the letter I read a few days ago from the student who said his mother never taught him to love or feel, just to mix drinks. Most nod or say yes and I tell them that the following letter is from the same young man. In it, he talks about his relationship with drugs; among other things, he recalls being introduced to marijuana when he was a fourth-grader:

I can't recall a time alcohol wasn't available to me in childhood, but I do remember when I started getting into weed. It was in fourth grade with some other friends at Longfellow. At this stage I had friends that either always had weed or had parents that shared with the kids (aren't Berkeley parents wonderful?).... My sophomore year...after three months doing one to two grams a day I scared myself into quitting coke, acid, weed—I resolved to forsake just about everything except alcohol. As I implied, this only lasted for a while and I then slipped into doing just about anything: crystal meth, crank, speed, quaaludes, dust, DMT, weed, acid, etc. Nowadays I drink occasionally, but I try to avoid it; my only remaining vices are coffee and cigarettes, and it looks as if these will be the most difficult to quit. I am not happy about what I have done to myself with drugs, and sometimes I feel as if I stopped too late. People that claim lucidity through drugs are fools; that's the last thing they foster. I do not pass judgments on those who do drugs, however. I am certainly in no position to do so. I do wish that people would be a little more honest with themselves about what they do (drugs) and their relationship to them. They have never been a blessing, just an escape.

As for the place of drugs in my life, you be the judge.
Male, 18

Cigarettes and Smokeless Tobacco

I ask if anyone knows which of the substances mentioned in the last letter is considered the "gateway" drug—the one that is most closely linked to experimentation with other drugs? Most students guess that it's marijuana and a few say alcohol. The correct answer is *cigarettes*. This does not mean that everyone who smokes will end up using other drugs, but when you ask people who *do* use other drugs which one they started with, they will almost always say cigarettes.

But not only is nicotine the gateway drug, it is also a highly addictive substance itself. There are many people who can use alcohol and some other drugs on a casual basis, but there are very few people who can just smoke a couple of cigarettes a day or a week. Among my speakers who are recovered addicts, most have stated that the hardest drug habit for them to kick is cigarette smoking. And, quoting from *Uppers, Downers, All Arounders*, "Tolerance to the effects of nicotine, a strong poison, develops quite rapidly, even faster than with heroin or cocaine.... Tobacco is the most addicting drug there is."

In addition, nicotine accounts for over 400,000 deaths each year. Taking all this into consideration, it seems to me that the government should take the money it currently spends on subsidies for tobacco farmers and use it on drug education and prevention programs instead. And more of the money currently spent on the "war on drugs" should be used for drug rehabilitation programs.

"SAVE THE COUPONS IN EACH PACK... THEY'RE GOOD FOR FREE FACE-LIFTS!"

Dear Cigarettes,

Well, I haven't seen you in quite a while. And I'm glad. You never gave me anything except an image. But you took so much. My money, my health, my intelligence, and other things. I hate you now. I hate the fact that you hang around my friends. They don't need you, but you won't let go. You tried to cling to me but I got rid of you. I don't need you. You've done nothing for me. I wish you would leave me and my friends alone. Goodbye.

S.

Male, 16

He imagined this response from the cigarettes:

Dear S.

Don't yell at me. I never asked you to use me. You had to listen to your friends. Anyways I don't need you, I got millions of others. Not to mention your friends. I don't care about you. You're a sucker—you spent money on something that kills you. Go ahead and leave, I know I'll see you again.

From,
Cigarettes

Recently I ran into one of my former students who was home from college. We chatted for awhile, and I noticed he had a cup in his hand. I kept wondering what he was drinking. Espresso? Then I looked more closely and realized the liquid was not going from the cup to his mouth, but vice versa. He was not drinking, but spitting! I asked him if he was "dipping," and he said yes. He proceeded to talk about how many of his college buddies are into dipping. He said that some of his friends have already had surgery on their gums. Some of his friends had thrown up the first time they used and never used again, while others became hooked the very first time they used. He knows that he should quit but says that it is just too hard to do. His advice to my students: "DON'T EVEN TRY IT—EVER!"

Dear Kodiak: [a brand of spit tobacco]

I use every day (sometimes twice, three, or four times a day). I have mixed feelings about you and I wish I knew what you might do to me! When I put you in my lip I feel good and the buzz I get from you feels great. It was a couple of weeks ago when I realized that I was addicted to Kodiak and when my lip hurts I use your lighter friend "Red Man." Sometimes I hate you, when I get home and pull down my lip in the mirror and see the sore areas that dig deep into my lip. I don't know when I will give you up but I don't think I will use you after college. I hate cigarettes but I worry that I will need the nicotine in an easier, faster, and less "disgusting" way. I wonder how you found your way to me and my friends. I wonder how you made me want more and

• According to the *University of California at Berkeley Wellness Letter*: "Though most people associate smoking with cancer, passive smoking accounts for 10 times as many deaths from heart disease each year as from lung cancer. In addition, children whose parents smoke (particularly if the mother smokes) have a higher prevalence of bronchitis, pneumonia, wheezing, coughing and middle ear disease. The lungs of young children whose mothers smoke may not grow and develop properly, leading to reduced lung function."

more. Kodiak, you are one crazy addiction, and if you give me cancer I will be so mad at you and myself.

Your faithful companion.

Male, 18

Each day the tobacco companies lose approximately 5,000 smokers—nearly 4,000 choose to quit and a little over 1,100 die from smoking related diseases. In order to attract new smokers, they spend nearly $11 million a day—$4 *billion* a year—in advertising and promotion to persuade consumers to begin smoking or to switch brands. In addition, the tobacco industry spends some $4 billion a year on promoting their products by sponsoring various sporting events.

Much of the current advertising is targeted at youth, women, and minorities, so I like to make my students aware of this. I pass around some examples of current cigarette ads and we discuss some of the ways in which advertisers deceive consumers. For instance, I point out that in most cigarette ads the cigarette is lit but there is no smoke. Generally, smoke looks unhealthy so it is simply airbrushed out of the advertisements.

I like to make sure that the nonsmokers in my classes understand that secondhand smoke can be dangerous (it accounts for some 53,000 deaths each year. I ask how many students live with someone who smokes cigarettes and about one-third of them raise their hands. I suggest that they try to educate the smoker as to the effect of passive smoking. Hopefully the person will be receptive and either do their smoking outside or restrict it to just one room in the house. Some parents who smoke are not aware that they are putting their children at risk. I teach a class called Teens Teaching Tobacco Prevention and through it have found that quite a few parents will give up smoking when their children educate them about the negative effects of both smoking and secondhand smoke.

Before class ends today, I tell the students that tomorrow we will have speakers from New Bridge, a residential treatment center for recovering drug addicts and alcoholics located a half block from the U.C. campus. The speakers are not trained as professional lecturers and may be quite nervous. Many have not been sober in front of a group of people for many years other than in their recovery group. I urge the students to listen carefully to the speakers because they will have more to offer than the obvious don't-follow-the-path-I-did message. They will also talk about the importance of not stuffing down one's problems, of talking to someone when you're depressed, and why you don't have to be "hip, slick, and cool" to be accepted.

In Recovery

Next morning the speakers are waiting for me when I arrive—they are early, and there are five of them—usually they only send three! One of them has spoken to my classes before; I introduce myself to the rest of the speakers and we find five chairs so that the panel is comfortably seated as the students begin to file in.

Each of the panelists gives a brief autobiographical sketch as to what led them to addiction and then to recovery. There are many "war" stories of gunshot wounds, overdoses, prison time, and prostitution. Most share that they grew up feeling unloved: low self-esteem and sexual, physical, and emotional abuse are common threads. Four out of five have a history of drug abuse in their families. One of the speakers tells us that in addition to a having history of drug use he is also gay and HIV positive.

One of the speakers asks the class if any of them has a friend or relative who is in prison. I am shocked that over one-third of the class raises their hands, but the students aren't surprised. The speaker wants the students to make the connection between drug use and prison. He says that addiction to using or selling drugs leads to one of three places: institutions, prison, or death.

The speakers continue and then we hear some noise from outside. I can't figure it out, but a student says that it is the PEACE NOW group protesting U.S. intervention overseas. Another student says,

"Kids use it as an excuse to get out of class," and another, "But our job is to be here." The noise subsides and the questions and answers continue until the bell rings, and the students give the speakers a warm round of applause.

After two more classes of the same, I hope to go hide at lunch, but a former student is waiting and I can tell she has been crying. We go to my office and I give the girl a hug and hand her a piece of Kleenex. I listen for a few minutes as she tells me how her mother has threatened to kick her out of the house. We go over some choices she has and I ask her to let me know what she decides to do.

I eat a few bites of my sandwich and take a few sips of juice and run to the restroom—if I don't go now I will not have another chance until after school—the bane of teaching and having a small bladder. I barely make it to fifth period on time. Personally, I would gladly have the school day extended by fifteen minutes to half an hour to have lunch longer than forty-five minutes. I would love to be able to get off campus, visit counselors, make a few phone calls, or just plain relax.

School over, I head for my car, which has some new graffiti on it (I later find out that it stands for a local gang). I say hello to a former student whose boyfriend was shot in the head when she was a student in my class. She had been riding in the car with him and had witnessed this horrific tragedy. I ask how he is doing; she says that he sometimes recognizes her, which amazes me since he has been in a coma for over a year.

Next morning, as soon as I arrive on campus, a student asks to talk with me immediately. She says that she can't stop going to the bathroom and when she does it is very painful—what should she do? I say it sounds like a urinary tract infection and she should go to the Health Center across the hall.

I teach a couple of classes and a former student comes up and says she must talk with me. I let her know that I have no time today—a third student is coming by at lunch—but tomorrow at lunch will work. She says "great." The third student and then Carla, another former student, comes in, obviously shaken. I send the third student into my office and ask her to be patient, and I proceed to talk with Carla.

Carla begins to explain some personal problems resulting from her abortion when *another* former student, John, says he needs to talk with me. I tell him I would like to talk, but there are two people ahead of him. Carla and I finally have about eight uninterrupted minutes together and she leaves. The girl in my office is explaining to me why she dislikes most white people. The bell rings, she leaves, and I see John at the end of the hall. I run to catch him and apologize for not being available. I ask him what is going on and he says, "Can a girl get pregnant from pre-cum?" I say yes and explain that there is a high concentration of sperm in it. His next question: "How much does an abortion cost?" The bell rings for class to begin and I realize that I have not eaten my lunch—nor gotten to the restroom.

Our new schedule now has us meeting with classes on two days of the week for ninety-five minutes. We were given very short notice that this would be going into effect. I have two ninety-five-minute classes back to back after lunch, followed immediately by an interview from a reporter from a local newspaper. At 4:00 P.M. I see the vice-principal to discuss my class size and I eat part of my lunch in his office. I finally get to the restroom at 4:20. On the way back to my room I stop in the mail room and pick up the latest communiqué from the administration:

> Two female BHS students were involved in an altercation that began on Shattuck Avenue and Allston Way around noon yesterday. One of the students allegedly pulled a knife out of her purse and began to pursue the other student down Allston Way. After catching up with her in an Allston Way store, the student allegedly stabbed the other student in the shoulder with the knife. The victim was sent to the hospital for treatment and the alleged perpetrator was arrested by the Berkeley Police Department.

What a way to end the day! The next day I find out that the victim is one of my former students. I call her, but the number listed in the school records is not correct. This is not unusual. Fortunately, she returned to school and apparently is okay.

Throughout the past few chaotic days, classes have gone on as usual. We pick up on several issues that the speakers from New Bridge brought up when they were here. The question of how easy or how difficult it is to overcome an addiction comes up, and I read several journal entries that have to do with quitting, including a thank-you note to the speakers that a former student wrote:

> Thanks so much for talking to us about the dangers of drug abuse. It has helped me tremendously to hear your stories and to feel your pain. I think that you are very brave to come and speak to us. I believe that what you have said has impacted me as greatly as anything I have learned at BHS. I wish you good luck in your recovery from your addictions.
>
> I believe that I may have a problem with alcohol abuse and it is good to see that people can recover and don't have to just give up to alcoholism. After hearing you guys talk about your lives I decided that I would take a weekend off from drinking and drugs to see if I have a problem. I'm not sure but I'm glad that I am addressing it instead of ignoring my possible problem.... I hope that it makes you feel good to know that perhaps I will be able to learn from your mistakes.... I find it very comforting to know that...if I ever realized I was abusing drugs I could go and get support.
>
> Thank you.
> Male, 17
>
> P.S. I hope that you continue to speak to high school classes because this topic is very important. I think that students tend to respond better to speakers than to statistics.

....

> I used to do quite a bit. I've done coke, speed, weed, alcohol. This was about one and a half years ago. I'm really glad that I'm out of that environment. What's really sad is that I thought the weekends would be boring if I didn't have any drugs. I couldn't just enjoy myself just by going dancing or something. I didn't think this was a problem then, but now that I look back on it, I know I had a problem. One thing that I've always been pretty lucky about, is that I never became addicted to anything. One day I just took a good look at myself and I didn't like it, so I quit everything all together. Now I'm really happy inside, I've made new friends, people that aren't so negative about life. Sure every now and then my boyfriend and I with a couple of friends will have a little pasta dinner party and have some wine or champagne, but that's all. I feel really healthy and clean now that I don't do drugs.
>
> Female, 17

Dear Bomb,

When I first tried you, I loved the way you made me feel. You relaxed my nerves and you calmed me down when I was angry or stressed. You were and still are being used by a lot of my friends. Your chemical is very addictive and I won't deny the fact that I was <u>very</u> addicted to you and you were something to look forward to every Friday, but now I've realized that it is not ladylike to smoke you. Also you destroy the brain cells, I already feel slow enough, so why do I need you to make me feel slower?

Recovered Bomb Smoker
Female, 15

P.S. I hate you for making my father addicted to you for 34 years. He is a computer technician and I wonder how he maintains his ability to work with you being sucked into his lungs and brain <u>EVERYDAY</u>!!

The next girl flunked my class the first time around due to excessive absences. She wrote the following piece when she repeated the class. In it, she speaks of herself in the third person and describes her "fall" and subsequent recovery:

HOW I FELL OUT OF BHS

Well, picture it. September 1991, Fall semester 10th grade. T. has just been kicked out of her house and has to go reside with her father. Her self-esteem is at an all-time low, and in the fourth week of school, she starts cutting madly, and is getting drunk and high every day. She is with her younger cousins, and their friends, who also attend BHS. She never talks to her mother, and her father is out of work and there are hints of cocaine in his room. Her crazy aunt lives there in the house with her two kids. This house only has three bedrooms. To escape the pressures from home, she smokes weed, and almost sleeps with horrible men, while she's high. But she has one inspiration: her best friend. This best friend has been by her since kindergarten, and knows her inside out. She encourages her to go to class, get out of the rut of smoking, and talk to her father. In a last ditch effort, T. decides to take her friend's advice. And everything from then on, went better, because T. got a job that summer, that did not allow drugs or alcohol. And that was the beginning of the beginning.

Female, 16

Luckily she was hired by a local firm that required regular drug testing, and for her, keeping the job was worth the effort to stay off drugs. It is very exciting to see a major turnaround in someone's life.

I have smoked marijuana,
I have drank my share of forties, Old E, Schlitz, Mickey's.
The weekends come, and before we go to a party, we stop by the liquor store.

"It makes me relax" I said.
"It makes me more brave" I said.
"It makes the party fun" I said.
"It makes me more social" I said.

But wait...
Without alcohol I can relax, I can have fun, I can be social,
and I can be brave.
Mushrooms I did once—it distorted my consciousness. I didn't enjoy myself.
Dank I liked for a while but it controlled my consciousness too much.
I will not let anyone or anything control my consciousness.
I've done no man-made drugs and don't plan on it.

Male, 18

As a young woman I never thought I had choices. I never thought anyone understood my way of thinking or that I belonged. I felt I had to keep most things a secret, hide them or make things seem like something they weren't. No one made it clear to me that I didn't have to "fit in" by compromising myself and my boundaries. No one showed me it was alright to be different from someone else, nor was I shown the validity in my ideas, hopes and dreams.

This is the seed I plant when I speak to young people—the fact that their feelings, ideas, hopes, fears, and dreams have validity and that it pays to be honest with oneself as well as with others.

Through my recovery I have received the knowledge of the choices I have, and the empowerment that has enabled me to push forward and accomplish goals I thought were unobtainable. Young people, especially, deserve to know and feel what has taken so long for me to realize, and they deserve to enjoy it now, *without going through the trials I have encountered. This is why I speak in schools.*

Marilyn F.
Recovering Addict

Some Say No

For many students, experimenting with drugs is just not an option. In the anonymous surveys I take at random intervals, about half the students report that they have either never used or no longer use. This surprises almost everyone, adults and teens alike. When I ask in class for estimates on how many students at this school have tried drugs, usual guesses are 98 percent, 100 percent, or 120 percent!

Students who stay away from drugs do so for various reasons, as the following letters show:

I will never, do drugs, ever. My morals are just too set against them, especially marijuana. My brother did pot, and it ruined his life. As far as I'm concerned pot is just a springboard to many various other drugs. My brother is now doing cocaine. He is 27, married, and has two kids. I think he's off it, I hope to God he is. Who knows what he did between pot and coke. It really doesn't matter now. He's also a severe alcoholic. Alcohol is a drug too. I've rarely heard of pot users that haven't tried or become addicted to another drug—including alcohol. Those few who do only use just pot—all I have to say to that is, I've never heard of an ex–pot user who regretted coming off the drug. I try to learn from the mistakes that I & the people around me make, I don't see why others can't do the same.

Female, 15

....

I don't take drugs. My friends are anything <u>but</u> drug addicts. What I don't understand is that I am under so much pressure, why wouldn't I want to take a break and get high? #1, I value my life. And I'm scared. I want to grow up to win the Nobel prize or make inventions, not to live off chemicals. #2, My parents have taught me that it is wrong to take drugs. Why should I think otherwise? My parents were hippies, and I'm <u>sure</u> took drugs at least 3 three times in their life, so why shouldn't I believe what they tell me? My friends are sweet, understanding, earthy. They range from about-to-go-broke poor to extremely rich. But we all love and support each other so that we don't need chemicals to make us feel high. I think weed once every three weeks is okay, but nothing else. Hell, I'm so paranoid that when I found out a good friend was a drug dealer, I dropped her like a hot potato. My fear of drugs is what makes me strong enough to resist them.

Female, 15

No one did or will ever put enough pressure on me to make me do what I feel is wrong. I have never "experimented" with drugs or alcohol, I've never even touched a cigarette to my lips. I feel it is stupid to allow a person to push me to do what I don't want to, it goes against all beauty and pride of being human and my own person. I have always been my own person—my own man.

Male, 15

People ask me if I want a drink or a smoke all the time but I am not even tempted to try them. I get a high out of life. If anyone tries to pressure me, I just tell them that I had so few brain cells when I was born that I can't afford to lose any. Ha! I feel that the main reason that I don't need drugs is because I am a secure, responsible, intelligent and loving woman. I don't need anything that is going to change the way I am.

Female, 15

Drugs have become very upsetting to me within these past two years, only because I've known several people killed over them and have seen two killed because of them. Lives are wasted over a one hour high and it's a shame. I went out with a drug dealer once and during that one date we were shot at by some fool, and chased by police. I didn't know why—I'm sitting in the car thinking he was just speeding.... Anyway, people are beginning to think drugs and alcohol are the exit to heaven, but I know personally if they keep on, they'll definitely miss that freedom train.

Female, 14

....

Drugs are killers. My father was an alcoholic and "was" isn't because he recovered and is not drinking anymore, it is because vodka killed him. People think drinking can't hurt you but it can kill you and also hurt the people around you.

...This experience in my life and my moral values have both contributed to me never using drugs. I have never drunk any alcohol or even took a puff of a cigarette. I know that my chances of becoming chemically dependent has increased since many generations above me are alcoholics. I have no interest and I wish they would just stay away from me.

Female, 15

Drug Dealers

Because drug dealers are an integral part of the drug scene, we always end up discussing them, too. Many of the speakers who come to talk about addiction admit that they also sold drugs. Most ended up having to do so in order to support their habits. But there are many people who deal in drugs purely for money, sex, and power. For them, *that* is their addiction.

Dear A.

Why did you have to try to be rich? Money is the main reason this world is so fucked up today. If you would not [have] tried to be rich fast and go to college instead maybe you'd be alive now. When I was little I looked up to you as a big play brother because I didn't have any real brothers. I was your little play sister, you'd never let anyone bother me. Then as you got older and started to hang with a bad crowd you messed your life up. You started selling drugs, lying, and stealing. Then after two years you had hella money and just had to have more. Well, whoever was after you caught you, stabbed the shit out of you, and left your ass in a van near Knowland Park. I have to end this it's too emotional for me.

Love,
Your play sis
Female, 15

....

I do not use drugs, I do not sell drugs. Last year I used to smoke weed a lot but I stopped because I didn't like the way it made me feel. It made me feel like I didn't have any control over myself. I've had a lot of dope dealers for boyfriends and I don't really like them either, they think that just because they have money they can do anything they want and it doesn't work like that. Don't they realize that when they sell dope they're oppressing the black population, their own mothers, fathers, sisters, and brothers. Realize this and maybe society wouldn't be in the shape it's in.

Female, 16

....

I don't really have a problem but I'm a dope dealer. I try to stop but the money is just too good. I sell a lot. I started with weed, growing my own plants, and then I started with my brother. We sell cocaine, base rocks, and weed. We usually just sell rocks. I don't give a fuck about nobody, that's the way I am. I make money and that's all that counts at the present time. On the weekend I make a lot of money. During school I don't let the dope get to me, but after school I start getting customers around 3:00 and they [are] so fucked up that all they want is more and more. I don't give a motherfucking thing about nobody. I cut my shit with anything, Ajax, baking soda, and sometimes powdered milk. I make my money any way I can. What the fuck, it's money-making time for me, and that's what I do. I try to stop but I can't. It feels so good to touch hundreds of dollars, but don't let the shit go to your head or you'll be dead. I'm not bullshitting. Girls around my part do anything for a rock and like I said, I don't give a fuck. It's money-making time right now.

Male, 16

Sometime during their presentation, the recovering addict speakers will often warn the students that drug dealers cannot be trusted. To any girls who have boyfriends who are dealers, they will say, "You are a fool if you think you are the only one your boyfriend is talking to." A couple of girls will usually say, "I know my boyfriend is faithful," and the speakers will just shake their heads in frustration and disbelief. And they warn everyone that dealers are always cutting their drugs with some additive or other. It could be something harmless like cornstarch or sugar, or something dangerous, like chemicals for cleaning swimming pools. Money is their motive, not the buyer's health.

I want to talk about a serious problem. I use to be a drug dealer, I thought it was fun all the money, women of all ages, I mean when you were up making money you had power and people respected you. For many young boys selling drugs, it give them a feeling of manhood and being tuff. But since then I've learned selling drugs in the black community is mental slavery. It keeps us down and oppressed. Drugs just didn't pop up in the black community it was put there. Drugs have two uses, one to make money, two to kill our people.

Male, 16

Mostly males have written about selling but it is not exclusively done by them. This girl wrote about "Life in the Fast Lane":

"LIFE IN THE FAST LANE"

What's really going on dope? I don't use you I only sell you to those in need of a quick fix. I started selling you at about the age of 14. I have been selling you on and off for 3 years now. I have dated drug dealers, I have loved drug dealers. But I don't let that get in the way of me getting mine every time. I have been shot at, robbed, etc., but I always seem to find my way back to my spot. I can stop selling drugs whenever I feel like it but until then I'll be seeing you when school gets out!

Female, 15

Cocaine is a thing of life that is just another part of life or another part of the 'hood. I started selling dope in the 7th grade. My parents didn't know what was going on until I got caught and even then I didn't stop. It was like the money was calling me. I didn't like going to jail but after making $600 a day it was hard to leave the dope game. I mean my parents sent me to a city that was far away but I still didn't stop. I don't know if I really want to stop. It is just like being addicted to crack. The money is my addiction and until I die I'll always believe in the saying money = power. And that's from the heart.

Male, 17

He later wrote:

If it wasn't for jail I don't think I would have stopped. But jail life is no fun life. Being shipped from prison to prison and cell to cell. Eating cold ass food and I think that being in a scared straight program made me think twice about going back to the dope game and the pain and hard times you put people through it's not worth it.

Todd's Letter

I save my heaviest message for last, and hand out copies of the following letter and ask the kids to read it to themselves. I don't attempt to read it aloud because, no matter how many times I have read it, I get too choked up. In it, the mother of a former student talks about her son's death and refers to the "time capsule" assignment where the students write a letter to themselves for future delivery. What she has to say clearly demonstrates that one does not need to be an addict to suffer major consequences from drug use. Most adults can use drugs recreationally without any problem, but there are no guarantees. Occasional use, or even one-time use can have disastrous effects.

Dear Ms. Rubin:

I'm afraid this letter will be the bearer of some very sad news. My son, Todd Crew, who was in your Social Living class in 1981 and who graduated from Berkeley High in 1983, died July 18, 1987, from an accidental overdose of drugs at a party in Manhattan.

He had been an aspiring rock star, and his band had played to sold-out audiences in San Francisco, Palo Alto, San Jose, Los Angeles and

Orange County. He had had a falling-out with his band in April, 1987, and so in July he had gone to New York with friends to attend a Rock Seminar in hopes of putting together a new band. Friday, the 17th, he called me to tell me how much he loved New York City, and that he enjoyed traveling so much that he had decided to go with another band as a music technician. He felt this band was about to become great, and he wanted to see how they did it. Their album was to be released the following week. They were scheduled to go on tour "all over." Late that night, a member of the band that had just hired him offered Todd what the autopsy was to call "an unnamed opiate." Todd normally did not use drugs, other than alcohol, which is of course extremely dangerous in itself. He had been drinking at the party, so his resistance was lowered, and at some point said okay to the opiate. They did not know Todd was not a user, and the dose they gave him, although not really very much, was not for beginners. Everyone else had the same thing; no one else was affected, but Todd was dead before the ambulance arrived.

New York has so many drug deaths that the police often do nothing unless someone presses charges. I was too numb with grief to do anything at all; it was all I could do for months just to make it through each day. The person who had given Todd the drug said Todd was his best friend, and he seemed so remorseful; by doing nothing, I hoped I was doing what Todd would have wanted.

That band did become great. Their songs went to the top of the charts, and their posters and CDs are found in record stores all over the United States, and in some foreign countries as well. Their music has been in movies with Tom Cruise and Clint Eastwood. Sometimes on MTV they are shown dedicating a song to Todd, Bob Dylan's "Knockin' on Heaven's Door." The band? Guns 'N' Roses. So in a sense Todd has been on MTV, but not at all in the way he would have dreamed.

Last September 2, Todd would have been twenty-five. A few days before, a thick envelope arrived addressed to Todd in familiar handwriting, with no return address. I opened it with some dread, because it was obviously from someone who knew him well—four pages it was—and who yet must not have heard that he had died. I looked to the back page to see a signature, but there was none, so I began to read. "Todd, How you doin'?" it began. "It's a fine day in September of 1990 by now. Well, have we made it? Are we out of college now?

Did we finish? I hope that we're happy now." By then the tears were streaming, and I soon realized the letter was from Todd himself.

The letter was of course part of your time capsule project, and he had written a letter in 1981 to be mailed to himself in 1990. It was mostly about how happy he was, and what a happy childhood he had had, and how many friends he had. He had signed it on the third page, and the last page he used for special quotes and names he wanted to remember. He listed you on that page as being a special person. If you would like, we could send you a copy. I cannot ever thank you enough for having assigned this project. I will treasure the letter forever.

Thank you for being such a good teacher, and for having been a special person to Todd.

Sincerely,
Todd's Mother
November 25th, 1990

One of my students was moved to write this in her journal after reading the letter from Todd's mother:

That letter really brought tears to my eyes. I've seen the video "Knocking on Heaven's Door." It really hurts me that he died so young, and had taken this particular drug from his best friend. I really feel for his mother. I dedicate this poem in memory of Todd:

Though life was short and sweet for you
You shouldn't have died a horrible death.
I keep your memory in my mind and soul and spirit
Though I didn't have the chance to meet you
I know someday we shall meet...

Female, 15½

Just Say Know

The best prevention to drug abuse is never to begin using but we are inundated by messages that tell us that it's okay—in fact, it's desirable—to enhance our lives with drugs: a glass of wine with dinner, a beer at a football game, a social drink at a party. Feeling anxious or sad? Take Prozac, Valium, or any other prescription antidepressant drug. You need to stay alert? Simply take No-Doz. There are many addictive substances that are legal and readily available in your local supermarket or drugstore. So let's be realistic. I think it's safe to say that we will never wipe out the use of mind-altering drugs or alcohol. The moment one substance becomes scarce or illegal, someone designs a new street drug to replace it, or devises a way to get around the law. Alcohol, I'm sure, will be with us forever (there have been laws against its use going back to 1700 B.C.). So if the use of drugs is not likely to stop, then it is imperative that we teach the truth about them so that young people will understand the risks involved and make intelligent choices. If you tell kids that marijuana will make you go crazy—as in the movie *Reefer Madness*—then they will not believe anything you say about drugs, so I will continue my Just Say Know campaign. I know that for some it has made a difference.

10 | Violence

ONE MONDAY MORNING a few weeks ago, I arrived at work feeling refreshed and ready to face the week ahead only to find the following interoffice memo in my box:

> At approximately 1:30 p.m. on Friday afternoon, there were "shots" heard by students, staff, and civilians on Martin Luther King Way near the breezeway between the G and H building. Administrators, campus monitors and Berkeley police responded promptly.
>
> Shortly after 2:00 p.m. Berkeley police did arrest an undisclosed number of suspects who had a gun in their possession. They were identified by several civilians who witnessed them firing a gun in other parts of the city. The description of the suspects and car were consistent with those reported by staff, students, and civilians in the area of the G building.
>
> We have no evidence to indicate that these were Berkeley High School students or that the shooting was directed specifically at Berkeley High School.

No longer were drive-by shootings just another story on the evening news or something that happens at other schools. One more terrible aspect of contemporary life was now a part of *my* work environment. Fortunately no one was hurt in that incident and the perpetrators were arrested, which is somewhat comforting. I have spoken with many other teachers about this incident, but so far, not one student has mentioned it to me. Just something else they must contend with in order to get an education. Sadly, for many, such random violence is all too common.

A few weeks ago, a former student who is a professional athlete came to talk to the seventh-period class about how she had dealt with being molested by her father's business associates and several cousins. She had just introduced herself when the bell started ringing repeatedly, then stopped. At first it sounded like the call for a janitor but it went on too long. Fire alarm? No, it was too short for that. I assumed it was a mistake. We continued on and then it happened again and I tried to find someone to ask, but all of the administrators and counselors were off campus. Eventually I found a student supervisor with a walkie-talkie who said that a bomb threat was called into the school and we should evacuate, but not to tell the students. Ignoring her advice, I walked into my room and announced that there was a bomb threat in the other building and we needed to evacuate. (If I said it was anything else, the kids would insist on hearing the speaker, as trash can fires and false alarms are standard pranks.) We went outside and waited for the all clear signal, then returned to our room only to be told that classes were canceled for the rest of the day and all students should leave the campus immediately. So much for the weeks of planning for my guest speaker. Since she would soon be competing out of the country, it was not possible to reschedule.

It wasn't until the next day that the strange bells made any sense. This notice from the principal was in our boxes:

A bomb threat was called into Berkeley High School through the registrar. An acting assistant principal was notified.... We decided to call a fire drill, notify the police, and have the building searched. This was done. When the police arrived they suggested that it was not wise to empty the building for a called-in threat as it encourages future occurrences. Thus the all clear was sounded and students sent back to class. After this had been done, it came to our attention that a few days before, a bomb had been found on campus. The police indicated that this then changed the seriousness of the situation. The superintendent was then called and informed of the events that had occurred and that a decision as to closing school for the remainder of the day was pending. The police did further checking into the prior incident and determined that the bomb was not an actual bomb, but the makings for a bomb. The principal was informed of the sequence of events by the acting assistant principal. We then decided to evacuate the building and encourage students to leave campus, which was done.

Considering that no one was officially left in charge of our 2,300 students, some good decisions were made. If there is ever a major earthquake in the Bay Area, I pray it does not happen while school is in session. Although many of us have begged repeatedly for a comprehensive evacuation plan, none exists.

I heard nothing further about the bomb incident until I read in the student newspaper that the girls who had called in the threat had been arrested. Again, none of my students inquired about the bomb threat.

Several days after this, a U.C. student was shot to death directly across the street from the high school. This had no direct connection to our school but it took place right next to our tennis courts and just a half block from classrooms.

In the midst of all this, I got a call from the PTSA (Parent Teacher Student Association) asking me to speak on how I help students cope with violence on campus. I laughed. The caller wanted to know what I found amusing about the topic. I said that my students did not seem to be worried about the violence on campus, but as a teacher I was very concerned. I said that I would be glad to speak about my feelings and reactions.

Speaking at the PTSA meeting to give the "student perspective" on campus violence, I began by reading a letter from the father of one of my students; in it he described the devastating effects that the violent atmosphere at school was having on his son. His tale was so disturbing and sad that I was overwhelmed by my feelings and had to stop and ask the psychologist sitting next to me to finish reading the letter. By the time he was done, I had regained my composure so that I could go on with my presentation. I spoke at length to the audience of some one hundred parents about the disrespect, anger, and hatred that students and staff experience every day at school.

The next day, one of the women who had addressed the panel approached me and said, "I know this is none of my business, and perhaps I am being too personal—but have you thought about hormones?" "Excuse me?" I said (I had no idea what she was talking about). "I thought perhaps that your emotional behavior might be due to being premenopausal," she replied.

I wish I could report that I withered her with some clever response, but all I could think of was to tell her thanks for your concern, and I'll look into it. I wondered if she had really heard *anything* I'd said at that meeting.

Several weeks ago, I previewed a video on how women are portrayed in rock videos and how this can influence behavior and expectations between the sexes. It consisted of a collection of clips from music videos with a voice-over describing the various images of women. It was one of the most powerful and disturbing educational films I had ever seen, and I decided to show it to my classes.

I told the first class that I thought the video was excellent, although I did have some concerns—it was explicit and intense, and it showed the gang rape scene from the movie *The Accused*. I said that anyone who wished to leave could go to my office, but no one left. When the video was over, I asked for reactions, and to my dismay, much of the discussion centered around the video being repetitious and boring—and too long. (In fact, I had to wake up some students.) And no one seemed to be disturbed by how women were depicted in the clips. After showing the video to the rest of my classes and getting the same overall reaction, I was even more upset. I concluded that kids are numb to the sexual and violent images they see. I do not get cable and therefore have seen very little of MTV, but I do know that TV's offerings today are far more violent and sexual than the "Gunsmoke" and "Ozzie and Harriet" shows of my day. However, hearing my students say that this video "just shows what we already know," that they are not disturbed because "we know that TV is not reality," really hit home for me. I guess there *is* a generation gap.

Many experts feel that there is a link between the violence that one sees on television and attitudes and behavior in children. My students can separate reality from TV fantasy, but at what age does this awareness set in? How many murders and violent scenes or lyrics were they exposed to before they reached this point of understanding? Too many students accept violence in our society as a given. This attitude worries me because it is usually followed by "...and there's nothing we can do about it.... It's only going to get worse."

So many of my students have lost friends and relatives to the violence of the streets, but most of them just shrug it off. One of my students once said, "Oh yeah, I hear another friend was shot and killed and I just take down the ol' black dress and go to another funeral." One guy told me, "Y' know Nancy, when one of my patnas dies, we just sit around and talk about him and cry and then the next day we just forget him and get back to whatever." I asked him if he wasn't afraid he might be next. "Yeah, sure," he said, "that's the reality of where I live." Life in the '90s? I find the kids' reaction—or apparent lack of reaction—to violence very disturbing, but maybe it is the best way to cope.

In 1992, all the students enrolled in the Social Living classes and the Teens Teaching Tobacco Prevention class were surveyed to get some idea of how safe our students felt while at school. Based on that survey, it would appear that students felt fairly secure on campus at that time.

At the end of the survey, when asked for their written opinions on the safety of the environment at school, 14 percent said it was pretty safe; 4 percent said it was okay if you mind your own business, don't walk alone on campus; 2 percent had witnessed assaults and cited the gym, bathrooms, slope areas, and empty hallways as unsafe; the balance did not respond.

But it seems to me that the campus environment gets a little more volatile with each passing year. The students generally just cope with the situation because it's normal school life to them, and their stay here is relatively short. But I always compare the present to the past, and, from my perspective, this year there were more problems than in any other of the twenty-four years I've been teaching here. In light of all the incidents that have occurred at school or nearby this semester, coupled with the fact that school safety has received so much press attention, I decided to add a question on violence to the Journal Assignments worksheet:

> **How do you feel about violence (at BHS, on TV, in your community, etc.)? Do you see yourself as a violent person?**

Most students expressed in their answer that they hate violence and wish that it didn't exist. Many said they would never initiate violence

---

Violence at BHS

1. Have you ever felt threatened at BHS?

Yes: 19% No: 74%
No Answer: 7%

2. Have you ever been verbally abused at BHS?

Yes: 29% No: 60%
No Answer: 11%

3. Have you ever been physically abused at BHS?

Yes: 7% No: 81%
No Answer: 12%

but acknowledged that they would do *everything* necessary to protect themselves. Overall, it appears that most of my students simply feel that violence is a part of life—always has been, and always will be. Here are some of the responses:

> Violence, where? Que? At Berkeley High? Oh! I get it, someone has been attacked. Well, violence exists everywhere and at Berkeley High it is not hidden very well. The Jacket [school paper] reads Gang Violence!—White Students Being Attacked by Angry Black Males! What can I say? I mean violence is everywhere—blacks attack whites—whites have killed blacks, Chicanos, Latinos, Asians, and other whites—blacks have killed, etc. Asians have killed. Chicanos/Latinos have killed. Everyone destroys.
>
> At BHS it is just not exploited like on TV. Violence—is a product of ignorance produced by an insecurity about oneself which manifests itself to an uncontrollable emotion which eats or embodies someone whole where it can not be reasoned with and since that person (one) is defined by others and not himself he therefore succumbs to the first reaction—not the right reaction to the probably ignorant but tiny incident.
>
> Male, 18

He also wrote the following:

> I don't have a problem with gangs because gangs involve [people] uniting and bonding together to become a family to depend on each other, to look toward each other for strength—No, I don't have a problem with gangs. I have a problem with gangs killing blacks, and other gangs start killing each other and innocent blacks and Latinos in the crossfire. See, with gangs, the problem isn't "the gang" itself, it's more of the gang's objectives or goals—what their interests are—that's a problem, because everywhere you look there are gangs. Besides the Bloods and Crips, Gang Disciples and Folks, Vice-Lords, we have the LAPD, OPD, BPD [Los Angeles, Oakland, and Berkeley Police Departments], Christians, Muslims, Jehovah's Witnesses, lawyers. So what exactly is a gang?

Yesterday, I went to five different sixth-grade classes to talk about Berkeley High School with the D.A.R.E. [Drug Awareness Resistance

Education] program. Most of the questions were regarding drugs, sex, school, and violence. I was really shocked to know that many of those kids are really terrified to come to high school. Many of the kids asked me if I had a gun? Do many people carry guns? Had I ever been shot at?

That was really sad for me because I have never seen a gun at Berkeley High. These kids are terrified that they are going to get beat up if they don't do drugs, or that you have to carry a gun to school just to be safe. This sickens me because all of this is brought about because of the media. They never show the good things we do in school. Or all the great curriculum we have at this school. I'm not really bothered by the violence because I don't see too much of it around me or at school. Yeah there's fights, but every school has fights. I feel bad for those kids that are afraid to come to high school because it's a wonderful experience even though it can be stressful at times. I'm glad I went in and talked to these kids because now they know from a student that goes to BHS that it isn't such a bad experience after all. It makes me sad to know that the media only cares about ratings and not what their perceptions are.

Female, 16

....

Well, violence affects everybody but I protect myself. I have a sharpened screwdriver in my locker at school and I have a butterfly knife with me so I am well protected. TV violence sucks, community violence stinks but in BHS it's something because of the gangs. If you are Mexican and in no gang you are in trouble so I consider myself in the middle.

Male, 16

....

I'm not a violent person and I don't carry a weapon but most people do. I don't bring a weapon with me to school even though I have been chased, fucked with and robbed. But it seems like so many people I knew in Jr. High that were nerds or just cool guys are now trying to be hard and to be down with everyone and carry guns or knives everyday in their backpack or in their pants! I just think it's all crazy and fucked up that people have to carry a weapon.

Male, 15

....

Violence is a form of entertainment. So it seems in this society that violence is the center of every TV show, newspaper, and radio show everywhere. Take the newspaper this morning, I opened right to the sports section expecting to see in bold the score of the CAL game yesterday, I was met instead with the shocking news that a prominent athlete was critically injured in an accident. The paper went on to describe how badly he was banged up. I figure if the sports section shows violence, everywhere shows violence. As for myself, yes I am an aggressive person. Not physically, but mentally. I am very, very competitive, and I enjoy paint-gun games. This is a form of violence made into fun, and I like it. I have people's back, I protect my friends by fighting. I am big and willing to beat ass for my friends, they do the same for me. Is that violence? I don't provoke fights, but I fight. A fighting man needs protection. I often carry a buck knife or my paint gun every day, everywhere. You may laugh and say "Paint gun?"—but you would be surprised at the reaction of people if they don't know it's a paint gun. Going to parties has become dangerous, I try to avoid fights by keeping a low profile. Some of my friends don't keep low profiles, and we all fight. Let me ask, do you think I am a violent person?

Male, 16

This next entry was the second one this young man wrote on the same topic. In class discussion, he told us that he had been jumped at school last year. Then he realized that he hadn't even mentioned this fact in his original entry. I asked him why he thought that incident hadn't come to his mind, and this is what he wrote:

At Berkeley High, so many small incidents of violence occur on a daily basis, it seems that the definition of violence has changed. A simple hit or slap seems insignificant. Even after being jumped, my ideas have not changed, if anything, I now think that everyday violence is more insignificant. There is little that can be done, and little consequence (for the person attacked) in "everyday violence." It seems like a waste of time to try to do anything about it. I don't necessarily believe it is a waste of time—but there is so little legal power and time, and so many larger crimes that affect people's lives in a much more severe way.

....

Well, violence to me is unnecessary, it's crazy, and stupid. People use violence as a way to earn respect. I never really just fought cause I am scared of dying. I let people talk all the shit they want as long as they don't put their hands on me. But when they put their hands on me it won't be violence it will be self-defense 'cause I don't believe in fighting over stupid stuff. I wasn't raised that way. Violence to me is a naive way of thinking. No, I don't see me as violent 'cause I try to avoid it. If I know my remarks are going to cause an argument I keep them to myself. I am just that way. But I am not saying that I don't be ready to buff or knock the shit out of somebody, 'cause I'm human, but I can't let my angered emotions get the best of me 'cause there is nothing but mixed emotions. If you let a person know what makes you mad then they will keep on doing it to aggravate you.

Female, 16

Most times I only learn about incidents through the school paper or occasionally through an interoffice memo. Rarely do I hear from the students themselves. Still, I get the sense that things are slightly more out of control, and the incidents I am aware of point to a heightened level of violence.

To help contain the problem, our school has hired a number of full-time student supervisors to patrol the halls and school grounds, to act as troubleshooters, and to keep nonstudents off the campus. We also have a student-run conflict resolution group.

But, as many of my students note, the problem is not confined to the school: it is really a community problem.

I try not think about the violence that goes on in our community. I've kind of grown numb to it. But every once in awhile when I think about when my parents were growing up, or some peaceful, tightly-woven country town I feel a twang of jealousy. Violence has become to me just another thing to deal with every day, nothing out of the ordinary.

Where to walk, where not to walk, but probably most importantly how to carry yourself in a dangerous situation, proud and strong but not too much so. I've gotten so used to this routine it is hardly anything out of the ordinary to me anymore. I wish it was.

Male, 15

How do I feel about violence? Hmmm…I really hate it. But it wasn't until a year ago that my father pointed out that I had adapted to it and no longer was very upset with it. I lived in between People's Park and Willard Park, one of the highest crime areas and it is rising. I remember last year when there were three robberies in one week. People were raped, car windows smashed, and tires, trash, and other odds and ends dumped into what we called our yard. It was and still is disgusting. Shootings, rape, kidnapping, and other crimes should not be adapted to. They are scary and inexcusable. I am not a violent person and never will be. Violence is one of the world's biggest problems. It needs healing.

Female, 15

"WHEN I ASKED YOU TO BRING YOUR FAVORITE MAGAZINE TO CLASS I DIDN'T MEAN THE ONE FROM YOUR UZI!"

Well, I feel violence is increasing in the nation in general, which affects urban areas like Berkeley, Oakland, the entire Bay Area. It actually affects everywhere—urban and rural. Violence affects me a lot. I limit myself because I'm scared of what can happen if I'm not extremely careful. Although I'm not directly associated with gangs and all the violence that happens I do feel the butt end of it. Why should I have to worry about what neighborhood I go into? What I wear? How I talk, act, respond to people? All of this can be directly related to the fact that I'm scared of violence. I don't want to have anything to do with it. In order to do that, I have to limit myself. It seems like a cycle that everyone is caught up in. TV doesn't help much either—even cartoons have so much violence it's unbelievable. How can our children grow up without facing violence everyday?

Female, 15

The word violence has shaken my family up. I hate violence, period. I have lost 2 real brothers 15 days apart because of violence.

As a result of violence we figured maybe we could get away from all of the drive-by shootings, robbery, etc. But it's not where you go. There's no way to escape it. It hurts like being trapped in a burning house and both the doors and windows are locked and there's no way to run. My neighborhood may seem quiet at daybreak but at night is when the real horror comes out. I fear so much for my ten-year-old brother as he fears for himself. I feel sad when some morning he wakes up praying that he will make it through the day constantly asking my mother will he make it through the day, or with the past 15 days staying in the house scared. I feel violence needs to be stopped.

Female, 15

There is all too much violence in the U.S. I hate to say that it comes from TV, but I have no other explanation. We're so used to watching people get beat up and killed that it doesn't matter anymore. Life has lost its value. Too many people I know have gone and hurt someone or gotten hurt by someone rather than talking it out. Some times you can't talk it out though, and you have no other recourse. But too many times people have gone for their guns or fists instead of their mouths. Or all they can say is irrational and just provokes more violence.

Male, 15

....

I'm afraid of nighttime and kidnapping but I'm trying not to live in fear. Society's violence affects me in that I'm careful, and I don't live freely—but I don't know anyone who's been killed.

Female, 15

....

Violence has no real impact on my life. I see it on TV and I see my friend threatening to kick someone's ass but none of these have anything to do with me. I'm not a violent person at all. I don't need to hurt someone physically to express my anger. I've never been in a fight and I don't plan on it. As a child I was only spanked once and I remember it fairly clear. My mother felt so bad about it that she never did it again. I guess that put the image in my head that violence is wrong. I've never even felt the need to hit someone. I can do a lot of yelling and it shows through my eyes when I'm mad so I don't feel a need to hit someone.

I do think there's a big problem with violence in our society and it needs to be changed. I think if more parents stopped spanking then violence wouldn't even be in the child's head and he/she would grow up peaceful!

Female, 15

....

TWO ELEMENTS IN A PARTY:

When I go to a party, I look at the most important things, such as where is it at? Is there going to be a lot of violence? If so I will not go. All these things can be determined by whose party it is and the neighborhood.

Once I have decided whether or not to go when I first get there I just look around to see what type of party it is. If I see something that I do not like then I will leave, to prevent any problems that may occur afterwards.

I also look at what kind of people are going to be there. Hopefully not people that are under the influence of alcohol or drugs, they tend to act crazy. If they don't cause any problems or bother me then I do not care because that is none of my business.

Female, 15

Many of the older journal entries speak of the link between violence and drug dealing:

Dear Little Brother,

As I watch you grow up I have many frustrations. I know it's hard for black males to grow up. With gangs and drugs. I'm really glad you hate all drugs and can't stand to be around them. But you think that selling drugs is cool too!! It really hurts me that you take that attitude. I've tried to talk to you repeatedly about it, and you ignore me.

It's not cool to be watching over your shoulder at all times. Whether it's for the police, dope fiends, someone you burnt, or a member of an enemy gang. Mom has brought you up teaching you that shit isn't cool. I don't care how much money you'd make or how many cars you'd have. You are 12 years old!!! If you want to live to see at least 20 you better snap out of this phase you're going through!!

I love you! Even if it doesn't seem like it at times. From the day they brought you back from the hospital—you were <u>MY LITTLE BROTHER</u>!! I've experienced a lot more than you think. You can come and talk to me about everything and anything.

I love you—always remember that—no matter what!!

Love,
Female, 16

....

Drugs are bad because they do bad things to your head and your mind. I never tried drugs. I used to sell drugs but I stopped because I almost got shot over drugs. People will do anything for drugs even kill for it. Now there are drug rehabilitation programs to help people with their drug problem and that's good.

Male, 16

I really hate to see drug dealers! It's stupid they get hooked up into this fast money and most of them are from the ghetto and are as dumb as hell, and don't even live to see the age of 21 because someone else is jealous and shoots them or their dumb asses die in jail! And girls who fuck with drug dealers is also stupid. They're not doing nothing but risking their lives for a nigga who obviously don't care much about her 'cause if he did, he wouldn't have her around the danger.

Female, 18

....

I am fifteen years old. About ¾ of the girls I grew up with are mothers or will be shortly. The guys are getting killed off. Everyone is either smoking or selling crack. In jail or dead. This shit depresses me so much. People in my generation whom I once looked up to are slowly falling down. Why is everyone fucking up?

This world is dying and we aren't even trying to stop the bad shit we're doing!

Oh well.

Female, 15

Y.

Last year, Y., one of my former students, was involved in a shocking incident—the murder of another young man over a drug deal that had gone bad. It was a tragedy that defied logic—one life ended, another put in limbo, two families shattered, all over a small amount of money. I kept in touch with Y., and when I told him about this book, he offered to write something for it. Along with this letter to me, he sent his explanation of the incident, and included some advice for young people everywhere:

Dear Nancy,

How have you been doing? Well, I've been doing pretty good. I had messed up a little bit and was on lockdown for about five to six weeks.

I seemed kind of crazy at first, but I got used to it real quick. I've been off for about three weeks now and I've been doing real good.

This place is mostly for people that haven't graduated yet. Since I've already graduated I'm probably going to be given a job within the institution. I'll get paid about 25–30 cents an hour. Not that much, but it's still money you know. Can't even complain.

But yeah, I just wanted to let you know that I think it's hell of cool the way you've kind of kept in touch with me. I've been staying in touch with all of my friends and family. Me being locked up has brought me closer to some of the people in my family. So that's good.

It's alright in here though. I'm <u>hell</u> of used to it now. It just seems like the way my life is now. For a little while. I have to do seven years, until my 25th birthday. If I do real good and get all of my time cuts I can get out in five. I'm about to start trying to do good now though. What I did before, it might get me in some more trouble. I have to go to court and if they decide to charge me then I get an extra year and have to go to a penitentiary. What happened was I was stressing and ended up beating up one of the guards. Everyone, even these CYA [California Youth Authority] people think they're going to just drop the charges. I'm just trying to do good now though…. And so far since that incident I've been doing real good.

But yeah—I'm 'bout to go now, just let you know how things have been going. I'm doing good now though. I wrote a little something for that book you're writing. I think that book is a pretty good idea. But anyway we should keep in touch though so I could let you know what's going on in here. You might be able to let some people know it's not even a cool way to be living you know. But yeah—I'm 'bout to go though. Take care—and Merry Christmas and a Happy New Year.

Y., 18

....

Ever since I was a little kid I've always liked getting into trouble, getting over on somebody in some way. It was just fun to me. As I got older my troubles became more serious. I always stayed in school though. It was out of school where I got into my mischief.

This last year 1992 through 1993, I got caught a few times for selling crack. I decided to stop selling that and instead sell marijuana. I

Children and Guns

From a 1993 Harvard University national survey of 2,000 children in grades 6–12:

- 15% had carried a handgun in the last 30 days;
- 11% had been shot at during the past year;
- 39% know someone who had been killed or wounded by gunfire;
- 35% believe they are likely to die by gunfire;
- 59% said they could get a gun if they wanted one.

figured there wasn't much wrong with selling marijuana. It didn't seem like that much of a risk as far as getting in trouble with the law. But sometimes things that seem like nothing at all can turn into a lot more, due to action [that] people like myself have taken that turns that little trouble into more than one might think he or she could get into.

In May 1993 my little trouble turned into the biggest trouble ever in my life. This whole year I wondered if I'd make it through. Sometimes I would think of what I'd do if someone robbed me. I knew if I kept up with selling sooner or later someone was bound to try and set me up to get robbed. And somewhere deep inside of me I knew I might end up killing that person for doing so. Finally it happen. Thursday night, May 6th, 1993 I was set up in a drug deal by my own friend. I didn't know what to do. I never told anyone about it because I didn't like people in my business. The next day I went to talk to my friend at his work and asked if he'd give me my money back. He said no. I shot him point blank in his heart. He died a little while later and later that night I was arrested. Now I'm in CYA until September 2000 and my victim's family as well as mine are living in great grief all over something that seemed to me to be no trouble at all in the beginning.

The point I'm trying to make is that if you think what you're doing isn't so bad right now the next day can completely change your life around. I'm not trying to preach, but if ya decide you'd like to live the rest of your life messing up, getting into trouble, living in jail, and maybe causing your own death, then do what you have to do. But if you decide you'd like to do something with your life, be a success in your future then do your best to completely keep yourself away and out of trouble. Little or big trouble is trouble and in the end either you'll end up dead, someone you love could end up dead, or maybe you'll end up killing someone else. So the best thing is to just keep away from it. The only thing that could have prevented me from doing what I did is if I had never started getting into trouble from the beginning, because the truth is what I did or the death of myself was bound to happen sooner or later if I had continued living as I was.

It took this incident in my life to make me realize that I can't go on living, and making my money the way I was.... I don't want to spend the rest of my life going in and out of jail or dying an early death. What I've done is done. The only thing I can do is take it as a learning experience of how not to live my life and change it for the better. When I get out I plan to find a job and go straight. It may be hard for awhile but as long as I, or anyone else for that matter, puts their mind to it, they can in their own way become a success in their lives.

    Y.

This note was on Y.'s release form:

> Thank you for letting me express what I had to say. It may seem a little harsh...but it's to the point and the message is simple, just don't get involved with any trouble.

One way that students can make up work or get extra credit is to write a letter to an editor, a TV station, or someone in government about an issue that is important to them. They show me the letter and then mail it. Shortly after the killing occurred, one of Y.'s classmates decided to write the following letter as a makeup assignment:

> Dear President Clinton,
>
> I'm writing to you today about Y., a 17-year-old high school student. Y. killed another teenager. I know Y. and he is not a murderer. Events or circumstances led to the death of one person and the end of life for another. All I can speak to is the Y. I saw in my class, the shy, slightly insecure individual who shared his dream about a grapefruit with the class, the one whose friends always told him he looked like a rat, the one who always walked in the door with a sheepish smile on his face. I never spoke to Y., so I won't pretend I have, but I've seen the innocence on his face, heard him speak so candidly, and I tell you he is not a murderer.
>
> The problem here is not the case of murder, but the case of a system that allows young men to kill, young men to obtain a gun at all, and then pull the trigger in a flash of irrational thought. Where does this hate come from, this hate of oneself that allows the life of another to mean so little to you? Why is self-respect and self-knowledge not encouraged in school? There are so many individuals asking, "Why do those minority students bring guns to school? Don't they know better than that?" IGNORANCE is what breeds these kinds of thoughts, and unwillingness to accept the psychological manifestations that lead to this behavior. People don't just randomly choose to carry guns, there's always a reason.
>
> I don't mean to ignore the death of the victim, rather to show how I

feel about its enactment and how it might have gone either way. Y., if convicted will probably live the rest of his life behind bars, abandoned of the education he had been working at in earnest. Why? Because he was never taught otherwise.

Thank you for your time, whoever's reading this,

Female, 16

When young people get in trouble, their parents are almost automatically blamed for having failed to raise their children properly, but I think this is a simplistic view. If we want to break the cycle of violence in our society, I think we must search for solutions in many directions. In the very thoughtful piece that follows, Y.'s mother gives her point of view:

Dear Nancy:

I am writing out of concern for what is happening to the young people of this country and to share with other parents what I have leaned through the tragedy of two young men—my son and the boy he killed.

The night of May 7, 1993, three police officers knocked on my door and told me that my son had killed another young man. They were looking for him. The next hours were spent collaborating with the police on a plan to make contact with and arrest him. The shock of the news and the terror of those hours shook me to the core as I felt for the other boy and his grieving mother and wondered if my son would soon be dead too. I never thought I would be one of those mothers I had seen on the evening news. I never thought the most severe of the problems facing today's youth would march into my home and change my life forever.

After all, my son was not a latchkey kid. I didn't live in a ghetto in West Oakland. I came from a respectable white, middle-class family— the kind that thinks it's insulated from the problems of the larger society. I had worked out of my home raising my son as a single parent and earning two college degrees in the same town in which I grew up. My son and I had a close relationship and good communication which I valued. He had had a few minor incidents with the law which I had handled through appropriate consequences. I was a responsible parent. He knew that I had a thing about being honest in one's affairs and working things out peacefully, that I was against drugs and guns. We had strug-

gled over these issues in what I had thought were simple clashes between generations. My son was to graduate from high school in only six weeks and was doing well in school. I thought we had finally made it.

The hardest thing for me to understand was what could have brought my son to the act itself. How could he have actually taken another life? What had occurred in these decisive moments between two boys? What had gone on inside his head? By his own description, this was a boy he considered to be a friend—someone to hang out with. There was no history of tension between them. I soon learned the facts. Without my knowledge, my son had bought a gun for protection long ago. The two boys had been involved in a drug deal that went bad. Now one is dead and the other in jail. But these facts didn't answer my questions. I searched myself to discover where I had failed as a parent. I ruminated over the things I could have done better or different. I could have done more to help him fill idle time; I could have insisted he get a job. I got angry at his father who had never met my expectations although he had remained involved and concerned in his own way.

I talked to many young people. We discussed the ease with which they can obtain guns, the violence they have experienced, the attraction of selling drugs for easy money, the fact that many had done "stupid things" and felt they could easily have been my son or the boy who died. I began to understand the frightening circumstances our children deal with alone and with very limited life experience.

I have learned that there is much I didn't hear my son trying to tell me. I was too afraid to confront his reality and I didn't know how to help. The press has recently given a lot of attention to the connection between drugs and teen violence, a connection that is blatantly obvious. But I think the problem goes deeper than drugs and guns. From the time my son was in sixth grade, he was trying in many ways to tell me that he didn't feel safe in the world. He felt the need for protection. He wanted to learn to fight better; he carried a stick with him when he walked by himself to protect himself; he learned to run very fast. I thought he was exaggerating or that these were just expressions of a youthful masculine bravado. I never grasped the gravity of the fear my son experienced. I also never understood the disturbing loss of control and personal power that accompanies that kind of pervasive fear nor the desperate need to take back control, to prove oneself when outside help appears unavailable.

At the same time, I have looked at the ways in which I abandoned my son through my own fear and helplessness. I was so overwhelmed with the details of daily life and providing the bare necessities. I was so overwhelmed with the task of dealing with my own son and his problems. I hoped the problems of the outside world would never come too close. It was too scary to really inquire into situations that concerned me or to seriously involve myself with other kids or their families. It was not that I lacked concern but that I felt isolated and personally powerless. This experience has made me question the need to take personal responsibility for our communities and for all children, the need for involvement, for inquiry, for listening, and for sharing of ideas and solutions.

I am convinced that the two boys involved were not so different. They were both raised by single mothers, both involved with younger siblings, both motivated to complete high school, both had dreams for the future, both attracted to excitement and daring, and both involved in activities they knew would bring them trouble. At the same time, I fully recognize that there is a big difference in that my son still has life and I can still touch him, while the other mother will never again touch her son, and has been deprived of all her hopes and dreams. But on another level, I have often felt that in some ways, both boys have died. The real tragedy is that no one was there to help.

Sincerely,
Y.'s Mom

Shortly after sending me this letter, Y.'s mother accepted an invitation to come speak to my classes. The students were very receptive to what she had to say—this was one presentation that everyone stayed wide awake for—and I think everyone admired her for trying to get her message across and for not climbing into a shell at this difficult time in her life. Later she shared some of her thank-you letters with me. I do not know who wrote them:

> Thank you for coming in and talking to us. That took a lot of courage. At first I was like "Oh, her son is a murderer" and I really felt sort of weird, but when you talked to us, I didn't see you as a murderer's mother. I saw you as an intelligent human being. You made me think a lot about violence and because of that you made a difference. So I'm going to give you some advice.

If you continue to speak at schools maybe you won't change the kids' minds right away, but at least you'll give them something to think about!

....

I really appreciate you coming to our class and sharing your problem. A few months ago I got robbed and I was thinking about committing a murder on them, but I feel that you changed my life by letting me know how my mother would feel if the same thing happened to her.

....

Thank you for coming and speaking to our class. Even though I hate violence, I have so much sympathy for you and your son and what you are going through. The news and the government, whatever, try to make people who commit murder like animals that are different from everybody else, but they just don't understand. I know so many people that have been in the same type of situation where shit gets out of hand and it can change their whole life. One thing that I thought of when you were giving your talk is that the drugs and the violence are really two separate issues. Drug deals and cash can lead to violence, but when it comes right down to it, when you're in that situation, it's your personal choice if you're gonna pull the trigger or not. That comes from the inside, from the way that person has grown up and the examples that they see. If their parents and friends think it's ok to smoke somebody because they took your money, then sometimes those attitudes could affect the person. I'm not saying there's something wrong with the way you raised your son. It's the society that's f—ed up and that's what we have to change. Good luck to both of you.

11 | Death

INSTEAD OF IMMEDIATELY revealing what we're going to talk about today, I ask my students to guess what it is. The only hint I give them is that it's the one subject parents are least likely to talk about with their children. As always, the first guess is sex. I say no. Drugs? Birth control? The guessing continues until they run out of ideas and I tell them the answer is *death*. This is greeted with mumbles, sighs, and "do we have to talk about this?" but when I point out that we will all have to deal with the loss of loved ones many times throughout our lives, it begins to make sense. In fact, I doubt that there's anyone in the class who has not already experienced such a loss. In our society, we tend to avoid the subject and cripple ourselves by bottling up all our feelings. Most of us are even uncomfortable around people who have just suffered a loss and don't know how to give comfort. So the purpose of this discussion, and the journal assignment that goes with it, is to share feelings and get some of this out in the open.

> Describe a personal loss of a friend, relative, pet, etc. How did you deal with your grief? You may wish to write this in letter form.

There is really no better way to start than with a story of my own, and so I tell the class about the biggest loss in my life. My grandfather lived to be 102 years old, and because I was so close to him for so many years, his death left a void in my life. I looked upon him as my mentor; I would visit him after school several times a week and he would listen and respond as I told him of my problems at school. He had an incredible sense of humor and so much knowledge. I could rationalize that I was lucky to have had him in my life for so long, but the fact is that I will always miss him—he can't meet the man in my life, he's not there to visit after a difficult day at school, nor can I get his opinion on current issues as I used to.

In other words, I tell my class, grief can be an ongoing process—you don't necessarily get over it after a certain period of time. In fact, you may think you're over it only to be overcome with grief again years later, often in response to some incident or on a day that has special meaning, like a birthday or holiday.

Most of us have been brought up to accept Hollywood's typical funeral scene as the proper way to deal with death—family and friends grieving at the cemetery—it is usually raining and people are quietly crying or openly sobbing—and then everything goes back to normal. In truth, there are many ways people express grief, and one's life rarely returns to normal quickly.

I ask what other feelings someone might experience besides sadness. Many students are familiar with the stages of grief either from reading or hearing about it or from their own personal experience, and the responses are varied. They talk about anger, guilt, a sense of relief, and even happiness. I ask them to give some examples. One girl volunteers, "You might feel angry if your mother died from cancer due to cigarette smoking. She should have quit, so you're pissed off that she left you." Someone else adds, "And then you might feel guilty that you're angry because after all, she's dead and you shouldn't be feeling sorry for yourself."

Another student talks about a classmate who lost his mother and returned to school the very next day as if nothing had happened. I ask the class if they think he was heartless and uncaring. "No, he just isn't ready to feel the pain," offers a young woman. "I know, I acted the same way. You feel that if you start to cry you will never stop so you just don't allow yourself to begin." Right, I say, and sometimes people are in shock or so numb that they can't deal with the death at the time. This happened to me when my grandmother died. She had been in a coma for a long time, and when she died I did not cry, and I thought it was because her death was not unexpected. But years later—to this

---

Five Stages of Grief

1. Shock

2. Awareness (often marked by emotional outbursts, anger, denial)

3. Withdrawal (a period of recovery from the awareness stage; often a time of despair)

4. Healing (gaining control, overcoming feelings of guilt and anger)

5. Renewal (finding a new focus)

day I do not know what triggered the memory—I thought of her and suddenly burst out crying. This kind of delayed grief is very common, I tell the class. Several students have mentioned it in their journals:

> I haven't had any serious problems until last year. Last year was the worst year of my life. Two of my favorite people died. First went my Daddy and then went my favorite aunt. My problem with this is that I haven't had a really good cry. Sure, I cried at the funerals, but not the way that I wanted to. Right now, I feel a swelling in my chest but not a teardrop to be found. Is this normal? Am I holding back on something? Am I doing this because I don't want to believe that they left me forever?
>
> Female, 16

> A few years ago my grandmother died. She was not a really special person to me because she was very rich and very mean. She favored me greatly over my sister, which made me feel hurt. She did this because she felt that because my sister was adopted, she was not her real granddaughter. This hurt me greatly. I knew she was going to die, because she had terminal cancer, and yet I did not feel bad. I was even a little glad, which I loathe saying, because I hated her for the things she did to our family. But, the day came, when she died. I realized that I never knew her. There was a whole person I would never know. This person who I am related to had left my life forever, and I had never really met them. That was when I realized I had to make the best out of what I had.
>
> Female, 15

> My grandmother died of cancer. It was in her liver then it spread to her lungs. She lived for two years and died at home with the family. I was in a very bad state of shock. I didn't cry until they put that damn white sheet over her face. I didn't cry at the funeral, but every once in awhile at least once a week I cry...not hard or long, the tears just come.
>
> Female, 16

I want my students to understand that grief is very personal and can be expressed in many ways. One person's experience can vary greatly from someone else's. Crying is an excellent way to release sadness but not the only way. I tell the class about my friend Mike whose sailing buddy died in a boating accident in the San Francisco Bay. Mike was angry for two reasons. First of all, he was angry at his friend for not wearing a life jacket even though he knew about the strong currents that flow through the Golden Gate. Secondly, Mike was angry because he never had a chance to say good-bye to his friend. I told Mike it might help to write his friend a letter and tell him all this, and that's just what he did. He put the letter in a bottle and threw it out into the bay. I think this gave him some feeling of at last being able to say good-bye—a sense of closure.

A student raises her hand and asks what is the best thing to do when someone tells you that their friend or someone in their family has died. I tell her to just give them a hug and let them know you care. See if your friend wants to talk, and don't be afraid to mention the person who died. It's best not to say, "I know just how you feel," or "You'll get over it in time," because people may resent this.

About two years ago, my mom died of a cancer tumor on her adrenal gland. It happened real fast. She went into the hospital on her birthday and died about two days later. Me and my brothers never got to say good-bye. The last word we heard from [her] was "don't worry, I'll be fine." She was as white as a ghost and hunched over in her bathrobe. I tried to convince my brothers that she was just sick from her trip to Hawaii (which she had just come back from) and had to get her stomach pumped. We were all real nervous. I could never explain how I felt when my dad told me. They were divorced and he had flown down from New York (we were living in another state at the time). When he told me I just sat there numb all over, literally, and the first thought was, she won't be able to see us grow up. It was definitely the worst day of my life. It didn't really hit me until her funeral. Up 'til then I was in shock. I cried and cried, almost went into convulsions. It was terrible. I'll never forget it. We were so close, we were like best friends. I couldn't have been any closer. I don't know how I've been dealing with it. Just keep on truckin' I guess. But I'll never forget her, and every chance I get I think about her. I hate when people say, "You <u>have</u> to get on with your life; it's in the past now." I say fuck you. Who the hell do you think you are to tell me to forget my mom. That's a load of crock. I think about her all the time and look at old pictures, it helps so much. The weird thing is that sometimes I feel like she's right next to me. Like right now for example. It is a real warm feeling. I don't know why God took her. Sometimes I get mad because the doctors said she died from something that happens to one in a million. Can you believe it? And it had to be my mom. I'll never get over her loss and I can't get rid of the grief, I just know how to deal with it.

Male, 16

....

Dear Mom:

I wish you were here now, I'm finding this part of my life the hardest. I sure could use some of your advice and wisdom and understanding to help me deal with these things. I miss your love for me very much you know. Dad's all right but as you always said, we are too much alike and we get along every now and then, but he tries, but not hard enough. Now it's time to decide my future and I wish you were here to help. Since your death three years ago, it took so much out of me mentally. I can't deal with things like I could when you were alive. Holding all of it in after you died and the things those other people put me through, it ate me up mentally…. But since your death things get me down faster and it's hard to get back up again…. I try not to think about you, because I would crack up most of the time. My mind still doesn't accept that you're not here and that I'll never see you again. It's tearing me apart to write this letter, but maybe my mind thinks you're really going to read this. I just wish you were here. Life is like a game now and I'm losing. I could never stand losing and if it wasn't for you I'd have taken myself out of the game long ago.

Male, 17

When my grandfather died, one of my students gave me this poem on a piece of bright orange stationery:

Put your best foot forward!
What?
You say they are both
Too weak…

Let the tears flow
Although you believe
They can never cease.
Express the pain
Or it will keep returning.
Self-pity is not a
Quality of desire.
Balance the thin line
Between.
Remember that this
Is not a triumph made
In solitude.
Know that we love you
And that will never be
Challenged.

Enjoy the cookies and be good to yourself! (call if you need to)
Love you,
Melanie

I didn't call her, but just knowing that she was thinking of me, had taken time to bake some cookies, made my day a little brighter. I suggest to my students that if they cannot figure out what to write, there are many beautiful sentiments printed on cards—or just writing a simple "thinking of you" will show that they care.

Perhaps what made Melanie so understanding was that her mother had recently died of a diabetic stroke:

As a sophomore in high school my life went fairly well. I knew lots of people and whenever there was a problem I could talk to Momma, about anything. As the year came to a close I began worrying about growing up and making an independent life for myself. But I always knew, because Mom had such confidence in me, that she would be there for support....

I went to graduation thinking that oh, God, in two years that will be me up there. It scared me. Because my best friend and I had gone to the ceremony together, and she was going to spend the night, we walked home together sharing our mutual fears toward becoming adults.

We walked into the living room of the apartment and both said "Hi Mom" as we went into my room to talk more "girl talk."...As it got later my friend fell asleep on the bed as I talked on the phone to a cute guy from French class, just before I crawled under the covers I headed toward the kitchen to get a glass of water and as I turned into the entrance, there, on the kitchen floor lay my mother, pale and still....

I guess my friend must have called her mom, because the next thing I remember is once again being in the living room answering a lot of questions to a cold, impersonal police officer. All I could think of was why were they being so cruel to me—why wasn't Momma here consoling me?

The first week afterwards I slept for maybe five hours altogether. My head kept thinking the same thought over and over..."Momma, where are you?" I didn't cry until the funeral. I was afraid if I started I wouldn't stop....

I spent my summer getting organized for school, keeping busy and occupying any moment of spare time. For the most part I could keep in control, with the exception of hearing certain songs or watching certain shows.... Now, school has started and I am trying to find motivation, but nothing <u>can</u> or ever <u>will</u> fill the gap that leaves me feeling so empty. Nothing can take her place, though I try so hard to convince myself it'll be okay.

My feelings are varied and extreme: I still don't believe it; I find myself wanting to share things with her. Guilty; wishing I had found her sooner or let her know how much she means to me. Hurt; she left me.

But my logic contradicts all of that...feeling content knowing she isn't suffering anymore and knowing I need to get on with my life, so, if for no other reason, that <u>hers</u> is <u>important</u>.

I can't talk about it and I seldom cry until the pain is too much, and her image still haunts me at night, but if I spend the rest of my life in mourning I'll never be that person Momma was so proud of and looked so forward to me becoming.

I have a long way to go until I can accept it, but I will never lose my mother's inspiration.

Melanie, 15

The next semester, Melanie repeated the class as my proctor, and she wrote another letter to her mom, whom she still obviously missed:

Dear Mother,

Last semester I wrote to you and I have the need to write again. It's so hard growing up without you here. One minute I can smell your perfume and the next I have to force myself to know that you were my entire life—you really <u>did</u> exist.

It hurts so much. You are supposed to see my graduation, you are supposed to meet the guy I've fallen in love with, you are supposed to talk to me when things get tough.

Sometimes I think I'm trying to forget too much. I'm so extreme, either driving myself crazy with all those memories, or wanting to shut everything out completely.

You understood me. We were a team, we faced and challenged the world together.

Sometimes this whole thing is a dream—a nightmare—and I'll wake up and you'll be there holding me. Sometimes my pride takes over and I think that I was so lucky for the times we did have. So many kids would have given the world for someone to listen the way you did.... Some kids would love to have their parents be their best friend. I think that makes it hurt more. Through most of the holidays I managed not to cry, but my birthday was so lonely. You are supposed to watch your little girl grow up and with the memories I'm trapped in youth. That little girl in me <u>needs</u> you.

I love you Mommy. I miss you too.

With love and remembrance,
Your Little "Look-Alike"
Melanie, 15

She thoughtfully added a note to me:

P.S. I think this should be read, so that those who have lost someone know they're <u>not</u> alone. It might ease the pain.

Melanie's situation was a precarious one because she had no family to fall back on. She knew nothing about her father and her only immediate relative was a brother who lived on the streets and was so strung out on drugs that he often did not recognize his sister. She had not seen him in two and a half years. Her stepfather was an alcoholic. Somehow, though, she was able to rise above all this. She was the first member of her family to graduate from college, and she now has a job working with young people. On occasion, she comes to speak to my classes about her experiences.

> I don't know if this is really a problem, but my dad died two years ago when I was thirteen. I sometimes get very confused about it. Sometimes I think I don't miss him or love him enough because I usually don't cry anymore. He died from radiation sickness, basically. He had cancer years ago and they treated him for it. But, unknowingly, they overdosed and he got sick. They had already cracked his ribs and taken out one lung, and then he had to deal with this. I was there when he died. Unfortunately, it was a quite uncomfortable death for him. He didn't go easily. I remember feeling sick at the thought of being in the same house as a corpse. Can you imagine? This was my father and I was thinking of him as a corpse! But anyhow, I still get confused.
>
> Female, 15

I ask for a show of hands and discover that one-third of the students in the class has had to deal with the loss of someone their own age or younger—brothers, sisters, schoolmates, or friends.

> I think that the one thing that I can relate to best is death. My father died when I was six years old. For years I hated the world. I could never get close to anybody. When I was in the eighth grade I lost my only boyfriend to cancer, a football player whom I loved very much, and over the years have lost two very close friends to the senseless cruelty of the streets. Both shot down in cold blood, both very near my heart. However, several times in my life I have been very near death. I'm not scared of it happening to me, but I wish my friends could live forever. If I knew I [was] going to die, I'd plan to spend what was left of my life doing what I wanted, being with those I loved.
>
> Female, 14

Death is something I find very hard to accept because eight months ago my boyfriend was killed in a very tragic way and it's still hard for me to deal with. He was killed over money, ten damn dollars. He was very special to me because he was basically my first love and I can't explain my feelings but I loved him very much and still do. A lot of people fail to realize that after a person has died, or just gone away from your life that you're still going to have feelings for them if the bond of love was strong. Every time I talk about the subject I begin to cry, just the word death upsets me. When I cry it seems that I can never get all of the tears out of my system, but I now realize that life must go on.

The other day when we were talking about death my mind just filled with all of the pain and agony his death caused me. I was really mad when he first died, because he always said that no matter what happens between us, he'd always be there for me, and when he died I felt as if he had lied to me in some sort of way. I think the hardest part for me to accept is realizing that it was the time for him to go and that I know he'd be going to a better place, but at least I'd know that I've always had a special place in his heart because true love never dies, if it's a strong bond.

Female, 16

....

My brother was killed instantly in an automobile accident three years ago—he was just nineteen…. Most people feel bad when somebody dies, they feel like they have lost something they really loved and will never have again. Well I felt worse, because I feel that I never quite had him to lose. The last thing I said to him was "Fuck, no, you can't ride my bike." Of course I didn't know that was the last time I would ever see him. Both him and me had a hard time showing our love. I think that when the time had come for him to die, he was generous enough to help me get over my fear of how to love, and I have come over it. I think that when he died he gave so much to everyone that it is overwhelming. Me and everyone in my family were bettered by his death. My parents especially were changed. They had never gotten along with younger people (generation gap) before his death. But after, they became in touch with themselves and my brother's friends…. I just feel that I never got to know him and when I look at the only picture (recent) we have of him (he is playing the harmonica), his face is blurred, as if he is not really totally alive and I break up in tears, because I know that he was really unhappy because of the way I

ASK ME IF I CARE

treated him. He was kind of the black sheep all the time, but now he would fit in perfectly. Right now I am breaking up in tears, I guess because this is the first time I have ever really realized how much of him and his life slipped out of my hands when he was here. I thought I had gotten it out of my system, but I guess not as you can see by the length of the letter.

Female, 15

Although they initially complained about having to discuss death, after listening to these last few journal entries, many of the students are anxious to talk about the losses in their lives. I am always deeply moved, not only by the profound losses that so many of them have experienced at such a young age, but that they are willing to share their feelings, and often tears, with a group of their peers most of whom they have known for only a few weeks. I remind them of my friend Mike and suggest that writing a letter to the person you miss can help. It's a way to unburden yourself of sorrow or express remorse over things you wish you hadn't said or done (or wish you *had*). Some people use it as a symbolic way of saying good-bye. Many of my former students have included such letters in their journals.

Dear Sister:

I really miss you. When I used to hear about death and violence in the streets, I didn't believe it could happen to someone in my family. You was only nineteen when you was killed three years ago, going out with some of your friends. I will always wonder who killed you, was it your friends, or was it someone off the streets who killed you, and your friends left you to die alone. I never got to tell you how much I really love you. You're gone now and I still can't believe it's true.

Love always,
Your sister
Female, 16

....

Dear T:

There was so much I wanted to tell you. I never gave you a welcome back to Berkeley. We were best buddies in fifth grade but when you left we never wrote or tried to see each other. Face it, we just grew apart from each other. I will always cherish the good times we shared.

When I first found out you were murdered I felt incredible guilt for not being your best buddy again. We had nothing left in common. I cried when you died. I cried for all of your dreams and ambitions. You had so much life ahead of you. I hope you are happy wherever you are. Rest in peace.

I miss you. Really I do.
Love, R.
Male, 15

....

Dear Baby Brother,

I wish you were here with us right now, instead of lying in the ground with your white satin robe on. I wish you were here so I could talk to you and play with you. I was your "big" sister and you were my brother. I loved thinking how it was going to be. I was going to make you one of the best dressed kids on the block. I gave you one of my favorite stuffed animals...my little mouse named Mortimer. I wish you could have met him. He was grey with pink ears. You would have enjoyed his company. He was in your bassinet waiting for your arrival. But since you never came home again I had to put him away, back in the closet.

Baby Brother, I miss you so much! I'm glad you're resting though. Because it hurt me so much to see you hooked up to those machines that breathed for you. It was so artificial looking. I wanted to hold you close to me and smell your "baby smell." We do have pictures of you, so we'll always be thinking of you. We buried you very close to home so we will be able to visit you often. Last week we planted flowers for you. Baby Brother, I love you so much and you'll always have a place in my heart.

Love always,
Your sister
Female, 16

Dear Brother,

I will try and write this letter without breaking up in tears. As I guess you already know grandaddy died a couple of months ago. I don't want this to sound like I am blaming it on you because I am not. The day you died grandaddy's health started to go downhill. He hadn't even found out yet. I want you to know that he really loved you as I do and everyone else does. I think that your death left an empty space in his heart. It sure did in mine.

Brother, I want you to know that I think you had a lot to offer and I am really sorry that I didn't take it, instead I took the pleasure out of it. As you and I both know you had a bad temper, but I think that you had so much love to give that it got all bundled up inside of you and when you asked for help and didn't get it your love was rejected. Yes, I remember the many times you teased me and at the time I was hurt. But you didn't hurt me half as much as I hurt you, when I didn't appreciate your love you had to give. I was too dense to see it. You would probably be so amazed at the change in mother and daddy, that you might even get along with them. I hope you are happy now, because I think people are unbearably unhappy when they die.... I love you and I wish I had gotten to know you. Please be good to yourself in your next lives to come. I will never forget you and I will never stop loving you, and I will never stop crying for you. If we meet again in another life or even in this one, please let me know it is you so I can tell you in person. If you feel like it, anytime you want I am here so you can talk to me. I would really like to be in touch with you and communicate to you. Somehow you seem to be alive to me, yet not quite within reach. I think of you constantly and I am frustrated by your constant hovering over my mind. I feel you are around at all times. I miss you.

Love,
Your sister
Female, 15

....

Dear J.

I really miss you, man. Really. When I first heard about your accident, I was so shocked, and upset, and angry. You wouldn't believe how much

I cried. I really wish we could finish our photography book and maybe get it published. I'll still try to do it for both of us.

I just heard that B., the guy driving the car, showed up at school the day after you died—WITH A BRAND NEW BMW AND A SMILE ON HIS FACE!! I was fuckin' amazed. I know the accident could have happened while anybody was driving, I mean, shit, who doesn't speed. I'd still like to kick B.'s ass! What an asshole. He got my best friend killed and shows up at school with a new car and a smile!?!

FUCK!

I really wish I could talk to you again. Just so I could tell you how much I really love you. Still. Even though you're gone. You're still my best friend and I'll never have a friend as special to me as <u>you</u> are. You knew me so well. And I knew you. I love you man. I'll see you in my dreams!

Love,
Male, 16

He imagines his friend's response:

Dear T.

I'm sorry for flaking on you that day at the BART station but I had other things on my mind that I couldn't change—no matter what. I wish I had worn my damn seat belt. Fuck. I got your letter and don't worry man, I know that I was your best friend and you were mine. We had the greatest friendship man. It was so cool. Sorry I had to die. But I love you man. Always.

Oh! By the way I saw Ghost, the movie, they show a lot of movies up here in heaven. Just kidding. Being dead is so peaceful, man. It's not as bad as I thought. Don't get me wrong, man, I'd much rather be alive but it's not as bad as I thought. Anyway I gotta tell you something. Try your best to take care of my mom for me. Don't forget about her. My dad too, man. Take care of them. Oh, yeah, don't go kick B.'s ass just because he's an asshole. I know—I'd love to kill him too, but he can't help it. He's a joke man, forget about him. But hey, remember me always!! Don't forget about US (ME and YOU).

Love,
Your friend always
J.

Monday was the second year anniversary of your death. I miss you so much G., but your death also taught me so much. Why the fuck did you have to drive that night, drunk, 80 mph around that curve? I thought you were smarter than that, G. I used to cry because your life wasn't meant to be taken so soon. I hate to sound like a bitch, G., but what you did was so fuckin stupid, it's almost like you asked for it. When you left me, my life was OVER (so it seemed)—everything was so superficial—nothing was stable or secure. Now, the worst part about it is, I feel like even though I was shown the horror of drunk driving, I can't pass on my knowledge to anyone. I try to keep people from doing it, and I can't. I feel so helpless—I've gotten into millions of fights with people because they want to drive after they've been drinking. Can't they see how much it hurts me? Can't they see the hole in my heart that is so empty, so black without you. G., you were my dream husband. I had planned to marry you. I loved you so much. You were the best person—I love you still. I really can't cry over you too much anymore? I actually can't really even think about you very much anymore—it's all too painful. I really do miss you and I know that you're in heaven, in peace. Please take care of yourself now.

Love always,
Female, 17

By the time I finish this last series of letters, everyone is feeling rather depressed. In some classes, the mood is too heavy, and I don't even read them all. Sometimes I'll substitute a few letters about pets who have died: there's sadness here, too, but it is not so intense. I usually preface the reading by saying that it's perfectly normal to grieve for our animals and that the process is just the same as when a person we care about dies. Since pets can give unconditional love (they don't care if you have bad breath, get D's or F's, or don't clean up your room), their absence can be a terrific loss. In fact, some of my students have said that they felt far more of a loss over the death of their cat or dog than they did over a relative. We seldom recognize that people need to grieve over the loss of any object, animate or inanimate, that has meaning to them, and that includes animals. When a pet dies, there is little public acknowledgment, if any, and the grief can be compounded because it is not shared.

Dear Kimmy,

Wherever you are I love you! We love you! You were the best pet anyone could ever ask for. You were the queen of the house and I love all the moments you gave me your love when I was down. When you died a piece of me died with you. I love you Kimmy, I love you. I'm crying now and I'll have to say see you later. I'm praying for you. I love you!

Male, 15

....

Last year right before finals, my cat was killed by a car. It was the only death I'd experienced. I'd raised that cat for five years. My grief was unbearable. I still haven't gotten over it totally, but I got a new kitten this fall. This is one problem that did have a happy ending.

Male, 15

....

I have never had the experience of a very close person dying. However, last Easter my cat died. You may not think this is such a big thing, but I was almost as close to him as I was to the rest of my family. I had him for 12 years and though we couldn't talk to each other, I felt we could communicate. Unfortunately, he got cancer and had to be put to sleep. I had grown up with him and spent almost all of my life with him and I doubt I will ever be as close to another animal again. As for how I was affected, I handled it better than I thought I would. My whole family was very upset. I still miss him.

Male, 15

....

My favorite pet was my bunny named Puffin. He was a runt and he was soo little! He was angora. He was all brown and really fuzzy, except he had grey ears, a grey tail and little grey feet. His fur was soo long I had to comb it and I kept all the hairs that came out in the comb. I have a big bag full and some day I'm gonna make a pillow in his honor. He was the absolute sweetest guy, he was soo cuddly. When Puffin died I cried for days. I buried him in our backyard and I wouldn't let anyone near. And then (now when I think about it, it's kinda gross but...) I picked some ivy leaves from his favorite place to play, two flowers, and (this is the gross part) a handful of his little poops and put them all in a jar. I kept the jar by my bed until the poops molded.

Female, 16

Losing a loved one is always a time of great sorrow, but when the death is the result of a suicide, it adds another dimension to the grief. Even as people are grieving over the loss, they may feel angry, betrayed, or abandoned. They may also feel guilty, as if somehow they could have prevented this from happening but failed. If there was no apparent reason for the suicide, lingering questions as to *why* may make it hard for the survivors to work through their grief.

It is not uncommon for students to share in class that a close relative or friend died as a result of suicide. Even more common are journal entries on this painful loss. I tell the class that we will talk about suicide prevention later on in the course, but I want to read the following entries now to give a sense of the devastation left behind when someone takes their own life. There is a tendency to romanticize suicide; I hope that what I read will put this act of self-destruction in better perspective.

Dear R.

That's what everybody used to call you because you were such a tough guy. No one ever expected this from you. You were such a sweet man and a great person, a joy to be around. You brought a smile to people's faces whenever they saw you. You never seemed to be upset, you always looked happy. I guess that has something to do with why you killed yourself. I suppose you were hurting on the inside and just not letting it slip to the outside. You should have seen your funeral on Monday, all those people there cared about you, they loved you. I used to go over and play with your son everyday. The three of us would often go and play baseball or football together. So why the fuck did you have to go and kill yourself. You had so many friends that you could have talked to. They all would have listened. I still can't believe you're dead. At this time of the year you would normally be helping out with Little League and getting ready for a summer full of your favorite activity, sports. I wish I could bring you back and show you how much other people cared about you. Then maybe you would think that you had made a mistake when you killed yourself.

Male, 15

....

My father was an extremely intelligent man; he taught history in college and he sat for long solemn hours at a chess game with his brother, he could compose the funniest line on the spur of the moment, and I admired him very much. But later I saw murky dark sides of him which lowered my respect for him (perhaps for myself, too) and was my basic introduction to the ongoing eternal process of trying to figure out the human being at large.

Exactly four years from today he said good-bye and jumped, putting an end to all his qualities leaving only vague memories and vivid emotions where a person used to stand. So that's my father.

Female, 16

A few years ago, one of my students offered to bring in her personal diary and read parts of it to the class. We had been talking about suicide in class, and our discussions had triggered her memories about a friend who had committed suicide. She wanted to share her thoughts with us:

In Social Living today we talked about STRESS and suicide. Mark, I miss you and knowing that you're around. I mean, if you were still alive I very well might have never seen you this year…but just knowing you're alive would be enough…just to know you were still out in the universe being your cheerful self, or maybe not, maybe feeling down one day—but eventually getting up—hey, that's okay, we all feel down—we all feel low, deep into the dregs of the earth of the world of ourselves, down and depressed, down and out, below low—yet we don't go so low and drift and drift so far—dislocating bonds of love, friendship, potential happiness, hope, support—trust—we don't pull in-in-in-inward until we can't see this love and hope and happiness and high times and success and opportunity and wonders of this wondrous universe and life and life dammit and life—we don't fucking kick the face of life—throw dirt in the eyes, the caring, gentle eyes of life—why did you man— why? why? It pains, literally, physically pierces and gouges my entire person and soul.... I feel in the dark—I feel miscommunication 'cause if you weren't able to receive and hear my call, your family's and friends' call of happiness of your being here with us on this planet at this time...well you must have had a misinterpretation of a major, major size—or maybe it was something that was gnawing at your gut day in and day out, some little creature of undescribable intensity and influence.... Maybe this was some lesson—some lesson, eh?! Like someone had to do this—someone significant/special/outstanding/unexpected had to shock us/scare us/confuse use/pain us/harden us/make us think and ask questions/maybe someone will write a book, maybe someone will become a therapist, maybe this will give me a real true emotion I've felt to draw from for my Oscar-award-winning performance—well, you can fuck that—take the Oscar—I WANT MARK. I WANT YOU. It wasn't worth it. It wasn't fair. It's not fair—who said life was fair?

My parents hate each other's guts—who said life was fair?

My SAT scores weren't 1600s—who said life was fair? I'm getting a B+ in English and a B in math—who said life was fair?

Drugs are rampant and crime is high—who said life was fair?

People in our city are starving and mentally ill with no place to live, no food to eat, no place to get psychiatric help—who said life was fair?

I have no control over nuclear war—who said life was fair?

The guy I was going to go to the prom with when I came down with the chicken pox is Mark. The same Mark I've been talking about. Who said life was fair? At the young age of 17 he threw his life away, but hey—who said life was fair?

Female, 15

....

Dear Papa,

When I look at pictures of you and me together when I was a baby, the expressions you had on your face looked like you loved me so much. I have nothing but good memories about you.... But if you loved me as much as it seemed like you did, how could you fucking kill yourself? I've thought of suicide more than once, more than even twenty times, but I couldn't do that to the people I love. It makes me wonder if you were really the wonderful person I think you were. You fucked my brother completely. He went from a happy, cute little boy to a man who thinks constantly of suicide, draws artwork of death, monsters, and killing, and is just about the most unstable person I know. I used to have nightmares that your ghost came back and I didn't know what to do because I knew it was a ghost and not the real you. I can't talk about you without crying, I can't even write about you without crying. Did you even think about your kids when you did it? All my life I've felt nothing but sadness for you, but now when I think about it, who the fuck do you think you are? Didn't you care about anyone but yourself? Your entire family is still suffering. Your parents, my mom, and especially me and my brother. Didn't you even want to watch us grow up? There have been so many times in my life when I wanted a daddy so bad, and all I had was a shitty stepfather who molested me. I

don't even know what else to say to you because you didn't even give me a chance to know you. I don't know if I should end this letter with I love you, or shove it up your ass. I guess both.

Female, 17

As angry and frustrated as she was at the time, she was eventually able to come to terms with her feelings. Many years later, she wrote to tell me how she was doing:

I have a job that I love, I'm finishing school where I'm planning on getting a teaching credential, and I have a wonderful relationship with a guy who is truly the best. The point I want to make is that my problems did not just go away. The reason I am where I am is very hard work. I had a lot of therapy and dealt with a lot of hard times. You have to really want to help yourself, and it's not fun when you're in the process. One very important thing I've learned is that there are some things that will <u>never</u> go away, I am going to miss my dad forever. I still have days where I hate him for not being here. But at the same time I am resolved to the fact that I will always feel this way.

Feelings don't go away, but they get better, and easier to deal with as time goes on. I think anyone has the power to be happy and have a good life. You just have to want it bad enough to do it.

Female, 23

Frequently when we are talking about death, we will also get into discussion on guardian angels, communicating with those who have died, reincarnation, near-death experiences, and life after death. Many students have strong beliefs due to personal experiences or because someone in their family has described an incident. When I first taught Social Living, one of my students told me that her mother had "visited" her shortly after her death. She said her mom appeared in her bedroom and told her not to be afraid, that she was safe in heaven. She said this was very comforting to her. This was the first time anyone had ever told me of such an experience, but since then, I have heard countless similar stories from my students. Today, the discussion bounces around from haunted houses to donating organs, and as the bell rings, a football player asks, "How much can I get *right now* if I donate my body to science." There are some joking remarks directed toward him, and I'm thankful that the mood has been lightened as everyone heads for their next class.

12 | Self-Image, Stress, and Suicide

SOME PEOPLE WONDER WHY I bother with the topic of self-image or self-esteem, since I am always complaining about how much material I have to squeeze into the nine-week session. My answer is that having a healthy self-image is every bit as important as understanding the facts about sex and drugs. It seems to me that people who have major problems steering their way through life, or who get into serious trouble, almost invariably suffer from poor self-esteem. At its worst, the problem can manifest itself in antisocial or self-destructive behavior or in severe depression and suicidal tendencies. On the other hand, people who have a strong positive sense of themselves generally lead much happier lives. They rarely suffer from eating disorders, are less likely to become alcohol- or drug-dependent, are able to handle stress well, and get along well with other people. If there are stresses, they believe they can deal with them (or will forgive themselves if they can't). If their bodies aren't "perfect," they can accept that, and a negative comment doesn't mean the end of the world.

If only there were a way to inject everyone with a strong positive self-image! But the world just wasn't built that way. So many of my students are burdened with problems that would undermine almost anyone's self-confidence—the kinds of things we've been talking about in class—violence, alcoholic parents, sexual abuse, fathers who have disappeared from their lives. And I have had far too many students tell me (often in front of the whole class) that their mothers told them they were not wanted, that they should have been aborted, or that they were a "mistake."

I'm not sure there's any way to repair the damage from that kind of psychological abuse, but I do what I can in my classes to help my students build self-esteem and inner strength. I always treat each student with respect, always give positive reinforcement and support, both in talking to them and in the comments I write in their journals.

Describe yourself...how do you see yourself? Explain how your outer and inner images differ. How do others see you?

Sometimes when I announce the journal topic for the day, I get a few mild complaints, but when I assign the topic of self-image, the objections seem the most heartfelt. Over and over, my students have told me that they find this topic one of the hardest to deal with. "I don't know what kind of impression I make—*you* tell *me*." I acknowledge that it is not an easy question and urge them to do the best they can. As usual, I turn to my collection of student writings for inspiration, starting with some very positive entries.

Some students seem to radiate self-confidence: they may realize they have a few faults but feel good about themselves anyway. Where do these students get their high self-esteem? My guess is that it comes from home where, from a very early age, they no doubt received a lot of love, affection, and positive reinforcement. It is always refreshing to read these entries:

I like a lot of things about myself. Heh heh heh. But most of all, I like my ability to communicate on a more mature level when I need to. I like to be able to make a good impression on people that have a lot of influence in my life. My teachers, my parents, my employer, etc. This is something that will help me be somebody when I'm older. It already has helped me a lot in high school. Being able to talk to my teachers in private and be respectable really makes a good impression and makes them think more highly of me. It also works with my parents. They give me respect when I give it to them (which actually isn't that often).
Male, 15

How do I see myself? Well, I see myself as a lot better person than I was last year at this time. My haircut did a lot for me because cutting off all that excess shit opened up the real me. I am totally myself and no one else. I set trends/styles that people follow and I don't give a fuck what anybody thinks of me. I'm very honest and sensual. It's very important to me that I don't lie to myself or anyone else. I think I have a great body except for the fact that I'd rather be naked than wear clothes and I wish I could lose about ten pounds. I guess I am self-conscious but I'm normally not insecure. Sometimes I think that if I could lose that ten pounds I'd be damn near perfect. But I am pretty happy with myself as of now. I'm often asked if I'm a model and told how pretty I am—so I assume—well, I know I'm attractive. My life is pretty satisfying.

Female, 16

I like myself. I don't fully understand my emotions and ways, but I try. I think of myself as a young black beautiful woman, with the same chance in life as a young yellow or white beautiful woman. I feel that I can reach my goals in life if I put forth effort. I don't believe in three points off for being black. I think that a person is a life and it is regardless of skin color, sex, or age…. Each can do what we really want to do. We are all equal as human beings.

Female, 16

I see myself as a tree growing. With each new branch a direction taken, I become more enlightened. I learn every day what is right and wrong for myself. I am always trying to better myself. Whether it be physically (with exercise), or it be mentally (education & life experience), I am striving to develop a strong existence. I am a positive person & a person with good morals. I try not to worry about how others view me. If I'm not happy with myself, no one else can make a difference. If I am satisfied and happy with myself, then my feeling will spread and transmit that message to others. If I transmit this message of confidence, others usually cannot view me in a negative manner.

Male, 18

I like the way I dress and look, and if other people don't like it, that doesn't bother me, cuz if I'm satisfied then their criticisms are only secondary to my feelings, usually it's their own insecurities reflecting on how they feel about themselves.

Female, 14

....

This is a hard topic for me because I'm never really sure what outer image I project. I know that I have a lot of friends but I'm not sure how they see me. I often try to figure it out but it's hard. Discussing my inner image is also difficult because I'm a teenager that about says it all. Like most teenagers I'm sometimes frustrated with school, guys, friends, clothes, beauty, my parents, and especially my body. There are times when I feel great about my body and other times when I just hate it. It could happen overnight, at night I could look in the mirror and think "gosh I wish I could look this good all of the time," and then in the morning, look in the same mirror and [feel like I] look horrible. Sometimes when I eat right/healthy and exercise and not stuff myself I feel wonderful.

Female, 15

> *To fall in love with one's self*
> *is the beginning of a lifelong romance.*
> —OSCAR WILDE

Most teens worry about being too fat. The next writer is unusual in that she feels good about her body, even though her stomach is not flat. I find it refreshing in this day and age where other women are doing hundreds of stomach crunches to tighten their stomach muscles (Demi Moore reportedly does 2,500 a week, Shannen Doherty, 1,250).

My clothes usually reflect my inner feelings. When I feel energetic and happy I wear bright colors and full skirts that swish and flash when I skip. When I'm tired or unhappy I wear darker colors, and I tend to hide behind my hair (if I lean forward my hair covers my face). I like my body, especially my tummy. A lot of why I like my tummy is 'cuz its round curve reminds me that someday I will carry babies in my womb (I hope!). I appear to most people to be giving and "sweet" (yearbook phrase I often see) and happy. I am most of the time. I feel more together during the summer. That's when I sleep enough, exercise properly, eat properly.

Female, 16½

My greatest strength lies in the maturity I have for the slim number of years I have had to gain knowledge and experience. At a very early age I related to people very well, and I never allowed other people to stray me away into any trouble. Unlike most people, peer groups never bothered me, I don't fall into trends easily, for I have very good judgment as to what is bad, good, stupid or stylish. In fact some of my peers hated me or rather resented me for this. But most looked up to me for the same reasons and I always made friends easily.

Male, 15

I'd like to believe that I'm a leader, that's most important to me. I'm strong, both physically and mentally, and have a deep relationship with G-d. I pray a lot, not always in Hebrew, but usually sincerely. I suppose many people would classify me as power hungry or egotistical, but I am proud also of my sensitive qualities. I believe in the last few years, a time when many teenagers experience confusion, I have matured. I used to be very afraid of social situations and therefore try to act tough to camouflage this fear. Fortunately, I have grown up before I got into real trouble. I attribute this increased maturity to my father, a very intelligent person, and an excellent role model.

The little boy qualities in me are released on the football field. I love football.... I don't think it's insulting G-d to say that football is a religious experience. It combines everything I adore: pain, love, and leadership. I love the players on my team, and often get into fights defending them.

I list as my weaknesses fear, a lack of modesty, and self-consciousness. I feel, however, that my good qualities outweigh the bad, and I hope to pass on the good qualities that my father passed on to me to my children.

Male, 15½

My strongest personal power is my self-satisfaction—it's not to mean that I'm always satisfied with myself—but that I don't need to occupy my time being with other people all the time.... I like being alone. I can always keep myself busy drawing, reading magazines, playing the piano and just plain "thinking." I don't feel guilty if I stay home alone on a Saturday nite, watching TV and eating, while my other friends are out partying and having a ball. That is not to say that I'm a loner. I love to be with my friends. But I don't need to have someone to be with all the time. I'm pretty proud of that. I think that people who always have to be with someone, must be really insecure about themselves. Being alone is great. I get to know myself better that way.

Female, 16

My inside and my outside are as different as night and day. Although not different at all. I never really view my body. I feel like I am not writing this paper, I am not looking out of these eyes. I am merely a spirit, a soul floating above myself. I am not completely satisfied with my body, it is a little overweight but sometimes I love the way the highlights in my hair glimmer in the sun, or the way my skin looks after I've been hiking in the sunshine. I am at peace with my higher self. I am bold and outgoing. I google at strange babies and introduce myself to attractive people that I get good feelings about. I am friends with almost everyone in the school and I love my neighbors. The world is full of beauty, and I always give everyone a chance. I care and I give. Sometimes too much. Unfortunately, sometimes I end up roping people into caring about me, and they stick to me like glue and I end up having to tell them to back off, because I not only love being with people, I also love being with myself. My music expresses the beauty, the pain, the sorrow I feel. When I sing I don't think about my past....

Female, 15

When I sense that I'm losing the class, I begin to read some entries that are not so overwhelmingly cheerful, letters that most of my students are actually more likely to identify with. I comment that appearances can be deceiving, that many of us walk around with masks on. Time and again, the students I perceive as confident and outgoing will describe themselves as insecure, while someone who appears to me to be unhappy will write about their contentment.

Who am I? On the outside I'm a happy, giving, friendly, shy person. Basically a normal teen who seems to have the normal teen problems. I share a lot of my feelings but never do get "down right dirty" and spit 'em all out. On the inside I see myself as a complete failure striving to find something I can fit in with and accomplish. Even when I do accomplish something I always question myself, wondering whether or not what I'm doing is what I really want to be doing. Sometimes I feel like I should just put myself and everyone else out of misery and kill myself. But that would just prove that I'm a failure and I'd only be giving up. Giving up on me, my friends, my family, and the whole world. Sometimes I get so confused with myself and everyone around me that I feel like I'm going crazy. Especially since my whole family is already crazy. As bad as I am, I must be the best in my broken and demented home.

With my mom, brother, and stepfather all dope fiends and a father that never has time for me, I feel alone inside. I feel like no one knows exactly what I'm going through and how it affects me. Especially when she smokes that SHIT in front of me. I can't imagine anyone's mother smoking/sniffing speed or any drug in front of their child. And the fact that she got my brother hooked and offers it to me really pisses me off. But there's not a whole lot I can do. She's not going to listen to me. The fact that I was unexpected and somewhat unwanted makes me feel even more unloved and rejected by society and my family, especially my mother. I know she loves me but it seems more like a guilt love than a true love. I just can't handle that but I can't handle downing a bottle of pills either. So I guess I'll just suffer or deal with it the best way possible.

Female, 16

On the outside I appear to be a smart, attractive, social, organized, happy girl who has a lot going for her. On the inside I feel rejected, sad, lonely, isolated, fat, dumb, unpopular, ugly, and most of all naive. I don't always feel this way. I mean I always think these things when I'm depressed (about 60% of the time) but when I'm happy these thoughts are only in my subconscious. I am very, very hard on myself. I am never satisfied with anything I do because I am a perfectionist. I hate myself for being so damned neurotic, paranoid, sensitive, and hypocritical. I find myself telling people "Hey, life's hard, take it easy, you're too hard on yourself." I don't even come close to doing this myself though. But ya know Nancy, sometimes I really am happy and am able to accept myself. I switch back and forth, it's like I'm in between stages of development during these good ol' motherfucking adolescent years. Maybe in ten years I'll look back on these confusing circles I've been running in and say, "Hey, it was good exercise." Until then I say, "Take that, world." But it's not the world's fault. It's my fault for being so immature. And here I go again running in circles—circles—circles.

Female, 15

....

I am very athletic, intelligent, pretty, and popular. I have many trophies (forty-nine to this day) for track, tennis, cross-country, and basketball. This is the outside person! Inside I am insecure. This I often cover up by being bold, and acting mean. In order to not let anyone see inside me, understand the REAL me, I act mean. At school, everyone wants to be me the athlete's friend, but what about ME, the person. These are the kinds of things I keep deep inside my heart. When I am at home I am extremely sensitive, and I go into my room and cry a lot. I think I am insecure because I grew up with a mother who was sometimes there, but for the most part not. My father was always there for me, but I needed to have my mother show love toward me, it always seemed like she hated me.

Female, 15

....

I am extremely self-driven, very perfectionistic. I am by society's standards very successful. I am intelligent, have very good grades, am athletic, artistic, pretty, talented, popular. I have a string of awards plus honors attached to my name. I've done all sorts of volunteer work, and have accomplished many notable things. I tend to excel at most everything I do. Inwardly I am very stressed, not very happy, sort of a bitch. I tend to manipulate people. I rarely show emotions in public, except sometimes anger, and very rarely share my problems. When I am alone I sometimes cry, have temper tantrums, sulk, or do destructive things to myself such as cut my hair, or throw up. I rarely live up to my expectations, am very rarely satisfied, and am often frustrated and angry.

Female, 17

Rejection

I am a 17-year-old mother-to-be. Other than me being pregnant most people seem to think I have things pretty much under control. No matter what happens, my mother seems to know what to do. She keeps telling me to strive for perfection and that I'm too fat, I need to go on a diet, and all that stuff. I tell her that I'm just fine just the way I am.

But on the inside, I'm screwed completely. I can't seem to live up to anyone's expectations, not even my own. I don't even make expectations for myself anymore. I live for my Mom and try to live up to what she wants me to be. I know that I'll never have a model perfect body or something near my mother's. I'm not smart enough, nor cute enough just for my mom to be at least somewhat satisfied. The only thing that made her happy was that I was graduating early. But not for long. She makes me so insecure that I only feel comfortable when I'm by myself. And even then her voice enters my brain saying "Look at those ham hocks. You have too many marks on your body. If you knew how to keep your legs closed you wouldn't be pregnant now. You eat just like a pig. Just look at you."

And so on. And listening to this basically all my life makes me feel like I wasn't meant to be.

Female, 17

This last letter illustrates how rejection and constant criticism can damage the self-image to the point where the person on the receiving end begins to feel like a nonperson, as if they "weren't meant to be." This is a vicious form of psychological abuse, especially when it comes from a parent.

Of course we must all deal with a certain amount of rejection in the course of our lives, and most of us can handle it pretty well.

The following story is a work of fiction. Any resemblance between the characters and real people is purely coincidental.

...We heard it all: Geek, Nerd, Dork, Fool, Dufus, Suck Up, "Get a life" "Don't you have any fun?" "Your best friend is a calculator, isn't it?" "You're such a teacher's pet, you know that?" "Add a little fun to your life" "You don't get out much, do you?" and the ever-so-witty "I went out with some friends last weekend and got falling down drunk, what did you do?" So, naturally, I was inclined to pass this off like I did all the other times. But there was something about this day, something that made me decide to finally react and tell him—and anybody else he'd gossip to—exactly what I thought of his eternal question—the 37 million peso question.

I was still thinking at the speed of light, but now my thoughts turned to the present and how I'd phrase my answer. I knew the question was purely rhetorical...and I was sure I was expected to fold under the "emotional strain" it presented to a wimp like me,...to counterattack with a generic insult, only to be left with a dumb look on my face. "Nah," I mumbled to myself, "I think I'll choose my own answer." So, I opened my mouth and replied...

"Why do you and your friends insist on constantly asking me that question? Exactly what purpose does it serve to you? I mean, you seem to pride yourself on having a life—in fact, you've made that very clear to the entire school, so how, how is it possible for you to have such a fulfilling life if you spend half your time putting down 'dorks' like me and my friends? Are you that unstable and insecure that you need to put yourself above others to give yourself that boost of pride you so desperately need to uphold your reign of arrogance? Sure, it's true that I don't have a life in your sense of the word, but why don't you try this: Next time you start to act so high and mighty, stop and think—if your brain hasn't been too atrophied by years of dormancy—think of which people are the ones who, while you carry on with your pitiful acts of so-called defiance, argue with teachers, fight the system, and have absolutely no regard for the rules of modern-day teenage society. When you're done with that, think of yourself, and what you are. Do you actually think for yourself? Are you really the rebel against authority that you make yourself out to be? Or do you just "go with the flow"? Maybe you might realize that you're not really much at all, you're stuck in a state of suspended adolescence—no matter what you do, it's not really you. Someday you'll realize that you—and me—don't know everything, someday you'll figure out that you have 70 or 80 more years to live, and that life is more than just parties, music, cars, and those 'trendy' arguments with your parents that you love so much to brag about, and then, and only then might you break out of your present existence and really begin to do something with yourself—

something you can actually call your own.... Have a great summer!"
With that I left him either to acknowledge my words or to just let
them pass through the void of his mind. Whichever choice he made, I
didn't care—I'd had my say. When I looked back about twenty feet
away from him I saw he was still standing there with a dumb look on
his face—nothing unique.

Male, 14

....

I am afraid of rejection from girls. Over the years I have some rejection,
but I can deal with it. Girls are sometimes very funny. They look at you
and judge you in thirty seconds without even talking to you. I know if a
girl would stop looking at the way I dress and gave me a half of a
chance, I could show that I am a fantastic person inside.

Male, 17

Whenever I hear the word rejection I am reminded of two things. One
is the Ziggy cartoon which states: "If you're not rejected at least three
times a day, you're not really trying." The other is a personal story of
rejection I told when I first started to teach Social Living and then I
promptly forgot. Years later I ran into a parent who said, "The only
thing my son remembered from your class was the story you told about
your graduation night experience." So now I always try to tell this story
in case someone else finds it comforting!

I was not invited to my senior ball at Los Angeles High but that did
not bother me. However, I really did want to go to Disneyland on grad
night, when the park was only open to groups of graduating high school
students. I asked six or seven guys to accompany me (it felt more like
dozens), but they all said they had other commitments. Finally, a friend
of a friend did say yes. We arrived at Disneyland around 10:00 P.M.,
and within twenty minutes, the guy had deserted me—dumped me, van-
ished. Somehow I managed to pull myself together, telling myself that
"he had done me wrong" and it wasn't my fault. Years later we ended
up running into each other. He now has a beautiful wife and three kids,
and I forgave him for ditching me.

To me, life is meant to be experienced and you can't let fear of failure and rejection immobilize you. I always share with students my most

current rejection—like applying for a Fulbright and not getting it. Successes are fun to share but I think it is also important to model disappointment and the handling of rejection. I add that anyone who has been turned down is in good company because Elvis, the Beatles, Marilyn Monroe, and many, many others were rejected over and over before they achieved their goals and dreams.

Body Image

For teens, whose bodies are going through radical changes, the issue of how they look is typically a vital aspect of their self-image and a source of great stress. In fact, for many, their appearance almost amounts to an obsession:

Dear Mirror,

I wish you'd stop lying to me. Every day I wake up and look into your face hoping against hope that you'd finally reflect my true deadly sexy appearance, but instead you insist on lying. You show me a new zit on my face every day. You show me my legs as being skinny with knobby knees. Once I woke up feeling great and you showed me a scratch on my face I never remember getting. I'd take a hammer and smash you into pieces with it, but I'm afraid of the seven years of bad luck it would bring.

Definitely Not Yours and Completely Fed Up.
Male, 15

....

Dear Glasses:

Thank you for helping me see better but I don't really like you as much as I thought. You make me look like a nerd (I do like to be a nerd but not look like one). Sometimes, I feel like because of you there, that's why nobody looks at me. But if you aren't there then I couldn't even notice that nobody looks at me. I wish I don't have to wear you but I want to be your friend.

Female, 15

....

Dear Makeup,

I hate the way I have come to depend upon you, but I'm glad you're around. I love putting you on in the morning—you are an aesthetic and psychological boost for me. I know it's silly, but I _feel_ better when you're on. I wish I was one of those people with "natural makeup" on all the time—you know, the kind with beautiful dark eyelashes, naturally red lips, and built-in eyeliner, but if everyone was like that, Maybelline would go bankrupt.

I won't even leave the house without putting you on now. I sound like a foolish victim of advertising, but you do make a huge difference in how I look. Let's keep it our secret how different I look without you, okay? Besides, I wouldn't want to scare anyone when I left the house in the morning now would I?

Love,
Female, 15 (your always faithful customer)

Dear Fat,

Do you know how much trouble you are always causing me? I hate you so goddam much that I just want to take a butcher knife and stab you to death! I thought about it thousands of times before but I didn't do it. So I've been on many diets before to get you the hell away from me but it just didn't work. What does it take to kill you! I don't have enough money to get that liposuction done and diets are too fucking hard!! You make it hard to buy clothes that fit and be in fashion at the same time. The only type of clothes made for people who are fat are those ugly big gabardine fabrics. Also people are always calling me names because of your stupid ass. I hate you so fucking much. Bitch. And boys, no boys want a fat ugly girlfriend. They want one of those Christie Brinkley, Whitney Houston-looking girls. So it's been hard to get one that likes me for who I am, not for what size I wear.

Female, 15

....

I know that a lot of people see me as pretty, smart, nice, etc., and I know some people who are jealous of me because of that. Sometimes I wish they would just look a little deeper. Actually, I wish that all the time. I'm tired of being liked because of my looks. I wish that guys wouldn't harass me, and I wish girls wouldn't talk about me behind my back. Some people think because I'm blond and blue-eyed, I can't possibly be smart or amount to anything besides being a cheerleader, which I would never do because I find it demeaning to women. I'm sure I get better grades than everyone that thinks that. I have a lot of pretty bad things in my past that people assume would never happen to me. They can't understand why "someone like her" would be depressed or unhappy with her life. It bothers me that people assume so many things about me without cause. Sometimes it bothers me so much that I get really depressed and then people think I'm a bitch, which doesn't make it any better.

Female, 14

I like to comment that physical beauty can create its own problems. As another of my students wrote, "I wouldn't ever want to be really, really beautiful, because then that becomes your entire identity, and people view you differently." I had a friend who constantly turned heads when we were out together. She was gorgeous, and extremely talented and intelligent as well. And she often stayed home on weekends. She felt that men were intimidated by her because of her beauty. They probably felt they weren't good enough for her and may also have assumed that she already had a boyfriend and that she must be a snob. They may also have thought she must not be very smart.

The talk turns to how we arrive at a standard for physical perfection and how easy it is to fall into the trap of comparing ourselves to the ideal images we see in magazines, newspapers, movies, and on TV. Then, when we look in the mirror, all we see are our imperfections and flaws. We're too fat, too thin, too tall, too short, ugly…. I tell my class that yesterday I glanced at some magazine covers in a bookstore—*Cosmopolitan, Essence, Vogue, Elle, GQ, Playboy, Mademoiselle*—and all I saw were perfect faces and perfect

> *No one can make you feel inferior without your consent.*
>
> —ELEANOR ROOSEVELT

bodies. There were no dark circles under the eyes, no pimples or freckles, not an ounce of fat. I show them some spreads from a *Sports Illustrated* swimsuit issue, and for equal time, a few perfect male specimens, such as Marky Mark in a Calvin Klein ad and Sylvester Stallone on the cover of *Vanity Fair*—both featuring bulging muscles. Very few of us will ever look like the models in the magazines—in fact, the models themselves may not look like that either. One girl says that her friend does some modeling and sometimes she does not even recognize this friend in the photo spreads because makeup, lighting, and airbrushing have all gone into creating a new image.

I read a recent article in which the author states that the "preferred female dimensions" (with Cindy Crawford as the example) is 5 feet 9 inches tall and weighs 120 pounds. However, the average American woman is 5 feet 4 inches tall and weighs up to 138 pounds. The author asks, "Why then do we think of the model's weight as *normal?*"

Our discussion goes on to the effect of advertising and its intent. I tell the class some of the things I've learned from a friend of mine who is a director of an advertising firm in San Francisco. He says that the advertiser is out to put the sizzle in the ads and most of them are totally contrived. For instance, women's breasts are sometimes taped together to create cleavage that really isn't there. In over 60 percent of ads, the hands holding the featured product are not the hands of the model whose face and body are shown. My message, of course, is that what you see in an ad may very well be nothing but an illusion created through the magic of editing.

I don't look at you with my eyes, honey,
I look at you with my heart.

—CHICKEN GEORGE

Eating Disorders

Tomorrow we'll have a speaker who is recovering from bulimia, so I want to give my students a little background on eating disorders in preparation for this. We talk about weight problems and crash diets and how they don't work. I stress that much of our body shape and weight is determined by genetics and cannot be altered no matter how much we starve ourselves or work out, and that the only safe and effective way to lose weight is to make sensible changes in our eating habits and to exercise regularly.

Bulimia Danger Signals:

- binging, or eating uncontrollably
- purging by strict dieting, fasting, vigorous exercise, vomiting or abusing laxatives or diuretics in an attempt to lose weight
- using the bathroom frequently after meals
- preoccupation with body weight
- depression or mood swings
- irregular periods
- developing dental problems, swollen cheek glands, heartburn and/or bloating
- experiencing personal or family problems with alcohol or drugs

Anorexia Danger Signals:

- losing a significant amount of weight

- continuing to diet (although thin)
- feeling fat, even after losing weight
- fearing weight gain
- losing monthly menstrual period
- preoccupation with food, calories, nutrition and/or cooking
- preferring to diet in isolation
- exercising compulsively
- binging and purging

One of the girls says that she can't gain weight, and I tell everyone that for some of us it is just as difficult to gain weight as it is for others to lose it. I recall that in junior high school, I was elected Class Pole. I was so skinny—not slender, svelte, or thin, just skinny—that friends threatened to buy me a padded girdle from Frederick's of Hollywood. Straight skirts were in, and I needed some help in keeping mine up. In high school I began to tower over my girlfriends and most of the guys. I hated being tall almost as much as I hated the well-intentioned remarks of my parents and their friends who said, "You're so lucky you're tall. Someday you'll appreciate it." They were right. By the time I was in college, being tall and thin was just fine. It helps if we can learn to accept our bodies as they are, rather than to strive for an unrealistic "ideal."

Most of the students already know something about anorexia, but I read over the list of danger signals for it and make sure they understand that this condition can be fatal. I give a simplistic description of bulimia as a gorging-purging syndrome, usually tied up with a desire to lose weight. Some stressful situation sets this cycle in motion: the person overeats to relieve anxiety, then feels guilty because they've stuffed themselves and gained weight, and then gets rid of the food by forcing themselves to vomit, taking diuretics or laxatives, and/or exercising excessively. Unfortunately, this process can quickly become a habit, and this "perfect solution" can have serious consequences. Not only are there emotional side effects, but it can harm the heart, esophagus, teeth, digestive organs, and other parts of the body. Bulimia is three times more common than anorexia, and it too can be life threatening.

- 1% of teenage girls in the U.S. develop anorexia nervosa and up to 10% of those may die as a result.

- Up to 5% of college women in the U.S. are bulimic.

- Up to 40% of people who are obese may be binge eaters.

Eating disorders are fairly common among teens, and I have many entries that revolve around them:

> When I look at myself I see a well-known girl in high school at the prime of her life. Happy, carefree, and young. My friends always ask me for advice, they think I never have any problems. Yet when I'm at home, I reach into my closet and my biggest problem begins. Pulling out twelve bags of potato chips, and cookies, chocolate by the pound and ice cream that I dash to the store for. The greatest feeling is to be so stuffed I can barely move. Lying there in bed, sadness takes over my body. I know how the world looks upon heavy people. I know how my mother feels about being heavy. Last year she went on a diet, if that's what you want to call it. I never saw her eat food, yes, she ate, if you call eating one thing of yogurt and a slice of cheese eating. After I eat all I could fit into my body, I would roll out of bed and take that long walk to the bathroom. I lock the door and turn on the water, as I relieve all the pain and fear of ever becoming fat or heavy!
>
> P.S. To all of the teenagers that share my problem, and I know I'm not alone, please seek help; if not help, then advice.
>
> Female, 16

I ask if anyone knows why she would turn on the water. Several girls raise their hands and one says, "So that no one will hear her throwing up." There are no outcries of disgust at this, but rather the realization of what she, and so many like her, suffer in privacy.

> It seems to me that most people today have at least heard about anorexia and bulimia, even if they don't really know quite what they are. I think that's great, because people should know about these kinds of things, but with all the books, magazine articles, studies, movies, and whatever else on eating disorders, I feel that people are still leaving out a very important problem: overeating.
>
> At first you may say, hey, that's no big deal, it's not a disorder, just

a bunch of people who need an excuse to be pigs. You may think that it's not up there on the scale with anorexia and bulimia, but let me tell you, from the point of view of someone who's been there, that's not true. It's an addiction, and it is just as bad as any other addiction.

I don't really know where to begin my story. There once was a time when I didn't have problems with food, but that was a long time ago, when I was maybe nine. I wasn't fat as a child, yet I went on my first diet when I was ten or eleven, and since then I've been on and off of diets so many times. There was a time when I was really good at it, too, when my willpower was strong and I could go for days measuring my food and counting calories, restricting myself to perhaps a plain bagel for lunch, an apple for a snack, and a small dinner—sometimes less. I've gone for as long as seventy-two hours without eating. Sometimes after a slip I wouldn't let myself eat for a day or two to make up. I wasn't an anorexic. I was, however, seriously screwing up my eating habits and my thoughts and feelings about food, my body, and myself. I've always been hard on myself, and coping with all my slips OVER THE YEARS made me feel like I couldn't even stick to a diet, a blow to my self-esteem. And because of this, my willpower began to erode and it got that much harder to stick to diets. I'm not really sure why I started to lose my control; it was a gradual thing. I started eating for comfort, out of depression, out of boredom, because the people around me were eating, because it looked too good to pass up even if I wasn't hungry, because I was frustrated, because I was lonely, because I was feeling insecure, because I was mad at myself, because eventually it just became a habit. There are probably other reasons I'm not aware of too. It gets to be a vicious cycle: I'm feeling bad, so I eat. It gets out of control and becomes a binge. And when I stop, I feel guilty and fat, and it reinforces all the bad feelings which caused me to eat in the first place.

Maybe there are some people out there who know how this feels, stuffing yourself even though you're not hungry. Hell, sometimes you get so far that you can't even tell anymore if it's your stomach that's hungry or your heart. You try to fill a void inside of you with food, but it can never work. And you don't have to come from a screwed-up family or anything for this to happen to you. I don't know the cause of my problem and by looking at me you'd probably never even know that I have one. I'm not always depressed—like everyone, I have my up days and my down days. You won't see me stuffing my face at lunchtime; eating disorders are very private things and people learn how to hide it well. I'm not fat, either; maybe I'm ten pounds overweight. I look normal, and I think of myself as pretty normal; I know that I have a problem but I consider my eating disorder a mild one, and I'm trying to correct it myself. I hope that if there are other people in my situation, that they get help. If you can look within and provide the help for yourself, like I'm trying to do, then that's great, but I know it's hard, too. It isn't easy to ask for help, especially [for] someone so stubborn and independent as I am, but if I can't solve my problem myself then I'm prepared to go to an Overeaters Anonymous meeting and see if they can help. I know how hard it is, feeling like you're the only one with your problem—I never even heard the term "compulsive overeater" until a year ago, although I've known of anorexia and bulimia since I was seven or eight.... That's why I wrote this...to let anyone who might be an overeater know that you're not alone.

Female, 16

She was correct in saying "by looking at me you'd probably never even know." She was an active participant in class and dressed in a manner which seemed to me that she felt good about her body.

Eating disorders are not confined to females, I tell my classes, just more common among them. My father told me that he first heard of bulimia in association with jockeys, as they have to keep their weight down. Since I've mentioned this in class, some guys have told me privately that they know wrestlers who purge because weight classification is very important to them.

I am totally obsessed with my weight. I am physically active and am not at all overweight, yet I hate myself if I gain a few pounds. Sometimes I will go a day and eat only small amounts of raw vegetables just to lose weight. Other times I will pig out and then feel guilty. I don't think my situation is very common among males.

Male, 15

This next letter shows how interconnected the issues of poor self-image, stress, and depression can be. It is easy to see from her story that when feelings get buried and problems are not addressed, they can build and feed on one another and the person can get sucked into a downward spiral rather quickly:

> I am a bulimic. I am always depressed, so I eat to try to fill my emptiness and loneliness. After I binge I vomit so I don't gain any weight. I have no boyfriends, I am still a virgin and in today's society I feel as though this means that I am abnormal. (There is so much pressure to have sex.) My family and I don't communicate. There is no one I can talk to. I hate being alone and miserable. More often now I think about killing myself. I have this bottle of headache pills in my dresser drawer and I am really tempted to overdose. I always dream about being reincarnated into a much better person and having a better life. I am really self-conscious. I hate to be laughed at or talked about. All I ever wanted was to be accepted!
>
> Female, 15

....

When I was in Nancy's class during my sophomore year, she mentioned that I could come and speak to her classes some time. At the time I was not ready. It had been about six years since I had been hospitalized for anorexia and all that time I had always kept it hidden. I had since kept the two parts of my life separate, before and after. After I had gotten out of the hospital I had gone to a new school and basically started over and never talked about my anorexia. As a high school junior, I finally decided to deal with my problems from that time. I thought speaking to Nancy's classes would be the easiest way because psychiatrists had never really helped me. Also I thought by speaking I might be able to help some other people or at least help them understand. Another reason I finally decided to speak was because it seems like no one ever wants to hear about eating disorders and I decided people need to hear about them.

My main message was basically that in order to survive you have to do whatever it takes and it doesn't matter if anyone likes you, you have to like yourself. My other message was that eating disorders such as anorexia and bulimia are not just worrying about your weight, they're more a way out, a way to show people you're unhappy and, most of all, a way to end your life.

I never really thought about how people would act after I spoke to the classes or how they'd treat me and talk to me. It was rather a spontaneous decision. Afterward I was surprised that almost all of the responses [I] got were positive and talked about bravery. I thought people would talk about eating disorders more but most tried not to. I guess that's easier, that's what I'd always done. I guess people never deal with what they don't want to deal with no matter how brave they are.

Katya Cengel, 17

I would like my name printed so that anyone who I might be able to help could contact me if they wanted to.

Anyone with an eating disorder should seek professional help. I also recommend that teenagers consult a physician or professional nutritionist before going on a diet. What goes into the body—or what the body is deprived of—during adolescence can have lifelong consequences. For example, many young women will cut out dairy products when they diet, not realizing that if they do not take in enough calcium as teens, they may suffer from osteoporosis later in life (the U.C. Berkeley *Wellness Letter* reports that up to age twenty-four females need the equivalent of a quart of milk a day).

Living with Disabilities

Over the years I have had many students with a variety of disabilities integrated into my classroom. Some of the handicaps were hidden—diabetes, dyslexia, brain tumors, heart problems, for instance—but many were very noticeable. I have had deaf students, blind students, and wheelchair-bound students.

Some of these students have spoken to my classes about their disabilities. One former student who was blind was a guest speaker many times while she was attending Berkeley High. She told the class that her dream was to free-fall from an airplane—and she accomplished this, making a tandem jump with her instructor. I have also had outside speakers with various handicaps. One young man, who had been in a serious car accident, would remove his glass eye about halfway through his presentation! This was nothing short of dramatic and I doubt if anyone will forget his "eye-catching" demonstration.

Not only do these speakers demystify some of the stereotypes we have about various disabilities, they are also very inspirational. They make us look inside ourselves and see the artificial barriers we place in front of ourselves. So often we tell ourselves "I could never do such and such..." and we don't even try.

Almost inevitably, a handicap becomes part and parcel of the self-image, and whether the disability is viewed constructively or not is a very individual thing. Some people with disabilities seem quite bitter about what life has dealt them, while others are very accepting of themselves. Years ago, I had a guest speaker who was born with cerebral palsy; someone asked him, "If you could take a pill and be able to walk, would you choose to do this?" From his wheelchair, Neil responded, "No, my whole identity is tied up with this image of myself—this is who I have always been." The same question was asked of the blind speaker, and she said that her blindness made her unique; she was very content and would not choose to be sighted.

Nancy invited me to come speak in her class and I decided to talk about diabetes because it was, unfortunately, a topic on which I could profess to be an authority and because it seemed to touch on some of the issues of adolescence. Like many of the problems teenagers face, diabetes is mostly invisible; it touches on existential issues, causes one to reflect on mortality and justice, and it sometimes requires help, which is never easy to ask for. And diet maintenance requirements get you into peer pressure issues. It's also the kind of thing for which a little information goes a long way—you can save someone's life just by being able to make the connection between hypoglycemia and sugar.

The class was just the way I remembered it: intelligent and aching to be entertained. I wanted to tell them everything I thought I knew about life, wanted to touch them the way I remember being touched by speakers in that class. In the end I gave them my experience and the information I had, and we gossiped a little, too, about college and the work force. It was nice to be able to bring a little bit of the world in to them. I think I could have talked about shoe polish and as long as I'd been honest, it would have mattered to them more than algebra.

Female, 23

The scientific term that the doctors use to describe what I have is "Springles Syndrome." They, as well, refer to it as some kind of handicap. I, being the person who actually has this "handicap," properly call it one of the greatest learning tools of all time....

It is to the people who cannot, for any reason at all, fathom my condition, that I am writing this paper. For those who have poked at my emotions, for those who look in my direction, but who cannot see me, this is for you. I suppose I should start by explaining what happened to me, and where it has taken me.

In 1979, when I was five years old, I had gone into surgery for my birth defect (I use this term strongly because so many kids over the years have formed their own ideas on how my shoulders came to be as they are now. I might add, all of their ideas are both far from the truth, and stupid). My shoulders were too high.... The doctors...lowered my shoulders a little, but not as much as they were hoping, or expecting.

Through the years, off and on, my peers had taken the opportunity to direct their aggression on me through a number of words and/or phrases to make me feel like sewer water. They succeeded in doing what they had wanted to do. I felt bad. Their satisfaction had been clearly granted. But, a funny twist had been added to satisfying the people who...put me down. That twist is, I find it difficult, to say the least, to trust, or to take a liking to, anyone who is twenty-five years of age, or younger. I now believe that I look into the eyes of this age group, and all I can see is a hollow figure, walking and talking without any real meaning, and without any real understanding. This may be immoral on my part, but it has shaped me during the nineteen years of my life. I discriminate against this age group for a reason. This was the age group—adolescence—and still is the age group, that teases me the most.

That is not to say that adults occasionally don't say something that might interrupt the good mood that I was in on that particular day. Because adults, too, have said a few things that were thoughtless.... Adults in their forties and fifties who work in grocery stores or hardware stores will ask me a thoughtless question like "Are you cold today?" I know that this question is more out of an ignorance that interrupts their ability to understand.... There are similar stories such as mine, where "normal" or "better" people put tags on people to lessen their morale.

Male, 19

Sexual Harassment

Sexual harassment, whether it is physical or verbal, is demeaning and tends to undermine the self-esteem of the person who is the target. Only a few journal entries have centered on this topic, because I have not specifically assigned it. (On the school survey on violence *[see chapter 10]*, 12 percent of those who were asked reported that they had been sexually harassed at school.) My sense, however, is that many young males have absorbed the message from the media or from their elders that it's okay to treat women as sex objects. I usually talk about this a little in class, and read a few journal entries on the subject:

> …I am also verbally attacked because of my sex. Either I have some man, usually old enough to be my father stop what they're doing to watch me pass. Many times they whistle or call out something foul or just yell. It annoys me and makes me feel like an insignificant sex object. I'm either discriminated this way or when I play coed sports. I'm usually picked last for any team sport even though I can swing a bat harder and more accurately than most boys and can run faster. Usually when I'm up to bat, the outfield moves in and the coach will pitch underhand and slow. Then they are surprised when I hit the ball over their heads.
>
> Female, 15

THE MAN ON THE CORNER

What gives you the right to look at me like that?
Your eyes suggesting some secret understanding
Between the two of us
When all I see are two beady pupils
So pitch black
That if I dared look into them,
I'd be sucked into their hellish depth
Without so much as an utterance of consent.
Those devilish eyes burn holes into my clothes,
Dancing upon the vulnerable flesh underneath
Until that, too, has disintegrated.

My soul is left exposed,
Unprotected from your probing stare,
Unable to fend you off
As you rape it and toss it aside.
Who told you it was okay for you to look at me like that?

What gives you the right to nod your head at me
And part your lips
In a feeble attempt to disguise your
Ill-willed intentions
With a friendly grin?
The evil hunger inside of you is obvious.
Behind the smile that plays on your lips
Are sharp, dagger teeth
That gnaw greedily at my dignity,
Washing down each bite
With my pride.
Who told you it was okay for you to smile at me like that?

What gives you the right to speak to me like that?
Rattling off empty words
And meaningless lines
About how beautiful I am
Or what a pretty smile I have.

You don't know me!
You've never seen me!
This whole time you've been looking right through me,
So how can you stand there
And tell me that I'm beautiful?
I never have
And never will
Smile at you,
So how can you tell me
That I have a pretty smile?
Who told you it was okay for you to speak to me like that?

You're just some man
I happened to pass by
On the street today.

There is no secret understanding
Between the two of us!
What gives you the right to think there is?
In overstepping your rights
You are stripping me of mine.

So the next time
I pass you by,
Before you wink your eye
Or begin to smile,
Think!
Think long and hard!
What gives you the right to look at me like that?

Female, 18

The next young woman describes how a rape destroyed her self-esteem:

Having been raised through a strict religious upbringing illicit sex is
morally wrong to me. I had always looked upon it as something I would
not experience 'til I was married. Unfortunately at the age of 13 I was
violently raped and thus lost my virginity. In the months that followed I
lost all self-esteem, respect, and confidence and surrendered to boys'
advances without resistance as I felt that they would hate me and never
want to speak to me again if I didn't give it up. When they did have
sex with me, I would usually lie lifeless, crying to myself wondering how
I was ever going to respect myself again. Being raped has ruined my
chances of ever feeling good about sex.

Female, 16

STRESS

On my way to a stress-reduction meeting a few weeks ago, a counselor
stopped me in the hall. She informed me that one of my students had
just been charged with murder and I was supposed to call his mother.
Murder! I was shocked; I could not imagine this student committing
any type of crime. I couldn't believe it. I got the mother's number and
headed upstairs to the meeting feeling numb.

When I reached the second floor, I smelled smoke and saw a burning flyer on the wall. I grabbed it by the one corner that was not on

fire, threw it on the floor, and looked around for something to put out the flames. My lunch, which was balanced precariously in my left hand, was on a paper plate, and I had on brand new suede shoes! I ruled out the plate and my shoes. The flames were almost out by now anyway, but I ran downstairs for help.

Down the hall, I could see all the student supervisors blocking the entrance to the Health Center. I caught their attention and shouted, "There's been a small fire upstairs. Someone set fire to one of the flyers on the wall." They all had walkie-talkies and I figured one of them would come back up with me or send a custodian or something. The only response I got was, "I told them not to let kids put flyers up on the walls." Just then, another counselor came by, and he quickly ran upstairs with me to make sure the fire was out.

Later on I found out that some kids from another school had attacked some of our students. The injured students were being treated in the Health Center, and I heard that the student supervisors were stationed there on the alert for possible gang retaliation. I rarely get any official word on such incidents, just rumors, or I may read about it some days later in the school newspaper. But it is probably better that I don't know all of the problems that security and the administration deal with on a daily basis. There's enough stress in the average teaching day without this added information.

By the time I got to my meeting, I was late, my lunch was cold, and I was definitely in need of stress reduction! After the meeting, I hurried back to my next class where Lisa Sterner, the school's health educator, was going to show the STD slides. One of my students had her head down on the desk: she said she didn't feel well. I suggested that she go to the Health Center but she preferred to rest in class. About

Reprinted with special permission of North America Syndicate

ten minutes later she headed for the door, then abruptly sat down on the floor. She said she felt faint. We made it as far as a chair outside my room. I told her to sit there with her head as low as possible and ran to the Health Center. I asked the receptionist to send over the nurse. The nurse was absent and so was the substitute. The receptionist suggested I call 911, but I didn't think this was necessary: the girl hadn't eaten anything all day and just felt faint. Somehow I found the director of the Health Center and she let the student lie down in her office. By then I could have used a second stress-reduction meeting!

A typical day in my life? Not exactly, but even on the "normal" days, I feel a constant pressure. I know from my students' journals that most of them do too. For them, there are the pressures of getting homework done on time, taking tests, getting good grades, problems dealing with teachers, parents, siblings, and friends, and the whole question of planning for the future. Add to this the fear of violence, racial tensions, financial concerns, worries about health, and it's no wonder the school feels like a pressure cooker at times, with students blowing up every now and then.

I think it's very important for my students to learn how to cope with stress, because unrelieved stress can have serious consequences, both physical and psychological. Somewhere during each nine-week course I take time to

> **Living with Stress**
>
> In a recent survey, BHS students reported they had dealt with these situations in the preceding year:
>
> - 39%—1 or more failing grades on a report card
> - 25%—witnessing or being involved in a violent fight or crime on the street
> - 33%—holding down a job
> - 32%—loss of a close friend or relationship
> - 27%—a serious problem getting along with family or others
> - 26%—major problem with a boyfriend or girlfriend
> - 18%—experiencing racial harassment
> - 13%—pregnancy (or getting someone pregnant)
> - 11%—family divorce, separation, or death
> - 11%—being involved with a serious crime
> - 7%—having sex when they didn't want to

talk about stress—what causes it, and how to deal with it. Usually I start with a stress quiz on which the students rate themselves from 0 to 5 (0=never; 5=always) on a number of stress-related items. For instance:

____ **I have trouble communicating with teachers, friends, family, etc.**

____ **I am a couch potato—I don't get much exercise.**

_____ I have muscle tension in my neck, shoulders, or back.

After they've taken the quiz, we discuss some of the items on it, and talk about positive ways to deal with stress. Listening to music seems to be the favorite method, but other frequently mentioned outlets include writing out your feelings, running, taking part in sports, and talking with friends. (Yelling at younger brothers and sisters is another favorite; I'm quick to point out that this may not be too positive for the person on the receiving end!)

Then I read a few journal entries from other students in response to the journal question on stress:

What causes you stress and how do you deal with it? Describe both positive and negative ways. Is this similar to the way that your parent(s) handle stress?

My main stress is money. I always have to have it. The only way I could get it is by getting a job. But every fucking time I put in an application I never get a call back. So that really burns me up, so I could go out with my friends and throw lemons at cars and run. That lets out the stress about the job and money. The other stress is gambling. I'm addicted to it like it's a drug. It's like I need it every day. For an example: today I was gambling—I lost all my money and then I started to ask people can I borrow money to play. I'm trying to stop, but it's hard to do. But it seems like I'm not going to stop because I always see dice because they're in my room on my desk.

Male, 16

When I read this letter, we usually get sidetracked on the topic of gambling. I'll mention that some people can bet for fun and just do it occasionally, but others will go on to do it compulsively, and the ensuing problems can wreak havoc on family and finances. I tell the class that there are support groups for people who can't control their gambling (Gamblers Anonymous and Gamanon are two).

I got a lot of stress—when I get stress or think about my stress (because I have it all the time), I like to swear a lot, so if I'm writing and I'm swearing a lot, I have a lot of stress or just thinking about it. I deal with stress my own way. I don't need to talk to nobody, fuck that,

that's for suckas who can't handle anything. I just keep my problems to myself and don't need no fucking shrink telling me I gotta talk. Man, fuck that shit—I ain't no punk. I'll take care of my own shit.

Male, 16

I wrote in his journal that I disagreed with his statement that talking is "for suckas who can't handle anything." I was pleasantly surprised and very touched when he later sent me this note:

Dear Nancy,

I'm writing you this letter so that you can understand why I do some of the things I do. First of all, I want to apologize for the way I've been acting. I've taken a good look at myself and have come to somewhat of a conclusion of why I've acted so badly to you. I think I am intimidated or scared of your classroom—I'm afraid I'll open up and look like a fool, so instead, I put up a mask to cover the real R. Again, I want to apologize, Nancy, for my poor behavior. You've got to understand I have secrets that are very hard for me to deal with. One of my ways of dealing with them is acting like I don't care and acting like an insensitive asshole. In one of my journal assignments I wrote that I don't need no one, I can take care of my own problems. I was wrong. I need a friend. I need someone to talk to. Nancy, I think you're a beautiful person, and I wish you really knew me so that maybe we could be friends.

Love, R.

I think that most students know when they are coping with their problems in negative ways (destroying things, destroying themselves, overeating or starving, using drugs, etc.), but often it is not easy to change bad habits. I read some entries by students who have found some positive ways to cope with their stress, and I hope that perhaps other students will follow their examples:

I have tremendous stress in my life right now. Some of it is from school, college applications, and parents, but most of it I inflict on myself. I mean, I strive for high goals and I work like a madman to get there. I love to be constantly active and reaching for dreams, but in the process I go through a lot of strain and stress.

On the whole, I can maintain a pretty calm head, but this semester has been a real test. I always thought that senior year would be less pressure and I was excited to begin working on applications, and having interviews. However, the whole college issue has been dominating my life. I have so many deadlines to meet, decisions to make plus I have to keep my grade point up. Since I am active in many activities, I use those to ease my stress. If I'm feeling particularly stressed, I practice singing and let my emotions flow with the notes; or I go play tennis and sweat and work out really hard; or I put my Walkman on full blast with an upbeat tape and go jogging. Stress has caused me much anguish but it often makes me work harder. But if I go crazy, I have many ways to deal with it.

Female, 18

....

I am not usually a stressed person. I am honest, so I don't have to keep up a charade of lies. I don't take drugs or alcohol and I don't smoke, never have, so I'm not worrying about hurting my body or my mind. I love my mother and my brother and I like my stepdad, so I have no problems family-wise. I can talk to my mother if I ever have problems. Sometimes I stress about grades and college, even though I'm a sopho-more. I call my friends and ask them for a study date and I catch up on grades. I never mess around with the wrong crowd. I have good intu-itions about people and what is right/wrong so I never put myself in a situation where I or someone else could get hurt emotionally or physi-cally. I am a pretty well-balanced person. I take care of myself and if I get stress over my period or a guy or whatever I just run around the house and scream or turn on the music and dance. Sometimes you just have to spend a little time by yourself to get in touch with your feelings.

Female, 15

....

I could write for 400 pages on stress. I've been stressed out on every-thing possible—I used to take life so seriously. Now, I feel that stressing will not solve anything. Sometimes it's unavoidable but you have to get it out of your system before it gets you. Usually I start to cry and then I stop and say "Hey—this isn't helping me." If I'm stressed about my body—I go and do something about it—work out, eat healthy. The one thing which I have trouble working out is my boyfriend's stress. When he gets angry, (or stressed) it stresses me out because I feel so out of control. Basically, I can control all my own inner-generated stress (even though it sometimes seems like I can't) but when his stress creates conflict between us, there's nothing I can do about it. I have to just leave him alone for a while, while he deals (tries to deal) with it. But I guess that's what he does to me also—leaves me alone while I deal with it. The best way is to sleep, exercise, study.... If you're stressed about not getting enough sleep, then sleep. If you're stressed about your body, exercise. If you're stressed about your relationships, work to do something about it. Work to change it rather than worry about it.

Female, 17

I get stressed out by tests I don't know how to study for, my parents fighting with each other and with me, having to wait for other people in just about any situation and probably a lot of other things that I can't think of unless they are actually happening to me. My body reacts by getting sleepy and feeling sluggish, and my attitude gets pretty bad. When I notice my body reacting like that I take a good look at what is causing the stress, take a deep breath mentally and physically, and try to analyze what I can do about solving the problem causing me stress. Then I do my best to get rid of it. Usually if I take an objective approach I can get rid of the stress easily.

Female, 15

....

A lot of things give me stress, but I deal with it much better than I used to. I think one of the reasons I have less stress now, is that I'm more self-assured. I used to be extremely insecure. I dealt with stress by drinking heavily, smoking pot (which made me feel even more self-conscious), biting my fingernails, and smoking. But then I got out of a stressful home where I fought with my mother and got in trouble all the time and moved here to live with my dad and his girlfriend. Since I moved, I've quit drinking and smoking and I get rid of stress by first confronting the problem, and meditating, then I exercise, which helps tremendously. And when things get bad I tell myself "things could always be worse." Then my problems don't worry me too much.

Male, 15

At this point, I like to zero in on the idea of relieving stress by removing the cause of the stress itself or, as the last writer put it, confronting the problem. I ask the students to look at the areas on the quiz where they showed the highest score and come with up a couple of ideas for working on at least one. We go around the room and each student makes an agreement that will bring about a positive change. For example, one girl who was stressed out over getting her homework done might say, "I agree to do my homework before I turn on the TV, and if I don't get it done tonight, I will get up early and finish it." For the next few days, time permitting, I have each student check in as to whether or not they are keeping their agreement. Hopefully, the daily public disclosure will help keep them on track.

Before having the class write their journal entries on stress, I let them know that I have relaxation tapes they can borrow, and I take them through a short relaxation exercise. I ask them to close their eyes, relax their bodies gradually and completely, and visualize something positive for themselves. Only a couple of times have students ruined this exercise by coughing, laughing, or loudly chanting "om." In fact, in some of my most difficult classes, you can hear a pin drop as students gradually let go of all the pressures and stress that they feel. I hope they will use this exercise at home to help them relax.

Over and over again, students describe themselves in their journals as being confused and having drastic mood swings. I hear this more from girls, but the boys complain of it too. I assure my students that they are not going nuts, that, to a certain degree, this is quite normal, and it's partly their hormones kicking in. As one girl wrote, "I'm schizophrenic, and don't know who I am anyway, because I'm a teenager, and all teenagers are neurotic and insecure and are in the middle of an identity crisis." An overload of life problems and pressures can also bring on mood swings or feelings of depression. I advise my students to talk over their problems with a friend or a trusted adult before these problems become unmanageable. I also point out that a deep and prolonged state of depression is not normal and that they should not be afraid to seek professional help for this.

SUICIDE

> My problem (or at least one of them) is that I have incredible mood swings and they really bother me. At times I'll be happy, energetic, on top of the world. Everything seems to be going right and I feel like I'm a wonderful person and I have a wonderful life. Then, all of a sudden and for no obvious reason, I'll become totally depressed. One little thing will go wrong and then everything will cave in. When I get in these depressed states of mind, I feel like it will never end and I can never think of anything positive to help pull myself out of the state of depression. I feel like my life is miserable and not worth living, although I've never seriously considered suicide. Usually I deal with this depression by doing something that can keep me from thinking about my life: I blast my stereo, smoke a joint, or just go to sleep. Usually it wears off by the next morning, and I go back to living my regular life, and everything is fine.
>
> Male, 17

> Sometimes I feel so mixed up. Generally about people. Is it normal to have no idea about oneself, what's going on? There are times when I

think I am the only thing that matters, that I don't need anyone. Usually this is when I'm hurt or in an angry mood. Then there are times when I know I need other people. It's scary to depend on other people. Why then do I start to hate or avoid anyone (boys) who likes (loves?) me. I'm really scared of getting close to someone. With good friends (males) I'm fine, but when someone pushes for something more I get this sick feeling in my gut. Maybe I really am a thousand different people.

Female, 14

....

I'm fourteen years old, almost fifteen. Pretty damn young. Why do I feel like I have to know everything about myself—who I am, what I'll be doing when I'm twenty, etc....by the time I wake up tomorrow? I hate being pressured like this. My mother calls me "ignorant" and tells me I'll be a McDonald's employee forever every time I exhibit even the slightest sign of youngishness, and now people are starting to tell her I'm "old before my time." Who do I listen to? I know you'll say "listen to yourself" but myself is wandering around saying "oh HELP." Am I too old, or am I too young? Or am I just experiencing one of the phases of adolescence (the great disease)? Please read this—I'm so lost.

Female, 14-year-old senior citizen

It is normal for teenagers to feel sad, lonely, and depressed on occasion, but far too often these feelings lead to thoughts of suicide and to attempted suicide. The rate of teenage suicide has increased dramatically in recent years; it's a topic that warrants discussing in class.

I've never told anyone. No one would guess that I've thought about killing myself.... It was so internal. I kept everything to myself as usual. I think I always knew even when I was really depressed, that I couldn't go through with it. But I was so scared. And really just depressed. About everything. Life, school, grades, you name it.... This may sound really weird, but I just wanted to stop living for awhile, not die. God, dying is so final. The end, of everything. Stopping living sounded real good for awhile. Maybe everything would go away. I was really down for awhile, and then it just changed. I couldn't tell you how or why, but I decided I didn't want to be depressed anymore. I came to school and all my friends said I was glowing. They thought I was in love. I'm real glad those feelings went away. Every once in a while they come back. But I don't think I could ever kill myself.

Female, 15

....

Much of the time I feel upset, depressed, and tired. I have been depressed for as long as I can remember. I've totally ruled out suicide because I know I want to live. I have come severely close to committing suicide, but I was crying so much I couldn't kill myself. Now I love my dad and mom so much that I will not let go. I do not want to hurt them.

Female, 15

Sometimes I get so depressed. I feel like committing suicide. I tend to play off my feelings, to a certain degree. I dampen them so they don't sound so severe. I try to tell my best friend I'm depressed but I don't say it in the way I really feel. I'm really good at covering up my feelings. Sometimes it gets so bottled up inside that I start to cry, but I don't cry like everyone else. I cry on the inside, very quietly and without even dropping my head down so people won't know something's wrong. I look out on the street and I feel like going for a bike ride. When I ride my bike 30–40 miles my mind gets cleared and I can even cry out loud, but sometimes I don't ride to clear my mind but I contemplate death. "What would it be like to be dead?" "What would my friends think?" I think of them being depressed for me and wishing I were back.

Male, 16

There is help for those suffering from depression, but each person must find their own way toward healing. For some, a doctor or psychiatrist will determine if antidepressant medication will be beneficial. Others find help through counseling or support groups. Sometimes I will ask students who said they were suicidal in the past how they overcame their depressed state. Sometimes they will say that they just don't know, or something like "I outgrew it," or "My problems didn't seem as bad as I got older," "I moved out," "I felt better after a summer away from school, friends, and family. I had a new perspective on life."

Each of us has a different level of tolerance for the emotional pain and setbacks that are an inevitable part of life. Some people are able to bounce back, but others have a harder time. They are handling their problems—or ignoring them—but then an additional stress makes everything seem overwhelming, out of control, hopeless. Feelings of despair set in, and suicide seems the only way out.

> My life hasn't been too cool. I feel like nobody wants me. My mother treats me like shit. She acts like she don't like me. Things like that make me hella sick. One day I will kill myself and I won't have to worry about these troubles.
>
> Signed, Shitty
> Female, 16

....

Even though I feel good about how I look, I'm not really comfortable with how I feel inside. I'm really insecure, I suppose you could call me almost schizophrenic. Maybe it's just puberty but I wake up a completely different person every day. Some days I wake up and I go out and meet strangers and other days I'm so secluded I can barely stay in school cause I think everyone's looking at me. Sometimes I really have doubts about how I stand with other people. I feel like people (in general) don't want me around. I get so I don't know if my best friend wants me to go away. Sometimes I can't go up to people because I know in my mind they don't want me around. I think to myself that it's all in my mind, that people like me more than that. I try to cover up my insecurity by cracking jokes and trying to be funny, but it feels like life is an act and I'm on a day-time soap, not ready for prime-time. Nobody knows me, not my mother, my best friend or anybody, except one of my ex-girlfriends.... To me she's the only person that I truly love. If I ever have loved anyone it certainly was her.... But it didn't last. She didn't love me as much as I loved her. It seems that's the way all my relationships are.... From all my reactions I've become insecure.... Whenever I'm with someone I just feel stupid and I can't talk. Being alone makes me sad but somehow it gives me satisfaction. My heart aches so much sometimes! I just get so sad. So sad I can't bear to go on. I've thought about suicide. I think about suicide a lot. I think to myself: "It's not the way out." But it really is. I could just end all my problems by one act. By just a handful of pills, a tub with only six inches of water in it. So many ways. But I can't, sometimes the good outnumbers the bad…. I'm insecure, confident, happy, sad, and alone but at the same time crowded in. All at once I'm dying.

Male, 16

....

Suicide, what an interesting subject. I would love to be dead. I'm constantly hoping I have a fatal disease or maybe someone will shoot me, etc. I almost tried to commit suicide. I had about seventy pills in front of me and I was totally depressed but all I could think of was how my parents would feel, I wanted to take them so badly but I also wasn't selfish enough to cause the pain that I knew would occur if I did die and all the time I was thinking about whether or not to take them I was writing in a journal which was what finally made me decide to wait awhile before I actually did kill myself. Then the next day I found myself once again with the pills but I didn't take them. I don't know why, it was partly because I'm not strong enough, selfish enough and I was scared about what could/would/might happen. But then I do want to die but I want it to happen some other way.

Female, 16

....

I can't take my family, we are all going crazy! My grades are going down, I tried killing myself again! Life right now is too much. I am being pressured too much and it is really too much for me to handle right now. My teacher tells me that there is no way I can make up a grade on one of my essays and he has told other people that they can! I guess he didn't like the topic, Comparing Older Teachers to Younger Teachers. I just wish that he would give me an equal chance.

I have tried to kill myself before, I know that it is useless, but there are just times when I can't take it! My mother recovers for maybe a couple of months but then something upsets her and she loses control. She has lost all her moral standards. I can never now know what to expect out of her. She has been in the hospital many times but it doesn't work! She knows what she is doing to our family but she doesn't really care. My father now realizes that I am going nuts and since my brother is living in [another state], he is going to put me in my brother's old apartment and I will take over his old job as aparment

In a recent study of 11,600 students in grades 9–12:

- 27.3% had seriously considered suicide;

- 16.3% had made a specific plan;

- 8.3% had attempted suicide;

- 2% had made a suicide attempt that resulted in an injury or poisoning requiring medical attention.

manager of a fourplex. WOW! What fun I will be on my own big deal I have been on my own all my life. The only thing I regret is that I have missed being a child!

Female, no age given

....

If I killed myself tomorrow I don't think anyone would really understand why I did it. I really can't talk to my friends about some of my problems because I don't think they would understand. I tried to talk to my family but they usually ignore me whenever I have something to say so I gave up on them. I'm not sure if I want to die or if I'm just trying to get someone to listen. I tried calling one of those suicide hotlines but I got scared and hung up. Sometimes I try to forget my problems and sometimes it works but it is getting harder and I feel like I'm running out of time. Am I normal or crazy?

Male, 16

Whenever I get letters like the preceding ones, or when a student appears to me to be severely distressed, I will try to approach them and ask them to see me after class. My frustration is that there are only five minutes between classes where thirty-four or more students are leaving as the next group is entering. It is almost the only time I can connect with a student on a one-to-one basis in order to set up a time to talk. It is a common occurrence that when I try to reach a student at home, I will find a disconnected phone or an incorrect number. Often the student is not home, and I hesitate to leave messages with a younger brother or sister, or on an answering machine, because sometimes this can work against the confidentiality I want to ensure. In this case, I have to hope they will show up in class the next day so I can hand them a note.

I try to arrange for the student to come by my room at lunch that day or after their last class. If they are having a problem at school, I will ask them for permission to talk with their counselor or perhaps with the specific teacher who might be frustrating them. I'll listen and suggest some of the possibilities of getting help; once again I'll remind them that we have free counseling at the Health Center, and we'll look at the community resource sheet together to see what other agencies or hotlines might be helpful. They can use my phone if they wish to call right then, or I'll call for them, or they can think about it overnight. Instead of forcing the issue, I like to keep the line of communication open between us.

Although it may take them awhile to express their problems, they are usually anxious to unload whatever it is that is troubling them. Often the tears will come before the words do. It is very common for teenagers to feel that no one understands them, and in these situations, sometimes the best thing I can do for them is to listen to what they have to say, nothing more.

Whenever possible, I have a speaker from the local suicide prevention organization come to talk. I couldn't make the arrangements this quarter, so I talk about suicide prevention myself. I ask the class how many of them know someone who has attempted or committed suicide, and a fair number raise their hands. I tell them that *they* are the main line of prevention to suicide for their friends, because when teenagers have suicidal feelings, they will usually confide in a close friend first, if they confide in anybody at all. This is too much of a burden for them to handle alone, and they should seek out an adult to discuss what should be done. They can also call the suicide prevention hotline to ask for advice. Crisis hotlines get thousands of calls a month, and staff are accustomed to talking things out with people who just want advice.

We go over the signs of depression and suicide risk:

- change in personality—sad, withdrawn, irritable, anxious, tired, indecisive, apathetic
- change in behavior—can't concentrate on school, work, routine tasks
- change in sleep pattern—oversleeping or insomnia, sometimes with early waking
- change in eating habits—loss of appetite and weight, or overeating
- loss of interest—in friends, sex, hobbies, activities previously enjoyed
- worry about money or illness, either real or imaginary
- fear of losing control—going crazy, harming self or others

- feeling helpless, worthless—"nobody cares," "everyone would be better off without me"
- feelings of overwhelming guilt, shame, self-hatred
- no hope for the future—"it will never get better, I will always feel this way"
- drug or alcohol abuse
- recent loss—through death, divorce, separation, broken relationship, or loss of job, money, status, self-confidence, self-esteem
- loss of religious faith
- suicidal impulses, statements—plans, giving away favorite things
- previous suicide attempts or gestures
- agitation, hyperactivity, restlessness that may indicate masked depression

Then we talk about some positive steps to take. I tell my students that they know their friends best, and when they see behavior that is so different that it concerns them, they should encourage their friend to talk about their problems—and should listen without being judgmental. They can tell their friend that it's okay to feel sad and lonely and suggest that they reach out for help—from a teacher, school or church counselor, or a local crisis intervention hotline, for instance. Very rarely do hotline calls involve someone who is about to kill themselves. I tell the class this because it is common for a person in a depression to think that their problems are minor and not deserving of a counselor's time, and so they don't make the call.

We do some role-playing to get an idea of what to say to a friend and what not to say. I ask for a volunteer to play the part of someone who is very depressed and a young woman comes up and sits across from me. We talk about why she is feeling so terrible for a few minutes and then I say to her: "But you are so pretty, and you have so much going for you." I stop the role-playing and ask her, "How did it make you feel when I said, 'You are so pretty...'?" She says that it made her feel more depressed because that just meant she was an even bigger failure. I tell the class that this is generally how someone would interpret this—you say it in all sincerity to make the person feel better but often they don't accept it this way. So just talk to them about how they are feeling and let them know that you care about them and you are there for them during this difficult time.

I always tell my students that I don't take their journals home every day—imagine me walking to my car with 175 journals tucked under my arm! But anytime they wish to communicate with me—to ask a question, to seek advice, or just to get some feedback—all they have to do is leave their journal with me after class, and I will read whatever it is they want me to read and get back to them right away. When the next young woman was in my class, she left her journal with me several times. This was one of her letters:

> Today I feel extremely depressed. In English class today I almost had to get up and leave because I started to cry. All of a sudden I felt everything was hopeless. So I just started to cry and couldn't stop. I hid my face in my book so that no one would notice. Then I just wanted to get out of there and go home. But I cut my last two classes yesterday and I really shouldn't do it twice in a row.... The pressures of school are really getting to me. I read that everyone's life has ups and downs. Where are the ups in my life? Nothing as drastic as my parents being alcoholics is happening to me. Like that poor girl in class. Why do I feel this way? I just walk through school like a zombie. I don't feel like going to class most of the time. I want to stay in bed and cry all day. I have nobody to talk to that will understand. But if I did I probably couldn't think of anything to say. I'm not very good at talking to people face to face. I can't talk to either of my best friends. I'm mad at both of them.... Mom, I never could say anything to. And my sister wouldn't understand. Hearing the alcoholics talk to the class reminded me of something I have done. One night a few weeks ago I was really depressed. I went into my mother's liquor cabinet and took out a few bottles. I drank up a storm; nobody else was home. I was there on our couch, played a record and cried. For about a year when I was about twelve I used to cry every night. I feel like the same thing is happening again only worse. I want to cry in school, walking down the street at home, in bed.... I don't have a boyfriend or someone special to me. My sister and mom are no help.... School is a drag. I'm not going anywhere with my life. I don't even enjoy sitting on the grass in the sun. I don't like

the little things I used to like. Sitting in class I contemplated going home and slashing my wrists instead of thinking about class work. Each day seems like forever. I don't know if I want to hang around anymore waiting for something good to happen. It might never happen. If I decide to commit suicide I wouldn't call suicide prevention. To me the whole idea of it is to end your life, not try to salvage what's left. I might call if I didn't really want to die and wanted someone to talk me out of it. If you're not too busy Nancy—maybe I could talk with you about all this. If you don't want to, that's OK.

Maria, 15

At the end of the course, Maria turned in a record 144-page journal, which I read through from cover to cover and kept for her at her request. She became my proctor for the next nine weeks, and after that I continued to keep in touch with her. Unfortunately, about a year later she attempted suicide by taking an overdose of aspirins. She was fortunate that someone discovered her and carried her to a nearby hospital where her stomach was pumped. The doctors said she came very close to dying. Since then, she has gone through many changes and I admire her for having overcome many obstacles in her life. She is now in her thirties and working toward her master's degree. Recently I asked her to write about herself and this is what she sent to me:

Life is an evolution of events, a struggle, with many challenges. What I have found to be important is how I respond to those challenges. I have a choice. Sometimes I make good choices, and sometimes I make poor ones. As an adult, I find that I still make poor choices at times. But I do feel that my overall direction in life is a positive one. I have spent my adulthood trying to overcome negative patterns established as a teenager—but rooted in childhood. Life is a struggle. I never hit a plateau, where I may rest long. Perhaps the key is to embrace change, rather than fight it.

Nancy, you know my history...a mother unable to love, who was self-absorbed, distant, remote—almost absent really. My father died suddenly in an accident. The absence of love is profound; the result— a feeling of worthlessness and self-loathing. In high school, I was very sexually active. I slept with my doctor, a Berkeley High School guidance counselor, a construction worker, etc. After high school, I began to make healthier choices—I attribute the change to three years of intensive counseling (my own awareness and acknowledgment of this past), and the support of a boyfriend and others. Today I can count many accomplishments for which I am proud—among them are—a successful career and achievement in higher education—and yet, I struggle still. I continue to have feelings of complete hopelessness and depression, at times.

You were one of the people who, early on in my life, gave me encouragement—gave me love. Thank you, Nancy, for your help to find a better path. I sometimes fall back to what is unhealthy, but familiar. I believe that, slowly, this is changing.

Love,

Maria

When I read these letters in class I emphasize that Maria felt totally alone. After her suicide attempt, none of her friends spoke to her and no one in her family ever mentioned it again. The hospital followed up with one session with a psychiatrist, but Maria felt that it was just routine and that no one really cared.

I asked her what advice she would give to someone who is feeling suicidal. Her response:

I would advise [them] to reach out for help—to a teacher, to a counselor, to a friend. Establish ongoing contact and support. Create ties to others through sports, activities, or support groups. (My isolation and sense of "separateness" exacerbated my depression.) Also, remember that life can change dramatically with time.

The next young woman's letter echoes many of Maria's sentiments:

I was 15 years old when I tried to take my life in my own hands. For a year I had been experiencing a severe depression and I was about to attempt suicide for the second time. In my eyes the world hated me, they didn't care about me, and I might as well not exist. I held a bottle of Tylenol in my hand and thought back six months ago when I tried to slit my wrists. That night I downed twenty Tylenol. I didn't know it would take a week for me to die if I kept my mouth shut. At the hospital I was told I had a chemical imbalance and that it runs in my family.

Now a year and one half later I love life. I'm on Prozac, an antidepressant. Seeing a psychiatrist helped incredibly. Because I told my

friend how I was feeling I'm alive today. If you're experiencing a
depression and having thoughts of ending it all; hang in there! There is
a way out. It hurts and it's a long way out but it pays off in the end.
Talk to someone, take things day by day, and stick in there. Suicide is a
permanent solution to a temporary problem.

Jessica Ruth Johnston, 17

The following young man expresses passionately how it feels to deal
with the aftermath of a suicide attempt by a loved one. I read it because
I think it might touch someone who is feeling unloved and has even
the remotest thoughts of committing suicide:

By far the event that had the greatest impact on my life was a day in
seventh grade. I came home from school, and found my sister had slit
her wrists. I grew up in a small town, and things like this just didn't
happen there. I still remember every second of coming home. I think
that event caused me to grow up more than any other event in my life.
My sister lived, although she would not have if it weren't for me. I
remember the feelings. I hated her for doing it. How could she do that
to me? to our mother? We always loved and cared for her and this was
her response. Nancy, please try to make it clear to students that suicide
is quitting. It is giving up on life. It is the most selfish act imaginable
and while sympathy is a response, there is still a level of resentment for
doing it. Suicide is not a solution. It is a cheater's way out. And anyone
who thinks suicide is "romantic" is dead wrong. It is painful and gory
both physically and emotionally. If not for yourself, for those around
you: don't take the shortcut out of life; play out your hand, you never
know what lies in the cards.

Male, 15

....

*I don't really have a specific answer why I was suicidal.... It has been
quite some time since I've had to discuss such a topic.... Thinking
about this brings back a lot of pain, anger, and frustration. However,
as I've stated earlier, it has been years since this incident occurred. Over
the years, I have gained a tremendous amount of knowledge from therapy sessions, books, and conversations that I've had with people who
are close to me.... I am very aware of my past and I have put my
experiences in perspective.*

With help from my family and friends, I have been able to speak about incest and suicide to Nancy's students. What I have to gain from making guest appearances in her classrooms is HOPE. If I hadn't had any hope left in me when I was younger, I really doubt that I would be here today writing about my feelings....

My future is not a reflection of my past, but rather a symbol of strength, optimism, perseverance, and HOPE. My childhood scars continue to help me strive for so much more out of LIFE and all the experiences I've had also reminds me how lucky I am to be alive....

Female, 25

....

The suicidal gesture is a cry not only of distress, not only a cry for help,
not only a prayer, but it is a pleading: I want to live:
help me find a way to live. We say that where there is life
there is hope. In a sense, one could say that
where there is hope there may be life.

—KARL MENNINGER, M.D.

13 | Your Choice

I**T SEEMS THAT NO MATTER** which topic I pick on any particular day, there are always a few students who are not in the mood to write about it (and may never be). Most students say that they like to use the assigned questions because it forces them to think about a particular issue even though it may be painful or difficult to come up with an answer, but some students have suggested on their evaluations that they be allowed to write on whatever they feel at the moment. In response to this, I've added a list of alternate questions to the course outline. These questions can be used in place of the assigned ones and can also be used for makeup assignments or for extra credit. There are even blank entries so that students can create their own questions.

Actually I never expect to assign all the questions listed in the course outline because there isn't enough time in any nine-week period. But this allows for a certain amount of flexibility, because I can vary the course content or take the opportunity to focus on a school event or current news item.

There are some days when the "your choice" alternative has been the perfect solution, for instance when a scheduled speaker has had to cancel at the last minute, or when I've planned to cover a certain topic and forgot to bring in the former students' journal entries to read to the class, or feel that somehow it just isn't the right day for it. Today is a good example as there's going to be a basketball rally: each class period will be few minutes shorter and most of the time the bells will not ring. We have so many different schedules: morning assembly schedules, afternoon assembly schedules, rally schedules, test schedules, minimum-day schedules, and so on. The tardiness skyrockets on these days as the kids wander in saying, "The bell didn't ring in our building." In this technological age one would think we could program the bells—or ask a reliable human to ring the bells—according to the particular day's schedule. What irritates me most is to spend hours on the phone lining up a panel of speakers weeks in advance only to find out at the last minute that we are on a totally different schedule. Fortunately that's not a problem today.

It is now two and a half weeks before finals. I remind the class once again that journals will be due in two days, and they must be handed in to me with all assignments completed inside a properly prepared journal folder. As a final inspiration, I read the next piece:

WHY AM I WRITING THIS?

I am writing this because if I don't write this I will have an incomplete folder. If my folder is incomplete then I will flunk this class. If I flunk this class I will not graduate because Social Living is a required course. If I don't graduate I won't find a good job. If the job I get doesn't pay enough money I will go rob someone. When I get caught the police will probably charge me of numerous false crimes. I won't be able to get a good lawyer because I won't be able to pay for one because I couldn't get a job because I didn't have a high school diploma because I had an incomplete folder in Ms. Rubin's tenth-grade Social Living class. When I go to jail for the false charges of crimes I did not do, the prison guards will not like me and tell the warden to keep me in there longer. The warden will forget that I was supposed to get out. I will never get out of prison and I will rot in a cell unnoticed. So the answer to my question is: I AM WRITING THIS BECAUSE I DON'T WANT TO SPEND THE REST OF MY LIFE IN PRISON!

Male, 15

Journals are due by 2:40 P.M. on Friday, without exceptions, I tell them. This elicits the usual barrage of questions and comments. Between this and the rally schedule, it seems like a perfect day for a "your choice" assignment.

Following are some "your choice" questions together with a few of the entries that I might read for each:

How has TV influenced your life? Estimate how much time you spend watching TV (include videos). How do you feel about this?

Over the years, I have noticed a direct correlation (my personal totally nonscientific study!) between the amount of time spent watching TV and whether or not students get their journals in on time.

Although I do not assign the TV questions, the students are required to keep track of what they watch on television for an entire week and log in the name of the program and the number of hours spent viewing. I also devote a little class time to a discussion of TV-viewing habits and the influence that TV has on our lives.

For starters, I pass out a sheet entitled Facts about Television that was put together by a Sonoma County organization called TV Turn-Off. On one side are dozens of facts about the effects of watching TV, and I go around the room and have each student read one out loud. These items invariably draw reactions:

- Asked which they would keep if forced to choose between their dad and their TV sets, over half the children chose television.

- By the age of 14, a devoted viewer will have seen 11,000 TV murders.

- 72% of scripts are simple sentences or sentence fragments. Scripts are written on a 7th-grade reading level.

- 250,000 Americans wrote to Marcus Welby, M.D., to ask for medical advice. (I have to explain that Marcus Welby was a character in a very popular TV show, and thousands of viewers believed he was a real doctor.)

- When a Detroit newspaper offered $500 each to 120 families if they'd turn off their televisions for a month, 95 families turned down the offer.

At this point someone always speaks up to say that they would be happy to do it for a hundred bucks.

There are always a couple of students in each class who do not have television sets, usually because the families chose to get rid of them. But in general, TV watching occupies a good deal of many students' free time. From the moment they get home until they go to bed the TV is on. They channel-surf, or they watch one sitcom after another. Rarely do they watch any of the programs that I suggest. (One option the students have for makeup or extra credit is to watch any show that is relevant to Social Living and to write a brief summary and personal reaction to it.)

The TV log has proved to be a worthwhile exercise. I often get comments like "I didn't think I watched much TV, but when you add it up it seems like a lot." This, and journal entries like those that follow, lead me to believe my students do take what I say seriously—at least some of the time. Very few students feel that television has been a positive force in their lives.

> Television had influenced me tremendously before I read some of the facts concerning TV viewing. To tell you the truth, I was appalled, truly shocked and stunned at the same time. I suppose I had been pulled into the hypnotic state of TV for so long that I didn't even realize it. I considered the "tube" as a friend, a trusted one whom I can call on every time I push a little button. Pure paradise. But the more I thought about it, the more came to light.
>
> I realized how much time I have wasted on this thing called TV, I regret it tremendously. I wish I could take it all back now, but that appears not possible. After the experiment we had conducted on the amount of TV viewing, I have hardly watched any TV, perhaps less than an hour every month. Can you believe it? This figure has dropped twentyfold. I just hope this effort is not too late.
>
> Male, 15

A NEW WARNING SYSTEM: HOW TO TELL WHEN THERE IS EXCESS SEX, TRASH AND/OR VIOLENCE ON TELEVISION.

Reprinted by permission of Tribune Media Services

TV CHART: KEEP TRACK OF WHAT YOU WATCH FOR ONE FULL WEEK!

SUNDAY	MONDAY	TUESDAY	WEDNESDAY	THURSDAY	FRIDAY	SATURDAY	
30 min Scooby Doo	The $25,000 Pyramid 30 min	T $25,000 Pyramid 30 min	Beverly Hills 90210 1 hr.	Saved By The Bell 30 min	Saved By The Bell 30 min	Cartoons (Ch. 2) 2 hr.	
Martin 30 min	Saved By The Bell 30 min	Saved by The Bell 30 min	Melrose Place 1 hr.	The Simpsons 30 min	Mama's Family 30 min	PBA Tour 1 hr. 30 min	
Living Single 30 min	Mamas Family 30 min	Mama's Family 30 min	Saved By the Bell 30 min	Sinbad 30 min	Boy Meets World 30 min	Nickolodeon 3 hrs	
The Lipton (Tennis) (2hrs)	Jeopardy! 30 min	Roseanne 30min	Cartoon Express 1 hr.	Cartoon Express 1 hr.	Cartoon Express 1 hr.	Wide World of Sports 1 hr. 30	
Married With Children 1 hr.	Wheel Of Fortune 30 min	Silk Stalkings 1 hr.	Silk Stalkings 1 hr.	Silk Stalkings 1 hr.	Silk Stalkings 1 hr.		
Basket ball	MONDAY NIGHT RAW 1 hr.	3 hr.	4 hr. 30 min	Basketball 2hr. 30 min	Real World 1 hr.		
Duck				6 hr.	4 hr. 30 min	8 hrs.	HRS. PER DAY
5 hrs. 30 min	4 hrs.	3 hrs.	4 hr. 30	2hr 30 min	4 hr. 30 min	8 hrs.	

FINAL TOTAL # OF HOURS YOU WATCHED THIS WEEK: _____

9 hrs 30 min + 7 hr. 30 min + 7 hrs. + 8 hrs.

17 hrs + 15 hrs

32 hrs. total

Once upon a half decade ago, there was a group of animals who called themselves homo sapiens who spent the majority of their time staring stonily at little black boxes. Actually, the black boxes weren't all so little. They varied in size, some were small enough to cup lovingly in one's hand, while others were so gigantic they had to be stared at reverently from afar.

The black boxes could talk, sing, dance, tell jokes, unravel the mysteries of the world, and dissect the lives of transvestite vegetarians who used to be cops. As time grew on, more and more people began putting down books, newspapers, and magazines to sit on their couches and stare like zombies at the black boxes. Some stonily munched on stale bags of half-eaten potato chips, while others made fleeting attempts to do history homework during the brief five-minute interludes in which large companies tried tirelessly to get people to buy things they really did not want or need.

Teenage girls ogled the plastic soap opera stars and dreamt of their gorgeous male counterparts. Men, young and old, inducted each other into watching professional men exercise for a living—then generally did this while eating high-fat snack foods, drinking beer, and smoking cigarettes. Young humans sang along with a purple dinosaur who taught them that imagination was the most valuable thing a human could possess. This was ironic since watching the black boxes required no imagination whatsoever.

This story has no point—but then again neither does TV. Pick up a book and read, America!

Female, 16

I think that television has played a larger part in my life than my parents have. I have been watching a lot of television even before I was five years old. I wish my parents had not let me watch too much television. Sometimes I confuse television with reality. I get confused most of the time. Television had the perfect families, perfect anything. I never realized until now that the people were actors. They always said the right things at the right time. I lived in Nigeria and so I thought that America was heaven on earth from the images I got. The houses, people, everything was perfect.

When I came to the U.S., the only way I could find out about this country was through television. At least that's what I thought. It took me a year to realize that television was not reality. Now, I am starting to know the realities in this country. That's because I stopped watching television a month ago (except of course for 90210, Star Trek, and Roseanne). To whomever may be reading this, television is an addiction and it can ruin your perspective of reality. Turn off your television.

Female, 15

Both of my parents are completely against TV. They used to keep our TV in the closet so we wouldn't be tempted to just plop down and watch any time. Productive activity was always encouraged in my house, such as art and reading. But to me and my younger brother TV was exciting, a forbidden thing that we would sneak and watch against our parents' wishes. I am happy to say that I no longer feel this way. There is nothing good on TV these days and I just feel that it is completely brainwashing and stereotypical in every way. TV is used for the exact opposite of what it should be used for. Regardless of how I feel I still watch at most two hours of TV a week. I have a TV in my room but I feel I have it completely under control. There are times I feel I have been watching too much TV and I make a conscious effort to cut back.

I'm glad I have not fallen into the trap that my younger brothers have, which is watching as much TV as they can get in. My parents have almost given up hope on controlling the amount of TV they watch. The sad thing is they are brainwashed. They constantly talk of TV, and violence and danger excites them. Especially the older of my two younger brothers, TV is such a part of his life and I feel that it has done a big part of making him the negative violent person he is and the constant source of pain he brings to our family. I hope it's just a stage and that he'll grow out of his obsession with TV because it really is an evil thing. I'm glad that I have realized this fact.

Female, 15

DINNERTIME

Describe dinnertime at your home. How do you feel about the situation? When you are a parent, will you keep the same patterns?

This journal question came out of something I heard over the radio recently—that most American families have the TV on during dinner. This was disturbing news to me, but when I mentioned it in class one day, no one was surprised. When I was growing up, dinnertime was a time for the whole family to be together. The TV definitely was not on. In fact we were the last I knew to get a television. My brother and sister and I each had a chore to do—to set the table, clear the table, or wash the dishes. We always ate at the same hour, and the whole family sat down together to eat a balanced home-cooked meal—no fast food or TV dinners ever graced our table. My mom was (and is) a great cook, but I was a terrible eater. I could not be excused until I at least tried everything on my plate. I used to swallow lima beans whole and smother most of my food with a salad dressing made of mayonnaise and ketchup. Still, apart from the lima beans and occasional liver and brussels sprouts, dinner was a very pleasant time for me—an integral part of my childhood memories.

• 1 in 6 meals is eaten in a car.

Unfortunately, times have changed. With so many women working outside the home now, and most everyone on tight schedules, dinnertime for most of my students is catch-as-catch-can. It is the exceptional family that eats together, but what's even more depressing to me is that very few of my students describe family mealtimes as a pleasant experience.

I get home at various times in the afternoon and stuff myself silly. Then around eight or nine my family gets together for the dinner that daddy dearest has prepared. The reason we eat so late is that my dad feels that he has to wait for my mom to get home from work before he starts cooking. For my family, dinner is a necessary thing; if you miss it or are late coming to it after you've been called, you get yelled at seriously. I hate it! I hate my parents and their over-obnoxious uptightness. They suck. I wouldn't even talk to them if they were my age. I don't care whether they live or die as long as they pay for my college education. They can get hit by buses for all I care. Dinner is when they get to ask me about school and everything and nag and bitch at me. If I'm lucky we watch TV. Dinner is the time when I most have to talk to my parents and lie to them and pretend to care about them more than shit on the bottom of my shoe. It's lame. I do like the food, though.

Male, 15

....

"Marsha, dinner."

"I'm not hungry."

"It's dinnertime."

"Okay. I'll be down in a minute. Get out of my room."

It's rare when my whole family eats together. When everyone is home and sits down together. Maybe once or twice a week.

"What are we having?"

"Ravioli."

"I don't like ravioli."

There's always at least one person who doesn't like what we are having.

"Then you can have cereal."

"I don't want cereal."

"Then make something else."

"We don't have anything good to eat. At Tony's house they have take-out Chinese every night. Why can't we ever have steak like at Julio's?"

"Because we don't have a grandma who lives with us who stays home and cooks all day. Sit down and stop complaining."

My parents proceed to talk about something that doesn't captivate the interest [of] my two younger brothers, so they start kicking each other under the table. This goes on until one screams.

"He kicked me."

"No, I didn't."

My mom or dad gets mad. "Can't we ever sit down to dinner together without you two always fighting? Stop it or you will be sent away from the table."

"Hey, that's just like this thing that happened on the Simpsons. And—"

"Henry, be quiet. We don't want to hear your TV talk."

Sometimes dinner is a success, other times one or two are sent to their rooms and everyone is mad for the rest of the evening.

Female, 15

There is no dinnertime. I hate it. We sit down together for dinner maybe once every two months and it usually goes well. But of course no one has time. Shit, I'd make time. It seems like the only time everyone can find out what's going on in everyone else's lives is at the dinner table. I go to friends' houses and love being in their conversations. I know people say if I wanted it badly, I would make it happen. But I don't think I have the ability or the time myself. I know that these types of things are supposed to carry on through my life but I'm putting a stop to it. If I ever have a family, dinnertime together will be enforced majorly. If I had to, I'd hire a cook to make sure the food was enjoyable enough for the conversation. I always talk too much whenever we do have those two-times-a-month dinners. Well, I hope it will change soon because my younger sisters need a better lifestyle.

Female, 15

The holiday season...what kinds of feelings do you have about family expectations, presents, religious rituals, traditions, pressures, joys, finances, etc.?

When the holiday season approaches I always spend time in class talking about the image of the holidays as portrayed by almost every TV commercial and print ad. It goes something like this: Mom and Dad and the two perfect kids are sitting in front of a roaring fire. Dad has on his monogrammed robe and is smoking a pipe. Mom is handing him a fresh cup of coffee or a brandy or a gorgeously wrapped gift. The puppy is sitting near a new bike with its red ribbon. The huge tree is perfectly trimmed with beautiful decorations.

The typical American home on Christmas morning? Not according to very many of my students. The holidays are supposed to be a time of togetherness for family and relatives, and I wish that were true for everyone but I know the reality is different. The holidays are an excuse for those who drink to drink even more. There may be an increase in family violence. Stress builds due to financial strain, finding the perfect gifts, last-minute shopping, dealing with relatives who don't really like each other (or don't speak to one another). For many students there's extra pressure and attendant guilt because they must choose which parent they will spend Christmas with. The holidays can also remind us of those who are no longer with us. In other words, it's no wonder many people find it a very unpleasant time of year. The hype of the holidays that begins around Halloween usually means that our own experience never quite measures up to our expectations or to our memories of past holiday celebrations.

On the plus side, there are some students who love the holidays and all of the traditions and good feelings that go with them. Some will talk about baking cookies and taking them to the homeless, singing in rest homes, and enjoying themselves with their families during the holiday season. It's unfortunate that this experience is not universal.

> I fucking hate this holiday. First it brings out all the kept-in pain of my parents' divorce because I fucking travel to my mom's gathering then my dad's gathering, then my mom's AND fucking it's not supposed to be like that. Then you have to fucking stuff your face (a total AMERICAN tradition) then be on your phony, fake behavior! It's such shit.

And on top of all that, it's a fucking tradition to eat a dead bird. I fucking don't eat dead birds. I whistle at them, watch them fly, look at their nests. I don't fucking eat them.

Male, 15

....

The holiday season has become a veritable bombardment of commercialism and capitalist advertisements. Not being religious, I have nothing to grasp onto during the holidays—no traditions that haven't been commercialized. My family celebrates Christmas, but I find the very idea somewhat ridiculous. And Santa Claus, or St. Nicholas...am I supposed to believe that there is a patron saint of mechanical toys? Or Nintendo games? Yeah, okay.

The holidays put a pressure on you to be very family-oriented. You get dressed up, and go to one or another family member's house. I have a HUGE family, but I'm not very close to anyone. I'm supposed to act like the fourth oldest cousin, instead of the black sheep, which I often think I am. Oh well. Happy holidays.

Female, 15

....

The holiday season conjures up memories of sleepless Christmas Eves and a pine-smelling home. That was a long time ago. I moved to Ohio from Maryland when I was seven. Christmas stayed at Grandma's. Sleepless nights remained until twelve but pine houses stopped at seven because Grandma has a plastic tree. Now Christmas is stressful because I feel "on" all the time. I feel like I have to be cheerful, happy, and polite all the time. Now pre-Christmas is more enjoyable than Christmas itself. I've learned to enjoy giving gifts almost more than getting them. And now I sleep on Christmas Day.

Female, 15

GREATEST IMPACT ON LIFE

What event/circumstance/person has had the greatest impact your life? Explain.

Today instead of going to school, I experienced something that will always stay with me: I witnessed the miracle of birth. No matter how many stories or films you hear about or see, nothing can be compared to actually being there when a child is born. It was my stepmother who gave birth. At 10:30 p.m. on Tuesday, her water broke, but she wasn't sure if it was going to happen right away. Then at about 5:00 a.m. the next morning my dad came in and said that we had to go to the hospital because she was in early labor. We stayed at the hospital all day, and then she started to go into real labor around 6:00 p.m. For about two and a half hours she pushed hard and we could see the baby's head. Finally, the doctor had to use a vacuum pump to pull him out.

He was a beautiful baby, 5 lbs. 11 oz. I felt so overwhelmed with waves of emotion, that I almost started crying. I think before you have a baby you should experience what I did and you'll realize how special it is. It's exactly what they call it—a miracle. To see this live human, being pushed out of the mother is so...wonderful. This has changed my life and now when someone says, "Oh, she had a baby," I can't help but to think what a fantastic experience birth really is.

Female, 16

In October 1991, a devastating fire raged through the hillsides of Berkeley and Oakland, destroying 3,354 single-family homes. Quite a few of our students, teachers, and counselors were directly affected: almost everyone in our school knew someone who lost everything in the fire.

Well, I think that my house burning down probably had the biggest impact on my life recently. Last October 20th, eleven days before my fifteenth birthday, my house burned down, and at the time, it felt like my memories, things that I treasured, had all burned with it. Now I realize that NO ONE and NOTHING can take away your memories. Twenty-five years of my dad's artwork went up in those flames including a bust that he did of me when I was eleven years old, as well as my grandma's art. Now I am coming to realize that all of those material possessions really do not matter that much. I will always have my memories and, although it does hurt to think of all my stuff destroyed...what does not kill me, can only make me stronger, really. I started going to a support group at Berkeley High though, and it really helped me deal with my loss. I feel much better about the whole situation now, and I can talk about it without crying now.

Female, 15

Loss is something that I have come to know very well in the past year and a half. I lost my home in the Oakland firestorm and with it many aspects of my life before Oct. 20th. One was the physical dwelling I had lived in for most of my life, the many irreplaceables like my baseball card and memorabilia collection, and gone was my home and the psychological comfort and safety, something I have yet to feel in the homes that I have bounced one to the other since the fire.

During the actual fire I dealt with it like anyone in emergency services would: calmly and methodically. First I started clearing brush and debris from the house and then eventually watering the roof, which was futile. Then when I got word that there was an invalid living down the street who needed to be carried out I got a friend and we went to his house, carried him from his bed to his wheel chair and then carried him and his chair 3 flights of stairs to a waiting car.

ASK ME IF I CARE

Once the elderly man was taken care of my father and I stayed with the house 'til it started to rain hot embers on us and the house. Then because there were two vehicles and only my father and I, I drove with no license and no one in the car in a complete daze to friends of my parents in Berkeley.

Since then I have had my moments of feeling stressed and depressed and even cried a little but never in front of anyone. I really haven't expressed much emotionally. And now with our insurance company trying to stall and jerk us around I have this never-ending feeling of being stressed and not having closure to this whole ordeal.

The most expressive thing I have done as far as the fire is concerned and the thing that has offered me somewhat of a feeling of catharsis is a portfolio of photographs that I took about two to three weeks after the fire. I ended up having some of them displayed in firestorm art shows around the Bay Area.

Male, 17

Describe your spiritual/religious background and beliefs.

Religion is not covered in the Social Living course, but the topic is brought up by students all the time. We have had some fascinating discussions, with students who are Muslims, Orthodox Jews, Catholics, Fundamentalists, and atheists, among others, stating their religious beliefs and how these beliefs influence their values and outlook on sex, homosexuality, drugs, or whatever we happen to be working on. Students are very outspoken on this topic, but they are also very respectful of other people's religious and philosophical convictions. Replies to this "your choice" question are usually very serious and thoughtful.

I'm not really religious, but I think that I'm very spiritual. I believe that you can make your own destiny, and control your own life, but I believe that there is some force or power, maybe an intelligence, that has planned much of what goes on. My mom's dad is Jewish, her mom is Protestant, my dad's mom is Seventh Day Adventist and his dad is Catholic. This is why I do not claim a religion.

Female, 15

I don't believe in any real GOD. I believe there is something but I would like to think of it as love. I guess I believe that there is something divine but I like to see it expressed as singing and dancing and especially laughing and smiling.

Female, 15

....

I believe that there is a God but I don't have a religion. I went to church when I was little but I found it to be more of a fashion show than anything else. But I believe that there is a God and that I have a guardian angel.

Female, 15

Sometimes I'll ask the class how many of them feel that they have a guardian angel and several will share that they do.

I do believe in God. I go to different churches because I would like to pick the religion I would like. I grew up going to a Pentecostal church. I liked the church but didn't like the people. I figure that I really don't have to go to church to worship God because God is wherever I go. My life may not be all that fantastic but I figure God put me here for a reason.

Female, 16

....

I do believe in God and I go to church on Sunday. I'm in a high school group that meets on Wednesdays. We talk about the bible and how we can use it in this day and age. We learn and try to understand what God wants for us. Sometimes it's hard for me to believe in God, even though I've grown up in a Christian family. I wonder what kind of plan he has for the world and why bad things go on when there seems to be no good in it or any good will ever come of it. With all the influence around these days in school and on TV, I think that there is no use for me in the world. I don't see how I can make a difference. I believe in the Trinity and I love to sing in the choir to praise his name. I love to be with Him by myself and I just feel that He is the one person who totally understands everyone and me especially.

Female, 15

God—My Inner Self:

You know, you are not a religious part of my life. I don't go to church to see or worship you, because you are inside of me—you are a spiritual part of me—you're not a human who looks down upon the earth like Zeus or Athena. I feel I have a personal relationship with you—I don't need to read the Bible or pray because in my mind you aren't related to the Bible, you are related to me (not in a hereditary way). You are related to every human being. You are a part of everybody and each person sees you differently in their own mind—I see you in no form—you are my guide—you could be a light, an animal for all I know—but one thing I do know is you are inside of me, not in a church or in heaven.

Female, 17

I never told my own religion nor scrutinized that of another. I never attempted to make a convert, nor wished to change another's creed. I am satisfied that yours must be an excellent religion to have produced a life of such exemplary virtue and correctness. For it is in our lives, and not from our words, that our religion must be judged.

—THOMAS JEFFERSON

Dear God,

You are very special to me. But You aren't like the god that gave Moses the Ten Commandments, or the god that will punish someone if they aren't good. You are a personal thing, something that's part of me. To me You represent the comfort and solace that I find deep down inside of me when everything seems to be going wrong. You are that feeling of exuberance that I get when I've done something good, or the excitement I feel when everything is working out and I'm so happy to be alive. You are the feeling of the perfect symmetry of my body when I do the breast stroke. You are the rush of blood coursing through my body when I flirt with guys I like. You are the feeling of calm contentment I experience when I float in the water on a raft with the sun shining down on me. You are the pure happiness when I look up and smile at someone and they smile back as if they know exactly how I feel. I love You, and by loving You, I love myself, because You are the reason that I'm here on this earth. You are the reason that one particular egg and one particular sperm came to make me what I am.

Female, 16

....

I cannot name what I believe in, it has no name. It is the total awareness of everything, it is the guide that brought about the beauty of the earth. It does not reside in a building, or listen to certain people, it is neither evil nor good. It is the shape of a rock or the shape of a thought. It neither seeks followers nor seeks to rid itself of followers. I feel closest to it in the wilderness, I feel a large part of it is nature, but I will never be sure. It helps to have it there.

Male, 16

....

My religious beliefs are more ethical than spiritual. My background religion is essentially about 600 to 700 different minor religions and cults, loosely bonded together as "pagan." I personally worship the Goddess in all her forms—from the Virgin Mary to Demeter the fruitful, to Binah, the keeper of knowledge, the wise woman. But, I also admit that there are male aspects of divinity, such as Jesus, Krishna, Buddha, Shiva, Pan, etc. The idea behind all this confusion is to restore balance. Male god(s) tend to be aggressive and dominant when they are "overworshipped"— the world as we know it tends to go to hell in a handbasket—for example, the last 10,000 years. Female gods are usually pacifying and fertile (but not always), so we are trying to swing the pendulum the other way, and restore peace and balance. I believe in using magic (earth magic, not "black" magic—there is a difference) to achieve this goal, and do call myself a "witch," but I haven't "sold my soul to the devil" or anything, since that would demolish the whole principle of the thing. To explain the workings of magic would fill well over 200 heavy tomes but it does work. I've used it often when my life is going to pieces.

Female, 16

Regarding God: I'm not very sure about how I feel about God. Unlike my father, who is an atheist, I do believe that there is a god—but not in terms of modern organized religion. I do not condemn organized religion because I realize that while it may not represent my personal ideas and beliefs, and that while there are many evils in organized religion (the religious wars, for example), organized religion does help some people. For some it gives them the spiritual support they need, and for their sake I do not condemn it. My stepmother is a pagan and from what I know about her beliefs, I lean more towards them, seeing God through nature in the world. For myself, I am a more logical and scientific type of person rather than artistic and some part of me thinks that it is logically impossible for such a being to create and exist in our scientifically set universe. Yet I feel that this being does not really exist in any physical way at all—that it is a spiritual part of me that comes from my beliefs. My god exists in myself solely because I believe in it and have faith in it. I don't pray to this god, or think about it very often even, but I feel that when I am very depressed, or joyously ecstatic, that there is a presence that is always with me—inside of me. I like to think of it as an inner strength that I can call upon in a time of need.

Female, 16

....

God is the most confusing subject. Although I can't honestly say that I believe in the Bible's theory of God, I find myself praying a lot, and worrying about what God thinks of me. My family is Jewish, but not really religious. Sometimes when something really wrong and unfair happens to me, I yell at God, or when I don't want something to happen, I stay awake all night praying that it won't. When it's all over, I pray again apologizing for putting all my problems and fears in God's hands when I know that I have more control over my life than anyone else. Even God.

Female, 15

....

It really bothers me that people, no names mentioned, get on our TV, ask for money and preach about God—their own, systematic views about Him. This is not religion—it is soliciting and cheating the people—it is wrong. God is a father—someone who watches over me—tells me and guides me so that I will experience the fullness of my life. Each God is different to each person. God is who you need most at the time—he fills the gaps in life—the holes in my mind. I love my God!

Female, 15

....

I don't believe in God. Sometimes I wish I did—it would be something to hold on to, something to help me through bad times, to help make decisions. But I don't. I believe the Earth is just one tiny planet among many billions and trillions in the universe—created not by supernatural forces but by the natural actions of our solar system. I believe humans evolved, along with all other life forms on the earth—not that we were created by God or gods. What happens in my life is determined by me, and by luck and chance, but not by some omnipotent, omni-scient being. Sometimes I am rewarded or punished for things—but not by God. Maybe there is a God—for many people there is—but not for me.

Female, 16

....

I have never been brought up in a religious environment. I am not reli-gious at all but I have nothing against those that are. I was born Jewish and I guess if I had to pick a religion to follow, it would be the one I would have chosen. Even though I don't go to temple and I don't fast or even celebrate any of the holidays, I still can identify with being Jew-ish. I guess I can identify with it because so many people discriminate against Jewish people and I was born with many qualities that many people are prejudiced against. Judaism is a very open, accepting religion and that's the way I think a religion should be. I don't think people should try to force their beliefs on others.

Female, 16

....

I swear, the easiest way to get your child involved in sex and drugs is to make them a Catholic.

Female, 15½

I am a Catholic, in that I'm baptized as one. I see myself as Christian but there are many Catholic "laws" which I find unloving, prudish and far from what Christ was all about. These mainly dealing with birth control, sexuality, homosexuality, and the idea that the Catholic Church is superior. I have a lot of trouble with my faith recently but I always believe that there is a "force" which binds the universe together. I don't believe in hell or heaven exactly, but I see death simply as a transition between life on earth and life in some other existence or plane. I believe most strongly in reincarnation, that you come back to earth for whatever number of lives it takes to learn all you can from the earth. When you have finished, you simply move on to another level of learning.

I have many different beliefs and I can understand most beliefs other than mine. There are a few I have a big problem with; Fundamentalism especially, and also Muslim beliefs dealing with women.

Female, 15

....

I'm not sure if I do or if I don't. Sometimes I feel He is with me and that there always will be a God. On the other hand, it seems as if God sometimes takes a break, so you don't know if He is there. In the end, if I really think about it, and weigh all my ideas back and forth, there is a God. It just takes an occasional sabbatical. After all everybody gets tired of their jobs at one time or another.

Male, 16

....

I am extremely active in the synagogue. I chant Hebrew and dance. I don't believe in God though, well, not the God I pray to in temple. I believe everyone has their own god, sort of like a supernatural superego. But I just love the feeling of religion. I love the overwhelming feeling of community and the sense of ethics that comes out of religion.

Female, 15

....

I once taught a Sunday school class when I was thirteen. By then I had read three different Bibles (a children's version, the King James version, and the Catholic version) and found fundamental ideological and moral differences and hence my lack of interest in that divinity called God. I no longer have a religion.

Male, 15

....

I don't believe in God or most religions. People created God so they had something to believe in and blame things on or make excuses for. I feel most religions are hypocritical. You commit adultery, go to church and confess, and God will make it alright. I believe that everyone has their own spiritual guidance within them. I personally am pretty superstitious and think that different things that happen to me are signs or signals of some sort. I also believe in fate. What is going to happen is going to happen whether you are the perfect Catholic, Jew, or whatever. If God was who everyone says He is—wonderful, can make everything better—why is there war and hunger in the world?...But in a way, God is good for some people. Some people can't express themselves very well to other people but can "talk to God." Maybe this can solve their own internal problems. But I don't feel the need to go to church every Sunday just so God won't get mad at me. God is just there for people to depend on.

Female, 15

....

My spiritual trust lies within myself—I have [a] strong will to do things that are good for me. I feel like God is not really a "god" but more of a force inside me. It is the happiness I feel, and the strength I have. It doesn't tell me what to do, but it encourages me for what I have chosen to do. It has no laws that say, "If you want to be a good person, you have to be married before you have sex," or "You must come to a church and listen to a priest babble on and on...."

The time I worship is the time I spend alone. I don't have to utter any special words, or read a special book, or hold special beads. All I have to do is think about myself, and other people. I cherish the time I spend at home alone. It gives me a feeling of freedom from the hectic society we live in, and gives me a chance to consider me. I don't even need to think...—it can be sleeping, listening to music, or reading. If I'm doing something good for myself, then I can be a much happier person.

Female, 16

What advice would you give to other teens? to the opposite sex? to anyone?

One reason I encourage class discussions and spend so much class time reading journal entries is that the students are much more likely to pay attention to what their peers say than to what I say. This is especially true when it comes to taking advice! There have been many times in class when you can just feel that minds are being opened and viewpoints changed by something a fellow student said. One time one of my students begged me to tell her how to keep her virginity—her hormones were in direct conflict with her moral beliefs. Before I had time to answer, three other students—a teenaged mother, a minister's daughter, and a young woman who had a long-term sexual relationship with her boyfriend—all offered their advice. Basically, they were all saying, "Keep your virginity." Undoubtedly, their input had a far greater impact than anything I could have said.

In the following entries, teens give advice to their peers. Each entry touches on a common life experience or contains some little gem of philosophy.

On Relationships

I guess some girls think that love, sex, dating, etc., is a breeze for the guys. I'd want them to know that that's not necessarily true, at all.

Male, 16

....

Stop being crude. Contrary to what you may think, we women do not like to be stared at and yelled to as if we were on auction, to be sold to the highest bidder. So cut it out, we are human beings and we demand to be treated as such.

Female, 16

....

Not all boys want only sex, or are promiscuous yet jealous, or are self-centered and selfish and uncaring. Don't get discouraged from one failure, and make generalizations about boys. And be more honest when you are interested in a boy, but don't "push."

Male, 15

One thing for sure, get your <u>right</u> and your <u>wrong</u> straightened out. If you love him, then stay with him. That's important. The most important thing is to love yourself. If you think you're doing wrong, stop. If you think you're doing right, God, don't stop!

Female, 16

....

Someone told me, "Never change, or act a certain way to make someone like you. An act can only last so long and what if that person falls in love with <u>that</u> person? The whole relationship will be based on a lie and can't possibly be real, or last long." I think it was the best advice I've ever gotten. There have been so many times when I begin to act differently, thinking it'll get this person to like me—then I think of that advice, and realize there's no point. What if I do get that person to love me? It won't be me they love, and there's no way I'd be happy. Now I'm always myself from the very beginning—either they like me or they don't. But if they do, then it'll be me they truly like!

Female, 15

....

On Forgiving

Forgiveness is important, and often very hard. Sometimes you put blame on somebody and hold a grudge, and then realize how stupid grudges are. If there was no forgiveness, everyone would walk around hating each other all the time. That would be a drag. If there was no forgiveness, nobody could stand to be alive. I love to be forgiven, and I like the feeling I get from forgiving somebody. It is definitely one of the most gratifying and sacred qualities for one to possess.

Male, 15

....

Ultimately what it comes down to is the ability to forgive—that's what makes close relationships possible. Forgiving doesn't mean giving in; in fact, it means the opposite. Forgiving someone removes you from the victim position and helps you to regain your personal power by reclaiming your emotions; apologizing is a way of forgiving YOURSELF—it says, "I'm human."

Female, 15

Forgiving someone is showing that there is still a bonding edge to the relationship with the person being forgiven, and proves that you still have respect for that person. And that is a very strong and great quality for anyone to have.

Male, 18

....

Sometimes to forgive someone is very difficult. But holding a grudge does nothing. When one forgives somebody, he or she shows that there is still love. It is so easy to bottle up and hold a grudge, but most rewarding to take the first step, reaching out to break the silence. Dear Mom and Dad, I forgive you both for breaking up your marriage and ultimately the whole family went different directions, each individual fending for themselves. I wish we could all reunite as a family, but I must face reality. Thank you.

Male, 15

....

I don't really know what to write about because I feel that I am an extraordinarily happy person. I don't have any family problems that are pressuring me now. (I did in the past but that was resolved by going to therapy and finally being able to communicate and understand one another's feelings.) I have many close friends with whom I am very open and I just recently got a boyfriend who I'm hella sprung on. Of course, I have pressures but I feel that I'm able to cope with them. I realize that everybody has problems and these problems are sometimes extremely difficult to deal with and seem to go on endlessly. I just want to say that if you take this problem one step at a time, try to under-stand why it arose, how it came to be, and how to settle it, and be open with your feelings both to yourself and others whom you can trust, it is much better than if you try to ignore it, stress over it and cover it up.

If you don't have anybody you can trust, go to a counselor—you are not a freak if you do. I went to one and I certainly don't think I'm a freak.

Enjoy life—problems are learning experiences that will come and go.

Female, 16

On Life and Self-Knowledge

Hold fast to dreams because they might become real, make sure you study hard because your education is a very big deal; instead of fighting with your work make love to it; instead of trippin' off our parents' derogatory remarks, tell them to shove it; so close your eyes and make a wish, and tell the world to watch out because you're coming and you're one crazy son of a bitch!

Male, 17

....

I think strengths and weaknesses are forever changing as your increasing trust or distrust of the world broadens to show you new ways. If you're aware and you watch, life takes you where you need to be and ultimately your weaknesses are going to serve you just as well as your strengths. Anything that pushes you closer to the truth about yourself—as long as you know, you're very strong.

Female, 15

Experience as much as you can, life's short.

Female, 16

The best advice that I have ever received was to love and believe in myself and my abilities, and to be proud of who I was. The reason...is because if you don't love yourself, then you cannot expect others to love you. Also, there are some people in the world who will insult you, or put you down, and try to convince you that something is wrong with you so that they can feel a sense of power, and if you don't believe in yourself you'll start to believe them, and you'll let it destroy you.

Female, 15

_____

The best advice I would want to give someone is something that is said time after time. Do not make cutting a weekly or daily habit. I would never say don't cut at all because that is a part of high school but once it becomes a habit it becomes a problem leading downhill. I can say this from experience at first I started cutting with friends & then I started cutting by myself going home and going to sleep. It wasn't worth it. I used to be in honors classes at my old school Piedmont High and then I came here and now I can't get into a four-year [college]. I didn't even try. I'm mad at myself but that is life, but I don't think it was worth it.

Female, 18

_____

My advice to teenagers is to slow down! Too many teenagers try to grow up too fast. I believe that they should enjoy life at a slow pace, instead of trying to be all grown up, (which they really are not). It isn't bad to grow up, but some teenagers try to grow up much too fast. Why can't they take life step by step?

Female, 15

_____

I read a piece of advice the other day, it said something like look and listen with an open mind and then develop your own opinion. This is great advice for all aspects of developing character. Don't just follow people, lead yourself. If you're going in the right direction you'll know it.

Don't diss a style, a person, or a point of view, unless you have given it a fair shake first. If you have truthfully given someone or something a trial run, then make your stand or point of view.

Male, 18

I think the best advice I could give is this: If you want something done right, you have to do it yourself. This advice can be used in many forms, but the main idea is that nobody is going to live your life for you, so if you have a problem it is best to solve it yourself. I'm not saying people shouldn't help one another, it's just that here at Berkeley High, most of the administrators and counselors don't have time to make sure every single person is doing what they should be doing. If you need something, you should always check up and make sure, because otherwise it's not going to get done. Out in the real world, it's pretty impersonal, so you should get used to being independent and self-reliant. If you depend on others to do the job, either it's not going to be right or it won't get done at all. I think I've learned this from going to Berkeley High.

Female, 16

What is success? To laugh often and much; to win the respect of intelligent people and the affection of children; to earn the appreciation of honest critics and endure the betrayal of false friends; to appreciate beauty, to find the best in others; to leave the world a bit better, whether by a healthy child, a garden patch, or a redeemed social condition; to know even one life has breathed easier because you have lived; that is to have succeeded.

—RALPH WALDO EMERSON

When I talk with former students who have gone on to colleges and universities in other parts of the country, they echo just what the last girl wrote. BHS really prepares you for being independent. Of course, the downside of this is that there isn't always a safety net for those who fall through the cracks, those who don't know how to work the system or to do it on their own.

Advice I would give to any person is to strive for what you want. Don't ever give up on anything you're trying to achieve, although it is normal and necessary to be weak and feel like giving up at times. Use that to your advantage as a booster, feel bad and sorry for yourself and use that as a reason to strive harder. Also it is very important to never keep your feelings bottled up. Develop strong friendships which are more than just outward. Use your spirit to look into other people's spirits and relate to them from the inside, not just the outside. Voice your feelings and opinions. Love yourself most importantly and remember that God is always there for you. If you trust in Him he won't let you down.

Female, 16

From what I can tell this last writer practiced what she wrote as I know that she was dealing with extreme personal trauma having been violently raped and subsequently kicked out of her house. I find her inner strength and positive attitude very inspirational.

I don't remember the exact quote, but it was something like, "If you haven't felt pain, then you can't fully experience joy." This quote reminds me, when I'm sad, that there will be better times. It also makes me treasure those moments when I am happy.

Female, 16

....

I would like to tell <u>both</u> sexes to relax! Everybody seems so uptight and so many people lose themselves trying to impress others, when honesty and openness would make things go over so much more easily. I wish people would stop trying to be what they're not, accept what they are, and work from there. The smallest lie, to oneself or to others, can cause the deepest and cruelest pain. In general, I think a deeper self-aware-ness and realization would make life a lot easier; and openness, honesty, and friendship would make for a smoother running "world in one peace," which can cope with itself for the benefit of everyone and everything live and beautiful.

Female, 16

....

This is really a hard question for me because advice is something I love to give, even when people don't ask for it. Safe Sex, Don't Drink n' Drive, Cover your chest when you have a cold, Don't wear blue pants and a black shirt to an interview, Get your hair cut before an audition— it looks awful. I feel like I might not be perfect, but I also see the faults in others very easily. Perfection is something I'm constantly striving for, so even if intellectually I can understand how others don't feel the way I do, physically it bothers me to see people screwing up. SO, ADVICE...hmmm? I guess the best advice in life is to LIVE 'n' LET LIVE, but if someone is fucking up, don't be afraid to tell them—NICELY. My second best advice is, "WHEN IN DOUBT, READ DR. SEUSS." Because he knows lots and he is always happy and beautiful and creative. And he accepts everyone, no matter how—Yeah! I like that advice!

Female, 18

Life is hard but it's harder if you're stupid.

—ANONYMOUS COMMENCEMENT SPEAKER

On Time

Re Time: The only time I can control is right now. The only moment I can control is right now, at this millisecond. So I can't spend too much time worrying about the future or dwelling on the past. Of course you have to think about the future and plan for it. But you shouldn't live in the past or future. You have to live for the present or else you're wasting your life.

Male, 16

....

Time comes
and time goes,
It passes as the wind passes,
sometimes soft and sweet
with a cushion to soften its parting.
Other times it will pass hard and cold
reminding us of the little time that we have left.
As it passes I wonder whether I use it wisely,
or do I waste the precious time that I have,
Time often passes so quickly that I start to worry about
where it goes
And yet, I realize that I cannot live for time,
I must use that time to live for
Laughter
and tears,

I must use that time to live for
the joy of meeting,
and the sorrow of parting,
I must use that time to live for
the wonder of birth
and the acceptance of death,
I must use that time to live for
the love of liberty,
and the hatred of slavery
I must use that time to live for life.

Male, 15

14 | **Finals**

THE DAY THAT JOURNALS ARE DUE is always one that tests my patience. Even though I have explained every day for the past week that journals must be turned in today (the date has been in bold letters on the board all week!), and have shown examples of the correct way to organize them, and provided easy-to-read instructions and a checklist, the endless questions make me wonder what grade I am teaching. "Is it okay if my work is not in order?" (Sarcastic replies run through my mind: Of course the numbers were just there for decoration, and the instructions to number everything and have all work in order were just to fool you!) "I couldn't find a photo of myself." I usually respond, "Fine," and they look pleased until I add, "I can't find any A's or B's for your journal grade then!" (They have had seven weeks to find one photograph that looks like them—or even a photocopy of one.) "Nancy, I left my journal on the bus." "Nancy, my backpack was stolen last night." And "Ms. Rubin, someone pissed in my locker last night. Really!! Do you want me to hand it in AS IS?" Do I dare call his bluff?

Journals are due by 2:40 P.M., but I end up lingering at school until 4:00 P.M. In the morning I will find a couple of journals under my door, and the owners will claim they got them in by 2:40, but I know differently.

It will take me every school night for two weeks, plus two full weekends, to "do journals." I read every word of every journal, adding comments and questions throughout, and I write each student a personal letter. When my friends call and I say I'm doing journals, they sigh as if to say, Not again—you always seem to be doing them. It

Top Problems in
Schools

In 1940:

1. talking

2. chewing gum

3. making noise

4. running in the
   halls

5. getting out of line

6. wearing improper
   clothing

7. not putting
   paper in the waste
   baskets

In 1988:

1. drug abuse

2. alcohol abuse

3. pregnancy

4. suicide

5. rape

6. robbery

7. assault

In 2000?

seems like I'm always doing journals because it happens four times each school year. I rarely do any socializing when I'm working on them. Basically I stay at home and hope for rain! I keep wondering if this is a worthwhile use of my time and if it is really beneficial to my students. But when the students evaluate the class at the end of each nine weeks, they are asked if the journal is important, and the response is always an overwhelmingly YES. So I persevere.

Somehow, I read all the journals and figure out grades for some two hundred students. As a student, I never liked being graded, and as a teacher, I like giving out grades even less. It is a long, tedious process; unfortunately, it is also an unavoidable one.

During these two weeks, I usually schedule speakers for the classes and show a video or two having to do with one of the topics we have been discussing. I also take this time to answer any questions that were not addressed earlier in the course, or to go back to any topic that I feel was not completely covered. Even though the journals have been turned in, there is always plenty to do.

The last few days of each semester are set aside for finals—the regular schedule is replaced by two-hour time blocks. At various times during the nine weeks of Social Living, students will ask if we are having a final. I tell them that there will be no test, but they will have some papers to fill out, and there will be a special final activity. They are required to come to class and stay for the entire two hours—and they should bring something with which to write.

One of the things the students have to do for their "final" is to grade themselves based on the criteria listed on the "Don't Say I Never Told You This!" sheet that they got at the beginning of the course. Some 90 percent of the students are very good at determining their grade; many of them are harder on themselves than I would be, and a few are a little too generous. So I not only lower some grades but raise others. It is helpful for me to see how the students evaluate themselves in such areas as participation, behavior, attendance, punctuality, and journal work. There are always a couple of students asking to borrow a pen—you would think that somewhere in their huge backpacks they would have an extra pen or pencil to bring to their final.

After this, I have the students write me a note evaluating the course.

I put a list of all the topics, speakers, videos, activities, worksheets, etc., on the board and ask them to tell me what worked, what should be dropped, added, or changed, and anything they wish to say regarding my teaching. I make it very clear that I want their honest feedback and any helpful criticism: they do not need to sign the letter unless they want to. The notes range from vicious to glowing—with many balancing one another out. For example, it is not unusual to get several notes saying we spent too much time on drugs and several others complaining that I should have covered drugs in more depth because it is such a big problem—all from the same class. One student wrote, "The activity we did on the first day, asking the opposite sex questions, was one of my favorite things (I came up with a few more interesting questions)," while someone else wrote, "One thing I would change would have been the first day of class. That first impression was not very good, a majority of the people didn't like the activity and their negativity rubbed off. Please consider making a better first impression for yourself and this class." One of the lessons I learned early on is that you can't please everybody.

The last thing we do is what I call, for want of a better name, the "envelope activity." I pass out large envelopes which have been used many times before—sometimes with dozens of names on them. Each student is to make sure all of the old names have been crossed out,

I suppose it's only fair to warn both of you: I've been keeping a journal the whole time!

then they are to put their own name on it with a brief description of clothing or something by which they can be easily identified. It could be as simple as Tyrone—A's cap; Carolyn—fuschia hair; or Tymeka—CAL sweatshirt. Then everyone is given a stack of scratch paper. To begin, each student passes their envelope to the person on their right, and then each student writes a personal note to the person whose name is on the envelope. They write the person's name at the top of a piece of scratch paper, then write something POSITIVE to them. I tell them that such comments as "You have the worst breath" or "Ever since second grade I thought you were gross" are unacceptable, and vague remarks like "Have a nice summer" or "You seem like a nice person" aren't good enough. For many weeks the classmates have been listening to one another and most of them also spent nine weeks together in Driver's Education, so they should have a sense of the other people. "Think of how the person will feel when they read your special message." They may sign the notes or give their initials, or write male or female, secret admirer, or anything they wish, or they may simply choose not to sign it. The note goes in the envelope, and the envelope gets passed to the right again. Each envelope will go around the room until the "owner" gets it back, by which time it should have a note from every person in the room.

Just in case someone should receive a nasty note—this doesn't happen very often—I tell the class that put-downs reveal more about the writer's own insecurity than anything else and should be ignored. I answer several questions and everyone begins to write.

This exercise certainly has to be less stressful than most of their other finals! One of my former students, whom I had not seen in over ten years, recently started working at BHS and the first thing she said to me was, "Do you still do the envelope activity?" I said yes, and she said she still has the notes her classmates wrote to her. I continue to do this activity because it seems that so few students get enough positive feedback. I remember the first year I did journals I wrote a note to one of my students, Steve, to say that he had the most beautiful eyes. He told me—years after he graduated—that that was the first compliment anyone had ever paid him. It had obviously meant a lot to him. These compliments and encouragement are even more meaningful because they come from peers. I think most of us can remember all of the hurtful comments we received as children and teens from our peers, but imagine getting a note that says, "You should talk more in class because you seem like such an interesting person." I have some of my own favorites tacked to my refrigerator, and they always give me a lift. "You is a good teacher"—"Nancy, if you weren't my teacher I'd ask you to marry me!"—and a short poem, "Nancy is great, Nancy is hella cool, I hear everybody say that cause Da Shit Be 4 Real."

Today, while the students are writing, I pack up my belongings, because I was told that most likely I will be moved to another room. I have been in this one for thirteen years and have accumulated decorations (all the photos, posters, and album covers that grace the walls and ceiling), educational materials, and "stuff" that needs to be filed— some in folders, some in the trash. I hate leaving this room—it is probably the best one in the entire school. It is directly across from the Health Center and close to the Main Office. This building is quite bright and cheery because of the many murals in the hallways that were painted by the students, and my room has the luxury of windows and doors that open onto a sheltered area so that I can adjust the room temperature. (The central heating has been a major problem: some classrooms end up like saunas while others have little or no heat.) I know that any room after this one will be a little less pleasant but it seems that I have no choice. So I continue to box up all of my books, supplies, and personal treasures, and I try not to think about the reality of when and where we will find a new home.

Someone jolts me back to the present and alerts me that everyone has received their own envelope back and someone hands me my envelope of notes. A girl asks me why *I* didn't write any notes and I explain that late last night I finally finished writing a personal letter to everyone in their journal. I have already written everything I wanted to communicate! We all read our notes and many students are complaining that their notes are not signed. "I want to know who said this, it is sooo sweet." "This guy said he wanted to talk to me and gave me his number—but didn't put his name on it! Who wrote this?" Silence. I ask if anyone wants to read some of their favorite notes but without naming the author, who might prefer to remain anonymous. There are some very creative notes and beautiful, personalized comments. It appears that everyone is enjoying their little recycled scratch paper sentiments and some of them will keep theirs for a long time—on their mirrors, in their memories, in their hearts. On this note—these notes—I collect the empty envelopes and say good-bye. I tell them to have a great summer, don't drink and drive, just say NO—or use condoms, always buckle up, and always wear a helmet! Someone shouts back at me, "Nancy, don't get pregnant!" They file out, smiling and talking to one another, and a few stop to say thank you or to wish me a happy summer.

Finals are now over and on this very last day of this school year two of my students come by. They are rather shocked to see my room. It is almost completely bare. It took me and Fran, a loving student who volunteered to help, almost five hours to carefully remove all of the remaining items from the walls, drawers, cabinets, and my desk. The room now looks like any other institutional classroom. The girls ask "What happened?" and I say that my room will be used for summer school and I was advised to remove everything—for security. AND, I might have to move to another room.

The girls have patiently listened to my saga and I enthusiastically ask them what they have planned for the summer. One girl says, "I don't know. I ran away from home last night." Immediately, my possible room change is put into its proper perspective.

The room is empty, and I rush to the Main Office to hand in grades, my roll book, and my keys. I always find the last day of school anticlimactic as students and teachers all check out at different times and everyone seems to quietly disappear. The school is basically deserted. There's no one to say good-bye to.

But then there is graduation. Berkeley High must have the most beautiful setting for graduation of any high school in the country. It is held about a mile up the hill from the high school, in the majestic Greek Theatre at the University of California. The campanile looms gracefully in the distance behind the stage. This is always a joyous occasion for me—not only does it signify that I survived another year of teaching, but the pride and excitement of the graduates is infectious. Often I assist backstage and I get to see each student right before they walk onto the stage and get their diploma. I recognize most of them from my classes and feel honored to have had their trust and to have been part of their educational experience. They also survived.

Specifically, I will always remember the girl who came up to me one Friday afternoon about five weeks before the end of the school year to say that she had been kicked out of her house. Her uncle had awakened her at midnight and said that she could no longer live with him and his wife. She had already been abandoned by her mother. Together we stayed in my office for over three hours trying to find a place that would take her—she was too old for some shelters and too young for others. She walked across the stage in her cap and gown having spent the last weeks of high school living in a homeless shelter. Did anyone from her family see her graduate? I certainly hope so, but I doubt it.

Sometime during the summer break, I take stock of the year that has just past, reflect on the successes and failures, and think about how I can improve the class. I read all the evaluations: along with the notes I get in my envelope, these evaluations are often the only reward I get for the many hours of teaching and reading and writing in journals, time spent lining up speakers, the endless day-to-day frustrations, and the feeling that sometimes all of the effort is just not appreciated. I often feel that I am only putting a Band-Aid on the deep wounds that so many young people carry with them. I barely touch the surface of so many of the issues that I squeeze into a typical quarter. However, I am always encouraged whenever the evaluations indicate that it is worth the effort, that the course can be effective. For some, it may only be an awareness of their situation, but others may take the knowledge they gain here and use it to begin to break a cycle of addiction, teen pregnancy, abuse, or drug use—or decide never to let it begin. When I start to doubt myself, letters like the following three give me the reassurance I need:

> Ms. Rubin, this class was very interesting, helpful and powerful. It has created a major impact on my life. I feel really good that I talked and shared my innermost feelings in the class. I would have never done it without this class, the students and your help.
>
> Your Sixth Period Student

I have learned a lot this quarter in your class, especially about myself and others around me. I think I've learned more about sex than I've ever learned in any class or church. The journal was very helpful by opening me up to talk on paper rather than words. I'm aware of a great drug inheritance risk that I'm at and I'm sure of myself that I'm not headed in that direction. Thank you for teaching and for your support. I wasn't at anytime concerned about my grade but rather I learned something everyday and it wouldn't matter if I got an A+ or F-. I think that this class should be required for a year.

In my opinion the journal was very valuable. Not only will it show how I was as a teenager, but, it will be a memory of my first year here at Berkeley High. I really liked the letter that you wrote to me and I took your advice about going to see the college advisor. Thanks!!!

I learned a lot about myself and I finally got a chance to tell someone the feelings that I had been hiding. The best assignment that you ever gave was the one where we write a letter to ourselves for the future. That's something that will always have some kind of sentimental value to everyone of us because it's almost like our own private psychic prediction. Well Nancy, since we had to grade ourselves today I'm going to grade you. I give you and your class an A+.

Love ya! And thanks for the great advice.

So many times during the school year I spend my lunch hour or time after school listening to a student and trying to help them with their problems. Often I don't learn what they decided to do or what was the outcome of their situation. I loan students books and never see the student nor the books again. But then I receive a note like the next one, and I know that the extra time was definitely worthwhile.

> It is really incredible to me that someone can give so much of themselves to one person. Life is so hard sometimes but just knowing that whenever I want I can come and open up to you. I have so many problems, and I let them build up until it's become an incredible depression, but having a journal and someone who listens is wonderful. You are like the mother we never had, the older sister who wasn't there, the aunt who wasn't there either. For me you are all of those things. You are so special and you dress, my god so very, very vogue! Take care—I know you will!

There are always evaluations that state that the student already knew all of the material and it was a waste of time, the class was boring, and they did not like my attitude. There are usually several complaints about my being so strict—"Ten absences in nine weeks and you flunk? Your attendance policy sucks—lighten up!" "You should let us chew gum." I read and take into consideration each evaluation and figure out how to improve the class.

> You run your class like it has to be the same every semester. Relax! I felt like I was compared to every past semester. Maybe you have been working here too long. You seem like you're bored. You've done these same things over and over, it's nothing new to you. After you read so many journals to me before I even start writing I feel like I am writing just like the past people except in my experience. Don't you want people to find new and exciting angles? Anyways, it was fun but now I get to leave! Thanx.

....

> Dear Social Living "Want-to-Be-a-Psychologist Person"—
>
> I hate this class so much it's amazing. In fact as a person I find you utterly repulsive. Damn—that felt good—thanks. I cannot express to the

degree that I think this class is a complete utter waste of time. Maybe if I was a molested batterer psychopath basehead with genital warts this class would be for me. As far as I can tell I'm not. Oh well.

....

You look like a wax doll and class was hella boring.

....

Your class is pointless. I didn't learn anything.... Why do you need to know all this shit? Why should we tell you? You get a good grade in this class by revealing yourself to you. Is that fair? Maybe I didn't want to share something with you. I don't have time to watch any of your fucking makeup assignments. Grading should be on class participation. It should be individual as well.

Unthankfully,
Wasted time.

Even though some feel the grading is too harsh, others realize that they need to change their attitude toward rules that have been set out. It seems to get harder and harder to stick to what I consider are minimum standards but I think that students really need to be held accountable.

I'm not going to beat around the bush. This class was valuable in two ways: the facts I learned and getting caught for my biggest four problems: laziness, procrastination, arrogance, and my lack of organization. There are few teachers ever that have told me not only how they feel about me or my work directly and you are the only teacher who got this feeling of letting someone else down stuck firmly in my head. I know I often don't have the "balls" to confess orally so I'm doing it on paper. Please forgive my being a jerk. I do need more people in my life like you to not only guide me in the right direction but other problem-riddled students, too. I have learned a lot about what I am and what I want to be thanks to the class.... The only way I can redeem myself to you beside kissing butt is to become a responsible, selfless, and a better person. You should know who I am.

Thank you.

Notes like the following are what motivate me to keep reading journals into the early morning hours:

I thought this class was very good and helpful. I think for those who don't always get to share things the journal entries were great. I have ten journals [at home] so far and another almost done but somehow focusing on topics in class was very helpful.

....

I really liked doing the journal—I was skeptical at first, but I really think I've been able to relieve a lot of bottled up anger.

....

You are one of the nicest teachers I know. You are also pretty enough to have a better job. Bye

....

I think it was okay. I don't like the Social Living but this Nancy ran the dumb class well. It must be a tough class to teach.

Surprisingly, the class that I thought had the best discussions and seemed to flow the easiest for me often gives me the most negative comments. In contrast, a difficult class with a lot of discipline problems, and one where I felt that much time was wasted and that I probably came across as annoyed and impatient, might give far more positive feedback.

> IF EVERY CHILD IN THE WORLD WAS A WANTED CHILD WHAT A WORLD OF DIFFERENCE IT WOULD MAKE.
> (seen on a bumber sticker)

I always appreciate the positive evaluations and the notes from the "envelope activity," but what I really enjoy the most are the unexpected encounters with former students or their parents. Most often these chance encounters happen somewhere in Berkeley, but I have run into students in such far-flung places as a remote village of Indonesia, a trail in the Sierra, and a museum in Mexico City. Recently the following note from a former student was delivered to my room by my proctor:

Nancy—

I was working at the BCT [Berkeley Community Theatre] and got an opportunity to say hello. Hope you are well. I am. I have a beautiful six-year-old daughter named Michelle. I've never forgotten you and the positive energy of your class. Someday I hope to see you again.

Love,
Steve, Class of 1979

It is always wonderful to hear from my students and find out about their lives. I usually ask if BHS prepared them for college or the real world. Most often they say yes and that they did not realize what a great school Berkeley High was until they had left. They usually feel that they are more independent and open minded than their peers who went to other high schools. They tend to appreciate the diversity of the student body and staff and the variety of courses and activities that were offered. I get the feeling that most students are very proud of BHS—once they graduate. I know the feeling. While walking through the hallways, I can get overwhelmed by the ugliness of the graffiti, garbage, and broken fixtures. I silently curse the blasting heat, no bells, and last-minute meetings and assemblies, but when I talk with people who are not connected to the school, my perspective changes. Then I, too, feel very proud of what we do accomplish and the fact that we have such a wonderful mix of students and dedicated teachers, counselors, and staff.

> 25% of all children in the U.S. between the ages of 10 and 17 grow up under conditions that limit their development, endanger their health, and damage their self-esteem. Primary factors contributing to this are increased financial insecurity in the family, the need for parents to spend more time earning money, and the growing number of teens living in single-parent families. Contributing factors are an inadequate child welfare system, neighborhood deterioration, poor health and mental health services, gaps in schooling, and an overburdened juvenile justice system.

I am often asked how I would solve the societal problems that our young people face daily. I say that if I had a magic wand I would put a loving father in every home. Many single mothers are doing a great job, and some loving fathers are unable to be as involved as they'd like to be in their children's lives, due to work demands, custody restrictions, or distance. But I do think that a loving parent (ideally, two parents) present and active in every home would do wonders toward resolving many of our current crises. It's too bad you cannot mandate love.

I would make parenting a mandatory class. I would put more money into education than into prisons. I would pay teachers more money to attract the very best of our university graduates into education. I would build dormitories with loving houseparents along with college students to be big brothers and sisters, so that all the abandoned, neglected, and abused children could have a safe and caring environment—whether they needed a place to stay for a few nights or for several years. I would encourage the elders in the community to become more involved with our schools. I would urge parents to monitor their children's television viewing and to encourage more challenging and educational use of leisure time. I think we *all* need to work together—parents, schools, businesses, religious organizations, and government and law enforcement agencies—to make our neighborhoods safe for our children and to improve recreational opportunities for them.

> Community organizations are not reaching millions of young adolescents whose after-school hours are often unsupervised and who therefore are more likely to engage in early sexual activity, drug use, gang activity, and violence.

In the final analysis, it always comes back to the critical need for love and support, and if it can't come from a parent, then let it come from another caring adult. Any of us can be that person—someone to connect to, someone to care, to love, to teach, and to set limits for the young person. Too many of our kids see themselves as "throwaway" children, and it takes more than a self-esteem workshop, a nine-week Social Living class, or a few counseling sessions to undo years of neglect, self-hatred, or abuse. But we have to start somewhere. The family, the school, the community, the churches and synagogues, all must come up with solutions that are appropriate for each unique individual and situation.

As for me, I will listen to my students and attempt to keep finding new ways to inspire them and connect with them on a personal basis—even if it is only through a few lines in their journal. I will go to the mountains for part of the summer to get some perspective on what transpired this particular school year and to get reenergized. I will look forward to what each period, each day, each semester presents me in the way of new and constantly shifting challenges. I never know what to expect—and this is what continues to excite me about teaching.

I used to say that if you offered me a million dollars a year to do something else, I couldn't imagine anything I would love as much as this job. I must say that I am not quite that enthusiastic anymore: most of the time I find teaching a real joy, but it seems to get more and more difficult each nine weeks. I always thought that the longer you stayed in a profession, the easier it would get, but this has not been true for me. Sometimes I worry about the generation gap, which keeps widening on me: after all, I get older every year, but my students are always in their teens. There have been moments—sometimes even days and weeks—when I have felt completely burned out. But it always passes: there are still so many fulfilling moments, so many small victories, that they outnumber the frustrations and irrational decisions I am forced to cope with regularly.

When I run into former students, they usually ask, "Are you STILL teaching at Berkeley High?" (I'm not sure if they think I am quite amazing for having survived there so long, or if they think I should have moved on to something bigger and better.) The answer is, Yes, I am still at BHS and most of the time I love it—and as long as I know I can make a difference, I will continue to teach, to learn, and to be there for those who need me.

If you are a parent, recognize that is the most important calling and rewarding challenge you have. What you do every day, what you say and how you act, will do more to shape the future of America than any other factor.

—MARIAN WRIGHT EDELMAN

APPENDIX

AUTOBIOGRAPHICAL INFORMATION SHEET

JOURNAL ASSIGNMENTS

SEXUALITY WORKSHEET

HOMOSEXUALITY WORKSHEET

Autobiographical Information Sheet

Legal name: _____ Period: _____

Name you liked to be called/nickname: _____

Where were you born: _____ If ESL, how long in U.S.: _____

Your Age: _____ Your Grade: _____

What kind of career/job are you considering for your future? _____

What do you like best about BHS? _____

What do you dislike about BHS? _____

Choose five words to describe yourself: _____

Your family situation. I live with: _____

_____

What are some of your interests, sports, activities? _____

_____

What famous person(s) would you like to meet? _____

_____

Last book you read for pleasure and/or favorite TV show(s): _____

_____

Do you have a job? Describe: _____

Favorite music/group/singer: _____

Additional facts/information you would like to add: _____

_____

Journal Assignments

All writing is confidential except if you write about abuse or sexual assault. It is mandatory that I report all cases. You may fold/staple any entries that you do not wish me to read. I suggest that you keep your journal to look back on (especially when you are a parent of a teen!).

_____ A. Autobiographical sheet: handout to be filled out.

_____ B. When I graduate from BHS… (explain your plans for life after high school—job? college? military? children? marriage? travel? etc.) How realistic are these plans?

_____ C. Describe yourself. How do you see yourself? Explain how your outer and inner images differ. How do others see you?

_____ D. AIDS: how has AIDS changed your view on intimacy? Do you know anyonewho is HIV positive or who has AIDS? Has this changed your relationships? Has this epidemic changed your life in any way?

_____ E. How do you feel about drug use/abuse? What experiences have you had or been around? peers influence your behavior? Is there a history of drug use in your family?

_____ F. What event/circumstance/person has had the greatest impact on your life? Explain.

_____ G. What is the biggest disappointment you've ever had? Explain.

_____ H. The holiday season: what kinds of feelings do you have about family expectations, presents, religious rituals, traditions, pressures, joys, finances, etc.?

_____ I. What do you feel are your strengths and weaknesses? Explain.

_____ J. What causes you stress and how do you deal with it? Describe both positive and negative ways. Is this similar to the way that your parent(s) handle stress?

_____ K. Sex: when and how did you learn about it? What was your reaction? How do you feel about sexuality now—in the media, teenage sexuality, homosexuality/bisexuality, romance, virginity, etc.?

_____ L. Current self-appraisal (school, health, family, body, relationships).

_____ M. Racial identity/feelings about race relations: have you ever experienced any racist attitudes? How do you feel about your race/ethnic background?

_____ N. Create your own question and write it in the space provided. Answer it in your journal!

_____ O.   Right now I feel... Describe your emotional/physical state.

_____ P.   Describe your spiritual/religious background and beliefs.

_____ Q.   New question: _____

The following assignments are done in letter form and remain in your journal. They do NOT require an envelope. These letters should express both your positive and negative FEELINGS about the person/issue/item and any suggestions for improving the relationship.

_____ R.   Write a letter to your mother.

_____ S.   Write a letter to your father.

_____ T.   Write a letter to anyone else: sister/brother, relative, pet, friend (imaginary or real), stepparent, God, romantic interest, drug, skateboard, musical instrument, body part, music, hormones, ETCETERA.

_____ U.   Take one of the people/items you wrote to in R, S or T and imagine what they/it would write back in response to your letter and write it!!

_____ V.   Write a letter to yourself. Say anything you want and enclose anything you want as long as it weighs under ½ oz. You might want to write about your feelings regarding your family, self-image, friends, dreams, fantasies, fears, etc. Think of it in terms of a time capsule of your life right now. You may want to have your friends write something inside or on the envelope. Place the letter in an envelope and seal it. Put the following items on the envelope:

1. Address the letter to yourself.

2. Put a different return address in the upper left-hand corner as a backup to your current address.

3. Put the date you wrote it AND the date you wish it to be sent on the back of the envelope.

4. Put $$$ or postage on the envelope—29 cents for the next couple years and figure 5 more cents for every two years thereafter. Please do NOT lick the stamps but paper-clip them to envelop. Enjoy!! Enjoy!!

_____ W.   Describe a personal loss of a friend, relative, pet, etc. How did you deal with your grief? You may wish to write this in letter form.

_____ X.   Contract for Life!!! You sign handout and then have your parent/guardian sign it. If you are unhappy with th e wording of the contract, change it to make it work for you. It is okay to make an agreement with yourself but write out your agreement.

_____ Y. Your personal goals for Social Living: What do you want to get out of the class? What do you want to learn? What are you willing to contribute to the class? What grade to you think you will EARN (due to your attitude, health, habits, etc.)?

_____ Z. Describe dinnertime at your home. How do you feel about the situation? When you are a parent, will you keep the same patterns?

_____ AA. Who is/are your role model(s)? (Use someone who you have known personally—relative, neighbor, priest/rabbi/minister, teacher, friend, therapist etc.) What is it about this person(s) that you admire and hope to emulate? What impact have they had on your life so far?

_____ BB. What major obstacle(s) have you overcome? What/who helped you work through it?

_____ CC. What do you like best about yourself? Explain.

_____ DD. What are your biggest fears (emotional, physical, social, etc.)?

_____ EE. How has TV influenced your life? Estimate how much time you spend watching TV (include videos). How do you feel about this?

_____ FF. How will you raise your children? What will differ from the way you were raised? What will be the same?

_____ GG. How do you feel about violence (at BHS, on TV, in your community, etc.)? Do you see yourself as a violent person?

_____ HH. Do you see yourself as a religious /nonreligious person, spiritual person, nonbeliever, etc.? Describe your beliefs.

_____ II. What area(s) of your life seems most in control? Out of control?

_____ JJ. Describe your journal cover. Why did you choose the items that you put on it? What does it say about you?

_____ KK. What did someone say or do to you that greatly affected your life (in either a positive or negative way)?

JOURNAL TRIVIA

Col. Ernest Loftus of Harare, Zimbabwe, began his daily diary on May 4, 1896 at the age of 12 and continued it until his death on July 7, 1987 at the age of 103 years, 178 days. George C. Elder (1889–1987) of Bethesda, Maryland, kept a handwritten diary continuously from September 20, 1909, a total of 78 years. Alisa Morris of New York City has a diary which comprised an estimated 15 million words in 238 volumes to date.

Sexuality Worksheet

1. The word "pregnant" was censored from TV in the fifties. True or False?

2. More than _____ teenagers become pregnant each year in the U.S.

3. At what age should a person stop having sex? _____ years old. Why?

4. For teens: 6 in 10 pregnancies result in live births; 3 in 10 are terminated by abortion: 1 in 10 ends in miscarriage; 1 in 6 is given up for adoption. True or False?

5. The U.S. has the highest teen pregnancy rate in the Western World. True or False?

6. Every day an estimated _____ teenagers have an abortion.

7. The cost of raising a single child from birth to 18 years averages $240,000. True or False?

8. Douching after intercourse, or at any time, is unnecessary and can be harmful. True or False?

9. Approximately what percentage of women have bleeding at some point during a pregnancy? _____

10. What percentage of women bleed the first time they have sexual intercourse? _____

11. You can't get pregnant the first time. True or False?

12. 1 in _____ sexually active teens gets an STD each year.

13. The CDC estimates that fewer than 14% of the estimated 1,000,000 Americans infected with HIV know they have it. True or False?

14. The typical baby has its diaper changed 6,608 times!!! True or False?

15. 11,000,000 children of divorce—half of the fathers do not pay child support. True or False?

16. What percentage of Berkeley High School teens use birth control the *first* time they have sex? _____

17. The best lubricant to use with a condom is: Vaseline Intensive Care lotion _____, Johnson's Baby Oil _____, Nivea hand lotion _____, all of the above _____, none of the above _____.

18. Use of oil-based lubricants can cause condom breakdown in _____ (amount of time) which allows sperm/HIV virus to pass through.

19. Percentage of sexually active girls from ages 14–18 years old in the Bay Area who were found to be infected with wart-causing HPV: 2%   5%   15%   20%.

20. The number one cause of infertility in America: abortion _____, drug use _____, birth control pill _____, chlamydia _____, IUD_____.

21. Percentage of all women who masturbate: 10–25%   40–60%   60–80%.

22. Percentage of males who masturbate: over 50%   over 75%   over 90%.

23. About 300–600 million sperm come out per ejaculation. True or False?

24. At what age do males begin to have erections? _ _____

25. Estimated number of gay/lesbian youth under the age of 18 in California. _____

26. A woman can become pregnant during her menstrual period. True or False?

27. A female can get pregnant even if the man withdraws his penis before he comes. True or False?

28. Urination after intercourse will help prevent pregnancy. True or False?

29. The penis must ejaculate into the vagina in order for pregnancy to occur. True or False?

30. The earlier a woman begins to have sexual intercourse and the greater number of partners, the greater her risk of contracting cervical cancer. True or False?

31. The most important attribute of a good sexual relationship is _____.

32. Smoking cigarettes acts as a sexual stimulant. True or False?

Homosexuality Worksheet

TRUE OR FALSE

1. We know the causes of homosexuality. _____

2. You can always tell if a person is gay._____

3. Most lesbians and gay men try to seduce straight people.____ _____

4. Homosexuality is not found in the animal world. _____

5. Approximately 10% of the population is gay, lesbian, bisexual. _____

6. A child of a gay person will most likely be gay. _____

7. Gay people really don't want to be gay. _____

8. If you have a homosexual experience it means that you are gay. _____

9. In a homosexual relationship, one person usually takes the role of the male and the other of the female. _____

10. Gay men want to be women, lesbians want to be men. _____

11. An estimated 30% of teen suicides are by gay/lesbian youth. _____

12. If I found out my best friend was gay, I would

_____

_____

_____

_____

_____

RESOURCES

Anyone can contact these resources for support, information, or referrals. If a San Francisco Bay Area resource does not have a national office or counterpart, I listed the local number. Call those numbers for referrals in your area or check the social services section in your telephone directory. Resources are listed as requested, and are in the order of topics in this book.

Planned Parenthood   SEXUALITY
 (800) 230-PLAN
 Callers can get referrals to local clinics.
 MEDICAL: pelvic and breast exams, pap smears, testicular exams, birth control instruction and supplies, pregnancy tests, confidential HIV/AIDS antibody test, diagnosis and treatment of vaginal and bladder infections and STDs, abortions, tubal ligations, colposcopy and cryosurgery
 COUNSELING: birth control, parent/child communication, pregnancy alternatives, sexuality, sterilization
 EDUCATION: pamphlets, films, videotapes, speakers and programs, reference library

National Adoption Information Clearinghouse
 (301) 231-6512
 11426 Rockville Pike, Suite 410
 Rockville, Maryland 20852
 Information on infant, special needs, and intercountry adoption. Referrals to adoption services, information about state adoption laws, and adoption expertise.

Pacific Center for Human Growth   HOMOSEXUALITY
 Gay/Lesbian/Bisexual/Transgender Switchboard   & BISEXUALITY
 (510) 841-6224
 For individuals with questions or thoughts about homosexuality, bisexuality, or gender identity.

Lavender Youth Recreation and Information Center
(LYRIC) Youth Talkline
(800) 246-PRIDE
For young people with questions about homosexuality, bisexuality, or gender identity.

Parents, Families and Friends of Lesbians and Gays (PFLAG)
(202) 638-4200
1012 14th Street N.W., Suite 700
Washington, D.C. 20005
Callers can get information on *The PFLAGpole* quarterly and PFLAG reports, as well as referrals to local chapters, affiliates, and youth programs.

AIDS

Centers for Disease Control National AIDS Hotline
English language (24-hours): (800) 342-AIDS
Spanish language: (800) 344-7432
TDD: (800) 243-7889
Information and referrals regarding HIV and AIDS.

San Francisco AIDS Foundation Hotline
Toll-free for Northern California: (800) FOR-AIDS
National: (415) FOR-AIDS
Hotline for questions and concerns about HIV and AIDS.

ABUSE

National Council on Child Abuse and Family Violence Help Line
(800) 222-2000
Crisis line for individuals with concerns about child abuse.

Childhelp/IOF Foresters National Child Abuse Hotline
(800) 4-A-CHILD
TDD: (800) 2-A-CHILD
24-hours, 7-days-a-week hotline for information and referrals for anyone with concerns about child abuse.

Bay Area Women Against Rape (BAWAR)
Hotline: (510) 845-7273
Business Line: (510) 465-3890
6536 Telegraph Avenue, Building A, Suite 201
Oakland, California 94609
24-hour hotline for concerns and questions about sexual assault, referrals, outreach programs, counseling, and support programs.

National Coalition Against Sexual Assault
(717) 232-7460
912 North 2nd Street
Harrisburg, Pennsylvania 17102
Referrals to local agencies and organizations.

Covenant House Crisis Line
(800) 999-9999
Hotline for runaways and for teenagers with substance abuse concerns.

New Bridge Foundation
1820 Scenic Avenue
(510) 548-7270
Berkeley, California 94709
Residential drug and alcohol treatment and teen day treatment.

Alcoholics Anonymous
General Service Office
Grand Central Station
P.O. Box 459
New York, New York 10163
Write for referrals to local chapters.

Alanon-Alateen Information Service
(800) 344-2666
Referrals for teens whose lives are affected by an alcoholic.

Marijuana Anonymous World Service Office
(800) 766-6779
Referrals to local chapters.

National Drug Hotline of the National Institute on Drug Abuse
(800) 662-HELP
Treatment and referral line for drug and alcohol abusers.

Narcotics Anonymous World Service Office
(818) 780-3951
Information and referrals regarding substance abuse.

Nar-Anon Family Groups World Service Office
(310) 547-5800
P.O. Box 2562
Palos Verdes, California 90274
Information and referrals for families and friends of substance abusers.

Gamblers Anonymous International Service Office
(213) 386-8789
Referrals to local chapters.

California Victims of Crime Resource Center
(800) 842-8467
McGeorge School of Law
3200 5th Avenue
Sacramento, California 95817
Statewide referral service for victims of violent crime and information
for victims of non-violent crime.

San Francisco Center for Living
(415) 252-1666
4054 18th Street
San Francisco, California 94114
Support for individuals (and their families and friends) living with life-threatening illness.

Center for Attitudinal Healing
(415) 435-5022
19 Main Street
Tiburon, California 94920
Support for individuals (and their families and friends) living with life-threatening illness.

Overeaters Anonymous World Service Office
(310) 618-8835
Referrals to local chapters.

American Anorexia/Bulimia Association
(212) 891-8686
425 East 61st Street
New York, New York 10021
Referrals to local support groups, physicians, and other national organizations that provide information about eating disorders.

Crisis Support Services of Alameda County
Berkeley/Oakland: (510) 849-2212
24-hour suicide prevention hotline.

ENDNOTES

What Is a Teenager?

8   "For instance...athletic shoes alone." *Business Week*. "Teens," April 11, 1994

8   "Number...12 million." As reported in *Seventeen*. July 1994.

Chapter 2: Sexuality

23   "Approximately 25%...by age 20." Center for Population Options (CPO). *The Facts: Adolescent Sexuality, Pregnancy and Parenthood*. Washington, D.C., May 1990

23   "1.1 million...age of 20." Ibid.

23   "3 million teens...every year." CPO. *The Facts: Adolescents, HIV and Other Sexually Transmitted Diseases (STDs)*. May 1993.

23   "At least 40,000...pregnancy." CPO. *The Facts: Adolescent Sexuality, Pregnancy and Parenthood*. May 1990.

24   "Every day 8,400...active." Children's Defense Fund (CDF). "One Day in the Life of American Children," in *The State of America's Children Yearbook 1994*. Washington, D.C., 1994.

24   "Every day teenagers...29 babies." Ibid.

24   "Every day an estimated...abortions." Ibid.

24   "Every day 480...gonorrhea." Ibid.

34   "I tell them...is 1.1 million." Ibid.

38   "Early legal...childbirth." CPO. *The Facts: Adolescents and Abortion*. February 1993.

38   "A 1992 study...abortion." Ibid.

38   "46%...care at all." CPO. *The Facts: Adolescent Sexuality, Pregnancy and Parenthood*. May 1990.

42   "5 in 10 women...conceived." Alan Guttmacher Institute (AGI). *Facts in Brief: Contraceptive Use*. New York, NY, March 1993.

42   "Studies have found...of the time." CPO. *The Facts: Condom Efficacy and Use Among Adolescents*. January 1993.

42   "Unmarried teenagers...pregnancy rates." AGI. *Sex and America's Teenagers*. 1994.

44   "66% of teenage...intercourse." AGI. *Facts in Brief: Contraceptive Use*. March 1993.

44 "50% of premarital...sexual intercourse." CPO. *The Facts: Adolescent Contraceptive Use.* June 1990.

44 "1 in 5 teenage...become pregnant." CPO. *The Facts: Adolescent Sexuality, Pregnancy and Parenthood.* May 1990.

49 "According to...sexual practices." World Health Organization (WHO). Geneva, Switzerland. Quoted in *The San Francisco Chronicle*, December 18, 1993.

55 "A 1991 Roper poll...junior high schools." CPO. *The Facts: Adolescents and Condoms.* October 1991.

55 "About 300–600...4 to 11 days." Planned Parenthood Federation of America. Current statistics obtained in telephone interview with Planned Parenthood of San Mateo County, Education Department. 1994.

71 "Whatever the rationale...twenties and thirties." CPO. *The Facts: Adolescent Sexuality, Pregnancy and Parenthood.* May 1990.

79 "How Can You Tell If Your Relationship is Abusive?" Levy, Barrie. *In Love and In Danger: A Teen's Guide to Breaking Free of Abusive Relationships.* Seattle, WA: Seal Press, 1993.

Chapter 3: Homosexuality and Bisexuality

87 "1 in 4...infection." CPO. *The Facts: Lesbian, Gay & Bisexual Youth at Risk and Undeserved.* September 1992.

87 "Of 289...students." Ibid.

87 "Gay and lesbian...annually." Ibid.

89 "Approximately 33%...of puberty." *The Kinsey Institute New Report on Sex: What You Must Know to be Sexually Literate.* New York, NY: St. Martin's Press, 1990.

89 "In 1973,...disease." American Psychiatric Association (APA). *Diagnostic and Statistical Manual.* New York, NY, 1973.

92 "Some studies...suicide are gay." CPO. *The Facts: Lesbian, Gay & Bisexual Youth at Risk and Undeserved.* September 1992.

92 "In fact...transsexual youth." U.S. Department of Health and Human Services (USDHHS). "Gay Male and Lesbian Youth Suicide," in *Report on the Secretary's Task Force on Youth Suicide.* Washington, D.C., January 1989.

94 "Are You Happy to Be Gay?" Ann Landers and Creators Syndicate. Syndicated column. Chicago, IL, 1992.

Chapter 4: STDs and AIDS

114 "Each year,...an STD." AGI. *Facts in Brief: Sexually Transmitted Diseases (STDs) in the United States.* September 1993.

114 "Chlamydia has...infertility." Ibid.

114 "STDs are less...in men." Ibid.

115 "Risk of pelvic...and older." CPO. *The Facts: Adolescents, HIV and Other Sexually Transmitted Diseases (STDs).* May 1993.

118 "Facts about Adolescents and HIV/AIDS" fact sheet. Centers for Disease Control (CDC). *HIV/AIDS Prevention* report. Atlanta, GA, October 1993.

119 "It was not until...had been infected." Shilts, Randy. *And the Band Played On.* New York, NY: St. Martin's Press, 1987.

119 "The Center for...law or policy." CPO. *The Facts: Adolescents, HIV and Other Sexually Transmitted Diseases (STDs).* May 1993.

119 "The state of California...until 1992...." Assembly Bill No. 11, Chapter 818,

attached to Sections 51201.5 and 51229.8 to the Education Code. Sponsored by Assemblymember Hughes, approved by Govenor Deukmejian. October 11, 1991.

121 "American teens see...or abortion." Ben Fishbaine and Sonoma County TV Turn-Off. *Facts About Television*. Sebastopol, CA, 1993.

135 "At most, 60%...they are infected." CDC. Excerpted from a speech delivered by Wanda K. Jones. "Non-Conventional Approaches to HIV Antibody Testing." Presented at ASTPHLD. Reno, NV, March 1994.

135 "In 1993, the rate...contact." CDC. *Morbidity and Mortality Weekly Report*, vol. 43, no. 9. March 1994.

135 "Lesions from STDs...of HIV." CPO. *The Facts: Adolescents, HIV and Other Sexually Transmitted Diseases (STDs)*. May 1993.

135 "Estimates of...to 125,000." CDF. *The State of America's Children Yearbook 1994*. 1994.

Chapter 6: Racial Identity

173 "In Germany...speak up." Attributed to Martin Niemoeller (1892–1984).

178 "Berkeley High School Population by Race." California State Department of Education. Survey by California Basic Education Data Systems. Sacramento, CA, 1992.

183 "Ethnic identity as defined by survey participants." Unpublished report by Johanna Metzgar. *Love, Lineage, and the Conflicts of Adoption*. Survey of 136 Social Living students conducted at Berkeley High School (BHS), fall 1992.

Chapter 7: Letters to Moms and Dads

186 "There were 9.7...nation." U.S. Census Bureau (USCB). Census report. Washington, D.C., 1992.

186 "10.5 million...single parent." Ibid.

186 "36% of black children...Hispanic children." Ibid.

186 "5% of all children...grandparents." Ibid.

186 "442,000 children...in foster care." Ibid.

189 "Children of divorce...married (34%)." Ibid.

189 "More than 80%...2-parent families." CDF. *Adolescent and Young Adult Fact Book*. 1991.

189 "11% of black...neither parent." Ibid.

197 "A National Research...their futures." CDF. *The State of America's Children Yearbook 1994*. 1994.

215 "A majority of teens...became parents." USCB. Census report. 1992.

215 "When Ann Landers...responded said No!" Heard by the author on *The Oprah Winfrey Show*, ABC-TV. April 1994.

Chapter 8: Sexual Abuse

218 "Approximately 20%...adulthood." American Medical Association. *Diagnostic and Treatment Guidelines on Child Sexual Abuse*. Chicago, IL, 1992.

218 "29%...11 years old." National Victim Center and the Crime Victims Research and Treatment Center. *Rape in America: A Report to the Nation*. Statistics cited from 714 cases. Arlington, VA, and Charleston, SC, 1992.

218 "32%...11 and 17." Ibid.

218 "1 out of 8...rape." Ibid.

218 "Teenage girls...abuse." Ibid.

219 "84% of rapes...stigmatization." Ibid.

219 "Fear of...HIV/AIDS." Ibid.

219 "39% are acquaintances." Ibid.

219 "36% are...uncle." Ibid.

219 "22% are strangers." Ibid.

219 "3% victims declined to answer." Ibid.

Chapter 9: Drugs

246 "Alcohol, Tobacco, and Drug Use in Preceding 30 Days." Institute for Social Research, University of Michigan. *Monitoring the Future.* Ann Arbor, MI, 1994.

247 "These are complex...illegal drugs." J. Michael McGinnis, M.D., and William H. Foege, M.D. *Journal of the American Medical Association.* November 1993.

247 "By comparison,...and heroin use." Telephone interview with Darryl Inaba, Pharm. D., Director, Drug Detoxification, Rehabilitation, and After-Care Project of the Haight-Ashbury Free Medical Clinic and Associate Clinical Professor at U.C. Medical Center, San Francisco. July 1994.

247 "What kills more people...and AIDS combined?" Americans for Nonsmokers' Rights. *Tobacco Advertising and Promotion.* Berkeley, CA, September 1993.

247 "50% of all Asians...if they drink." Editors of U.C. Berkeley *Wellness Letter. The Wellness Encyclopedia.* Boston, MA: Houghton Mifflin, 1991.

247–48 "Which of the following...none of the above." U.S. Department of Education (USDE). *Youth and Alcohol: Selected Reports to the Surgeon General.* Washington, D.C., 1993.

248 "I tell her...one alcoholic drink." USDHHS and U.S. Department of Agriculture. *Dietary Guidelines for Americans.* 1990.

248 "Alcoholism is...notably denial." National Council on Alcoholism and Drug Dependence. Definition by NCADD and the American Society of Addiction Medicine. New York, NY, 1990.

249 "Researchers estimate...college students." USDE. *Youth and Alcohol: Selected Reports to the Surgeon General.* 1993.

249 "In one survey...stoned or drunk." Ibid.

253 "If one parent...one alcoholic parent." Inaba, Darryl S. and Cohen, William E. *Uppers, Downers, All Arounders: Physical and Mental Effects of Psychoactive Drugs.* 2nd edition. Ashland, OR: CNS Productions, 1993.

260 "At the beginning of class...5. addiction." Inaba and Cohen. *Uppers, Downers, All Arounders.* 1993.

262 "Youth are more...substance abuse problems." Ibid.

262 "Adolescents have...drug disruption." Ibid.262

262 "Many current...or function." Ibid.

263 "The psychological...years of maturation." Ibid.

263 "The adolescent...some degree." Ibid.

264 "3 million students...in the previous month." USDE. *Youth and Alcohol: Selected Reports to the Surgeon General.* 1993.

264 "Junior and senior...beer each year." Ibid.

264 "A 12-ounce can...glass of wine." Ibid.

265 "Tolerance to marijuana...dramatic fashion." Inaba and Cohen. *Uppers, Downers, All Arounders.* 1993.

265 "Current street...early '70s." Ibid.

266 "All available…of the 1990s." Ibid.

266 "Chronic marijuana users…life's problems." Ibid.

266 "Some of the negative…sense of time." Ibid.

271–72 "And, quoting from…drug there is." Ibid.

272 "Every day…1 million annually)." American Cancer Society. Statistics compiled by the American Cancer Society Alameda County Unit for the 1993 Smokeout. New York, NY, 1993.

272 "70% of children…grade school." Ibid.

272 "The younger a person…in life." Ibid.

272 "At least 33%…first year is over." Ibid.

272 "Teenagers spent…in 1991." American Public Health Association. *American Journal of Public Health*. New York, NY, February 1994.

273 "According to the University…lung function." Department of Public Health, University of California at Berkeley (U.C. Berkeley). *U.C. Berkeley Wellness Letter*. Berkeley, CA, October 1991.

274 "It took the Viet Cong…every 44 days." Just Say No! to Tobacco Dough Campaign. *SAYNO* bulletin. Fremont, CA, April 1994.

274 "Each day…smoking-related diseases." Bartecchi, Carl E., M.D., MacKenzie, Thomas D., M.D., and Schrier, Robert W., M.D. "The Human Costs of Tobacco Use." *The New England Journal of Medicine,* vol. 330, no. 13, March 1994.

274 "In order to attract…switch brands." USDHHS. *Preventing Tobacco Use Among Young People: A Report of the Surgeon General.* 1994.

274 "In addition…sporting events." Federal Trade Commission. *Federal Trade Commission Report to Congress for 1990.* Washington, D.C., 1992.

274 "I like to make sure…53,000 deaths each year." Bartecchi, MacKenzie, and Schrier. "The Human Costs of Tobacco Use." March 1994.

Chapter 10: Violence

292 "Every day 5,703…violent crime." CDF. *The State of America's Children Yearbook 1994.* 1994.

292 "Homicide…leading cause." Ibid.

292 "Over 50%…violent crime." *Newsweek.* Poll conducted by the CDF. New York, NY, January 1, 1994.

292 "Children under 18…were in 1986." Federal Bureau of Investigation, U.S. Department of Justice. "Crime in the United States 1992: Uniform Crime Reports." Washington, D.C., 1993.

295 "Violence at BHS." Anonymous, written survey conducted and compiled by Marcia Brown-Machen. 309 Social Living students surveyed (a 12.8% sample of total BHS students), fall 1992.

305 "Children and Guns." School of Public Health, Harvard University. "Survey of Experiences, Perceptions, and Apprehensions about Guns among Young People in America" (Study 930018). Cambridge, MA, 1993.

Chapter 11: Death and Grief

314 "Five Stages of Grief." Sanders, Catherine M. *Surviving Grief…and Learning to Live Again.* New York, NY: John Wiley & Sons, 1992.

322 "Every day 7…homicide." CDF. *Adolescent and Young Adult Fact Book.* 1991.

322 "Every day 10…by firearms." Ibid.

322 "Every day 39…vehicle accidents." Ibid.

Chapter 12: Self-Image, Stress, & Suicide

388 "To fall in love...lifelong romance." Attributed to Oscar Wilde (1854–1900).

388 "I find it refreshing...Shannen Doherty, 1,250." *San Francisco Chronicle.* "Suffering and Being Beautiful." January 1993.

349 "No one can...your consent." Attributed to Eleanor Roosevelt (1884–1962).

349 "I read...120 pounds." *San Francisco Chronicle.* "The Ideal Woman." May 10, 1993

349 "However, the average...138 pounds." Met Life Height and Weight Tables. Metropolitan Life Insurance Company. New York, NY, 1983.

349–50 "In over 60...body are shown." Telephone interview with Ray Clemons, Associate Creative Director, Carol H. Williams Advertising, Oakland, California. July 1994.

350 "I don't look at you...my heart." Haley, Alex. *Roots.* From the television miniseries, based on the book of the same title. New York, NY: Doubleday, 1976.

350–51 "Bulimia Danger Signals" & "Anorexia Danger Signals." American Anorexia/Bulimia Association (AABA). "Eating Disorders" fact sheet. New York, NY, n.d.

351 "Bulimia is three...life-threatening." APA. *Diagnostic and Statistical Manual IV.* 1994.

352 "1% of teenage...die as a result." AABA. Informational pamphlet. N.d.

352 "Up to 5%...are bulimic." Ibid.

352 "Up to 40%...binge eaters." Ibid.

356 "For example, many young women...of milk a day)." Department of Public Health, U.C. Berkeley. *U.C. Berkeley Wellness Letter.* April 1994.

359 "(On the school survey...harassed at school.)" Brown-Machen. "Violence at BHS" survey. Fall 1992.

363 "Living with Stress." Anonymous, written survey is part of the Teen Health Needs Assessment for the BHS Health Center written by the BHS Health Center staff. Administered to 150 Social Living students by Nancy Rubin, February 1993.

370 "The suicide rate...4 decades." CDC. "Health Objectives for the Nation," in *Morbidity and Mortality Weekly Report,* vol. 40, no. 37. September 1991.

370 "500,000 teenagers...will die." Crisis Support Services of Alameda County (CSSAC). Informational flyer. Berkeley, CA, 1993.

370 "Suicide is the third...and homicide)." American Association of Suicidology. National Center for Health Statistics report. Denver, CO, 1993.

370 "Guns are the method...teen suicides." Ibid.

373 "In a recent study of 11,600...medical attention." CDC. "Attempted Suicide Among High School Students—U.S. 1990," in *Morbidity and Mortality Weekly Report,* vol. 40, no. 37. September 1991.

375–76 "We go over the signs...masked depression." CSSAC. List compiled from informational materials. 1993.

381 "The suicidal gesture...may be life." Attributed to Karl Menninger, M.D. (1893–1990).

Chapter 13: Your Choice

385 "These items invariably...turned down the offer." Ben Fishbaine and Sonoma County TV Turn-Off. *Facts about Television.* 1993.

386 "According to...59 hours per week." Nielsen Media Research. *1992–1993 Report on Television.* New York, NY, 1993.

386 "A recent study...273 punches." Center for Media and Public Affairs. "A Day of Television Violence." Washington, D.C., June 1992.

387 "TV log." Facsimile of Social Living student's TV-viewing log. BHS. Spring 1994.

390 "One in six meals is eaten in a car." NPR Weekend Edition. "Chrysler Announces No More Ashtrays." January 8, 1994.

395 "In October 1991,...homes." The East Bay Hills Fire Operation Review Group and the State of California Government Office of Emergency Services. *The East Bay Hills Fire: A Multi-Agency Review of the October 1991 Fire in the Oakland-Berkeley Hills*. February 1992.

399 "I never told...must be judged." Attributed to Thomas Jefferson (1743–1846).

410 "What is success?...succeeded." Ralph Waldo Emerson (1803–1882).

412 "Life is hard...you're stupid." Anonymous commencement speaker. NPR. June 1993.

Chapter 14: Finals

416 "Top Problems in Schools." Police Department of Fullerton, California, and State Department of Education, California. Information compiled from a straw poll taken at a conference of law enforcement officers and educators. Los Angeles, 1988.

426 "25% of all...justice system." CDF. National Research Council panel on High-Risk Youths, 1992, in *The State of America's Children Yearbook, 1994*. 1994.

427 "Community organizations...and violence." CDF. "A Matter of Time: Risk and Opportunity in the Nonschool Hours," in *The State of America's Children Yearbook, 1994*. 1994.

428 "If you are a parent...any other factor." Marian Wright Edelman (1939–).

Appendix

433 "Journal Trivia." Donald McFarlan, Editor. *Guinness Book of Records*. New York, NY: Bantam, 1992

INDEX

NOTE: "sb" denotes sidebar